Hellenic Studies 72

MASTERPIECES OF METONYMY

Recent Titles in the Hellenic Studies Series

Kinyras
The Divine Lyre

The Theban Epics

Literary History in the Parian Marble

Plato's Four Muses
The Phaedrus and the Poetics of Philosophy

Plato's Wayward Path
Literary Form and the Republic

Dialoguing in Late Antiquity

Between Thucydides and Polybius
The Golden Age of Greek Historiography

Poetry as Initiation
The Center for Hellenic Studies Symposium on the Derveni Papyrus

Divine Yet Human Epics
Reflections of Poetic Rulers from Ancient Greece and India

The Web of Athenaeus

Eusebius of Caesarea
Tradition and Innovations

The Theology of Arithmetic
Number Symbolism in Platonism and Early Christianity

Homeric Durability
Telling Time in the Iliad

Paideia and Cult
Christian Initiation in Theodore of Mopsuestia

Imperial Geographies in Byzantine and Ottoman Space

Loving Humanity, Learning, and Being Honored
The Foundations of Leadership in Xenophon's Education of Cyrus

The Theory and Practice of Life
Isocrates and the Philosophers

From Listeners to Viewers
Space in the Iliad

http://chs.harvard.edu/chs/publications

MASTERPIECES OF METONYMY

FROM ANCIENT GREEK TIMES TO NOW

Gregory Nagy

CENTER FOR HELLENIC STUDIES
Trustees for Harvard University
Washington, DC
Distributed by Harvard University Press
Cambridge, Massachusetts, and London, England
2015

Masterpieces of Metonymy: From Ancient Greek Times to Now
by Gregory Nagy

Published by Center for Hellenic Studies, Trustees for Harvard University, Washington, DC
Distributed by Harvard University Press, Cambridge, Massachusetts, and London, England
Production: Ivy Livingston
Cover design: Joni Godlove
Cover illustration: Zoie Lafis
Printed by Edwards Brothers, Inc., Ann Arbor, MI and Lillington, NC

Library of Congress Cataloging-in-Publication Data
Nagy, Gregory, author.
Masterpieces of metonymy : from ancient Greek times to now / by Gregory Nagy.
pages cm -- (Hellenic studies ; 72)
ISBN 978-0-674-08832-0 (alk. paper)
1. Greek literature--History and criticism. 2. Metonyms. 3. Figures of speech. I. Title. II. Series: Hellenic studies ; 72.

PA3052.N34 2015
809'.91--dc23

2015032428

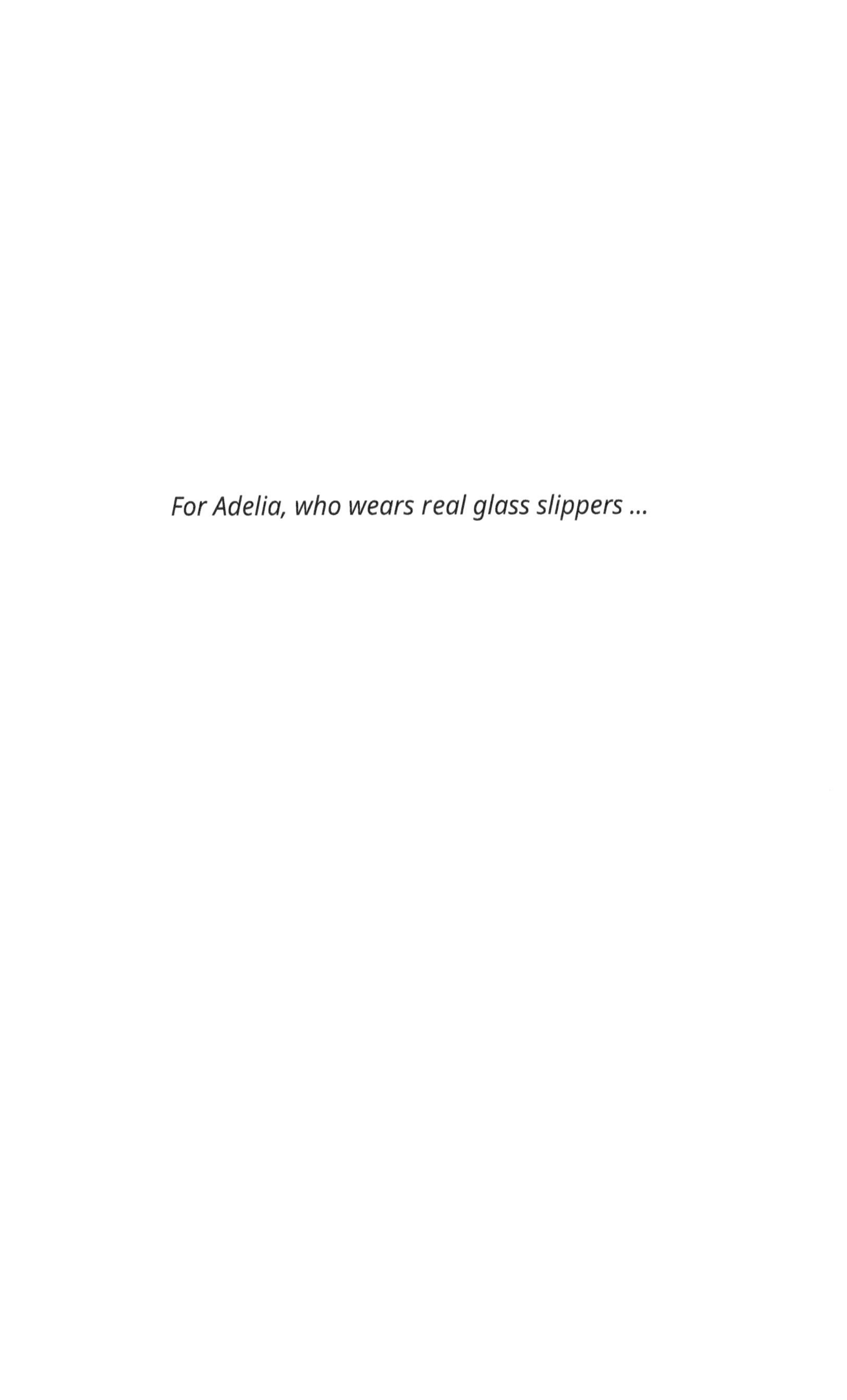

For Adelia, who wears real glass slippers ...

Contents

List of Multimedia Content

http://nrs.harvard.edu/urn-3:hul.eresource:Nagy.Masterpieces_of_Metonymy.List_of_Extracts

(Icons indicate content available only online.)

Acknowledgments

THIS BOOK STEMS from the Martin Classical Lectures that I presented in the spring of 2003 at Oberlin College (details in 0§02). I will be forever grateful to the intellectual community at the college for all their support and encouragement. Special thanks go to three colleagues there: Kirk Ormand, Tom Van Nortwick, and Nate Greenberg.

I also thank the following people for all their help: Daniel Cline, Kyle Courtney, Claudia Filos, Christos Giannopoulos, Zoie Lafis (especially for her cover illustration), Sarah Lannom (especially for creating a most helpful index), Ivy Livingston, Stefanos Loukas (editor of *Rizospastis*), Leonard Muellner, Ioanna Papadopoulou, Jill Robbins, Noel Spencer, David Stern, Keith Stone, and Jacqueline Vayntrub.

Introduction

0§01. Although my primary interest here is in *metonymy* and in the creations of metonymy—which I call *metonyms*—I cannot think of this word *metonymy* without correlating it with another word, *metaphor*. So, I begin with a working definition of the two words taken together:

- *Metonymy* is a mental process that expresses meaning by *connecting* something to something else that is next to it or at least near to it, thereby making contact.
- *Metaphor* is a mental process that expresses meaning by *substituting* something for something else.[1]

0§02. On the occasion of the Charles Beebe Martin Classical Lectures that I presented in the spring of 2003 (March 3, 4, 6, 7) at Oberlin College, I had already argued for the distinction I make here between *metonymy* as *connection* and *metaphor* as *substitution*. Now, over ten years later, I hope to consolidate and refine that argumentation in the format of a book that re-enacts in four parts the four lectures I had presented back then at Oberlin.

0§03. From the start, I confront an obstacle that may interfere with the flow of my project. The word *substitution* in my working definition of metaphor may be misunderstood. Let me clarify: when I say *substitution* here, I am referring not to the simple replacement of one word by another. Even the use of metonymy, as we will see, can involve replacements in wording. Rather, as we will also see, the process of substitution in the use of metaphor is something that transcends words: *substitution in metaphor is a mental process where one way of thinking is replaced by another way that is alien to the previous way.*

[1] This working definition of the two words *metonymy* and *metaphor* follows closely the wording in Hour 4 §32 of my book *The Ancient Greek Hero in 24 Hours* (2013). From here on, I abbreviate the title of that book as *H24H*, and I will cite references to it by way of indicating the given "hour" (in this case, 4) and paragraph (in this case, 32). At the end of the present book, before I give my list of bibliographical references, I insert a list of all bibliographical abbreviations such as *H24H*.

0§04. In developing my arguments in this book, I will make use of relevant terminology developed by my teacher Roman Jakobson, a leading figure of the so-called Prague School of linguistics, who describes *metonymy* and *metaphor* respectively in terms of *contiguity* and *similarity*, or *combination* and *selection*,[2] moving along *an axis of combination* in the case of metonymy and along an *axis of selection* in the case of metaphor.[3] The axis of combination in meaning can be seen as a horizontal movement connecting elements A and B and C ... to each other in a sequence that proceeds all the way to ... X and Y and Z; correspondingly, the axis of selection in meaning can be seen as a vertical movement that varies the elements in the same sequence by allowing substitutions of one variant for another, so that the element A can become A_0 or A_1 or A_2 or A_3 ..., or the element B can become B_0 or B_1 or B_2 or B_3 ..., and so on.

0§05. In the horizontal axis, for example, if A is "hand," then B can be "arm" and C can be "shoulder," and so on. As for the vertical axis, in an example starting again with "hand," we can say that A_1 and A_2 and A_3 and so on can stand for, respectively, "hand" and "claw" and "hoof" and so on.

0§06. In Part Two of this book, I will give my own reasons for visualizing the interaction of metonymy and metaphor as a coordination of horizontal and vertical axes respectively. Here in the Introduction, however, as also in Part One, which follows, I will avoid using these terms *horizontal* and *vertical* while I argue, more generally, that metonymy and metaphor interact with each other as coordinated mental processes.

Opening Remarks on the Coordination of Metonymy and Metaphor

0§1. Although I view metonymy and metaphor as coordinated mental processes, I find no explicit statement in ancient Greek sources about such a coordination. But I see at least the implication of a pattern of coordination between metonymy and metaphor when I read the working definition of metaphor in the *Poetics* of Aristotle, who lived in the fourth century BCE:

Extract 0-A

> Metaphor [*metaphorā*] is the application of a noun [*onoma*] that is *alien* [<u>*allotrion*</u>], by transference either from the general [*tò genos*] to the specific [*tò eidos*], or from the specific [*tò eidos*] to the general [*tò genos*],

[2] Jakobson 1956:60–62, 76 [1990:119–120, 129].

[3] See in general Ducrot and Todorov 1979:111, with references.

> or from the specific [*tò eidos*] to the specific [*tò eidos*], or [it is a transference] by way of analogy [*tò analogon*].
>
> Aristotle *Poetics* 1457b5–9[4]

0§2. For me the key word here is *allotrion*, which I have translated as 'alien', that is, 'belonging not to the self but to someone else or to something else'. In ancient Greek, the opposite of *allotrion* is *oikeion*, which means 'familiar', that is, 'belonging to the self or to someone or something that belongs to the self', as we see in further remarks made by Aristotle about metaphor (*Poetics* 1457b31–32 and elsewhere). Although Aristotle nowhere uses the term *metōnumiā*, which we translate as 'metonymy', it is attested in later Greek sources. And, in one of these sources, this term *metōnumiā* 'metonymy' is defined as a reference to the *oikeion*, that is, to whatever is 'familiar'. Here is the wording of that definition, preserved in an ancient commentary on the works of Dionysius of Thrace, a pioneer in the science of linguistics who lived the second century BCE:

Extract 0-B

> Metonymy [*metōnumiā*] is a part of speech that properly applies to one thing but indicates [*sēmainei*] another thing by way of what is *familiar* [<u>*oikeion*</u>] to it. Here is an example: ὑπείρεχον Ἡφαίστοιο [at *Iliad* II 426] "they were holding [the meat to be roasted] over Hēphaistos" instead of "[they were holding the meat to be roasted] over the fire". That is because fire is *familiar* [<u>*oikeion*</u>] to [the god of fire] Hēphaistos.
>
> Scholia for Dionysius of Thrace *Ars Grammatica* 461.5 Hilgard[5]

0§3. Building on this formulation, I now offer a second working definition of metonymy: it is a mental process of *connecting* things that are *familiar* to the self.

Reading Metonymically

0§4. Throughout this book, I will be reading examples of metonymy in a wide variety of forms. Some of these examples will come from literature—or let me call it not *literature* but *the verbal art of song, poetry, prose*. Other examples will come from *visual art*. Still other examples will come simply from the use

[4] μεταφορὰ δέ ἐστιν ὀνόματος <u>ἀλλοτρίου</u> ἐπιφορὰ ἢ ἀπὸ τοῦ γένους ἐπὶ εἶδος ἢ ἀπὸ τοῦ εἴδους ἐπὶ τὸ γένος ἢ ἀπὸ τοῦ εἴδους ἐπὶ εἶδος ἢ κατὰ τὸ ἀνάλογον.

[5] μετωνυμία ἐστὶ μέρος λόγου ἐφ' ἑτέρου μὲν κυρίως κείμενον, ἕτερον δὲ σημαῖνον κατὰ τὸ <u>οἰκεῖον</u>, οἷον "ὑπείρεχον Ἡφαίστοιο", ἀντὶ τοῦ πυρός, ὅπερ ἐστὶν <u>οἰκεῖον</u> τοῦ Ἡφαίστου.

of language—and here I mean *visual* as well as *verbal* language. So, I cannot say that all of my examples qualify as art. And that is as it should be: already in Part One of this book, which follows shortly, I will show that the mental process of metonymy—and the same goes for metaphor—is simply a fact of human life.

0§5. Yes, some of my examples of metonymy will come from masterpieces of verbal or visual art and, in some cases, the examples themselves can be appreciated as artistic masterpieces in their own right. That is one reason why I have given this book the title *Masterpieces of Metonymy*. But I also had another reason for this title, and here it is: any metonym, as a creation of the mental process of metonymy, may qualify as a piece of creativity, even if the metonym itself is no masterpiece. To take it one step further, a metonym can be a masterpiece even if the larger artistic creation that contains it fails to qualify as a masterpiece. And I can take it another step further: we can find masterpieces of metonymy even in contexts that have nothing to do with art in the first place.

0§6. That is why, wherever we encounter in this book an example of metonymy, I will try to concentrate on the potential creativity of that metonymy simply as a process, without worrying about the artistic status of that process. Although some of the metonyms we are about to encounter are in fact artistic masterpieces, I cannot really say such a thing about all of them. And it should not even matter if some of the metonyms we read may end up falling flat as artistic creations. What matters to me is not what we read but how we read it.

0§7. So, how are we to read? A model is the philologist's art of reading, described by Friedrich Nietzsche, who links the artistry of a goldsmith's delicate fingers with the attentiveness of the careful reader's eye:

Extract 0-C

> Philology is that venerable art which demands of its votaries one thing above all: to go aside, to take time, to become still, to become slow—it is a goldsmith's art and connoisseurship of the *word* which has nothing but delicate cautious work to do and achieves nothing if it does not achieve it *lento*. But for precisely this reason it is more necessary than ever today; by precisely this means does it entice and enchant us the most, in the midst of an age of "work," that is to say, of hurry, of indecent and perspiring haste, which wants to "get everything done" at once, including every old or new book:—this art does not easily get anything done, it teaches to read *well*, that is to say, to read slowly,

deeply, looking cautiously forward and backward, with reservations, with doors left open, with delicate fingers and eyes.

Nietzsche 1885, *Daybreak* (*Morgenröt[h]e*) Foreword 5[6]

A Metonymic Reading of a Scene from a Film By Miloš Forman

0§8. Keeping in mind my secondary working definition of metonymy as a mental process of *connecting* things that are *familiar* to the self, I choose as a first example a scene from the film *Hair* (1979), based on a musical by the same name (off-Broadway 1967; Broadway 1968). The film version, directed by Miloš Forman, captures most tellingly a performance of metonymy. The performer is singing and dancing the role of an ostentatiously egotistical Self whose exuberant head of hair connects to every imaginable part of his self-expression. This Self is a young man named George (acted by Treat Williams), who becomes an unwelcome intruder at an exclusive dinner party. Confronting George is an outraged hostess who scolds him for his boldness by intoning: "You've got a hell of a nerve, young man." Undeterred, George gets the nerve to test the limits further. He impulsively leaps on top of the dinner table, and right there he starts to sing and dance what he is all about, while addressing in the most familiar terms his alien hostess as "mother":

Extract 0-D1

I got life, mother. | I got laughs, sister. | I got freedom, brother. | I got good times, man. | I got crazy ways, daughter. | I got million-dollar charm, cousin. | I got headaches, and toothaches ... | And bad times too ... | Like you.

| I got my hair I got my head I got my brains I got my ears I got my eyes I got my nose I got my mouth, | I got my teeth. | I got my tongue I got my chin I got my neck I got my tits I got my heart I got my soul I got my

[6] *Philologie nämlich ist jene ehrwürdige Kunst, welche von ihrem Verehrer vor Allem Eins heischt, bei Seite gehn, sich Zeit lassen, still werden, langsam werden —, als eine Goldschmiedkunst und -kennerschaft des Wortes, die lauter feine vorsichtige Arbeit abzuthun hat und Nichts erreicht, wenn sie es nicht lento erreicht. Gerade damit aber ist sie heute nöthiger als je, gerade dadurch zieht sie und bezaubert sie uns am stärksten, mitten in einem Zeitalter der "Arbeit", will sagen: der Hast, der unanständigen und schwitzenden Eilfertigkeit, das mit Allem gleich "fertig werden" will, auch mit jedem alten und neuen Buche: — sie selbst wird nicht so leicht irgend womit fertig, sie lehrt gut lesen, das heisst langsam, tief, rück- und vorsichtig, mit Hintergedanken, mit offen gelassenen Thüren, mit zarten Fingern und Augen lesen ...* The translation here is adapted (with only slight changes) from Hollingdale 1982:5.

> back, | I got my ass. | I got my arms I got my hands I got my fingers—got my legs I got my feet I got my toes I got my liver. | Got my blood ...
>
> [By now George's song is accompanied by the outraged cries of the dinner guests as he continues prancing on top of the dinner table. But George does continue, recycling the connections of his song until it reaches its conclusion ...]
>
> ... got my guts, | got my muscles ... | I got life, life, life, life, life, life, life.
>
> From the script of *Hair* (1978; directed by Miloš Forman, choreography by Twyla Tharp) "I Got Life" (words by Gerome Ragni and James Rado, song by Galt MacDermot)

Extract 0-D2 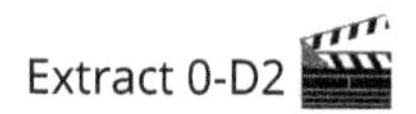

[The online version features a link here to the relevant scene in the film *Hair* (0:32:48).]

0§9. From a metonymic view of this performance as I have just transcribed it, we can see a lengthy sequence of monosyllabic words arranged in the pattern *I got my this I got my that*. What is most remarkable about this sequence is the absence of pauses that would otherwise be required by the syntax. This absence accentuates the continuity that is being expressed in connecting the hair to the head, or the arms to the hands, and so on. In the transcription I just gave of the sequence *I got my this I got my that*, I tried to approximate the absence of pauses by omitting punctuation at those points where a pause is syntactically needed but performatively omitted. This absence of pauses is especially noticeable in the part of the song that pours out the following stream of monosyllables: "I got my hair I got my head I got my brains I got my ears I got my eyes I got my nose I got my mouth I got my teeth I got my tongue ..." For the metonymy to work, the mind's eye has to visualize in rapid-fire sequence the parts of the human body as they connect to each other here. And the wording of the metonymy as we hear it can do the work of imagining for us these connections.

0§10. For George as the Self who is singing and dancing this extravaganza of organic continuity, it all comes naturally: his body, in all its connectivity, is his self, and this self extends metonymically from his own members—the members of his own body—to the members of the family that is being artificially created in the words of his song. This act of creation is most intrusive, since the self is boldly becoming all too familiar with everyone in the immediate proximity. So, the alien character of a hostess at an elite dinner party now becomes the familiar character of your own mother. And then your mother's daughter becomes your own sister. And then, the next thing you know, all these alien people are transformed into members of George's artificial family, becoming mother, sister, brother, and cousin to the Self. All get connected. When I say "your own mother," I am deliberately referring here to a personal "you" as the reader, not to an impersonal "one" as in the expression "one's own mother." After all, metonymy has the power to draw the unfamiliar toward the familiar, which verges on the personal.

0§11. Even if you add to the mix someone whom George addresses simply as "man," surely this man too must be somehow co-opted into a relationship of familiarity. As he sings the words "I got good times, man," the George of Forman's film *Hair* is looking at one particular man—looking him straight in the eye while addressing him as "man." This man is Claude (acted by John Savage), a young draftee who is waiting to be shipped off to the Vietnam War. A fellow intruder at the elite dinner party, Claude has been befriended by George and, by the time the whole story is finished, George will selflessly contrive to take the place of Claude on a transport plane flying off to Vietnam and carrying its cargo of draftees to their doom. So, in the end, it is George, not Claude, who will be killed in the Vietnam War. George will have given up his life for the man he is now addressing simply as "man" in his song. He will become that man's other self, and this selfless selfhood becomes his ultimate metonymic gesture of connecting with the familiar.

0§12. I should stress that the actual sequence of connectivity for George's would-be family members in this song and dance seems at first arbitrary, just as the sequence of his body parts, of his own bodily members, seems arbitrary—except for the one simple fact that George's wording starts from the top down, focusing on the shock of curly hair on top of his head. You would think that his hair became the first extension, metonymically, of his exuberant Self, and that his head came only second. And you would be right, since hair is what his story is really all about, as we can see even from the title of the whole story, which is *Hair*. In a variety of examples still to be shown, we will consider further the special metonymic power of hair. Metonymically, as we will see, hair has its own special attractions.

Part One

Making Metonyms Both Naturally and Artistically

1§0. The making of metonyms comes naturally. In other words, I argue that the human capacity for metonymy is inborn, natural. This is not to say, however, that the making of metonyms in verbal and visual art needs to be artificial. Metonymy can be artistic, yes, but the artistry of making metonyms—as well as metaphors—can still be natural. In what follows, I will explore the natural foundations of metonymy—as also of metaphor—and then I will show examples of artistic creations that are built on those foundations. As I get started, I will be concentrating on examples taken from verbal arts. Then, as the exploration proceeds, I will gradually take into account the visual arts as well.

An Inborn Capacity For Making Metonyms—As Well as Metaphors

1§1. My point of departure is something that Aristotle says about metaphor only. For him, metaphor is a certain something that you cannot really learn and you cannot really teach. To be a master of metaphor, you just have to have the inborn capacity, the natural ability, to engage in the right kind of mental process:

Extract 1-A

> But the greatest use of words is the use of metaphor [*tò metaphorikon* 'that which is transferable']. This is the only thing that cannot be learned from someone else; and it is also a sign [*sēmeion*] of a good quality that is inborn [*euphuia*], since the making of good metaphors [*eu metapherein* 'good transference'] is the same thing as the contemplation [*theōreîn*] of what is similar [*homoion*] to what.
>
> Aristotle *Poetics* 1459a5–8[1]

[1] πολὺ δὲ μέγιστον τὸ μεταφορικὸν εἶναι. μόνον γὰρ τοῦτο οὔτε παρ' ἄλλου ἔστι λαβεῖν εὐφυΐας τε σημεῖόν ἐστι· τὸ γὰρ εὖ μεταφέρειν τὸ τὸ ὅμοιον θεωρεῖν ἐστιν.

1§2. If the capacity for making a metaphor is inborn, then what about the making of a metonym? Surely the capacity for metonymy must likewise be inborn within the self—if it is true that metonymy, as distinct from metaphor, depends on what is *oikeion* or 'familiar' to the self, not on what is *allotrion* or 'alien' to it. And we already saw that much just from reading Extract 0-B (scholia for Dionysius of Thrace *Ars Grammatica* 461.5) in the Introduction.

1§3. For an example of this idea that metonymy and metaphor come from something natural inside us, from something we are born with, I bring up a scene from a subtitled film called *The Postman*, or *Il Postino* in the original Italian version (1994). In this scene, a shy and relatively uneducated Italian postman named Mario is engaged in a dialogue with a fictionalized version of the Chilean poet Pablo Neruda (1904–1973). The postman (acted by Massimo Troisi, who was also the writer of the screenplay) has been reading—in Italian translation—the poems of Neruda (acted by Philippe Noiret) in hopes of emulating the exiled poet. Mario is eager to impress Don Pablo, as he calls him, by quoting back at him some of the famous similes and metaphors invented by Neruda.

1§4. Mario is quoting similes and metaphors without knowing what they are. But the meaning of these terms *simile* and *metaphor* becomes clear as the conversation between the postman and the poet continues. Mario is gently scolded by the poet: why do you shower me with quotations of similes and metaphors taken from my book of 'elementary' poems—I've composed many other poems as well, maybe better than those poems. The wording of the Italian script here plays on the double meaning of the Spanish word *elementales* in the original Spanish title of this book of collected poems by Neruda, *Odas elementales* (1954), since *elementales* here means not only 'elementary': it refers also to the intended elemental force of these odes. And something elemental is actually being awakened inside Mario as he engages with the elementary principles of poetry, even though he does not understand that he has been quoting similes and metaphors. I use the word 'awakened' here quite deliberately: something elemental is literally being awakened in Mario, since the story makes it clear that the postman's capacity for understanding simile and metaphor is something that is inborn.

1§5. But the problem is, the self-education of Mario has been so elementary that he does not understand one of the two words for this elemental something that is inborn in him. The Italian word for 'simile' he understands, yes, since the meaning of the plural form *similitudini* is transparent in Italian—and so this word is familiar to Mario. When you make a simile or *similitudine*, something will be like *this* while another thing will be like *that*. This much is clear for now, though we will see in Part Two of this book that the making of similes is not as simple as it seems here. Still, the point for now is simple enough, and the meaning of *simile* is clear in the present context. But the other Italian word, *metafora* 'metaphor', is opaque in this same context. The word is quite alien to Mario. So, when Don Pablo uses this word in the plural, *metafore* 'metaphors', in referring to the poetic words that Mario has been quoting back at the poet, the postman asks Neruda plaintively for a definition, as if a definition from the poet could turn this alien word into something familiar—something that could now become a part of Mario himself. Here are the words of the dialogue:

Extract 1-Ba

DON PABLO [speaking to Mario]. *Elementary Odes* isn't the only book I've written. I've written much better. It's unfair of you to shower me with similes [*similitudini*] and metaphors [*metafore*].

MARIO [not understanding the word *metafore* 'metaphors']. Don Pablo?

DON PABLO. Metaphors.

MARIO. What are those?

DON PABLO. Metaphors? Bha! Metaphors are— How can I explain? When you talk of something, comparing it to another.

MARIO. Is it something ... you use in poetry?

DON PABLO. Yes, that too.

MARIO. For example?

DON PABLO. For example ... when you say, "the sky weeps [*piangere*]" [*Il cielo piange*], what do you mean?

MARIO. That it's raining.

DON PABLO. Yes, very good. —That's a metaphor.

MARIO. —It's easy then! Why has it got such a complicated name?

DON PABLO. Man has no business with ... the simplicity or complexity of things.

MARIO. Excuse me, Don Pablo, then I'll go. I was reading something yesterday: "The smell of barber shops makes me weep [*piangere*] and cry [*stridere*]" [*L'odore dei parrucchieri mi fa piangere e stridere*].[2] Is that a metaphor, too?

DON PABLO. No ... not exactly.

MARIO. I liked it, too, when ... when you wrote: "I am tired of being a man" [*Sono stanco di essere uomo*].[3] That's happened to me, too ... but I never knew how to say it. I really liked it when

[2] Here is the wording in the original Spanish: *El olor de las peluquerías me hace llorar a gritos*. From the poem "Walking Around," in: *Residencia en la tierra* (1931–1935) Libro 2, Parte II (1960). I have modified slightly the translation of this wording used in the English subtitles.

[3] Here is the wording in the original Spanish: *Sucede que me canso de ser hombre*. From the same poem "Walking Around."

I read it. Why "the smell of barber shops makes me weep [*piangere*]"?

Don Pablo. You see, Mario ... I can't tell you ... in words different from those I've used. When you explain it, poetry becomes banal. Better than any explanation ... is the experience of feelings that poetry can reveal ... to a nature open enough to understand it.

From the script of *Il Postino* (1994; directed by Michael Radford); my translation[4]

Extract 1-Bb 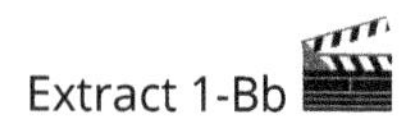

[The online version features a link here to the relevant scene in the film *Il Postino* (0:22:10).]

1§6. In this dialogue, the first elementary lesson to be learned is about metaphor. But the poet does not really teach you by explaining how to make a metaphor: he only awakens within you the inborn natural capacity for metaphor. "Better than any explanation," Don Pablo says to Mario, "is the experience of *feelings* that poetry can reveal ... to a *nature* open enough to understand it" (the highlighting of the words *feelings* and *nature* is mine). So, the capacity for understanding metaphor is natural. That is why the poet teaches not by explaining but merely by giving an example. In this example of a metaphor, the natural experience of seeing rain pouring from the sky is being compared to weeping, *piangere*, which is the natural experience of seeing tears flowing from someone's eye—or even from your own. You substitute the idea of weeping for the idea of raining, and, there it is, the metaphor comes to life.

1§7. Now comes the second elementary lesson to be learned in this dialogue, and it is about metonymy. After Mario quotes for Neruda another set of words once composed by the poet, "The smell of barber shops makes me weep [*piangere*]," he asks Don Pablo whether these words show another example of metaphor. The poet replies: "No ... not exactly." But Don Pablo does not say what this thing really is if it is not a metaphor. Clearly, we see here a metonymy. Something familiar to both the poet and the postman, which is the smell of talcum powder wafting from inside a barber shop where men get their hair cut, is connected here to something that makes a man sad about being a man, and that sad something makes you weep, *piangere*, and cry out loud. As before, when I was analyzing a scene from a film by Forman, I am deliberately referring here

[4] This scene, and the whole film, is based on the novel (and film) of Antonio Skármeta, *Ardiente Paciencia* (1983), later republished as *El Cartero de Neruda*.

to a personal "you," not to an impersonal "someone." After all, as I already said, metonymy has the power to draw the unfamiliar toward the familiar, which verges on the personal.

1§8. So, we have seen in this dialogue a deft interplay of metaphor and metonymy. In the case of metonymy, we can say that it comes from an inborn capacity to connect something that is familiar with something else that is familiar or can become familiar. And the familiarity here comes from personal experience, as when you smell the scent of talcum powder wafting from inside a barber shop. The mind has the inborn natural capacity to connect such a specific personal experience to other specific personal experiences, such as feeling tears flowing from your eyes. But the mind also has the natural inborn capacity to substitute for something that is familiar something that is alien, not familiar. That is what metaphor is all about, according to the working definition of Aristotle. So, in the case of the metaphor we have just encountered, about the sky that weeps, surely we would never know from personal experience that the sky is weeping when it rains. To think that tears are pouring from the sky is to transfer something familiar that we do personally experience, weeping, to something unfamiliar that we will never personally experience, which is what happens to the sky when it rains. While the experience of weeping is familiar to us, it is alien to the sky. While the experience of seeing rain fall from the sky is familiar to us, the idea of seeing tears falling from the sky is alien, because surely the sky does not have eyes.

Activations of the Five Senses in the Making of Metonymy

1§9. All five senses can be activated in the mental process of making metonymy: seeing, hearing, smelling, tasting, touching. Of these five, the sense of seeing is primary, and I will consider it together with the sense of hearing, which is secondary. Then I will consider the three remaining senses: smelling, tasting, and touching.

1§10. I consider together the senses of seeing and hearing because metonymy, which is primarily visual, is communicated through language, which is primarily verbal. Language is something that is heard, though special kinds of language may be read as well as heard. Also, I should repeat here something I said earlier, that visual arts have their own language. That is why, throughout this book, we will be considering not only the verbal arts of song, poetry, and prose but also the visual arts.

1§11. For the moment, in any case, I concentrate simply on the sense of seeing, artful or not artful, as combined with the sense of hearing. Of these two senses, seeing is not only primary but even primal for making metonymy. This sense is primal because sight is the primary source of imagination. Combined with the sense of hearing, which receives the sound that conveys what is being imagined, the sense of seeing creates the imagery of metonymy. As for the sound that conveys what is being imagined, it can come from everyday words or from the words of song, poetry, and prose. The sound can even be music, as we call it, which is abstracted from the words of song. Or the sound can be muted, as when we experience imagination simply by reading silently to ourselves.

1§12. What I have said so far about the activation of the senses in the making of metonymy applies also to the making of metaphor. The sense of seeing creates the imagery of metaphor, not only of metonymy. As in the case of metonymy, the primary requirement of metaphor is imagination. I return here to the example from the film *Il Postino*, where the metaphor of the weeping sky requires the picturing of tears flowing from the eyes: these tears can then be substituted for rain in picturing the sky when it rains. And the wording of the metaphor as we hear it can do the work of imagining for us this mental act of substitution.

1§13. Unlike metaphor, however, metonymy goes beyond imagination, activating not only the two senses of seeing and hearing. Also activated in the making of metonyms are the three other senses: smelling, tasting, touching.

1§14. As we begin to consider these three other senses, I note right away that there is something metonymical even about the way these senses are activated. What I mean is, each sense as it gets activated has a way of combining with other senses. And the mental process of making combinations, as we will see, is the essence of metonymy.

1§15. That said, I am ready to consider the first of these three other senses, the sense of smell. In terms of evolutionary biology, smell is almost as primal as sight, since the olfactory connection of nerves to the brain is secondary only to the optic connection. The power of this primal sense of smell comes through clearly in the metonym we have already read in the poetry of Pablo Neruda: "The smell of barber shops makes me weep and cry." And a sign of such primal power is the fact that, in some languages, the word for 'sense' in general is the same as the word for 'smell' in particular. That is what happens with the French verb *sentir*, which can mean not only 'sense' in general but also 'smell' in particular. Moreover, this same French verb can mean 'taste' as well as 'smell'. Next I turn to the Latin verb *sentīre*, meaning 'sense', from which French *sentir* is derived: this verb is even more versatile in meaning, since it can take as its direct object anything perceived by any one of the five senses, such as a flash, a noise, a smell, a taste, a touch.

1§16. As we consider the overlap in the specialized meanings of French *sentir* as both 'smell' and 'taste', I draw attention to other meanings that overlap by way of engaging the sense of smell in combination with the sense of taste. For example, the French word *doux*, meaning 'sweet', can refer to a good smell, not only to a good taste. In English as well, the word *sweet* can refer to a good smell, as when we speak of the sweet smell wafting from a fresh brew of coffee—even though the coffee has no sweetness to the taste. What we see here is not a *substitution* of taste for smell, which would be a mental process that is *metaphoric*. Rather, what is at work here is a *combination* of taste and smell, which is a mental process that is *metonymic*. There is a combinatory mental association going on here. Smelling and tasting go together organically. They are already familiar to each other. So there should be nothing alien to the mental process of tasting when you smell something good, and there should be nothing alien to the mental process of smelling when you taste something good.

1§17. By now I have touched on four of the five senses that can be activated in the making of metonymy: seeing, hearing, smelling, tasting. As for the fifth sense, *touching*, this one comes closest to the basic idea that I had built into my initial working definition of *metonymy*. As I said at the beginning, *metonymy* is a mental process that expresses meaning by *connecting* something to something else that is next to it or at least near to it, thereby making *contact*. I now highlight the word *contact* in this working definition, since its meaning depends on the idea of *touching*. And the sense of *touching* is the most inclusive of the sensory aspects of metonymy.

1§18. To show the metonymic inclusiveness of *touching*, I focus on the meaning of the English word *feeling*, which can be used to express the experience of *touching* or *being touched*. At this early stage of my argumentation, this word *feeling* is especially good to think with, since it can apply either to the sense of *touch* in particular or to all five senses in general, just as Latin *sentīre* 'sense'—and Greek *aisthanesthai* 'sense'—apply to all five senses. But the application of the word *feeling* to the other four senses besides *touching* needs to be mediated by emotions—such as loving, being happy, being afraid, being sad, being angry, hating, and so on. For example, I can say that I *feel* the emotion of love when I *see* someone I love. Similarly, I can *feel* love when I *hear* a sound or *smell* a smell or *taste* a taste that is lovable. But, ordinarily, I cannot say in English that I *feel* directly a sight or a sound or a smell or a taste. I can say that I *feel*, without the intermediacy of emotions, only when I *touch*.

1§19. The metonymic inclusiveness of the sense of touch is most evident in the variety of its combinations with the other senses. For example, in English we can say that someone has a *sweet touch*. Or, in French, the adjective *doux* can mean 'gentle to the touch', not only 'sweet to the taste'. Or again, to go back to

English, if we say colloquially that something has *a good look and feel to it*, we are thinking of a good feeling in general, connecting all the senses—not only the senses of looking and touching.

Differentiating Two Terms: Metonymy and Synesthesia

1§20. From this brief survey of linguistic evidence taken mostly from English, we have by now seen examples of words used metonymically in referring to all five senses: sight, sound, smell, taste, touch. What creates the effect of metonymy, as we have also seen, is the mental process of combining references to the senses. And in each of these combinations, what seems to be at work is a kind of fusion—some would even call it confusion. In neuroscience, there is an invented term that is meant to convey this kind of fusion or confusion of the senses. The term is *synaesthesia* or *synesthesia*. It is a modern linguistic creation, combining two ancient Greek words: the preverb *syn-*, meaning 'together', and a noun derived from the verb *aisthanesthai*, meaning 'to sense'.[5] The basic idea here is that the senses can be interchangeable in the process of perception. It is as if one sense could substitute for another.

1§21. But can we really say that metonymy is the same thing as synesthesia? I say no, if in fact the term *synesthesia* is meant to account primarily for the substitution of one sense for another. In terms of the working definitions that I used at the beginning of my project, the mental process of substitution creates metaphors, not metonyms, which are created instead by the mental process of connecting, combining. Although metonymy can produce the momentary effect of fusing one sense with another, the senses can still remain distinct from each other, since the fusion happens only in the actual moment of combining one sense with another—of connecting the senses with each other—but the same senses that we see being fused together in one moment can still get separated from each other in other moments. For example, Hungarian apricot brandy smells intensely sweet—but it has no sweetness to the taste. So, in this case, a sensory fusion at the moment of smelling is counteracted by a sensory distinctness at the moment of tasting.

[5] For comments on such concepts as *synesthesia* and *fusion* in the context of Greek ritual, see Bierl 2009:255, 259–264.

Two Kinds of Fusion: Sensory and Emotional

1§22. What I have argued here about the metonymy of sensory fusion, as an experience, is parallel to another kind of metonymy, which I will call emotional fusion. A classic example is this short poem by Catullus, who lived in the first century BCE:

Extract 1-C

> I hate and I love. Why I am doing it, you might be asking? | I don't know.
> But I feel [*sentīre*] it happening to me, and for me it is a torture.
>
> Catullus 85[6]

1§23. The speaker here is shown in a moment of actively engaging in the emotions of hate and love simultaneously, but this same moment is viewed also as a passive experiencing of these same two emotions, again simultaneously. Hating and loving are things I am doing actively right now, the speaker is saying, but these same things are at the same time also being done to me, and I am passively letting it all happen. Just as the fusing of senses at one moment can be contrasted with the separation of these same senses at other moments, so also with the emotions: what may be a simultaneous experiencing of hate and love in one context, as in the wording I just quoted, can be viewed as distinct experiences in other contexts. The emotions of hate and love are here metonymically combined with each other, just as the senses can be combined. What we are seeing, then, is not mutual replacement, where one sense or emotion substitutes for another, but mutual connectivity.

A Metonymic Exercise in Sensory Fusion

1§24. I return here to the colloquial expression *look and feel*. As I noted a few moments ago, this expression refers to a feeling in general, connecting all the senses—not only the senses of looking and touching. So, when a given situation has a really good look and feel to it, you could even take away the primary sense of eyesight and still be left with a good look and feel. The point I am making here conjures in my mind the celebrated "tango scene" in the film *Scent of a Woman* (1992; directed by Martin Brest, screenplay by Bo Goldman), where we encounter a blind man literally feeling his way around a dancing floor. What we see in this scene, as I will now argue, is a metonymic exercise in sensory fusion.

6 *odi et amo: quare id faciam fortasse requiris. | nescio sed fieri sentio et excrucior.*

1§25. As we join the scene, a blind man named Frank (acted by Al Pacino) is about to dance the tango with a beautiful young woman named Donna (acted by Gabrielle Anwar), whom he has persuaded to learn this dance from him. Before the dance begins, Frank leans over to Charlie (acted by Chris O'Donnell), a timid young man who has been hired to take care of the blind older man, and asks him to estimate the "coordinates" of the dance floor. Once this spatial framework is set in his mind, Frank can begin the dance.

Extract 1-Da

[The online version features a link here to the relevant scene in the film *Scent of a Woman* (1:22:35).]

The original song in this scene is "Por una cabeza," music and lyrics 1935 by Carlos Gardel and Alfredo Le Pera.

Extract 1-Db

[The online version features a link here to a survey of audio recordings of "Por una cabeza."]

1§26. So, dancing the tango here has a good look and feel to it, even for Frank, who cannot see and can only feel his way around the dance floor. But what does this tango scene have to do with the title of the story, *Scent of a Woman*? For an answer, which will require an extended exercise in metonymic reading, I return to the point I already made about the primal feel of the sense of smell. Earlier in the story of *Scent of a Woman*, Frank is having a conversation with Charlie about the attractive scent of a cologne, the brand name of which is attractive in its own right, *Floris*. Frank recognizes that scent wafting from the direction of an attractive woman who had served him a drink a moment ago. The aroma inspires Frank to embark on a crude meditation about women:

Extract 1-Dc

> Oh, but I still smell her. [Sniffing] Women! What can you say? Who made 'em? God must have been a fuckin' genius. The hair—They say the hair is everything, you know. Have you ever buried your nose in a mountain of curls ... and just wanted to go to sleep forever? Or lips—and when they touched yours, were like ... that first swallow of wine ... after you just crossed the desert. Tits! Whoo-ah! Big ones, little ones, nipples staring right out at ya ... Like secret searchlights. Mmm. And

legs—I don't care if they're Greek columns ... or secondhand Steinways. What's between 'em, passport to heaven. I need a drink.

From the script of *Scent of a Woman* (1992; directed by Martin Brest, screenplay by Bo Goldman) [0:36:35]

1§27. The scent of a woman, already foregrounded in the part of the script we are reading here, is what triggers the later tango scene. But, by the time we reach that later scene, the center of attention has become the scent of another woman. That woman is Donna.

1§28. Here is the setting. The dance floor for the tango is adjacent to a table where Frank and Charlie are having drinks, and Frank catches the scent of soap wafting from the direction of someone having a drink "from down there," at the next table. So Frank in his blindness interrogates Charlie, in order to get the big picture:

Extract 1-Dd

FRANK. Who are we drinking with? I'm getting a nice soap-and-water feeling from down there.
CHARLIE. Ah ... female.
FRANK. Female? You're callin' her female, must mean you like her or you wouldn't be so casual. Is she alone?
CHARLIE. Yeah, she's alone.
FRANK. Things are heatin' up. Chestnut hair?
CHARLIE. Brown ... Light brown.
FRANK. Twenty-two?
CHARLIE. Wh— What am I, a guy at a carnival?
FRANK. The day we stop lookin', Charlie, is the day we die.

From the script of *Scent of a Woman* (1992)

1§29. By now the older man, with the timid young man in tow, is moving over to the table where Donna is seated. Frank starts up a conversation with her, hoping to win her affections for Charlie. The conversation soon turns to soap:

Extract 1-De

FRANK. You know, I detect ... a fragrance in the air. Don't tell me what it is. Ogilvie Sisters soap.
DONNA. Ah, that's amazing.
FRANK. I'm in the amazing business!

DONNA. It *is* Ogilvie Sisters soap. My grandmother gave me three bars for Christmas.

FRANK. I'm crazy about your grandmother. You know, I think she'd have liked Charlie too.

From the script of *Scent of a Woman* (1992)

1§30. Soon after this exchange, Donna will get drawn into "giving it a try" by dancing the tango with the blind man, who reassures her that this dance is not like life—because the tango is forgiving of mistakes. If you make a mistake and "get tangled" when you dance the tango, you just "tango on." The reassurances are vital, since Donna has already confessed to Frank that she is mortally afraid of making mistakes.

1§31. So, the combinatory power of metonymy makes it possible for the mind to link the primal sense of smell with the look and feel of dancing the tango. The smell here metonymically triggers the mental association that leads to the dance.

1§32. I must stress here that such a mental association should not be mistaken for what is sometimes known as *free association*, since the elements that are now being connected follow an ordered sequence, a natural and organic continuum. Such an ordered sequence is like the ordering of steps that add up to a dance like the tango itself.

1§33. So, the scent of a woman can be a metonym. And I must add that the title of the film *Scent of a Woman* is in fact a metonym, since it triggers the mental associations that lead into the entire story by that name. Titles are like that. When they connect well to the connected parts of the story and to the story as a whole, they can become metonyms. In some cases, they can even become masterpieces of metonymy.

A Metonymic Activation of All Five Senses: A Muse Inspires a Poet

1§34. What I am about to analyze is a primal scene that gets replayed in many forms throughout the history of literature. I concentrate here on a form that derives from ancient Greek poetic traditions. In the scene I have chosen as the first example of this form, we will see a Muse inspiring a poet, and her act of inspiration will activate all five senses. What results is, I think, a masterpiece of metonymy.

1§35. The setting for this primal scene is exquisitely French. The text comes from the Epilogue of the romantic opera *The Tales of Hoffmann* (*Les Contes d'Hoffmann*), composed by Jacques Offenbach (libretto by Jules Barbier; world premiere February 10, 1881). Here is what we are about to see: a Muse, whose identity has been disguised up to now, reveals herself to a poet, whose persona is a fictionalized version of a real author named Ernst Theodor Wilhelm Hoffmann (1776–1822; he renamed himself E. T. A. Hoffmann and, pointedly, the new "A." of E. T. A. stands for "Amadeus"). We join the scene at a moment when the Muse, dropping her disguise as the poet's faithful manservant and now revealing herself in all her celestial feminine beauty, addresses Hoffmann in prose, and then the poet responds to her words in passionate song:

Extract 1-Ea

> **The Muse to Hoffmann.** What about me? Me, the faithful friend whose hand would wipe the tears from your eyes. The one who made your sorrow go to sleep, to be exhaled in dreams that soar to the skies. Am I nothing to you? May the storm of your passions subside in you. The man who was exists no more. Be reborn, poet! I love you, Hoffmann. Belong to me.
>
> **Hoffmann responds to the Muse by singing.** God, with what intoxication do you [= the Muse] set my soul on fire! | Your voice, like a divine harmony, has penetrated me. | My very being is devoured by a fire that is sweet as it burns. | The looks of your eyes have poured their flame into mine, | like radiant stars! | And I sense [*sentir*], ah, my Muse loved by me, | your perfumed breath passing | over my lips and over my eyes. | Muse loved by me, I belong to you.
>
> Jacques Offenbach *The Tales of Hoffmann* Act 5 [No. 27] [Dibbern 2000:138–139]; my translation[7]

1§36. A most memorable example of this scene from *The Tales of Hoffmann* was performed at Covent Garden in 1981. Claire Powell was the Muse, and Placido Domingo was Hoffmann.

Extract 1-Eb

[The online version features a link here to the relevant scene in the 1981 video-audio recording of *The Tales of Hoffmann*, with discussion.]

[7] **The Muse to Hoffmann.** *Et moi? Moi la fidèle amie dont la main essuya tes yeux? Par qui la douleur endormie s'exhale en rêves dans les cieux. Ne suis-je rien? Que la tempête des passions s'appaise en toi. L'homme n'est plus! Renais, poète! Je t'aime, Hoffmann. Appartiens-moi!*

Hoffmann responds to the Muse by singing. *O Dieu! de quelle ivresse embrases-tu mon âme, | comme un concert divin ta voix m'a pénétré, | d'un feu doux et brûlant mon être est dévoré, | tes regards dans les miens ont épanché leur flamme, | comme des astres radieux! | Et je sens, a ma muse aimée, | passer ton haleine enbaumée | sur mes lèvres et sur mes yeux! | Muse aimée, je suis a toi!*

1§37. I note in passing a detail in this clip that is purely coincidental to the story of *Tales*—though as we will see later it is not at all coincidental to other stories about human contact with the divine: as Claire Powell, acting the role of the Muse, removes the stovepipe hat she is wearing, revealing her true identity as a celestial Muse, we see a shock of curly hair, heretofore hidden underneath the hat, cascading down from her head and spreading luxuriantly around her neck and shoulders. In masterpieces of metonymy taken from other stories still to be explored in this book, we will see further examples of such cascading curly hair—and in these examples the image of the hair will be part of the story.

1§38. With this detail duly noted, I am now ready to focus on the central moment when the poet sings "I sense [*je sens*], ah, my Muse loved by me, | your perfumed breath passing | over my lips and over my eyes."[8] The verb *sentir* of the wording *je sens*, 'I sense', here refers to two sensations at the same time. First, there is the sensation of *feeling* the breath of the Muse who has finally revealed herself as the true object of the poet's desire. Second, there is the sensation of actually *smelling* the sweet scent wafting from this divine breath. And why is this scent sweet to the taste? It is because the wording pictures the Muse's breath at the precise moment of actually touching the lips of the poet, entering his mouth, and her voice can now penetrate him and devour him, inside out, with the sweetness of its fire: "With what intoxication do you [= the Muse] set my soul on fire! | Your voice, like a divine harmony, has penetrated me. | My very being is devoured by a fire that is sweet [*doux*] as it burns."[9]

1§39. In my metonymic reading, the feeling of the Muse's perfumed *breath*, which is literally a poetic *inspiration*, becomes an exquisite experience of physical contact with the poet's lips, which can now speak, and with his eyes, which can now see what is being spoken to be heard: "The looks of your eyes have poured their flame into mine, | like radiant stars!"[10] We can now finally understand that the contact of the poet's lips and eyes with the sweet-smelling breath of the Muse is the combined sensory experience of touching as well as seeing and hearing and smelling and tasting her divine presence.

1§40. So, by the time the Muse finally says to the poet, "Belong to me," and the poet responds in passionate song, "I belong to you," what has happened is a metonymy of physical contact with the divine. And this contact extends from an earthbound existence all the way up to the sky—which would be otherwise a most alien place for a mortal to experience. While the sky is alien to a mortal poet in metaphor, as we saw in the example of the weeping sky, that same sky

8 *Je sens, ... | passer ton haleine enbaumée | sur mes lèvres et sur mes yeux!*

9 *De quelle ivresse embrases-tu mon âme, | comme un concert divin ta voix m'a pénétré, | d'un feu doux et brûlant mon être est dévoré.*

10 *Tes regards dans les miens ont épanché leur flamme, | comme des astres radieux!*

can now become familiar to him in the world of metonymy, which makes it possible for the celestial Muse and the earthbound poet to make contact by way of physically touching each other, mouth to mouth. I see a vivid contrast here between the poetics of connection in metonymy and the poetics of substitution in metaphor. Although something alien that is substituted in metaphor can remain truly alien, as when tears flowing from the human eye remain alien to the rain pouring from the sky, that same alien something can become familiar—intimately familiar—when it is actually being connected to something familiar. That is what happens when the tears of a poet make contact with something in the sky—and when that something turns out to be a loving Muse who desires familiarity with the poet.

1§41. Such familiarity can be deceptive, of course. And, in fact, there is an alternative version of *The Tales of Hoffmann* where the poet sings his love not to the true Muse, as he does in the Epilogue of so many older versions as also in the new version performed at Covent Garden in 1981 (Act 5 [No. 27]), but to a false Muse. In this alternative version, which is actually closer to the original intention of the composer Jacques Offenbach, the song of the poet's totalizing love is sung not in the Epilogue (Act 5 [No. 27]) but in an earlier part of the narrative (Act 3 [No. 16]), and, in this earlier part, the immediate object of desire is not the real Muse but a perfidious courtesan named Giulietta.[11] In this alternative version, the concluding words where the poet sings "Muse loved by me, I belong to you"[12] are missing; also, the poet in this version does not sing "Ah, my Muse loved by me,"[13] as in the version of the Epilogue, but simply "O my beloved one."[14] All that is because the poet here is singing to Giulietta, and this woman is, as I said a minute ago, a false Muse.

1§42. Or, to put it more accurately, the poet in this alternative version is singing to a refraction of a false image of the real Muse. Here is what I mean. In the logic of the master narrative that connects the three tales of love that are told by the character of Hoffmann in *The Tales of Hoffmann*, the immortal Muse of the poet is displaced in his intoxicated mind by a deceptive reflection, a *diva* singer of high opera whose name is, appropriately, La Stella, or the 'Star', and this false reflection of the real Muse is fragmented into three refractions of the divine image. That is how the character of Giulietta as a false Muse takes shape: she is one of these three refractions, since she is one of the three women loved by the poet in the three tales of love that he tells in *The Tales of Hoffmann*. And, like Giulietta, the other two women in the other two tales are also false Muses.

[11] For documentation, see Dibbern 2000:139; also Nagy 2009c:88.

[12] *Muse aimée, je suis a toi!*

[13] *A ma muse aimée.*

[14] *Ô ma bienaimée.*

They are Olympia and Antonia, who as we will see later are likewise refractions of the false image of the real Muse. Even before this real Muse drops her disguise as Hoffmann's faithful manservant and reveals herself in all her celestial feminine beauty, she herself declares that all three of these women in Hoffmann's three tales are really one and the same woman, who is the operatic *diva* named La Stella:

Extract 1-Ec

> Olympia ... Antonia ... Giulietta ... they are all just one and the same woman, La Stella!
>
> Jacques Offenbach *The Tales of Hoffmann* Act 5 No. 25 [Dibbern 2000:136]; my translation[15]

1§43. I said a minute ago that the name of this *diva*, La Stella or the 'Star', is most appropriate. Here is why: this false Muse attracts the poet by looking like the real Muse—as if she too were a heavenly body. I recall the words sung by Hoffmann to the real Muse in the Epilogue (Act 5 [No. 27]): "The looks of your eyes have poured their flame into mine, | like radiant stars!"[16] In the alternative version, placed at an earlier phase of the narrative (Act 3 [No. 16]), Hoffmann is suffering from a tragic delusion when he sings these words to Giulietta instead of the Muse. This way, the poet is in effect singing to a refraction of the false Muse who is the 'Star' named La Stella. But the song remains the same song, intended for the poet's one true love.

1§44. For the sake of variation, I will now show an English-language text of this same song. In this case, the libretto for *The Tales of Hoffmann* adopts the alternative version for performing the song, and so Hoffmann sings it at the earlier point in the story (Act 3 [No. 16]) where, tragically, he is singing not to the real Muse but to the false one. Here again is the poet's passionate song, this time reworded into English:

Extract 1-Ed

> O heaven O joy divine | illumines all around me. | Let music from the spheres. | Your voice has pierced my heart. | A fervent eager flame | consumes my every part. | Your glances kindle mine | and tongues of fire surround me. | They burn as the stars in the skies | and I feel with my love ablaze. The breath of your passion that plays | on my mouth and on my eyes. | The breath of your passion, | of that passion that plays

[15] *Olympia ... Antonia ... Giulietta ... Ne sont qu'une même femme: La Stella!*

[16] *Tes regards dans les miens ont épanché leur flamme, | comme des astres radieux!*

| on my mouth | on my mouth | and on my eyes. | O heaven O joy divine | illumines all around me. | Your glances kindle mine | and tongues of fire | and tongues of fire surround me.

From the film *The Tales of Hoffmann* (1951; directed by Michael Powell and Emeric Pressburger; French libretto of Jules Barbier, translated into English by Dennis Arundell)

Extract 1-Ef 

[The online version features a link here to the relevant scene in the 1951 film *The Tales of Hoffmann* (1:13:47), with discussion.]

1§45. Even in this version where Hoffmann is singing to Giulietta instead of the Muse, the love of the poet is already intended for the true Muse. The poet will soon fall out of love with Giulietta, this refraction of La Stella, and, in the end, he will also fall out of love with La Stella herself, that false reflection of the true Muse. Instead, he will love the true Muse as the goddess who has always been there for him even if he did not know it.

Another Metonymic Activation: The Muses Inspire Hesiod

1§46. In the scene that I have analyzed from *The Tales of Hoffmann*, we have just seen a faithful transmission of a classical Greek model for poetic inspiration. A prototype of this model is a scene in the Hesiodic *Theogony* where the nine Muses, who are nine refractions emanating from a singular divine female source of inspiration, are shown in the act of *inspiring* Hesiod, thus making him a poet, by literally *breathing into* (*en-pneîn*) him an *audē* or 'voice':

Extract 1-Fa

They [= the Muses] breathed into [*en-e-pneu-san*] me [= Hesiod] a voice [*audē*]

Hesiodic *Theogony* 31[17]

1§47. This voice that the Muses breathe into Hesiod, thus making him a poet, is really their voice, which now becomes also his voice:

17 ἐνέπνευσαν δέ μοι αὐδὴν.

Extract 1-Fb

> Their voice [*audē*] pours forth from them [= the Muses] without ever running out of power, | and flowing sweet [*hēdu-*] from their mouths.
>
> Hesiodic *Theogony* 39–40[18]

1§48. Elsewhere too in the Hesiodic *Theogony*, the Muses are described as *hēdu-epeiai* 'having sweet words' (*Theogony* 965, 1021).[19] And the sound of their voice, which is literally sweet to the taste, is eroticized as well as estheticized by the beautiful desirability of their mouth, which is explicitly visualized:

Extract 1-Fc

> Sending through their mouth [*stoma*] a voice [*ossa*] that rouses desire, | they [= the Muses] sing-and-dance [*melpesthai*].
>
> Hesiodic *Theogony* 65–66[20]

1§49. The very vision of a Muse's mouth, if it is ever to be visualized, can be pictured as a singular female mouth. That is what happens in the description we have just read. And why does this vision need to be singularized? One reason is that the nine Muses can be seen as nine refractions emanating from a singular divine female source of inspiration, who is the goddess *Mnēmosunē* or 'Memory', their mother (*Theogony* 54, 915). But there is also another reason, which is more to the point. The mouth of the Muses needs to be pictured as a singular female mouth because the sweet-tasting voice that flows from such a single mouth is being poured into the mouth of one single male poet. And this pouring is mediated by the sweet-smelling breath of divine inspiration that emanates from the Muses. So, the sweet-tasting voice of these Muses makes contact not merely with the hearing of the poet. Because it is sweet-tasting, this voice can flow right into the mouth of the poet. Implicit in this mediation is a mystical kind of contact, a kind of touching, which makes it possible for the sweet taste to be poured directly from the desirable female mouth of the Muses into the desirous male mouth of the poet. It is some kind of cosmic mouth-to-mouth kiss.

18 τῶν δ' ἀκάματος ῥέει αὐδὴ | ἐκ στομάτων ἡδεῖα.
19 ἡδυέπειαι.
20 ἐρατὴν δὲ διὰ στόμα ὄσσαν ἱεῖσαι | μέλπονται.

Variations on a Theme of a Kiss: A Metonymic Reading of the Opening Words in the *Song of Songs*

1§50. Such a mentality is comparable to what we read in the 86 sermons of Bernard of Clairvaux (1090–1153) on the *Song of Songs* in the Hebrew Bible—a text that Bernard had read in the Latin Vulgate translation. In the mystical interpretation of Bernard, the Word of God reaches the human soul with an ineffable cosmic mouth-to-mouth kiss (*Sermons on the Song of Songs* 1.5, 2.2, 2.3, and so on), and, for textual support, he is thinking of the opening words of the *Song of Songs*. In the Latin Vulgate version that Bernard was reading, what we see is a syncopated re-enactment of an erotic dialogue between lovers. I offer here a working translation of the words as read by Bernard:

Extract 1-Ga

> May he kiss me with the kiss of his mouth.
>
> *Song of Songs* 1:1, Latin Vulgate version
> [= 1:2 in the Hebrew Bible][21]

1§51. Bernard of Clairvaux recognizes (as in *Sermons on the Song of Songs* 1.5) that the point of comparison in this lyrical passage that opens the *Song of Songs* is a sexual encounter between lovers, but for him the erotic dialogue between them is to be interpreted as an allegory about the initiative taken by God to establish contact between the Word of God and human nature. And the high point of this allegory is the reference, at the very beginning of the *Song of Songs*, to the mouth-to-mouth kiss shared by the lovers. For Bernard, it is this kiss that expresses allegorically the actual moment of spiritual contact between the Word and humanity.

1§52. I take this opportunity to offer a working definition of *allegory*: if we understand *metaphor* as an expression of meaning by substitution, then *allegory* is an *extended metaphor* that maintains the substitution, not letting go of it at any point. So, the presence of an allegory in a given narrative is the omnipresence of one single driving metaphor, which can pervade without limitations the entire narrative.

1§53. Even if the allegorical interpretation of Bernard goes far beyond the intent of the original Hebrew text of the *Song of Songs*, I think that he is right to see in this text some kind of reference to some kind of contact between God and humanity. In the logic of the Hebrew text, however, I think that the activation of such a transcendent contact is made possible by the explicitly sexual

[21] *osculetur me osculo oris sui.*

contact that is taking place between human and human. In terms of this logic, it is such sexual contact that makes it possible for humans to communicate with the divine. And, conversely, in the chicken-and-egg mentality of this logic, it is this communication with the divine that makes it possible for a human couple to experience the sublimity of sexual pleasure with one another.

1§54. Following this train of thought, I will now examine the larger context of the opening of the *Song of Songs*, reading it metonymically. I begin with a translation of the text that follows the version transmitted in the Latin Vulgate:[22]

Extract 1-Gb

> [She:] $|_2$ May he kiss me with the kiss of his mouth.
>
> [He:] [I kiss you] because [*quia*] your breasts are better than wine. $|_3$ They are scented with perfumed oils that are the best.
>
> [She:] Like [perfumed] oil when poured is [the sound of] your name. That is why girls have loved you. $|_4$ "Go ahead and tug at me! We will run after you, [following the scent of your perfumed oil]. The king has led me into his chamber."
>
> [He:] We [= I] will celebrate, finding joy in you, and we are [= I am] keeping in mind your breasts, which are better than wine. Those who are straightforward [masculine] do love you.
>
> *Song of Songs* 1:2–4, Latin Vulgate version
> [where the numbering is 1:1–3][23]

1§55. And here is the version as transmitted in the Greek Septuagint:

Extract 1-Gc

> [She:] $|_2$ May he kiss me with the kisses of his mouth.
>
> [He:] [I kiss you] because [ὅτι] your breasts are better than wine. $|_3$ And that scent of yours, the scent that comes from oil of myrrh, is better than all other perfumes.

[22] The parts of the translation that are labeled "[She]" and "[He]" are not, I must emphasize, a part of the textual tradition. The square brackets are meant to indicate that I am reconstructing these assignments of "parts" in a dialogue.

[23] $|_2$ *osculetur me osculo oris sui quia meliora sunt ubera tua vino* $|_3$ *fraglantia unguentis optimis oleum effusum nomen tuum ideo adulescentulae dilexerunt te* $|_4$ *trahe me post te curremus introduxit me rex in cellaria sua exultabimus et laetabimur in te memores uberum tuorum super vinum recti diligunt te.*

> [She:] Like oil of myrrh when poured is [the sound of] your name. That is why girls have loved you. $|_4$ They have tugged at you, [saying] "We will run after you, following that scent of yours, the scent that comes from oil of myrrh. The king has led me into his chamber."
>
> [He:] We [= I] will celebrate, finding joy in you, and we [= I] will love your breasts, which are better than wine. The essence of straightforwardness has loved you.
>
> *Song of Songs* 1:2–4, Greek Septuagint version [where, again, the numbering is 1:1–3][24]

1§56. My two working translations here, though they conform to the words transmitted in the Latin Vulgate and in the Greek Septuagint, do not conform in some ways to the words transmitted in the surviving version of the Hebrew text. This Hebrew version, which follows the Masoretic tradition of restoring the vowels that were originally left unwritten in the earlier textual transmission of the Hebrew Bible, shows some words that differ in meaning from corresponding words transmitted by both the Latin Vulgate and the Greek Septuagint. But these corresponding words, as we will now see, stem from an alternative Hebrew reading that was evidently the source for the translations we see in the Latin Vulgate and in the Greek Septuagint.

1§57. In the alternative reading of the Hebrew text as reflected in the translations I have just given for *Song* 1:2–4, a woman's breasts are ostentatiously foregrounded. In the Masoretic reading, on the other hand, even the visualization of breasts is absent. That is because the Masoretic tradition, in restoring the vowels that were left unwritten in the consonantal sequence *ddyk* found in the earlier textual transmission of the Hebrew Bible, gives the reading *dōḏeyḵā*, which would mean 'your [*masculine* your] love', instead of *daddayiḵ*, which would mean 'your [*feminine* your] breasts'—and which corresponds to the reading transmitted not only by the Latin Vulgate, which gives the translation *ubera tua*, meaning 'your breasts', but also by the Greek Septuagint, which gives the translation *mastoi sou* (μαστοί σου), likewise meaning 'your breasts'.

1§58. Some have argued, I should hasten to add, that the translation 'your breasts' in the Latin Vulgate and in the Greek Septuagint stems not from the form *daddayiḵ* in Hebrew, which would mean 'your [*feminine* your] breasts', but

24 $|_2$ Φιλησάτω με ἀπὸ φιλημάτων στόματος αὐτοῦ, ὅτι ἀγαθοὶ μαστοί σου ὑπὲρ οἶνον, $|_3$ καὶ ὀσμὴ μύρων σου ὑπὲρ πάντα τὰ ἀρώματα. Μύρον ἐκκενωθὲν ὄνομά σου. διὰ τοῦτο νεάνιδες ἠγάπησάν σε, $|_4$ εἵλκυσάν σε, ὀπίσω σου εἰς ὀσμὴν μύρων σου δραμοῦμεν. Εἰσήνεγκέν με ὁ βασιλεὺς εἰς τὸ ταμίειον αὐτοῦ. Ἀγαλλιασώμεθα καὶ εὐφρανθῶμεν ἐν σοί, ἀγαπήσομεν μαστούς σου ὑπὲρ οἶνον· εὐθύτης ἠγάπησέν σε.

from *daddeykā*, which would mean 'your [*masculine* your] breasts'.[25] The motivation for making such an argument can be traced back to a general desire to interpret the entire *Song of Songs* as an allegory. In terms of an allegorical interpretation, we would start with the general idea that the lovers in the *Song*, imagined as a bridegroom and a bride, are meant to be viewed as substitutes for God and Israel respectively, or, according to a Christian re-reading, for Jesus and his Church—or simply for God and the human soul.[26] Here I apply again my working definition of *allegory* as an *extended metaphor* that maintains the substitution created by the metaphor, not letting go of it at any point. As I already said, the presence of an allegory in a given narrative is the omnipresence of one single driving metaphor, which can pervade without limitations the entire narrative. At the beginning of the *Song of Songs*, for example, if the two lovers are viewed from the start as acting the parts of bridegroom and bride for the purpose of serving as allegorical substitutes for God and Israel, then the logic of any details about this amorous pair should conform to an overall discourse about God and Israel, not to any kind of realism that may be needed for achieving an artistic description of a sexual encounter between lovers. That is how, in terms of an allegorical interpretation of the *Song of Songs*, the object of erotic attention could become the breasts of a male lover, not of a female lover: after all, even God could be eroticized simply by being compared to an amorous bridegroom.

1§59. Responding to such a line of argumentation, I start by accepting the idea that God can be eroticized in the context of the *Song of Songs* writ large, and so I subscribe to the term *theo-eroticism* as used by some exegetes of the Bible.[27] But then I still need to dispute the argument that insists on a reference, by allegory, to the male breasts of God. Such an allegorical reading, with reference to the passage we have just read in *Songs* 1:2–4, is lacking in internal consistency. Nowhere else in the *Song of Songs* are male breasts eroticized—let alone mentioned. Moreover, if we consider the entire Greek version of the Hebrew Bible as transmitted by the Septuagint, nowhere else are male breasts ever even mentioned: in the Septuagint, the Greek word *mastoi* refers always to female breasts, never to male breasts.[28] The only exception would be the present example of *mastoi* in *Song* 1:2–4, and the only way to defend the interpretation of this word as referring to male breasts in this context would be to argue that the eroticizing of God justifies an eroticizing of his male breasts, linked to an

25 Such an argument is evaluated by Kaplan 2010:59–60, 134–135.

26 Kaplan 2010:iii, 28.

27 For the term, see Kaplan 2010:135, who describes as "theo-erotic" the trope of describing God or Jesus erotically.

28 Kaplan 2010:134–135n168.

eroticizing of the male lover. But there is no textual evidence for the idea of eroticizing God by envisioning his male breasts.

1§60. Granted, a possible exception could be cited from a Christian text, *Revelations* 1:13, where we read a description of a splendid golden sash worn around the *mastoi* 'breasts' of the glorified Son of Man.[29] But even this image, stemming from the early Christian era (*Revelations* was composed in the late first century CE), is not so much eroticized as it is estheticized, and it could be interpreted in an erotic sense only if we assume that (1) the Christian composer of this image is alluding to the passage we have read in *Song* 1:2–4, and (2) this composer understands the Greek wording *mastoi sou* 'your breasts' as referring to male breasts in that passage. But I do not find either one of these two assumptions compelling, and so I continue to argue for the interpretation of the Greek *mastoi sou* 'your breasts' and of the Latin *ubera tua* 'your breasts' at *Song* 1:2–4 as referring to the breasts of a woman who is loved by a man.

1§61. That said, I can resume my own ongoing interpretation of the opening of the *Song of Songs*. In the Latin Vulgate, the vision of a woman's *ubera* 'breasts' at *Song* 1:2 (numbered 1:1 in the Vulgate) is continued in the next verse, *Song* 1:3 (1:2), with an adjective: these breasts are *fraglantia* 'fragrant', smelling of the best perfumed oil.[30] So, in this version, the woman is already anointed with oil. In the Greek Septuagint, the same vision of the woman's *mastoi* 'breasts' at *Song* 1:2 is this time continued with an explanatory clause in the next verse, at *Song* 1:3: "And that scent of yours, the scent that comes from oil of myrrh, is better than all other perfumes."[31] So, in this version too, as we can see from the explicit reference to "your" scent, the woman is once again already anointed with perfumed oil. But then, what follows in both the Latin Vulgate and the Greek Septuagint at *Song* 1:3 is a reference to the perfumed oil that is poured to anoint the man who loves the woman. So by now both the man and the woman have been anointed with perfumed oil. In the Masoretic version, however, even the very first reference to the smell of perfumed oil applies not to the woman but to the man, whose "love" in *Song* 1:2 is the referent for the smell of the oil that is poured.

1§62. Elsewhere in the Hebrew Bible, we find other contexts that support the non-Masoretic alternative Hebrew version of *Song* 1:2–4 as reflected in the Latin Vulgate and the Greek Septuagint.[32] One such context is *Song* 4:10, where *ddyk* is interpreted in the Masoretic tradition as *dōḏayiḵ*, which would mean

[29] Kaplan 2010:133–136, with bibliography.

[30] $|_2$ ... *ubera tua* ... $|_3$ *fraglantia unguentis optimis* (your breasts, fragrant with the best oils).

[31] καὶ ὀσμὴ μύρων σου ὑπὲρ πάντα τὰ ἀρώματα. The numbering of this passage in the Septuagint is *Song* 1:2.

[32] See again Kaplan 2010:59–60, 134–135.

'your [*feminine* your] love'. But a non-Masoretic alternative version is *daddayiḵ*, which would mean 'your [*feminine* your] breasts'. This version, featuring a woman's breasts instead of simply her "love," corresponds again to the translations provided by the Latin Vulgate and the Greek Septuagint at *Song* 4:10, where the man exclaims to the woman: "More beautiful are your breasts than wine!"[33]

1§63. Also, at *Song* 7:13, where the consonantal sequence *ddy* in the Hebrew textual transmission is vocalized in the Masoretic tradition as *dōḏay*, which would mean 'my [*feminine* my] love', a non-Masoretic alternative version is *dadday*, which would mean 'my [*feminine* my] breasts'. Here too, such an alternative Hebrew reading was evidently the source for the Latin Vulgate and Greek Septuagint translations of the passage, where the woman says to the man that she will take him to a beautiful vineyard, and "there I will give my breasts to you."[34]

1§64. Finally, there is an attestation of *daddeyhā* in the sense of 'her breasts' in the Masoretic text of *Proverbs* 5:19. Here is the context: a loving father, instructing his son, is saying to him that a good husband should avoid having sex with women other than his wife, who is described as having desirable breasts: the husband should be "intoxicated" with this woman's breasts, that is, with *daddeyhā* in the sense of 'her breasts'. The Hebrew wording in the Masoretic text of *Proverbs* 5:19 is this: "May her breasts satisfy you always, may you always be intoxicated in her love."[35] In the Latin Vulgate version of *Proverbs* 5:19, we read: "May her breasts intoxicate you always, and may you always feel delight in her love."[36] Next, in *Proverbs* 5:20, the text goes on to say that the husband should not be intoxicated with the breasts of a woman who is a stranger to him.[37] The feeling of intoxication in response to a woman's breasts, as expressed here, is I think parallel to the feeling expressed in *Song* 1:2–4 (1:1–3), where the woman's breasts are described as superior to wine.

1§65. On the basis, then, of the comparative evidence that we can extract from the contexts I have just surveyed, especially from the context of *Proverbs* 5:19–20, I argue that the non-Masoretic alternative Hebrew version of *Song*

[33] Latin Vulgate: *pulchriora ubera tua vino*. Greek Septuagint: τί ἐκαλλιώθησαν μαστοί σου ἀπὸ οἴνου; For the Greek, a more precise rendition would be "How your breasts are more beautiful than wine!"

[34] Latin Vulgate: *ibi dabo tibi ubera mea*. Greek Septuagint: ἐκεῖ δώσω τοὺς μαστούς μου σοί. The numbering of this passage in both the Vulgate and the Septuagint is 7:12.

[35] The Masoretic text of this part of *Proverbs* 5:19 reads: דַּדֶּיהָ יְרַוֻּךָ בְכָל־עֵת בְּאַהֲבָתָהּ תִּשְׁגֶּה תָמִיד.

[36] *ubera ejus inebrient te in omni tempore, in amore eius delectare iugiter.* In the Greek Septuagint, the wording is not so explicit: ἡ δὲ ἰδία ἡγείσθω σου, καὶ συνέστω σοι ἐν παντὶ καιρῷ "May she be considered your very own, and may she be with you always."

[37] On these readings of the relevant Hebrew texts, I gratefully acknowledge the expert help and advice of Keith Stone 2013.12.28. On the *Song of Songs* in general, I recommend the judicious assessment of Stern 2008.

1:2–4 as translated in the Greek Septuagint and in the Latin Vulgate, where the breasts of a woman are highlighted, is more accurate than the Masoretic version in transmitting the traditional wording of this composition.

1§66. To back up this argument, I now argue further that the Masoretic version, where the image of the woman's breasts is not made visible, forces upon the reader an interpretation that lacks internal coherence. To make this further argument, I will first offer a literal translation of the Masoretic version and will then analyze briefly the problems I encounter in the course of interpreting the text of this version. Here, then, is my translation of the relevant Masoretic text:

Extract 1-Gd

> $|_2$ May he kiss me with the kiss of his mouth, because your [*masculine* your] love is better than wine. $|_3$ Your [*masculine* your] perfumed oils are the best. Like oil being poured is [the sound of] your [*masculine* your] name. That is why girls have loved you [*masculine* you]. $|_4$ Tug at me. We will be running after you, following the scent of your perfumed oils. The king has given me entrance into his chamber. We will celebrate, rejoicing in you [*masculine* you], thinking of your [*masculine* your] love as better than wine. Those who love you [*masculine* you] are right to do so.
>
> *Song of Songs* 1:2–4, Masoretic text[38]

1§67. The text of this Masoretic version, as we see in the translation I offer here in Extract 1-Gd, shows the same sensory experiences that we saw in the alternative version as I translated it in Extracts 1-Gb and 1-Gc. Both the Masoretic version and the alternative version highlight the smelling of perfumed oil and the tasting of wine—as well as kissing and touching. But there is a big difference between the two versions. In the Masoretic version, not only is there an absence of female breasts. More important, there is also an absence of participation by the man in the mutuality of amorous exchange with the woman. So, at verse 3, the Masoretic version formats the vowels of the Hebrew forms corresponding to the three instances of "you(r)" in such a way as to make all three of these forms masculine, though they could all be vocalized as feminine forms as well.[39] Also, according to the Masoretic vocalization, only the "love" of the man

[38] Masoretic text of *Songs* 1:2–4:

יִשָּׁקֵנִי מִנְּשִׁיקוֹת פִּיהוּ כִּי־טוֹבִים דֹּדֶיךָ מִיָּיִן.
לְרֵיחַ שְׁמָנֶיךָ טוֹבִים שֶׁמֶן תּוּרַק שְׁמֶךָ עַל־כֵּן עֲלָמוֹת אֲהֵבוּךָ.
מָשְׁכֵנִי אַחֲרֶיךָ נָּרוּצָה הֱבִיאַנִי הַמֶּלֶךְ חֲדָרָיו נָגִילָה וְנִשְׂמְחָה בָּךְ נַזְכִּירָה דֹדֶיךָ מִיַּיִן מֵישָׁרִים אֲהֵבוּךָ.

[39] Again, I thank Keith Stone 2014.01.04 for his help and advice. On the *Song of Songs* in general, I recommend the judicious assessment of Stern 2008.

is scented with perfumed oil, starting at verse 2, and only he gets anointed when the perfumed oil is poured at verse 3. Further, the pleasant thought of tasting wine is linked only with the pleasant thought of the love that comes from the man and goes to the woman.

1§68. So, we see that the woman expresses her feelings of attraction to the man, but we can find no corresponding expressions of feelings from the man. In the alternative version, on the other hand, the sensory experiences are associated with both the woman and the man. And, though there do exist some differences between the interpretations that are built into the texts of the Latin Vulgate and the Greek Septuagint, what matters for the moment is the simple fact that both these texts indicate an attraction that is mutual. Both the man and the woman express their feelings of attraction for each other, corresponding to the give-and-take of the dialogue that takes place between them. (Other examples in the *Song of Songs* where the man talks back to the woman, reciprocating her amorous feelings, include: 1:9–11, 1:15, 2:2, 6:4–9.)

1§69. But how can we be sure that there really is a dialogue going on in the non-Masoretic alternative Hebrew version at *Song* 1:2–4, as reflected in the translations of the Latin Vulgate and the Greek Septuagint? For me the most telling indication is the shift from the feminine "me" to the feminine "your" in the opening of this alternative version. The person who is speaking about the feminine "me"—saying that "I" desire to be kissed—cannot be the same speaker as the person who is speaking to the feminine "you" about "your" breasts. By contrast, in the Masoretic version, the person who is speaking about the feminine "me"—saying that "I" desire to be kissed—must be the same speaker who then speaks to a masculine "you"—in this case, to the man whose love is desired. There is no evident motivation, however, for the abrupt shift in the Masoretic version from an indirect address in expressing a desire to be kissed—"may he kiss me"—to the direct address that immediately follows—"because your [*masculine* your] love is better than wine." In the non-Masoretic alternative Hebrew version, by contrast, the corresponding abruptness of the shift from indirect to direct address could be motivated by the interruption of one speaker by another. I offer here just one possible rhetorical scenario for such an interruption. The indirectness of the woman, who is saying "May he kiss me with the kiss of his mouth," may be a gesture expressing the speaker's feelings of shyness about the boldness of her desire. But then she is interrupted by the directness of the man, who is not shy at all in responding to the boldness of the woman's desire. His response expresses his share in the desire for mouth-to-mouth kissing, but now one bold desire leads to another, as the "I" of the man speaks directly to the "you" of the woman about the beauty of her breasts scented with perfumed oil. What has just happened is an escalation in the boldness of mutual desire.

1§70. With this analysis in place, I now offer an experimental metonymic interpretation of the non-Masoretic alternative version of *Song* 1:2–4 as transmitted in the Latin Vulgate and in the Greek Septuagint (in both those texts, the traditional numbering is 1:1–3):

1§70-A. In *Song* 1:2 (1:1), a woman expresses her desire for the pleasure of mouth-to-mouth kissing with a man, which activates for both the woman and the man the sense of *touching*—as also the sense of *tasting*. At a later point, in *Song* 4:11, the woman is addressed as "my bride" by the man, and he goes on to tell her that drops of honey are flowing from her lips, and then, that both honey and milk reside under her tongue, while her garments exude the scent of incense from Lebanon.[40] At a still later point, in *Song* 7:9, the words of the man praise the woman's mouth by comparing it to wine, and then the words of the woman express the wish that the wine should flow into the mouth of her lover.

1§70-B. Back at *Song* 1:2 (1:1), before the woman can say anything more about her desire to be kissed, the man interrupts, continuing where she left off and intensifying the desire for mouth-to-mouth kissing by making this desire mutual. He too desires mouth-to-mouth kissing, but now there is something added to the desire of the woman: besides the desire that she expresses for her own reasons, the man expresses the desire for mouth-to-mouth kissing also for another reason—because [*quia*, ὅτι] he wants also the pleasure of *seeing* and *touching* the breasts of the woman. This pleasure of *seeing* and *touching* the breasts of the woman is then linked with the further pleasure of *smelling* the perfumed oil anointed on her breasts, which is further linked with the pleasure of *tasting* wine.

1§70-C. Next, at *Song* 1:3 (1:2), it is said that the *smelling* of perfumed oil is by comparison better than the *tasting* of wine, but this comparison is not metaphorical, since no substitution is required. The *smelling* of perfume can be combined with the *tasting* of wine, but, for now, the *smelling* is in the foreground while the *tasting* remains in the background, since the *smelling* is linked to the breasts, which have been decisively foregrounded.

1§70-D. Next, at *Song* 1:3 (1:2), the *smelling* of the perfumed oil is to be shared by the woman and the man as it is poured out from some kind of container.

1§70-E. Looking ahead, I highlight a relevant detail that we see at a later point, in *Song* 1:13 (1:12): visualized there is a small container, filled with oil of myrrh, which is suspended from the woman's neck and "residing" between her breasts.

[40] I admire the relevant formulation of Exum 1999:61: "[At *Song* 4:11] 'lips' and the more precise term 'tongue' are substituted for the mouth of [*Song*] 1:2 [1:1], and kisses, rather than being mentioned, are described metonymically as distilled nectar, milk and honey."

1§70-F. Having noted this detail, I come back to the present moment in the text, back to *Song* 1:3 (1:2). The next connection to be made in the ongoing sequence of connections is the pouring of perfumed oil, which is linked to the *hearing* of the sound of the man's name as that sound pours out from the mouth of the woman, whose voice is then echoed by the voices of girls who accompany the woman as her attendants. These voices, as we are about to see, are *quoted*.

1§70-G. When I speak of *quotation* in this context, I should say in advance that I have in mind a speaking voice embedded not within a *text* that is simply being read but, rather, within wording that is spoken by *speaking voices*. In the *Song of Songs*, there are two primary speaking voices, "his" and "hers," and, more important for the moment, there are also secondary speaking voices—voices that are embedded within the dramatic frame of wording spoken by the primary voices.

1§70-H. That said, I am ready to argue that the woman's voice in this passage is *quoting* the voices of young girls who are her attendants, and this quotation is preceded by a declaration that creates the effect of vicariously experiencing the collective amorous feeling of the girls in reaction to the perfumed scent of the man: "That is why girls have loved you," the woman says to the man at *Song* 1:3 (1:2). Now the quotation can start, at least in the Vulgate version of *Song* 1:4 (1:3), and the amorous girls are quoted here in the act of calling out to the man flirtatiously: "Go ahead and tug at me! We will run after you." In the Septuagint version of *Song* 1:4 (1:3), the words of the girls go further: "We will run after you, following that scent of yours, the scent that comes from oil of myrrh."

1§70-I. But the part in the Vulgate version where the girls say flirtatiously "Go ahead and tug at me!" in *Song* 1:4 (1:3) differs from the corresponding part in the Septuagint version. There the flirtatious words of the amorous girls—"Go ahead and tug at me!"—are not spoken. What is spoken instead is a narration, not a quotation, of what the amorous girls say and do. And the voice of narration is the primary speaking voice of the woman, who pictures the girls in the act of behaving flirtatiously and actually tugging at the man, hoping that he will let them follow him into the king's chamber. And, if any one of the girls succeeded, that girl could boast, as in *Song* 1:4 (1:3) "The king has led me into his chamber." So, in the Septuagint version, the girls are bolder: instead of tempting the man to tug at them, they tug at him.

1§70-J. We see at work here a mental process of self-identification, involving a psychology of *projection*. I start with the persona of the woman who is speaking. This woman *projects* her own feelings into the feelings of the amorous girls: she too desires to follow the perfectly scented man, who is evidently the king, into his royal bedchamber, but she is too shy to tug at him. So, as we see in the Vulgate version, she makes the gesture of asking him instead to tug at her. In the Masoretic version as well, the persona of the primary speaking woman in *Song*

1:4 is making the same gesture to the man, saying "Tug at me!" If the man now makes a move and tugs at the woman, thus responding to her gesture, she will follow him gladly. As for the Septuagint version, the desire to follow the king to his royal bedchamber is escalated, since the amorous girls have already been tugging at the king, flirtatiously hoping that he will let them follow along.

1§70-K. By now we can understand more deeply, I think, the mental process of self-identification that is going on here: the speaker to whom I have referred up to now simply as *the woman* can become simultaneously one of the amorous girls who desires to follow the king into his bedchamber. So, we now see here a *projection in reverse*: if I am one of the girl attendants, I can *project* my feelings into the feelings of the principal female speaker of the *Song of Songs*, and then I, yes, I will be the one who is chosen by the king to become his one true love.

1§70-L. Then, in both the Vulgate and the Septuagint versions of *Song* 1:4 (1:3), we come back full circle to the expression of a desire already expressed at the beginning, at *Song* 1:2 (1:1). The object of desire had been the pleasure of *seeing* and *touching* the woman's breasts, linked with the pleasure of *smelling* the perfumed oil that anoints the breasts—a pleasure that is now once again decisively foregrounded against the attendant pleasure of *tasting* wine. That is why the persona of the principal male speaker says in the Vulgate version of *Song* 1:2 that he is "keeping in mind" the breasts of the woman he loves: "we," he says, are *memores*, that is, "we are keeping them in mind." Those breasts that are even now kept in mind had already come into his mind at the very beginning, at *Song* 1:2 (1:1). And now, as a climax in the festive celebration has been reached, the Vulgate text at *Song* 1:4 (1:3) quotes the primary male speaker as saying *exultabimus* 'we will celebrate'.

1§70-M. As we can now see, what I said earlier about secondary speakers in the *Song of Songs*—that they are *quoted* within the frame of what is spoken by the woman and the man who are the primary speakers—applies to the primary speakers as well. That is to say, the woman and the man who are speaking to each other from the very beginning of the *Song of Songs* are themselves *quoted* by the outermost frame of this composition, which is the drama that quotes the parts, as it were, that the woman and the man say to each other.

Interpersonal Metonymy

1§71. We have just seen how the dialogic interaction between the persona of the woman and the persona of the man in the opening of the *Song of Songs* is complicated by further dialogic interaction—this time, between the woman as a primary speaker and the flirtatious girls as secondary speakers. And the interaction between the woman and the man as the two primary speakers is even more complicated, as we can tell from the vast variety of interpretations when it comes to assigning the speaking parts to the persona of the woman or to the persona of the man. Already at the very beginning of the *Song of Songs*, the casual reader can easily get confused about who says what. It is unclear whether the male persona does or does not respond to what is being said by the female persona. But such lack of clarity in the reader's mind cannot be blamed on any sense of confusion in the ancient verbal art that produced the *Song of Songs*. In that kind of art, what we see at work is a mental process of *fusion*, not *confusion*. Previously, we had seen examples of *sensory fusion*. And, yes, we see such examples also in the *Song of Songs*—in fact, all five senses are engaged in what we have read in the *Song*: tasting and touching and smelling and seeing and hearing. But now we can see another kind of fusion as well, affecting both the principal speakers and the secondary speakers: it is an *interpersonal fusion*, as when the feelings of the woman are projected into the feelings of the amorous girls who attend her—or the other way around. And, more important, we can see another example of such *interpersonal fusion* when we read the central words projecting the feelings of the woman into the feelings of the man—or the other way around. And such fusion, I argue, is metonymic, just as *sensory fusion* is metonymic. That is what I mean when I speak of *interpersonal metonymy*.

1§72. The most telling examples of interpersonal metonymy can be found in the uses of possessive personal pronouns. In what we have read from the Latin and Greek versions of the *Song of Songs*, for example, we see references to *his* mouth, *your* breasts, *your* scent, *your* name, *his* chambers, and (again) *your* breasts. To which we may add *your* love in the Masoretic Hebrew version. In order to appreciate more fully the interpersonal force of these possessive combinations, I focus here on one example, *his* mouth. When the female speaker expresses a desire to be kissed by the kiss of *his* mouth, that mouth-to-mouth kiss will become the kiss of *her* mouth as well. The kissing will create a fusion of ownership, of possession. The possession expressed by the possessive pronoun *his* can become the same possession as expressed by the possessive pronoun *her(s)*. So we see here an interpersonal fusion—even an exchange of identities. The *me* of the woman who desires to be kissed can become the *you* of the man who will kiss her on her mouth with his mouth, since the mouth-to-mouth kiss will be both *his* kiss and *her* kiss. Thus the lovers will have possession of one another, and that is why the woman in the *Song of Songs* keeps declaring that *he* is *mine* and *I* am *his* (*Song* 2:16, 6:3, 7:10).[41] Even more than that, the two lovers have projected their identities into one another, fusing themselves together.

[41] Exum 1999:62 gives a perceptive analysis of the "mutuality" that is built into this amorous declaration.

1§73. For another example of such *interpersonal fusion*, I proceed to a modern context that is historically unrelated but good to think with as a point of comparison. I cite here the words of a song composed in 1958 by Mikis Theodorakis (1925–), incorporating words from a poem composed in 1936 by Yiannis Ritsos (1919–1990). The poem of Ritsos, originally entitled *Miroloyi* (*Μοιρολόγι*), meaning *Song of Lament*, is lengthy, consisting of fourteen stanzas. In the final version, published in 1956, the poem was renamed *Epitaphios* (*Ἐπιτάφιος*), by now consisting of twenty stanzas.[42] The corresponding song of Theodorakis, by contrast, is short, consisting of the first four rhymed couplets of Stanza III. And the title of the song features wording taken from the last of the four couplets. I present here the text of the song, which is preceded by the wording for the title of the song:

Extract 1-Ha

> **Title:** Lips, those sweet-smelling lips of yours for me[43]
>
> || Hair, that curly head of hair, I would slip my fingers through it, | all those nights, while you were asleep, and I was awake, right there next to you.
>
> || Eyebrows, those eyebrows of yours for me, brows shaped like a curved scimitar, sketched with a pencil point ever so fine | —an arched chamber where my gaze could nestle and be at rest.
>
> || Eyes, those dreamy eyes in which would shine the reflection of a distant morning sky, | and I would try and make sure they never got blurred by even one single teardrop.
>
> || Lips, those sweetly scented lips of yours for me, when they made words, there was a blossoming | even from rocks and dried out trees, and nightingales would flutter.
>
> First four couplets of Stanza III of the poem *Epitaphios* (*Ἐπιτάφιος*), by Yiannis Ritsos (Γιάννης Ρίτσος); the poem was originally published as *Miroloyi* (*Μοιρολόγι*) on May 12, 1936, in the Athenian newspaper *Rizospastis* (*Ριζοσπάστης*); set to music in 1958 by Mikis Theodorakis (Μίκης Θεοδωράκης); my translation[44]

[42] For an illuminating introduction to the work of Ritsos, see Prevelakis 1983.

[43] Χείλι μου μοσχομύριστο.

[44] ||Μαλλιὰ σγουρὰ ποὺ πάνω τους τὰ δάχτυλα περνοῦσα | τὶς νύχτες ποὺ κοιμόσουνα καὶ πλάϊ σου ξαγρυπνοῦσα ||Φρύδι μου, γαϊτανόφρυδο καὶ κοντυλογραμμένο, | καμάρα ποὺ τὸ βλέμμα μου κούρνιαζε ἀναπαμένο ||Μάτια γλαρὰ ποὺ μέσα τους ἀντίφεγγαν τὰ μάκρη | πρωϊνοῦ οὐρανοῦ,

Extract 1-Hb 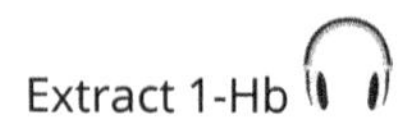

[The online version features a link here to the first recorded version of the part of the poem *Epitaphios* (*Ἐπιτάφιος*) as set to music by Mikis Theodorakis (Μίκης Θεοδωράκης), "Χείλι μου μοσχομύριστο," sung by Grigoris Bithikotsis (Γρηγόρης Μπιθικώτσης).]

And here I refer to a "recital" version of the same song, rearranged by the composer Manos Hadzidakis (1925–1994):

Extract 1-Hc 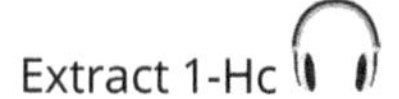

[The online version features a link here to a later recorded version of the part of the poem *Epitaphios* (*Ἐπιτάφιος*) as set to music by Mikis Theodorakis (Μίκης Θεοδωράκης), "Χείλι μου μοσχομύριστο," rearranged by Manos Hadzidakis (Μάνος Χατζιδάκις), sung by Nana Mouskouri (Νάνα Μούσχουρη).]

1§74. In quoting my translation of the song, I have used the notation of two parallel vertical bars, ||, to indicate the beginning of each one of the four couplets—and the notation of one vertical bar, |, to indicate the break between the two parts of each couplet. I draw special attention to the word that comes right after the notation || that marks the beginning of each couplet. Each one of the four English words that occupy that space in my translation corresponds exactly to each one of the Greek words that start each couplet. And each couplet, as we can see from my translation, begins with a word for a part of the body: head of hair, eyebrows, eyes, lips. There is a sequential logic to it all, starting from the top and moving downward from one body part to the next: head of hair to eyebrows to eyes to lips. The title refers to the fourth of the four body parts, the lips, and, by starting with the lips as a title and ending with the lips as the last of the body parts in the song, there is a coming full circle.

1§75. So we see a metonymy at work here, featuring a logical sequence of body parts combined with an activation of all the senses. From the very start, already in the title, there are lips that are sweet-smelling, waiting to be kissed by the loving lips of the speaker. Next there is the hair, a shock of curls waiting to be touched and fondled by the speaker's loving fingers. Next there are eyebrows, on which the eyes of the speaker may focus their loving gaze. Next there are eyes, which dreamily open in the morning and can now meet the gaze of the speaker's own loving eyes. Next there are the lips again, ready to be kissed one more time by the loving speaker. So we see here a metonymy of sensory fusion, activating all five senses. There is tasting, smelling, touching, seeing, and, climactically,

καὶ πάσκιζα μὴν τὰ θαμπώσει δάκρυ ||Χείλι μου μοσκομύριστο ποὺ ὡς λάλαγες ἀνθίζαν | λιθάρια καὶ ξερόδεντρα κι ἀηδόνια φτερουγίζαν.

even hearing—as words start to flow from the lips of the beloved, fused with the words flowing from the lips of the loving speaker whose role is sung by the singer of the song.

1§76. Besides the metonymy of sensory fusion, we see here also another kind of metonymy. It has to do with the ownership, as it were, of the lips, the hair, the eyebrows, the eyes, and then again the lips. The *I* of the loving speaker is addressing not the *you* who is the beloved but rather *your* lips and *your* hair and *your* eyebrows and *your* eyes, and then *your* lips once more. But the language of the original Greek wording here is saying not *your* but *my*. When the speaker addresses the lips of the beloved, those are not *your* lips but *my* lips, as if the lips of the beloved now belonged to the loving speaker as well, not only to the beloved. In the Greek, *híli mou* means literally *my lips*, but the persona who is addressed is clearly not *I* but *you*, the owner of the lips, the loved one. So, what we see is a projection of identity, a fusion of *I* and *you*, which is strikingly similar to the patterns of fusion we have seen in the *Song of Songs*. This pattern is an example of what I have been calling *interpersonal metonymy*. Another example in the original Greek of this song is *frídhi mou*, which means literally *my eyebrows*. In my attempt to render these examples of interpersonal metonymy into English, I have translated *híli mou* not as *my lips* but as 'those lips of yours for me', and *frídhi mou* not as *my eyebrows* but as 'those eyebrows of yours for me'. But the fact is, the starkness of the transfer of possession from the beloved to the one who loves is unmistakably clear in the original Greek.

1§77. Questions remain. In this song of Mikis Theodorakis, how are we to imagine the beloved? And what about the one who loves this beloved? Are the words of the song referring to a beloved man to whom a loving woman addresses her song? Or is it a beloved woman to whom a loving man addresses his song? In the original Greek of the song, there is no way of telling who is who, since there are no pronouns indicating the gender of either the beloved or the one who loves this beloved. In the version sung by the male singer, as I cited it in Extract 1-Hb, we could guess that the beloved is a woman and that the lover is a man. Or, in the version sung by the female singer, as I cited it in Extract 1-Hc, the beloved could be a man and the lover could be a woman. In Modern Greek popular culture, such questions are misleading. This song, ever since its first recording and continuing all the way to the present, has been appreciated and even loved by millions of Greek-speaking listeners, male and female, who can identify with the emotion of love expressed by the singer—regardless of gender. And this love, as we see from the wording of the song, is deeply eroticized as well as estheticized.

1§78. So, for anyone who is not aware of the song's origins, the obvious inference is that we see here an erotic description of a love shared by two lovers, where the *I* of the singing voice that describes this love is addressing the *you* who is loved by this loving *I*. Only those listeners who are aware of the poem of Ritsos, which as we have seen was the source of this song of Theodorakis, would know for sure that the *I* of the singing voice represents a *she*, and that the *you* is a *he*. And only they would know that the *she*, from the standpoint of the lengthy poem from which the short song was extracted, is Mary the mother of Jesus, and that the *he* is Jesus himself, whose death on the cross is being lamented by his mother in song. The poet Ritsos had based his poem on a lengthy song of lament attributed to Mary in the folk traditions of Christian Greek songmaking—a song entitled *Epitaphios Thrinos* (Ἐπιτάφιος Θρῆνος), which had crystallized into a poem dating back to the fourteenth century CE. The meaning of the title points to a lament sung at the funeral of the dead Jesus. It has been said about this medieval Greek poem:

> This traditional lament, based on early forms dating to the sixth century, is sung by entire congregations throughout Greece and all Greek Orthodox communities in the diaspora every spring during the Good Friday evening service. ... [Ritsos] reaches the broadest audience possible for a poet writing in Greek, for the *Epitaphios Thrinos* is known to nearly all speakers of the language: men and women, young and old, urban and rural, rich and poor, educated and uneducated, of all political persuasions. The Greek populace's personal memories of the lament, furthermore, are inextricably intertwined with its context, since it is sung as part of an elaborate service which re-enacts the funeral of Christ and his descent into Hades.[45]

1§79. In Greek folk traditions of lament, the dead person who is being lamented is conventionally eroticized as well as estheticized, and, in the case of laments sung at funerals for young men, the corpse can even be compared to a beautiful bridegroom who is getting ready for a wedding; moreover, songs of lament can in general be interchangeable with wedding songs.[46] In the *Epitaphios* of Ritsos as well, the corpse of Jesus is estheticized and even eroticized, as if he were a beautiful bridegroom at a wedding (X.1, XVIII.5).[47]

1§80. Earlier, I had mentioned the term *theo-eroticism* as used by some exegetes of the Hebrew Bible in referring to erotic descriptions of an idealized bridegroom who figures as the center of attention in the *Song of Songs*. By now we can see that this term can apply also, at least indirectly, to the eroticized male body in the song of Theodorakis.

45 Newton 2014:9–10; Alexiou 1974:62–69.

46 Newton 2014:12–13; Danforth 1982:74–90.

47 Newton 2014:13.

1§81. But we are not finished with the context of this song. The original poem of Ritsos was inspired by a historical event. On May 10, 1936, Ritsos saw a photograph in a newspaper. It showed a woman mourning over the dead body of a young man lying on the street. It was her son, Tassos Toussis, a factory worker who had just been killed by police at a demonstration by striking workers in the city of Thessaloniki on May 9, 1936. This image led Ritsos to compose the poem that is now known as the *Epitaphios*, imagined as a lament sung by the mourning mother in the photograph.

Extract 1-Hd

Photo: Tassos Toussis, lying dead on the street, is mourned by his mother. Originally published on the front page of the Greek newspaper *Rizospastis* (*Ριζοσπάστης*). May 10, 1936. Photo by kind permission of *Rizospastis*.

Extract 1-He

[The online version features a link here to an electronic version of the May 10, 1936 edition of *Rizospastis*, featuring the photo of Tassos Toussis on the front page.]

Defining Synecdoche

1§82. There is yet another kind of metonymy at work in the song of Theodorakis. When the beloved is addressed as *my lips* or *my eyebrows* instead of being viewed as a whole person, what we see is a highlighting of a part of the whole, as if the part could mean the same thing as the whole. There is a word for this specialized kind of metonymy, which is *synecdoche*. This English word is a latinized spelling of the Greek word *sunekdokhē*, which means literally 'getting a sense of one thing together with another thing'. In the ancient Greek lexicographical tradition, *sunekdokhē* is defined this way: 'when someone learns from a part of the whole' (Hesychius 2495, under the entry συνεκδοχή).[48]

1§83. This definition needs to be supplemented. I must add that synecdoche is not a *metaphoric substitution*, where a given something is replaced by something different, alien. Rather, synecdoche is a mental process of *metonymic connection*, where a given something is partitioned into parts of that something—and where any one of these parts, which stay connected to each other, can refer to that same whole something. Such a reference to the whole by way of any one of its parts is not a substitution for the whole, since all the parts, whether or not they are visible, can continue to participate in the mental process of referring to the whole by way of their interconnectedness with each other.

Contrasting Examples of Metaphor and Synecdoche

1§84. To show how *metaphoric substitution* is different from *metonymic connection by way of synecdoche*, I will contrast an example of metaphor with an example of synecdoche. For metaphor, I will now go back once again to a most useful example that we saw already at the beginning, back when we looked at that fictional exchange between the poet and the postman. In that example, the expression *it is raining* is replaced by the metaphor *the sky is weeping*. For the making of this metaphor, as we saw, the vision of rain pouring from the sky is replaced by the picturing of tears flowing from the eyes—so that tears of sadness can now be seen pouring from the sky itself in the listener's imagination. As for an example of metonymic connection by way of synecdoche, I will analyze a passage featuring not the sky itself but, instead, a god of the sky.

1§85. In the case of the metaphor about teardrops instead of raindrops falling from the sky, what is metaphorical about the substitution of tears for rain is the simple fact that something alien to the sky, weeping, has replaced something that is not alien to the sky, raining. As I noted from the start, surely

[48] συνεκδοχή· ὅταν τις ἀπὸ μέρους παραλάβῃ.

we would never know from personal experience that the sky is weeping when it rains. To think that tears are pouring from the sky is to transfer something familiar that we do personally experience, weeping, to something unfamiliar that we will never personally experience, which is what happens to the sky when it rains. While weeping is familiar to us, it is alien to the sky.

1§86. Now I turn to an example of metonymic connection by way of synecdoche. This example has to do with the picturing of the sky god Zeus in the Homeric *Iliad*. To think of the sky as Zeus, who is personified as god of the sky, is already a metonymy in itself, since the personification makes the sky more familiar and thus less alien to humans who worship Zeus. I will have more to say in a minute about the human motivation for worshipping Zeus, as described in ancient Greek sources, but for now I limit myself to observing the simple fact that this metonymy involving Zeus is also a synecdoche, since Zeus as a personalized god of the sky thus becomes part of the overall human experience of the sky. Zeus is a part of that whole experience, a most important part.

1§87. The familiarity generated by such a synecdoche about Zeus as god of the sky stands in sharp contrast with the unfamiliarity of a metaphor like the one we have just considered, which pictures tears flowing from the sky. Although our familiar human experiences of seeing tears flow from our eyes and seeing rain pour from the sky can get defamiliarized by way of metaphorically picturing tears instead of rain pouring from the sky, these same experiences can get refamiliarized by way of a metonymy that pictures these tears flowing from the eyes of a sky god. That is exactly what happens in a striking verse we encounter in the Homeric *Iliad*, where the god Zeus is mourning in advance the impending death of his son, Sarpedon. This hero is the only mortal in the *Iliad* whose father is the sky god himself. Here, then, is the verse describing the sky god as he weeps:

Extract 1-Ia

> He [= Zeus] poured down [*kata-kheîn*] bloody drops [*psiades*] to the earth.
>
> *Iliad* XVI 459[49]

Metonymies of Tears

1§88. The drops of blood that flow from the body of Sarpedon when he is killed in battle are metonymically linked, even fused, with the drops of tears flow from the eyes of Zeus himself as god of the sky. Metaphorically, we can say that the

49 αἱματοέσσας δὲ ψιάδας κατέχευεν ἔραζε.

sky weeps when we see rain pouring from the sky. But here, metonymically, the sky is personified as the sky god Zeus, who has eyes just as we mortals have eyes, and so, just as tears can pour down from our eyes, so also they can now pour down from the eyes of the god.

1§89. The verb that is used in this passage we have just read from the *Iliad*, *kata-kheîn* 'pour down', is used elsewhere in Homeric poetry together with *dakru* 'teardrop' as its direct object, as when the words of the hero Hector picture some future time when his wife Andromache, soon to become his widow, will be weeping for him after he is killed:

Extract 1-Ib

> $|_{459}$ And, one fine day, somebody will say when they see you [= Andromache] pouring down [*kata-kheîn*] your tears [*dakru*]: $|_{460}$ "This one here used to be the woman of Hector, who was best in battle $|_{461}$ among all the Trojans, horse-tamers, back when they were fighting to defend Ilion."
>
> *Iliad* VI 459–461[50]

1§90. Soon after these words are spoken, Hector and Andromache will part. This moment is the last time these lovers will ever see each other, speak to each other. And, as we see Andromache heading back to her chambers while Hector heads off in the other direction, going off to his imminent death in war, the wife cannot resist turning back again and again for one last glimpse of her beloved husband, whom she will never again see alive:

Extract 1-Ic

> She [= Andromache] was turning her head back again and again, pouring down [*kata-kheîn*] her tears [*dakru*], which were flowing thick and fast.
>
> *Iliad* VI 496[51]

1§91. What we see here are familiar human reactions to the deep sadness of suffering and dying. And these familiar reactions of mortals are experienced also by the deathless sky. That is because Zeus, potentially a remote sky god, is being personalized at the moment of his experience of sadness over the death of his mortal son, and thus he becomes familiar to humans. His bloody tears,

50 $|_{459}$ καί ποτέ τις εἴπῃσιν ἰδὼν κατὰ δάκρυ χέουσαν· $|_{460}$ Ἕκτορος ἧδε γυνὴ ὃς ἀριστεύεσκε μάχεσθαι $|_{461}$ Τρώων ἱπποδάμων ὅτε Ἴλιον ἀμφεμάχοντο.

51 ἐντροπαλιζομένη, θαλερὸν κατὰ δάκρυ χέουσα.

then, are not metaphorical. It is not that these bloody tears, which in everyday circumstances are alien to the sky, are a metaphorical substitution for rain. Rather, bloody teardrops are a metonymical connection. The teardrops connect not with the sky, which is alien to tears, but with the part of the sky that is the sky god Zeus—and with the part of Zeus that is seen as his own eyes, which are not alien to tears, just as the god's eyes are not at all alien to him. And the tears of Zeus are fused with blood because the bloody death of his mortal son is not at all alien to him. The god feels touched here by the human condition, and so his stylized weeping is not metaphorical but metonymical. The metonymy of the tears shed by the familiarized sky god overrides the metaphor of tears shed by an alien sky.

1§92. In Virgil's *Aeneid*, we see a cosmic extension of such metonymy—where the weeping of humans literally touches every single atom in the universe, as if every particle of reality had inside it a tear-filled story to tell. The hero Aeneas, breaking down in tears when he sees images that show all the suffering and dying experienced by his own people in the Trojan War, says it this way:

Extract 1-J

> There are tears [*lacrimae*] that connect with the real things [*rēs* plural] [of the universe], and things that happen to mortals touch [*tangere*] the mind [*mēns*].
>
> Virgil *Aeneid* 1.462[52]

1§93. So, we began with the weeping of the sky. Now we see the weeping of all the atoms of the universe. Elsewhere, I have analyzed in some detail the wording of this extraordinary passage from Virgil, focusing on the poet's allusion to atomic theory as articulated in the poetry of Lucretius.[53] Here I confine myself to comparing three of the relevant passages in Lucretius.

1§94. Before I turn to Lucretius, however, I need to highlight a word in the passage I just quoted from Virgil, the neuter plural *mortālia*, which I translate as 'things that happen to mortals'. We see here a universalizing reference to the *rēs* 'things' (genitive *rērum*) in the real world. I am using the word *real* here in the sense of its etymology as an adjective derived from the noun *rēs*, which refers here and elsewhere in Lucretius and Virgil to the world of reality.[54] In the wording of Virgil, the *rēs* 'things' (genitive *rērum*) of the real world are connected with the shedding of tears, and these realities are further connected with the

52 *sunt lacrimae rerum et mentem mortalia tangunt.*

53 *HC* 1§§178–196.

54 *HC* 1§180.

mental faculty of the *mēns* or 'mind'. The mental connection here is a matter of genuine contact with things that are real. These real things literally touch the *mēns*—and the word for 'touch' here is *tangere*. In the poetic world inherited by Virgil, the experience of touching cannot be insubstantial. If something touches and is touched, it must be substantial, real.[55]

1§95. That said, I turn to the first of the three passages I will quote from Lucretius. In this passage the poet speaks of reality as corporeality. What is substantial may be either visible or invisible, like the atom, but it must be a *corpus* or 'body':

Extract 1-Ka

> No single thing [*rēs*] can touch [*tangere*] and be touched [*tangere*] unless it is a body [*corpus*].
>
> Lucretius *De rerum natura* 1.304[56]

1§96. Now I turn to the second passage I will quote from Lucretius, where we can see clearly the relevance of the word *rēs* 'thing' to atomic theory:

Extract 1-Kb

> Nor should you think that the good colors of real things [*rēs* plural], colors that nourish [= are a feast for] the eyes, are similarly constituted in their atomic seed as the [bad] colors [of real things], which cause a sharp sting [for the eyes] and compel the shedding of tears [*lacrimāre*].[57]
>
> Lucretius *De rerum natura* 2.418–420[58]

1§97. In this description, the exterior stimuli come from invisible particles, but these particles are still part of the real world. Again I am using the word *real* here in the sense of its etymology as an adjective derived from the noun *rēs*, which refers to the world of reality.[59]

1§98. Now I turn to the third passage from Lucretius, where the use of the word *mēns* 'mind' helps us understand its use in the passage I quoted earlier from Virgil:

55 This paragraph is derived from *HC* 1§183.

56 *tangere enim et tangi, nisi corpus, nulla potest res.*

57 In translating this particular passage, I gave up on my usual practice of simulating the original verse-boundaries.

58 *neve bonos rerum similes constare colores | semine constituas, oculos qui pascere possunt, | et qui conpungunt aciem lacrimareque cogunt.*

59 *HC* 1§180.

Extract 1-Kc

> |$_{136}$ The *animus* and the *anima*, I say, are held joined together one with the other, |$_{137}$ and form one single nature of themselves, |$_{138}$ but the chief and dominant thing in the whole body [*corpus*] |$_{139}$ is still that faculty of reasoning that we call the *animus* or mind [*mēns*], |$_{140}$ which is lodged in the middle region of the chest [*pectus*]. |$_{141}$ Here is where fear and terror flourish; it is around these places |$_{142}$ that moments of happiness offer their caresses; here, then, is the mind [*mēns*] or *animus*. |$_{143}$ The remaining part of the *anima* is scattered throughout the whole body [*corpus*], |$_{144}$ but it obeys and is moved [*movēre*] according to the assent and the motion of the mind [*mēns*].
>
> Lucretius *De rerum natura* 3.136–144[60]

1§99. Returning to the passage from Virgil, I now focus on the genitive construction *lacrimae rerum*, which could be translated literally as 'tears of the real things [of the universe]'. Such a translation, however, is too specific—as if the use of the genitive case here implied some kind of ownership. But the idea of ownership is only tangential to the genitive case. The most general function of the genitive, rather, is simply to express a connection between one thing and another thing. In other words, *the most general function of the genitive case is to express a metonymic relationship*. So, that is why I translated *lacrimae rerum* this way: 'tears that connect with the real things [of the universe]'.[61]

Zeus and his Metonymic Contacts with Human Emotions

1§100. In paragraph 1§91 above, we saw how Zeus, potentially a remote sky god, can become personalized and thus familiarized through the metonymy of his tears. We may say that he is making metonymic contact with human emotions. To drive the point home, I return here to the verb that signals this metonymy, *kata-kheîn*, which means literally 'to pour down', as when Zeus 'pours down' bloody tears from his eyes to signal his emotional reaction to the impending death of his beloved son Sarpedon. We saw that this same verb *kata-kheîn* applies to

[60] |$_{136}$ *nunc animum atque animam dico coniuncta teneri* |$_{137}$ *inter se atque unam naturam conficere ex se,* |$_{138}$ *sed caput esse quasi et dominari in corpore toto* |$_{139}$ *consilium, quod nos animum mentemque vocamus.* |$_{140}$ *idque situm media regione in pectoris haeret.* |$_{141}$ *hic exultat enim pavor ac metus, haec loca circum* |$_{142}$ *laetitiae mulcent: hic ergo mens animusquest.* |$_{143}$ *cetera pars animae per totum dissita corpus* |$_{144}$ *paret et ad numen mentis momenque movetur.*

[61] Further argumentation in *HC* 1§193.

humans when they 'pour down' tears from their own eyes, as when Andromache 'pours down' her tears in her own emotional reaction to the impending death of her beloved husband Hector. What I find singularly remarkable about this parallelism between Zeus and Andromache is that we get to see, at a later point in the storytelling of the Homeric *Iliad*, that these two figures actually get connected to each other by the story itself. It happens at a most climactic moment of the storytelling, in a scene where Zeus himself shows that he feels an emotional connection with the weeping of Andromache over the death of Hector. It is this extraordinary scene that I have in mind as I start to elaborate on the metonymic contacts of Zeus with human emotions.

1§101. It happens in *Iliad* XVII, just after Hector kills Patroklos, who in turn had just killed Sarpedon, the son of Zeus. The sky god is watching from his celestial vantage point as Hector starts pulling off the armor from the corpse of Patroklos. This armor really belongs to Achilles, but Patroklos had put it on his own body when he went to battle as the ritual substitute of Achilles. And now, after pulling off this armor from the corpse of Patroklos, Hector proceeds to put it on his own body. Reacting emotionally, Zeus says to himself that Hector is now doomed to be killed by Achilles. And the god also says in the same breath—this is what I find so singularly remarkable—that Hector's wife Andromache is now doomed to feel the pain of never seeing Hector alive again. So, Zeus is in effect saying that he will now be the cause of grief for Andromache, making her weep, and the god expresses a certain sadness in the way he says this. I quote here the wording, within the context of the whole scene as I have just described it:

Extract 1-La

> $|_{194}$ He [= Hector] put on the immortalizing armor $|_{195}$ of Achilles the son of Peleus, which the skydwelling gods $|_{196}$ gave to his [= Achilles'] father near and dear. And he [= Peleus] had given it to his son [= Achilles] $|_{197}$ when he [= Peleus] grew old. As for the son, he never reached old age wearing the armor of his father. $|_{198}$ He [= Hector] was seen from afar by Zeus, gatherer of clouds. $|_{199}$ There he [= Hector] was, all fitted out in the armor of [Achilles] the godlike son of Peleus. $|_{200}$ Then he [= Zeus] moved his head and spoke to himself [= to his own *thūmos*]: $|_{201}$ "Ah, you [= Hector] are a pitiful wretch. Your own death is not on your mind [*thūmos*] $|_{202}$ —a death that is coming near. There you are, putting on the immortalizing armor $|_{203}$ of a man who is champion, one who makes all others tremble. $|_{204}$ It was his comrade [= Patroklos] you killed, gentle he was and strong, $|_{205}$ and his armor, in a way that went against the order [*kosmos*] of things, from his head and shoulders $|_{206}$ you took. All the same, I will for now put

> into your hands great power [*kratos*]. |$_{207}$ As a compensation [*poinē*] for this, you will never return home from the battle. |$_{208}$ Never will you bring home, for Andromache to receive, the famed [*kluta*] armor of [Achilles] the son of Peleus." |$_{209}$ So spoke [Zeus] the son of Kronos, and with his eyebrows of blue he made a reinforcing [= *epi-*] nod. |$_{210}$ He [= Zeus] fitted the armor to Hector's skin, and he [= Hector] was entered by Ares |$_{211}$ the terrifying, the Enyalios. And his [= Hector's] limbs were all filled inside |$_{212}$ with force and strength. Seeking to join up with his famed allies |$_{213}$ he went off, making a great war cry. He was quite the picture for all to see. |$_{214}$ He was shining in the armor of the man with the great heart [*thūmos*], [Achilles] the son of Peleus.
>
> *Iliad* XVII 194–214[62]

1§102. When Zeus nods his head here at verse 209, he is formally expressing his will, which is a plan for the outcome of this part of the story: Hector will be killed, and the hero's death will cause grief for Andromache. Only one other time does Zeus nod his head in the *Iliad*, and that previous nod of the head translates into the outcome of the whole story:

Extract 1-Lb

> |$_{528}$ So spoke [Zeus] the son of Kronos, and with his eyebrows of blue he made a reinforcing [= *epi-*] nod. |$_{529}$ Ambrosial were the locks of hair that cascaded from the lord's |$_{530}$ head immortal. And he caused great Olympus to quake.
>
> *Iliad* I 528–530[63]

1§103. When Zeus nods his head here at verse 528, he is formally expressing his plan to make the whole story of the *Iliad* happen. The Plan of Zeus is the

62 |$_{194}$ ὃ δ' ἄμβροτα τεύχεα δῦνε |$_{195}$ Πηλεΐδεω Ἀχιλῆος ἅ οἱ θεοὶ οὐρανίωνες |$_{196}$ πατρὶ φίλῳ ἔπορον· ὃ δ' ἄρα ᾧ παιδὶ ὄπασσε |$_{197}$ γηράς· ἀλλ' οὐχ υἱὸς ἐν ἔντεσι πατρὸς ἐγήρα. |$_{198}$ τὸν δ' ὡς οὖν ἀπάνευθεν ἴδεν νεφεληγερέτα Ζεὺς |$_{199}$ τεύχεσι Πηλεΐδαο κορυσσόμενον θείοιο, |$_{200}$ κινήσας ῥα κάρη προτὶ ὃν μυθήσατο θυμόν· |$_{201}$ ἆ δείλ' οὐδέ τί τοι θάνατος καταθύμιός ἐστιν |$_{202}$ ὃς δή τοι σχεδὸν εἶσι· σὺ δ' ἄμβροτα τεύχεα δύνεις |$_{203}$ ἀνδρὸς ἀριστῆος, τόν τε τρομέουσι καὶ ἄλλοι· |$_{204}$ τοῦ δὴ ἑταῖρον ἔπεφνες ἐνηέα τε κρατερόν τε, |$_{205}$ τεύχεα δ' οὐ κατὰ κόσμον ἀπὸ κρατός τε καὶ ὤμων |$_{206}$ εἵλευ· ἀτάρ τοι νῦν γε μέγα κράτος ἐγγυαλίξω, |$_{207}$ τῶν ποινὴν ὅ τοι οὔ τι μάχης ἐκνοστήσαντι |$_{208}$ δέξεται Ἀνδρομάχη κλυτὰ τεύχεα Πηλεΐωνος. |$_{209}$ Ἦ καὶ κυανέῃσιν ἐπ' ὀφρύσι νεῦσε Κρονίων. |$_{210}$ Ἕκτορι δ' ἥρμοσε τεύχε' ἐπὶ χροΐ, δῦ δέ μιν Ἄρης |$_{211}$ δεινὸς ἐνυάλιος, πλῆσθεν δ' ἄρα οἱ μέλε' ἐντὸς |$_{212}$ ἀλκῆς καὶ σθένεος· μετὰ δὲ κλειτοὺς ἐπικούρους |$_{213}$ βῆ ῥα μέγα ἰάχων· ἰνδάλλετο δέ σφισι πᾶσι |$_{214}$ τεύχεσι λαμπόμενος μεγαθύμου Πηλεΐωνος.

63 |$_{528}$ ἦ καὶ κυανέῃσιν ἐπ' ὀφρύσι νεῦσε Κρονίων· |$_{529}$ ἀμβρόσιαι δ' ἄρα χαῖται ἐπερρώσαντο ἄνακτος |$_{530}$ κρατὸς ἀπ' ἀθανάτοιο, μέγαν δ' ἐλέλιξεν Ὄλυμπον.

Will of Zeus. It is an executive order that determines the outcome of the *Iliad*—how the anger of Achilles will make the Achaeans lose their advantage in the Trojan War until they compensate this angry hero for the insult that their king Agamemnon had inflicted on him.

1§104. Likewise, as we saw a minute ago, there is another moment in the *Iliad* where the god nods his head and thus signifies his will, which is again the Plan of Zeus. That time, however, the Plan is equated not with the whole story of the *Iliad*, as in *Iliad* I, but only with a part of the story. That part of the story will begin with a scene in *Iliad* XXII where Andromache first sees the corpse of Hector and weeps over his death, singing a song of lamentation for him. Like some director of a grand theatrical production, Zeus himself is setting up that scene, already picturing Andromache as she helplessly waits for Hector to come back to her. It is the Plan of Zeus that Andromache will be kept waiting, since, sadly, Hector will never again come back to her alive.[64]

1§105. So the exquisite moment when Zeus makes his nod is pictured not once but twice in the *Iliad*. The first time, Zeus signals his metonymic contact with the emotions of Achilles—first there was sadness, and then there was anger—as the divine nod leads into the whole story of the *Iliad*. The second time, Zeus signals his metonymic contact with the emotions of Andromache—as his nod leads into the embedded story that tells how Hector was killed and how Andromache lamented him.

1§106. This signaling of the god's contact with human emotions was synthesized in the classical period, in the middle of the fifth century BCE, with the creation of a colossal statue of Zeus. This spectacular work of art, made of gold and ivory, dominated the Temple of Zeus in Olympia, and the creator of the statue was Pheidias the Athenian. I quote here a relevant story about him. The story is reported by Strabo (first century BCE/CE), who tells us what exactly it is was that inspired Pheidias to make this statue:

Extract 1-M (including a quotation of the text we read in Extract 1-Lb)

> Collaborating in many ways with Pheidias was Panainos the painter [*zōgraphos*].[65] He was his nephew and his partner in getting the contract [for making the statue]. The collaboration had to do with the adorning [*kosmēsis*][66] of the statue [*xoanon*], particularly of its fabrics,[67] with colors

64 *HC* 4§269.

65 The *zō-graphos* is literally someone who performs a 'filling in' [*graphein*] of outlines by way of painting, thereby 'animating' or making 'alive' [*zōi-*] what has been filled in.

66 At a later point, I will comment on the idea of "adding" inherent in *kosmeîn* 'adorning'.

67 This is a matter of simulating the fabrics by shaping the material that is being sculpted.

> [*khrōmata*]. And many wondrous paintings [*graphai*],[68] works of Panainos, are also to be seen all around the temple. There is this recollection about Pheidias: when Panainos asked him what model [*paradeigma*] he was following as he [= Pheidias] started to make the likeness [*eikōn*] of Zeus, he [= Pheidias] replied that he was going to make it after the likeness set forth by Homer in these words [*epos* plural]:
>
> Strabo 8.3.30 C354[69]

> [What follows here is Strabo's quotation of the Homeric passage:]
>
> |$_{528}$ So spoke [Zeus] the son of Kronos, and with his eyebrows of blue he made a reinforcing [= *epi-*] nod. |$_{529}$ Ambrosial were the *locks of hair* that cascaded from the lord's |$_{530}$ head immortal. And he caused great Olympus to quake.
>
> *Iliad* I 528–530[70]

1§107. According to this story, the creative impulse that leads Pheidias to make the statue of Zeus is a distinctly Homeric impulse. The moment captured by the maker of the statue is a Homeric moment. It is the moment when Zeus nods his head and thus signifies his divine will, that is, the Plan of Zeus, which is coextensive with both the overall story of the Homeric *Iliad* and the embedded story about the death of Hector and the sorrows of Andromache over this death.[71]

1§108. The Plan of Zeus will make Andromache weep, yes. Nevertheless, as we have seen, the god speaks of his plan in a way that reveals his compassion for the woman who will never again see her husband alive. As I said already, this is a sky god who makes metonymic contact with human emotions.

1§109. The picturing of Zeus at a moment when he makes contact with human emotions not only familiarizes the sky god by way of personalizing him: such a picture, as I will now argue, also estheticizes him, and even eroticizes him. In making this argument, I will consider not only the Homeric visualization of the contact that Zeus makes with extraordinary humans in the heroic

68 A *graphē* is the result of a filling in of outlines by way of painting.

69 πολλὰ δὲ συνέπραξε τῷ Φειδίᾳ Πάναινος ὁ ζωγράφος, ἀδελφιδοῦς ὢν αὐτοῦ καὶ συνεργολάβος, πρὸς τὴν τοῦ ξοάνου διὰ τῶν χρωμάτων κόσμησιν καὶ μάλιστα τῆς ἐσθῆτος. δείκνυνται δὲ καὶ γραφαὶ πολλαί τε καὶ θαυμασταὶ περὶ τὸ ἱερὸν ἐκείνου ἔργα. ἀπομνημονεύουσι δὲ τοῦ Φειδίου, διότι πρὸς τὸν Πάναινον εἶπε πυνθανόμενον πρὸς τί παράδειγμα μέλλοι ποιήσειν τὴν εἰκόνα τοῦ Διός, ὅτι πρὸς τὴν Ὁμήρου δι' ἐπῶν ἐκτεθεῖσαν τούτων

70 |$_{528}$ ἦ καὶ κυανέῃσιν ἐπ' ὀφρύσι νεῦσε Κρονίων· |$_{529}$ ἀμβρόσιαι δ' ἄρα <u>χαῖται</u> ἐπερρώσαντο ἄνακτος |$_{530}$ κρατὸς ἀπ' ἀθανάτοιο, μέγαν δ' ἐλέλιξεν Ὄλυμπον.

71 *HC* 4§96.

age. There is also a piece of evidence about visualizations attributed to ordinary humans in the post-heroic age. I am about to quote from a text that shows how ordinary humans can express a hope that Zeus will make contact with them as well. Such a hope is what Pheidias must have had in mind when he said, as we saw in the story reported by Strabo, that he was inspired to picture Zeus at the moment when he nods his head in the *Iliad*.

1§110. What I just said is not an attempt on my part to second-guess what Pheidias really thought when he made the statue of Zeus. No, the second-guessing comes from the ancient world, and we can see it not only in the passage I quoted from Strabo. I am about to quote another passage that explores even further the thinking of Pheidias. This passage is what I was describing a moment ago as a piece of evidence about visualizations attributed to ordinary humans in the post-heroic age. The author of the passage, as we will see, is exploring the emotional reactions of ordinary humans at the sight of the statue of Zeus by Pheidias. According to this author, the attempt of Pheidias to visualize the Homeric moment when the remote sky god makes contact with humans can be seen as a sincere artistic response to a basic human need. The need, in such a line of thinking, was to make this remote sky god reachable, even touchable.

1§111. The author of the text I am about to quote was an intellectual named Dio of Prusa, who lived in the first and the second centuries CE. In this text, which I extract from his *Olympic Discourse* (*Oration* 12), Dio is imagining a hypothetical speech delivered by none other than Pheidias himself, who is speaking here about his masterpiece, the colossal statue of Zeus that he created for the temple of Zeus at Olympia. In his speech, Pheidias explains his idealizing of the human form by creating the spectacular statue of Zeus. To justify this human form that he creates for Zeus, the sculptor speaks about a basic need felt by humans to go beyond imagining gods as they might exist in the sky or in the cosmos in general. More specifically, humans need to have a feeling of divine immediacy by getting near them, close to them—a feeling achieved by way of mental or even physical contact with statues and with paintings and with other images of the gods.[72] Here is how Pheidias says it, in his speech as staged by Dio:

Extract 1-N

> No one would argue that it would have been better if no statue or image of gods [*theoi*] had ever been set up in the realm of humans for them to look at—arguing on the grounds that humans should look only toward those things that are connected with the realm of the sky [*tà ourania*]. Here is why I say this. Granted, everyone with good sense holds in

[72] What I just said here matches my formulation in *H24H* 5§126.

worshipful reverence those things [connected with the realm of the sky], thinking that those things are blessed gods [*theoi*] as viewed from a vast distance. Nevertheless, because humans are attracted to whatever the divine thing [*tò daimonion*] is [that is unknown],[73] they all have a powerful erotic desire [*erōs*] to worship [*tīmân*] and to take care of [*therapeuein*] whatever the divine thing [*tò theion*][74] is [that is known], [and they do so] by getting up close to it and near it, as they approach it and try to touch it in an act of persuasion, and they sacrifice to it and put garlands [*stephanoûn*] on it. Quite simply, they are like disconnected [*nēpioi*][75] children who have been torn away from their father or mother and who, feeling a terrific urge [*himeros*] and longing [*pothos*], often reach out their hands while they are dreaming, in the direction of their parents who are not there; so also are humans in their relationship with the gods [*theoi*], loving them as they do, and justifiably so, because the gods do good things for them and have an affinity with them. And, in their love for the gods, humans strive in all possible ways to be with them and in their company.

Dio of Prusa ("Dio Chrysostom") 12.60–61[76]

1§112. Earlier, we saw that a god like Zeus, despite his remoteness in the sky, can still make contact with the emotions of mortals. Now we see that mortals have a deep yearning for such contact. They even yearn to make contact on their own with *tò theion*, which I have translated as 'whatever the divine thing is that is known'. In colloquial American English, we could call it *the "god" thing*. And, in the words of the sculptor Pheidias as staged by Dio, humans express their yearning for this thing by worshipping it, and I quote Dio again as he describes how the worshippers worship this thing: "by getting up close to it and near it, as

[73] This word *daimonion* is derived from *daimōn*, which refers to an unspecified god, whereas *theos* refers to a specific god: see *H24H* 5§1. That is why I translate *tò daimonion* here as the 'whatever the divine thing is that is unknown'.

[74] This word *theion* is derived from *theos*, which refers to a specific god. That is why I translate *tò theion* here as 'whatever the divine thing is that is known'.

[75] On this word *nēpios*, plural *nēpioi*, in the sense of 'disconnected', see Edmunds 1990, who shows that the disconnection can be mental, moral, or emotional.

[76] οὐδὲ γὰρ ὡς βέλτιον ὑπῆρχε μηδὲν ἵδρυμα μηδὲ εἰκόνα θεῶν ἀποδεδεῖχθαι παρ' ἀνθρώποις φαίη τις ἄν, ὡς πρὸς μόνα ὁρᾶν δέον τὰ οὐράνια. ταῦτα μὲν γὰρ ξύμπαντα ὅ γε νοῦν ἔχων σέβει, θεοὺς ἡγούμενος μακαρίους μακρόθεν ὁρῶν· διὰ δὲ τὴν πρὸς τὸ δαιμόνιον ὁρμὴν ἰσχυρὸς ἔρως πᾶσιν ἀνθρώποις ἐγγύθεν τιμᾶν καὶ θεραπεύειν τὸ θεῖον, προσιόντας καὶ ἁπτομένους μετὰ πειθοῦς, θύοντας καὶ στεφανοῦντας. ἀτεχνῶς γὰρ ὥσπερ νήπιοι παῖδες πατρὸς ἢ μητρὸς ἀπεσπασμένοι δεινὸν ἵμερον ἔχοντες καὶ πόθον ὀρέγουσι χεῖρας οὐ παροῦσι πολλάκις ὀνειρώττοντες, οὕτω καὶ θεοῖς ἄνθρωποι ἀγαπῶντες δικαίως διά τε εὐεργεσίαν καὶ συγγένειαν, προθυμούμενοι πάντα τρόπον συνεῖναί τε καὶ ὁμιλεῖν.

they approach it and try to touch it in an act of persuasion, and they sacrifice to it and put garlands [*stephanoûn*] on it." Such yearning verges on something that might as well be described as not only erotic but even *theo-erotic*.

1§113. Earlier, I had talked about the mentality of *theo-eroticism* in interpreting the *Song of Songs*. I see a comparable mentality when I think of Zeus as he was pictured in the Homeric *Iliad*—and, later, as he was shaped into the magnificent statue created by the sculptor Pheidias in Olympia. I focus here on one detail. As we saw in the description given by Strabo (8.3.30 C354), Pheidias lavished special attention on the cascading locks of divine hair at the moment when the god nods his head, as lovingly described in the Homeric *Iliad* (I 528–530).[77]

1§114. We can read surviving reportage about the strong impressions experienced by viewers attracted to the spectacular sight of this splendid head of hair. I focus here on just one example. In the early Byzantine era, the head of Olympian Zeus became a model for artists seeking to picture the head of Jesus himself, and there are stories that tell of dire consequences. I cite here one such story, which survives from ancient excerpts taken from the writings of the historian Theodorus Lector (*lector* is a latinized way of rendering Greek *anagnōstēs*, the oldest meaning of which is 'the one who reads out loud'), who flourished in the early sixth century CE.[78] We read in these excerpts a story about Gennadius, Patriarch of Constantinople from 458 to 471 CE, who mercifully and miraculously healed the withered hand of a painter [*zōgraphos*] punished by superhuman forces for painting [*graphein*] Jesus in the likeness of Olympian Zeus.[79] According to Theodorus Lector, the conventional *skhēma* or 'way of representing' as practiced by painters who painted pictures of Jesus in that period—the 'more true' way [*alēthesteron*]—was to show him with short, tight curls [*oulon kai oligotrikhon*]. By contrast, the hair of Olympian Zeus was long, with curls less tight and more flowing. Also, the hair of Zeus had a telltale parting at the middle of his forehead, leaving the god's face stylishly unencumbered by hair. According to Theodorus Lector, the painter [*zōgraphos*] had painted the hair of Jesus in this style, so that those who desired to worship Zeus could pretend to be worshipping Jesus instead.[80]

77 Other references to *Iliad* I 528–530 as the inspiration for Pheidias include Dio of Prusa 12.25–26. See further the analysis of Lapatin 2001:84–85.

78 On the meaning of *anagnōstēs* as 'one who reads the text out loud', see *PP* 149–150, 168, 176–177, 201. I note with interest a report claiming that Plato called Aristotle his *anagnōstēs* (*Vita Marciana*, Aristotle *Fragments* 428.2 ed. Rose).

79 Theodorus Lector 1.15 in *Patrologia Graeca* (ed. J.-P. Migne) vol. 86 (1865) p. 173; see Mango 1972:40.

80 Fragment from Theodorus Lector 1.15 in *Patrologia Graeca* (ed. J.-P. Migne) vol. 86 (1865) pp. 220–221; see Mango 1972:40–41.

1§115. The dating of this Byzantine story about Olympian Zeus as a model for Jesus corresponds to a major event in the history of art: at some point in the era of the Byzantine emperor Theodosius II, who ruled from 406 to 450 BCE, the statue of Zeus had been removed from the ruins of the Temple of Zeus at Olympia and transferred to a high-ceiling palace in Constantinople, hub of the Byzantine Empire, along with many other art treasures of the ancient world. This new home for Zeus was not to last. Sadly, the god's stay in Constantinople was all too brief, lasting less than even one single century, since the palace where his statue was exhibited burned down, Zeus and all, probably in the great fire of 475 CE.[81] Before Olympian Zeus finally went up in flames, however, he evidently managed to leave a deep impression on the artists of Constantinople at the time, as we see from the story of the painter who was punished for modeling his image of Jesus on the image of Zeus. And, despite the threats of divine punishment as conveyed by this story, the picturing of Zeus not only persisted but even prevailed in the end. Although Olympian Zeus had gone up in flames and was now lost for all eternity, his visual effects were destined to last: in conventional Byzantine art as it evolved beyond the early period when the statue of Zeus was still extant in Constantinople, the head of Jesus—especially in his role as Christ the *Pantokratōr* or 'ruler of the whole universe'—retained the look and feel of the old sky god whom the sculptor Pheidias had made accessible to all humanity—almost a thousand years earlier.[82] A most striking example of this look and feel is a mosaic dating from the late twelfth century CE, inside the Monreale Cathedral, Santa Maria la Nuova, near Palermo in Sicily, where we see Christ the *Pantokratōr* looking down from the celestial heights of the central dome.

1§116. In describing here the visual effect of seeing the flowing curls of Jesus and, indirectly, of Zeus, I deliberately used the colloquial expression *look and feel*, recalling what Pheidias as staged by Dio says about the desire of humans to worship *tò theion*, that is, to worship whatever is divine. I quote again the words, as we read them in Extract 1-P, describing how humans worship this divine thing, whatever it is: "because humans are attracted to whatever the divine thing [*tò daimonion*] is [that is unknown], they all have a powerful erotic desire [*erōs*] to worship [*tīmân*] and to take care of [*therapeuein*] whatever the divine thing [*tò theion*] is [that is known], [and they do so] by getting up close to it and near it, as they approach it and try to touch it in an act of persuasion, and they sacrifice to it and put garlands [*stephanoûn*] on it."

81 Mango 1963:58. For more details, see also Mango, Vickers, and Francis 1992.

82 Lapatin 2001:137 gives an admirable summary of the evidence, with further references.

Extract 1-Oa

Mosaic of Christ *Pantokratōr*. In the Monreale Cathedral, Santa Maria la Nuova, Sicily (near Palermo). Made available on Wikimedia Commons by the user Mboesch under a Creative Commons Attribution-Share Alike 3.0 license. Cropped version of color original.

Extract 1-Ob

[The online version features a link here to a color version of this photograph of the mosaic inside the Monreale Cathedral.]

1§117. I continue to focus here on the human desire, even erotic longing, for physical contact with whatever is divine: to be near it, next to it, touching it. And I note how the sense of touch is being foregrounded here. Such foregrounding leads us back to the topic of *theo-eroticism*: so what exactly is *theo-erotic* about this Jesus whose image is modeled on the image of Olympian Zeus? A simple way of starting to address this question is to quote again the words from the song of Theodorakis, taken from the poem *Epitaphios* by Ritsos:

Extract 1-P (repeating Extract 1-Ha)

> || Hair, that curly head of hair, I would slip my fingers through it, | all those nights, while you were asleep, and I was awake, right there next to you.

> || Eyebrows, those eyebrows of yours for me, brows shaped like a curved scimitar, sketched with a pencil point ever so fine | —an arched chamber where my gaze could nestle and be at rest.
>
> || Eyes, those dreamy eyes in which would shine the reflection of a distant morning sky, | and I would try and make sure they never got blurred by even one single teardrop.
>
> || Lips, those sweetly scented lips of yours for me, when they made words, there was a blossoming | even from rocks and dried out trees, and nightingales would flutter.
>
> From the poem *Epitaphios*, by Ritsos, turned into song by Theodorakis; my translation[83]

1§118. At the very beginning of this song, there is an erotic sensation of fingers touching a curly head of hair. And fingers are most relevant to the idea of metonymy, which I defined from the start as a mental process that expresses meaning by connecting something to something else that is next to it or at least near to it, thereby making contact. As I revisit here the wording of this working definition, I now highlight the last word, *contact*. To make *contact* is to *touch*. And that is how fingers become most relevant to the idea of metonymy. From the start, I showed as an example of metonymy the sense of connectivity that we notice in a sequence connecting the hand to the arm to the shoulder and so on. But now I can show a better example if I start again with the hand but then proceed in a sequence that is heading in the other direction, connecting the hand to the fingers to what the fingers touch—or, even better, to what the fingertips are used to touching. To touch is to become familiar, which as we have seen is a sign of metonymy. And that is what we see happening in the words quoted from the song of Theodorakis: "hair, that curly head of hair, I would slip my fingers through it." As I think about the ultrasensitivity of fingertips, my mind turns here to the interest of evolutionary biologists in the intense concentration of nerves situated at the tips of human fingers.

1§119. In quoting again the words from the song of Theodorakis, I focused on the sense of touch. But that sense connects in this song to all the other senses. And the senses all converge on a unifying experience in this song. That experience of sensory fusion comes very close, I think, to the experience of making

[83] ||Μαλλιὰ σγουρὰ ποὺ πάνω τους τὰ δάχτυλα περνοῦσα | τὶς νύχτες ποὺ κοιμόσουνα καὶ πλάϊ σου ξαγρυπνοῦσα ||Φρύδι μου, γαϊτανόφρυδο καὶ κοντυλογραμμένο, | καμάρα ποὺ τὸ βλέμμα μου κούρνιαζε ἀναπαμένο ||Μάτια γλαρὰ ποὺ μέσα τους ἀντίφεγγαν τὰ μάκρη | πρωϊνοῦ οὐρανοῦ, καὶ πάσκιζα μὴν τὰ θαμπώσει δάκρυ ||Χείλι μου μοσκομύριστο ποὺ ὡς λάλαγες ἀνθίζαν | λιθάρια καὶ ξερόδεντρα κι ἀηδόνια φτερουγίζαν.

metonymic contact with the divine. And the sensuality of the sensory fusion can be described as *theo-eroticism*. After all, the song of Theodorakis connects with the song of lament sung by the mother of Jesus over his beautiful body—as brought back to life in the poem of Ritsos. And the making of both this song and this poem is what I would describe as a masterpiece of metonymy.

Another Example of Divine Metonymic Contact With Human Emotions

1§120. Before we turn away from the *theo-eroticism* of the colossal gold-and-ivory statue of Zeus created by Pheidias, I must consider an equally famous statue created by the same sculptor in an earlier phase of his career. It is the colossal gold-and-ivory statue of the goddess Athena inside the Parthenon, that spectacular building situated on the Acropolis of Athens and revered as the home of the goddess Athena Parthénos or 'Virgin'. According to a reliable source dating from the fourth/third centuries BCE (Philochorus *FGH* 328 F 121), the statue of Athena Parthénos was inaugurated in 438/7 BCE, and the statesman Pericles himself was an *epistatēs* 'supervisor' of its creation.[84] Here I concentrate on a story that tells what ultimately happened to this statue—more than nine hundred years later. In this story, as we will see, there was something about the Athena of Pheidias that caused a man to experience the sensory fusion of simultaneously *seeing* and *hearing* the goddess herself. And the experience of this man, as we are also about to see, is another example of divine metonymic contact with human emotions.

1§121. The man is Proclus. He was a Platonic philosopher, a non-Christian, who is best known for the commentaries that he published on Plato's *Timaeus* and *Republic*, among many other works. And the story comes from *The Life of Proclus*, authored by Marinus of Samaria, a follower of Proclus (*Life* 1, 5, 9, 16–17, 20, 27, 30–35). This Marinus (*Life* 35–36) gives an exact date for the birth of Proclus in the context of documenting the man's horoscope—as also a date for his death. So, the philosopher was born in Constantinople on February 8, in 412 CE, and he died in Athens on April 17, in the year 485. And we know from Marinus (*Life* 10) that Proclus at a young age moved from Constantinople to Athens, where he eventually became the director of Plato's Academy. We also know that, from his place of residence at Athens, he could see the Acropolis (*Life* 29). So he could enjoy a view of the Parthenon, which, as I noted, was the home of the goddess Athena. This detail, as we will see, is most relevant to the story

84 In *HC* 4§§97–124, I analyze the rationale that led to the commissioning of Pheidias to make the gold-and-ivory statue of Athena.

that tells what ultimately happened to the statue of Athena in the Parthenon—and how this Platonic philosopher Proclus experienced a kind of sensory fusion involving that statue.

1§122. This story is roughly contemporaneous with the story that tells what happened to the statue of Zeus after its relocation from Olympia to Constantinople. As we are about to see, the fate that befell the statue of Athena in Athens was more ignominious than the disaster that happened to her father's statue at around the same time in Constantinople. In the case of Zeus, at least he was situated in a place of honor, however alien, at the moment when he finally went up in flames in the fifth century CE. In the case of Athena, by contrast, as we are about to read in the story told by Marinus (*Life of Proclus* 30), her statue in Athens was unceremoniously carted off by Christian zealots—never to be seen again.[85] In the story, this ignominious event is linked with an epiphany experienced by Proclus:

Extract 1-Qa

> How dear [*pros-philēs*] he [= Proclus] was to the goddess of philosophy [= Athena] was amply demonstrated by the fact that he chose for himself a philosophical life. But, even more than that, the goddess herself showed it when her statue, which had been until this time situated in the Parthenon, was removed by those [= the Christians] who move [*kineîn*] things that must not be moved [*akinēta*]. In a dream [*onar*], he [= Proclus] seemed to be seeing a woman of great beauty coming toward him and announcing to him that he must, as quickly as possible, get his home [*oikiā*] ready for her, "because the Athenian Lady wishes to live with you in your home [*para soi*]."
>
> Marinus *Life of Proclus* 30[86]

[85] By this time, in the fifth century CE, the original gold-and-ivory statue of Athena had undergone a series of remakings: see Lapatin 2001:89. So, the look and feel of the remade version that was finally removed from the Parthenon in the fifth century CE may have been a far cry from the glory days of the original statue as shaped by Pheidias in the fifth century BCE, over nine hundred years earlier.

[86] ὅπως δὲ αὐτὸς καὶ αὐτῇ τῇ φιλοσόφῳ θεῷ προσφιλὴς ἐγένετο, παρέστησε μὲν ἱκανῶς καὶ ἡ αἵρεσις τοῦ ἐν φιλοσοφίᾳ βίου, τοιαύτη γενομένη οἵαν ὁ λόγος ὑπέδειξε· σαφῶς δὲ καὶ αὐτὴ ἡ θεὸς ἐδήλωσεν, ἡνίκα τὸ ἄγαλμα αὐτῆς τὸ ἐν Παρθενῶνι τέως ἱδρυμένον ὑπὸ τῶν καὶ τὰ ἀκίνητα κινούντων μετεφέρετο. ἐδόκει γὰρ τῷ φιλοσόφῳ ὄναρ φοιτᾶν παρ' αὐτὸν εὐσχήμων τις γυνὴ καὶ ἀπαγγέλλειν ὡς χρὴ τάχιστα τὴν οἰκίαν προπαρασκευάζειν. "ἡ γὰρ κυρία Ἀθηναΐς" ἔφη "παρὰ σοὶ μένειν ἐθέλει." I disagree with the emendation Ἀθηναία proposed by Saffrey and Segonds 2001:165 for the manuscript reading Ἀθηναΐς. They argue that Ἀθηναία, meaning 'Athenian' in the feminine, is more appropriate for the goddess, since that form Ἀθηναΐς is a common name of Athenian women. But the dream itself indicates an ambiguity: the first impression of the

1§123. Goddesses have a way of talking like that. Even when they speak in the first person, they will refer to themselves in the third person. A classic example is the wording of Aphrodite in the *Hippolytus* of Euripides (verse 33).[87] As we consider further the story about the epiphany of the goddess Athena, appearing as she does to Proclus in a dream, I need to highlight the fact that the goddess here is following up on an earlier epiphany experienced by the philosopher. As we are about to read in a passage extracted from an earlier point in *The Life of Proclus*, Athena appeared to the philosopher already in his youth, when he was still living in Constantinople. In this earlier epiphany, the goddess had invited young Proclus to embrace philosophy as his lifelong passion. I will now quote the wording of this story, calling attention in advance to a striking detail. As we are about to see, this epiphany is meant to explain why the philosopher developed a special feeling of intimacy with Athena as the goddess of wisdom, as the patroness of philosophy. Here, then, is the wording, which explains why Athena cared so much for Proclus from the very start:

Extract 1-Qb

> You see, she [= Athena] appeared [*phainesthai*] to him in a dream [*onar*] and summoned him to a life of philosophy. And I think that this is why he experienced such great familiarity [*oikeiotēs*] with the goddess. As a result, he especially adored her and was observant of her rituals [*orgia*] with more of a passionate intensity of divine possession [*enthousiastikōteron*].
>
> Marinus *Life of Proclus* 6[88]

1§124. The intimacy that Proclus felt he shared with the goddess Athena is expressed here by the word *oikeiotēs*, which I translate as 'familiarity'. As we saw from the start, the Greek adjective *oikeio-* 'familiar', from which the noun *oikeiotēs* 'familiarity' derives, captures the basic feature of metonymy that distinguishes it from metaphor: the opposite of *oikeio-* 'familiar', which is indicated by metonymy, is *allotrio-* 'alien', indicated by metaphor.

1§125. To be *familiar* with something or someone is to be *at home* with that something or someone. After all, the adjective *oikeio-* is derived from the noun *oikos*, meaning 'home'; a related noun is *oikiā*, likewise meaning 'home', which

dreamer is that the beautiful lady is not the goddess but simply a beautiful lady who happens to have a typically Athenian name.

87 Analysis in *H24H* 20§13.

88 αὕτη γὰρ αὐτῷ ὄναρ φαινομένη ἐπὶ φιλοσοφίαν παρεκάλει. ὅθεν, οἶμαι, αὐτῷ συνέβη καὶ πολλὴ οἰκειότης περὶ τὴν θεόν, ὥστε καὶ ἐξαιρέτως τὰ ταύτης ὀργιάζειν καὶ ἐνθουσιαστικώτερον αὐτῆς τοὺς θεσμοὺς μετιέναι.

is used in the text I quoted in Extract 1-Qa (Marinus *Life of Proclus* 30) when Athena at the moment of her epiphany tells Proclus that he must, as quickly as possible, get his *oikiā* 'home' ready for her. Here I return one last time to the story about the removal of the statue of Athena from her home in the Parthenon on top of the Acropolis of Athens. As we saw in this story, Proclus experiences the sensory fusion of both *seeing* and *hearing* the goddess at the very moment when her statue is being permanently removed from sight. As her statue disappears forever, the goddess re-appears to Proclus in a final epiphany that recalls the primal epiphany that had bonded the philosopher to her forever. Though the statue of the goddess is gone, removed from her home in the Parthenon, the goddess of philosophy now finds for herself a new home in the heart of the philosopher who will love her forever and ever.

1§126. Here I return to the expression *enthousiastikōteron* in Extract 1-Qb (*Life of Proclus* 6), describing the passionate intensity felt by Proclus in worshipping the goddess Athena. My translation of this expression, 'with more of a passionate intensity of divine possession', was meant to reflect the etymology of this word, which is derived from the adjective *en-theos*, meaning 'possessed by a divinity' or even 'having a divinity inside' (as in Plato *Ion* 533e).

1§127. Such, then, is the power of metonymic contact with the goddess Athena. And such is the power of her *theo-erotic* attractiveness.

On the Idea of Epiphany

1§128. A moment ago, I used the word *epiphany* in describing the vision of Athena as she appears to her worshipful follower Proclus. The ancient Greek word *epiphaneia*, which I translate as 'epiphany', refers to the experiencing of something superhuman that makes itself known primarily by way of a visual appearance.[89] We will need to hold on to this word as we prepare for readings still to come.

1§129. In fact, we have already seen the verb from which this noun *epiphaneia* 'epiphany' is derived. It is *phainesthai* 'appear [in a vision]', as used in Extract 1-Qb (*Life of Proclus* 6), where this verb refers to the appearance of the goddess to Proclus in his youth, on the occasion of her first epiphany. Later in the narrative, we find the noun *opsis* 'vision' referring to that same epiphany (*Life of Proclus* 10). In that context (and also already in *Life of Proclus* 9), the first epiphany of Athena is described as the divine force that leads young Proclus to relocate to Athens, where he is destined to preserve the teachings of Plato and to become, eventually, the director of Plato's Academy (again, *Life of Proclus* 10).

[89] *H24H* 5§38.

Metonymic Contact with the World of Heroes

1§130. The sacred relationship of the Platonic philosopher Proclus with Athena is linked to further relationships that are also sacred. The metonymic contact of Proclus with the goddess of Athens extends to other contacts with other superhuman powers that resided in that city. As we are about to read in *The Life of Proclus*, Marinus goes on to say that Proclus developed a sacred relationship with the cult heroes of Athens. I must stress here that cult heroes, though they were not considered to be gods, were nevertheless traditionally worshipped as sacred superhuman forces in their own right.[90] Moreover, the cult heroes of Athens in the era of Proclus—and even in earlier eras—included Socrates and Plato. Here I rely on the relevant facts gathered by Stephen A. White in a perceptive and far-reaching study of initiatives taken by Plato for instituting a hero cult for Socrates; in that study, White also examines further initiatives taken by Plato's successors in maintaining a hero cult not only for Socrates but even for Plato.[91]

1§131. In the next section, we will consider White's arguments for the existence of hero cults established in honor of Socrates and Plato in Athens. But first, I propose to examine a relevant passage in *The Life of Proclus*, and I start by focusing on a point in the narrative where a youthful Proclus first comes to Athens. At this point in the narrative, a mystical event confirms his destiny as the future director of Plato's Academy, and I begin by summarizing here the main details of this event (*Life of Proclus* 10). As soon as he lands at the Athenian harbor of Peiraieus, Proclus proceeds to walk toward the city of Athens. Along the way, he becomes thirsty. He tells his companion Nikolaos that he needs a drink of water, which is then brought to him. Although Proclus does not yet know it, his first drink of water on Athenian soil comes from a *pēgē* 'spring' that flows from a plot of ground described as a *khōrion hieron* 'sacred space'. Sacred to whom? As we are about to see, this place is sacred to Socrates, the teacher of Plato. The name of the place, as we are also about to see, is *tò Sōkrateion*, 'the space of Socrates', and the spring is near a *stēlē* 'stele, pillar' that had been set up in honor of this philosopher, who is said to receive *tīmai* 'honors' there. The use of the word *tīmai* is essential in this context, because *tīmai* conventionally refers to the 'honors' received by cult heroes in hero cults.[92] When Proclus is informed about the source of the water that he just drank, he offers to Socrates 'a gesture of worship', as expressed by the verb *proskuneîn*, before he resumes his journey and continues his walk toward the city. Here, then, is my translation of the text

90 *H24H* 00§13, 8§44, 11§14.

91 White 2000. See also *H24H* 23§46.

92 *H24H* 17§1.

that tells about this mystical event, and I ask the reader to track with special care the words I have already highlighted:

Extract 1-Qc

> So, he [= Nikolaos] was escorting him [= Proclus] to the city [of Athens]. He [= Proclus] was feeling the effects of the exertion he was experiencing from all the walking along the way [to the city], and, in the space of Socrates [*tò Sōkrateion*]—though he [= Proclus] did not yet know and had not heard that this was a place where Socrates was the recipient of honors [*tīmai*]—he [= Proclus] asked Nikolaos if it was all right for him [= Proclus] to stop there for a while and sit down. He [= Proclus] also asked if he [= Nikolaos] could bring him some water from somewhere. He [= Proclus] was feeling held back, he said, because he was so very thirsty. He [= Nikolaos] most readily did as he was asked, and he had the water brought to him [= Proclus] from a place that was none other than that sacred [*hieron*] space [*khōrion*]. You see, the spring [*pēgē*] was not so far away from the pillar [*stēlē*] of Socrates. When he [= Proclus] finished drinking, he [= Nikolaos] addressed him [= Proclus]: "this is a symbol [*sumbolon*]," he said—only then realizing it for the first time. He [= Nikolaos] was referring to the fact that he [= Proclus] was sitting in the space of Socrates [*tò Sōkrateion*], and that it was in this place that he [= Proclus] first drank the water of Athenian territory [= Attica]. He [= Proclus] stood up, made a gesture of worship [*proskuneîn*], and then resumed his journey as he started walking again toward the city [of Athens].
>
> Marinus *Life of Proclus* 10[93]

1§132. The wording used in the narrative here indicates that Proclus has at this precise moment made contact with something sacred—that is, with a hero cult established in earlier times by Plato's followers in honor of Socrates. And this sacred contact is metonymic: the fresh water that Proclus is drinking

[93] ἦγεν οὖν αὐτὸν ἐπὶ τὴν πόλιν. ὁ δὲ ἐκ τοῦ βαδίζειν κόπου ᾔσθετο κατὰ τὴν ὁδὸν καὶ περὶ τὸ Σωκρατεῖον—οὔπω εἰδὼς οὐδὲ ἀκηκοὼς ὅτι Σωκράτους αὐτοῦ που ἐγίγνοντο τιμαί—ἠξίου δὴ τὸν Νικόλαον ἐπιμένειν τε αὐτόθι βραχὺ καὶ καθέζεσθαι, ἅμα δὲ καὶ εἰ ἔχοι ποθὲν ὕδωρ, αὐτῷ πορίσασθαι· καὶ γὰρ δίψει πολλῷ, ὡς ἔλεγε, κατείχετο. ὁ δὲ ἑτοίμως αὐτῷ, καὶ τοῦτο οὐκ ἀλλαχόθεν ποθέν, ἐξ αὐτοῦ δὲ ἐκείνου τοῦ ἱεροῦ χωρίου ἐποίει φέρεσθαι· οὐδὲ γὰρ πόρρω ἦν ἡ πηγὴ τῆς Σωκράτους στήλης. πιόντι δὲ αὐτῷ σύμβολον ὁ Νικόλαος, καὶ τότε πρῶτον ἐπιστήσας, εἶπεν ὡς τῷ Σωκρατείῳ εἴη ἐνιδρυθεὶς καὶ πρῶτον ἐκεῖθεν Ἀττικὸν ὕδωρ πιών. ὁ δ' ἐξαναστὰς καὶ προσκυνήσας ἐπὶ τὴν πόλιν ἐπορεύετο.

flows from a spring that is sacred by way of its contact with the sacred space of Socrates, who is worshipped as a cult hero within that space.

The Metonymy of Periodic Recurrence in Hero Cults

1§133. I emphasize another detail in this narrative of Marinus that I just quoted in Extract 1-Qc (*Life of Proclus* 10): as soon as he is told about the source of the fresh water he is drinking, Proclus makes a ritual gesture of worshipping Socrates. Elsewhere too in the narrative of Marinus, there are references to the ritual correctness of Proclus in observing the customs of worshipping cult heroes and of honoring the dead in general. This correctness, as we will see, has to do with the observance of rituals that recur year after year in honor of cult heroes. And the mentality of ancient reportage about such a periodic recurrence, as we will also see, is metonymic.

1§134. Marinus describes such a mentality in the context of noting that Proclus, toward the end of his life, had planned ahead for a traditional funeral, Athenian style, to be held in his honor after he died:

Extract 1-Qd

> He [= Proclus] deemed it proper that his body should receive the kind of ritual care [*therapeiā*] that accorded with the ancestral customs of the Athenians—and that accorded also with the arrangements he had made while he was still alive. You see, this was yet another thing that this blessed [*makarios*] man had in his possession, more than anyone else: he had an understanding and a practical knowledge of the rituals performed [*tà drōmena*] in connection with the departed. He neglected no date [*kairos*] marking the customary ritual care [*therapeiā*] of these [departed ones]. Every year, on properly determined days, he would make the rounds visiting the monuments [*mnēmata*] of the heroes of the Athenian territory [= Attica], as also the monuments of those who led a philosophical life, and, more generally, of those who had been his friends and acquaintances. He would ritually perform [*drân*] there the traditional things [*tà nenomismena*] to be performed—not by way of some intermediary but rather by activating [*energeîn*] the rituals himself. And, after having rendered the proper ritual care [*therapeiā*] in each case, he would go off to the Academy and, at a special space that was set aside for that purpose, he would supplicate the spirits [*psūkhai*] of his ancestors and, inclusively, all related spirits. Then, in general,

> at another [special] place, he would pour libations for, this time, the spirits [*psūkhai*] of all those who had led a philosophical life. In addition to all these things, that most holy man would mark out a third [special] space and, at that spot, he would pronounce a blessing on the spirits [*psūkhai*] of all departed humans.
>
> Marinus *Life of Proclus* 36[94]

1§135. This text of Marinus shows the great care taken by Proclus to visit in general the sacred spaces of the "Attic heroes," that is, of cult heroes who were worshipped in Athenian territory.[95] More specifically, as we see in this same text, Proclus also visited various other sacred spaces—especially monuments established in honor of heroized philosophers. The evidence of this text, then, backs up a point made by White, that the heroization of philosophers was not uncommon.[96] Here is an example: the philosopher Parmenides, who lived in the fifth century BCE, founded a *hērōion*, that is, a 'site for a hero cult', to honor his teacher, the Pythagorean philosopher Ameinias; the source for this information is Diogenes Laertius (*Lives of Philosophers* 9.21), who lived in the third century CE—and whom I will soon cite again for other such pieces of information.

1§136. I now come to a remarkable detail mentioned by Marinus in the passage we have just read in Extract 1-Qd (*Life of Proclus* 36) about the visits made by this philosopher Proclus to the sacred spaces of heroes. Such visits, as the wording of Marinus in this text indicates, were periodically *recurrent*, determined by ritual calculations of different dates for different yearly visits. The key word used here by Marinus is *kairos* in the sense of 'anniversary date'. This word, referring to the ritual observances practiced by Proclus, is directly relevant to the ancient Greek practice of worshipping cult heroes—and my terminology here includes philosophers as cult heroes. As Marinus mentions elsewhere in *The Life of Proclus* (23), two of the anniversary dates that Proclus observed were the birthdays of Socrates and Plato. We know the actual dates

94 καὶ θεραπείας τὸ σῶμα ἠξιώθη κατὰ τὰ πάτρια τὰ Ἀθηναίων, καὶ ὡς αὐτὸς ἔτι περιὼν διετάξατο. καὶ γὰρ αὖ καὶ τοῦτο ὑπῆρξε τῷ μακαρίῳ ἀνδρί, εἴπερ τινὶ καὶ ἄλλῳ, γνῶσις καὶ ἐπιμέλεια τῶν δρωμένων περὶ τοὺς ἀποιχομένους. οὐδένα γὰρ καιρὸν τῆς εἰωθυίας αὐτῶν θεραπείας παραλέλοιπεν, ἑκάστου δὲ ἔτους κατά τινας ὡρισμένας ἡμέρας, καὶ τὰ τῶν Ἀττικῶν ἡρώων περινοστῶν, τά τε τῶν φιλοσοφησάντων μνήματα καὶ τῶν ἄλλων τῶν φίλων καὶ γνωρίμων αὐτῷ γεγονότων, ἔδρα τὰ νενομισμένα, οὐ δι' ἑτέρου, ἀλλ' αὐτὸς ἐνεργῶν. μετὰ δὲ τὴν περὶ ἕκαστον θεραπείαν, ἀπιὼν εἰς τὴν Ἀκαδημίαν τὰς τῶν προγόνων καὶ ὅλως τὰς ὁμογνίους ψυχὰς ἀφωρισμένως ἐν τόπῳ τινὶ ἐξιλεοῦτο. κοινῇ δὲ πάλιν ταῖς τῶν φιλοσοφησάντων ἁπάντων ψυχαῖς ἐν ἑτέρῳ μέρει ἐχεῖτο. καὶ ἐπὶ πᾶσι τούτοις ὁ εὐαγέστατος τρίτον ἄλλον περιγράψας τόπον πάσαις ἐν αὐτῷ ταῖς τῶν ἀποιχομένων ἀνθρώπων ψυχαῖς ἀφωσιοῦτο.

95 For a full treatment of the local "Attic heroes," see Kearns 1989. To date, there are around 300 attestations.

96 White 2000:160.

from other sources: Socrates was supposedly born on the sixth day of the month Thargelion, while Plato was born on the seventh day of the same month. One of the sources for this information about the birthdays of Socrates and Plato is Diogenes Laertius (*Lives of the Philosophers* 2.44 and 3.2 respectively).

1§137. Once again I return to the study of White, who emphasizes that such observances in honor of Socrates and Plato had to do with hero cults that were instituted in honor of these two philosophers:

> Most families [in Athens] visited the graves of their closest relatives through the year to leave simple offerings of flowers and small gifts. Some also honored their parents and ancestors in private ceremonies. But heroes, like gods, were typically celebrated by wider groups than the family, with sacrificial meals, and on special occasions that often became known as their birthdays [*genethlia*]. It is therefore remarkable that later Platonists celebrated the birthdays of both Plato and Socrates with sacrifices and readings [Porphyry *Life of Plotinus* 2]. These are not merely Neoplatonist inventions. Plutarch [second century CE] earlier did the same. In fact, he records the dates in one of his sympotic dialogues, recounting how he and some friends celebrated Socrates' birthday [τὴν ... γενέθλιον (ἡμέραν)] with a feast on the sixth of Thargelion, and Plato's the following day [Plutarch *Table Talk* 8.1 717b].[97]

1§138. In the case of Socrates, as White has shown, the traditional dating of his birthday is identical with the date of the day when he actually died, the sixth of Thargelion, in 399 BCE, and such a dating of the philosopher's birthday was evidently formalized by his follower Plato and by Plato's followers.[98]

1§139. In general, the idea of celebrating someone's birthday even after that someone is already dead follows a traditional mentality that is typical of ancient Greek hero cults. To celebrate such a special birthday, as White has shown, worshippers of any given cult hero would gather every year to participate in a communal feast.[99] The occasion for such feasting in honor of cult heroes has aptly been described as "a consecration of conviviality."[100]

1§140. So, the connectivity for remembering a cult hero was made possible by celebrating the periodic recurrence of a communal feast, and this recurrence was pictured as something cyclical. In other words, the metonymy of connectedness here is circular, not linear.

97 White 2000:153.
98 White 2000:156.
99 White 2000:160.
100 Nock 1944:155–156. Comment by White 2000:172n46.

1§141. Here is my attempt at formulating such a circular connectedness: *the day of death for a cult hero could be rethought as a day of rebirth—a periodically recurrent or cyclical rebirth that needed to be repeated year after year, like a birthday, but, unlike an ordinary person's birthday, such a day of rebirth needed to be repeated yearly for all time to come.*

The Metonymy of Periodic Recurrence in Hero Cults of Philosophers

1§142. In the case of philosophers who were honored as cult heroes, the feast of celebrating such a notional birthday was the occasion for recalling, either directly or indirectly, the words of the philosopher himself. I cite, as the most striking example, a piece of evidence preserved in a remarkable text: it is the last will and testament of the philosopher Epicurus, who died in 270 BCE. In the wording of his will, which is quoted directly by Diogenes Laertius (*Lives of the Philosophers* 10.18), Epicurus stipulated that his birthday, even after his death, needed to be celebrated annually at a feast commemorating him as a cult hero. And, in fact, Epicureans continued these annual rituals of commemoration for many years to come, as we see from documented evidence extending well into the second century CE. The evidence has been studied in some detail by Diskin Clay,[101] who notes that one form of such commemoration was the practice of reading aloud texts relating in one way or another to the teachings of Epicurus, and these texts included even the instructional letters written for the Epicureans by their teacher.[102] Plutarch, who lived in the second century CE, makes a pointed reference to this practice of reading aloud the words of Epicurus at communal feasts of Epicureans (*Live Unknown* 1129a). As Clay observes, such commemorative readings, which he describes as a prominent feature of Epicurean philosophy, were "a part of the hero cults of Epicurus."[103] Here I will build on this observation by arguing that the practice of reading aloud the words of a philosopher in the context of celebrating his birthday was understood to be a substitute for bringing him back to life. To put it another way, the periodic recurrence of the philosopher's words could be substituted for a belief in his afterlife. Instead of continuing life, the philosopher would be dead, but his words as read by his followers could continue their own life by reconnecting metonymically with the words he actually spoke when he was alive.

[101] Clay 1983 and 1986.
[102] Clay 1998 [1986] 98–100.
[103] Clay 1998 [1986] 99.

1§143. Epicurus, as we know well from Epicurean teachings, strongly argued against believing in any prospect of a personal afterlife.[104] And yet, he stipulates in his will that he must be honored as a cult hero. There seems at first to be contradiction here. After all, hero cults were predicated on the idea that there is in fact an afterlife in store for the cult hero.[105] So, how can it be that the teachings of Epicurus about the finality of death did not stop him from endowing his own hero cult as a ritual expression of perpetuity for himself? The answer, as I will now argue, has to do with the practice of reading out loud the words of the philosopher on the occasion of seasonally recurring memorial celebrations in his honor.

1§144. In order to make this argument, I start by considering another example of yearly memorial celebrations held in honor of a dead philosopher. I have in mind a traditional yearly feast known as the *Platōneia*, celebrating the notional birthday of Plato. On the occasion of this feast, Plato's followers would read aloud various texts that were relevant to his teachings, as we see from the reportage of the Platonic scholar Porphyry, whose life extended from the third century CE into the first few years of the fourth. In a treatise he produced about the life of the Platonist philosopher Plotinus, who was his teacher, Porphyry reminisces about a time when he himself performed a public reading of one of his own essays on the occasion of the yearly memorial feast celebrating Plato's birthday, the *Platōneia*, and how Plotinus at that time complimented him on his effort (*Life of Plotinus* 15).

1§145. Elsewhere in *The Life of Plotinus*, we find Porphyry making another reference to such occasions of public readings at the memorial feasts celebrating the birthdays of Socrates as well as Plato.

Extract 1-R

> If we count backward sixty-six years from the second year of [the emperor] Claudius, then the date when Plotinus was born falls on the thirteenth year of [the emperor] Severus (204/5 CE). He [= Plotinus] never disclosed to anyone the month when he was born or the date of his birthday [*genethlion*], since he did not want anyone to make sacrifice [*thuein*] and to organize feasts [*hestiân*] on his birthdays [*genethlia*]. Nevertheless, at the traditional birthdays [*paradedomena genethlia*] of Plato and Socrates, he would follow the practice of making sacrifice [*thuein*] and organizing feasts [*hestiân*] for his companions, and, on

[104] These Epicurean teachings are clearly documented by Clay 1983 and 1986; see also White 2000:160.

[105] *H24H* 8§§43–44, 11§14.

> these occasions, every one of these companions who was able to do so was expected to perform a reading aloud [*anagnōnai*] of an argument [*logos*] in the presence of the group that was assembled.
>
> Porphyry *Life of Plotinus* 2[106]

1§146. I need to justify my translation of *logos* here as 'argument'. For Plato and for Plato's Socrates, as I show at length in another project, this word *logos* refers to the living 'word' of dialogue in the context of *philosophical argumentation.*[107] When Socrates in Plato's *Phaedo* (89b) tells his followers who are mourning his impending death that they should worry not about his death but about the death of the *logos*—if this *logos* cannot be resurrected or 'brought back to life' *(ana-biōsasthai)*—he is speaking of the dialogic argumentation supporting the idea that the *psūkhē* or 'soul' is immortal. In this context, the *logos* itself is the 'argument':

Extract 1-S

> [Phaedo is speaking:] I was sitting on a kind of stool, |$_{89b}$ while he [= Socrates] was lying on a couch that was quite a bit higher than where I was. So then he stroked my head and fondled the locks of hair along my neck—he had this way of playing with my hair whenever he had a chance. And then he said: "Tomorrow, Phaedo, you will perhaps be cutting off these beautiful locks of yours?" "Yes, Socrates," I replied, "I guess I will." He shot back: "No you will not, if you listen to me." "So, what will I do?" I said. He replied: "Not tomorrow but today I will cut off my own hair and you too will cut off these locks of yours—if our argument [*logos*] comes to an end [*teleutân*] for us and we cannot bring it back to life again [*ana-biōsasthai*]."
>
> Plato *Phaedo* 89a–89b[108]

[106] ἀναψηφίζουσι δὲ ἡμῖν ἀπὸ τοῦ δευτέρου ἔτους τῆς Κλαυδίου βασιλείας εἰς τοὐπίσω ἔτη ἕξ τε καὶ ἑξήκοντα ὁ χρόνος αὐτῷ τῆς γενέσεως εἰς τὸ τρισκαιδέκατον ἔτος τῆς Σεβήρου βασιλείας πίπτει. οὔτε δὲ τὸν μῆνα δεδήλωκέ τινι καθ' ὃν γεγέννηται, οὔτε τὴν γενέθλιον ἡμέραν, ἐπεὶ οὐδὲ θύειν ἢ ἑστιᾶν τινα τοῖς αὐτοῦ γενεθλίοις ἠξίου, καίπερ ἐν τοῖς Πλάτωνος καὶ Σωκράτους παραδεδομένοις γενεθλίοις θύων τε καὶ ἑστιῶν τοὺς ἑταίρους, ὅτε καὶ λόγον ἔδει τῶν ἑταίρων τοὺς δυνατοὺς ἐπὶ τῶν συνελθόντων ἀναγνῶναι.

[107] *H24H* "Hours" 22 and 23.

[108] ἔτυχον γὰρ ἐν δεξιᾷ αὐτοῦ καθήμενος |$_{89b}$ παρὰ τὴν κλίνην ἐπὶ χαμαιζήλου τινός, ὁ δὲ ἐπὶ πολὺ ὑψηλοτέρου ἢ ἐγώ. καταψήσας οὖν μου τὴν κεφαλὴν καὶ συμπιέσας τὰς ἐπὶ τῷ αὐχένι τρίχας—εἰώθει γάρ, ὁπότε τύχοι, παίζειν μου εἰς τὰς τρίχας—Αὔριον δή, ἔφη, ἴσως, ὦ Φαίδων, τὰς καλὰς ταύτας κόμας ἀποκερῇ. Ἔοικεν, ἦν δ' ἐγώ, ὦ Σώκρατες. Οὔκ, ἄν γε ἐμοὶ πείθῃ. Ἀλλὰ τί; ἦν δ' ἐγώ. Τήμερον, ἔφη, κἀγὼ τὰς ἐμὰς καὶ σὺ ταύτας, ἐάνπερ γε ἡμῖν ὁ λόγος τελευτήσῃ καὶ μὴ δυνώμεθα αὐτὸν ἀναβιώσασθαι.

1§147. For Plato's Socrates, it is less important that his *psūkhē* or 'soul' must be immortal, and it is vitally more important that the *logos* itself must remain immortal—or, at least, that the *logos* must be brought back to life. And that is because the *logos* itself, as I say, is the 'argument' that comes to life in dialogic argumentation.[109]

1§148. In terms of White's formulation, this *logos* is learned by Phaedo, who is figured as the narrator of the dialogue that we know as Plato's *Phaedo*, and this man Phaedo can then bring the original *logos* back to life by performing it all over again in the *Phaedo*: so, he performs the *logos* "rhapsodically," White says, "as countless others have done since."[110] When White speaks here of a *rhapsodic performance*, he evidently has in mind the medium of Homer, performed by professional *rhapsōidoi* 'rhapsodes'. At the festival of the quadrennial Panathenaia (traditionally known as "Great Panathenaia") in Athens, the Homeric *Iliad* and *Odyssey* were performed rhapsodically every four years, and such quadrennial reperformances were expected to recur for all time to come.[111] Similarly with the annual birthday celebrations of Plato and Socrates: they too were expected to recur for all time to come. White puts it this way: "Through Plato's writing, Socrates thus attains the immortality that epic song awards its heroes."[112] So, the *logos* of Plato's Socrates, like the epic song of Homer, is meant to be seasonally reperformed forever.

1§149. In Plato's *Phaedo*, such reperformance of the words of Socrates is imagined as an event that happened in the context of a real dialogue between a man called Phaedo, the student of Socrates, and a man called Echecrates: in terms of the text that we know as Plato's *Phaedo*, this man Phaedo literally reperforms for Echecrates, from memory, the words once supposedly spoken by Socrates and by the philosopher's interlocutors in the course of the last few days of his life. But we can imagine further reperformances in the form of reading aloud the text of Plato's *Phaedo* on the occasion of annual gatherings of students celebrating the birthday of their teacher. And the word for such reading aloud, as we have already seen, is *anagnōnai*. In this connection, I note with interest a report claiming that Plato called his most famous student, Aristotle, his *anagnōstēs*, that is, 'the one who reads aloud' (*Vita Marciana*, Aristotle *Fragments* 428.2 ed. Rose).[113]

[109] *H24H* 24§§44–49. My argumentation here was inspired by the earlier argumentation of Loraux 1982.

[110] White 2000:161.

[111] Supporting evidence comes from Aristotle *Constitution of the Athenians* (60.1), Plutarch *Life of Pericles* (13.9–11), Plato *Ion* (530a), Isocrates *Panegyricus* (4.159), and other sources. Further references in *HPC* I§26 p. 15n20. I offer an introduction to the subject of rhapsodic competitions at the Panathenaia in *H24H* 0§45; 7E§§1–4, 10; 8§§23, 25, 28–32.

[112] White 2000:161.

[113] Earlier, we saw this word applied to a historian, Theodorus 'Lector'.

1§150. Here I find it most relevant to note that Proclus himself, at the beginning of his Essay 6, which is a separate piece of argumentation within his overall *Commentary on the Republic of Plato*, refers to *logoi* or 'arguments' that are generated in the context of dialogues—or, at least, conversations—that take place at the recurrent memorial feasts held on the occasion of Plato's birthday:

Extract 1-T

> Just the other day, in the course of the conversations [*tà dialegomena*] that take place at Plato's birthday celebrations [*genethlia*], we had the opportunity of examining how someone could make arguments [*logoi*] on behalf of Homer that would be appropriate responses to the Socrates of the *Republic*, and how one could make a showpiece performance [*epideiknunai*] of (1) things that are in most complete accord both with the nature of the content [of Homeric poetry] and with the things that are most pleasing to the philosopher as also (2) things that offer instruction about matters both divine and human.
>
> Proclus *Commentary on the Republic of Plato* VI (I p. 69 lines 23–26 and p. 70 lines 1–3 ed. Kroll)[114]

1§151. In this case, Proclus is presenting his *logoi* or 'arguments' as words that were generated in the context of dialogues—or, at least, conversations—that took place on the actual occasion of Plato's birthday. In this way, the *logoi* of Proclus are dramatized here as a continuation of the *logoi* originating from Plato himself. I find it relevant that Proclus, as director of Plato's Academy, was officially known by the title of *diadokhos* or 'continuator', which is another way of saying that he was thought to continue the *logoi* of Plato in the context of his own *logoi*. And, in the last passage I quoted, Proclus is expressing his intent to make "a showpiece performance" that continues the actual words of Plato—or even of Homer.

[114] ἔναγχος ἡμῖν ἐν τοῖς τοῦ Πλάτωνος γενεθλίοις διαλεγομένοις παρέστη διασκέψασθαι, τίνα ἄν τις τρόπον ὑπέρ τε Ὁμήρου πρὸς τὸν ἐν Πολιτείᾳ Σωκράτη τοὺς προσήκοντας ποιήσαιτο λόγους καὶ ἐπιδείξειεν τῇ τε φύσει τῶν πραγμάτων καὶ τοῖς αὐτῷ ⟨τῷ⟩ φιλοσόφῳ μάλιστα πάντων ἀρέσκουσιν συμφωνότατα περί τε τῶν θείων καὶ τῶν ἀνθρωπίνων ἀναδιδάσκοντα. In translating *pragmata* here as 'content', I follow Lamberton 2012:59n76, who notes: "*pragmata* ... is regularly used to designate the content, as opposed to the language, of poetry." And I translate *logoi* here as 'arguments' in line with the use of the same word later on (I p. 71 line 22). And I note that Proclus, in making these *logoi*, is staging himself as actually 'speaking' them (*legein*: ἐμὲ δὲ τὸν λέγοντα at I pp. 25)

Homer's God

1§152. I started my observations on Proclus by concentrating on the sensory fusion that he reportedly experienced in making metonymic contact with the goddess Athena as the patroness of philosophy. After that, as we saw, the philosopher's experiences of metonymic contact extended further, including not only the goddess but also cult heroes in general and the heroized figures of Socrates and Plato in particular. And then the experiences extended even further, including Homer as a thinker whose thoughts could be connected with those of Plato.

1§153. As I now leave the world of Proclus, I bring to a close my collection of examples showing metonymic contact between the human and the superhuman—but not before I quote the words of another thinker who is named Homer. This time, the speaker is Homer Simpson, referring to an epiphany he experienced in a dream. Appearing to him, he says, was God, whom Homer describes in these words:

Extract 1-U

> Perfect teeth. Nice smell. A class act, all the way.
>
> From "Homer the Heretic" (*The Simpsons*, season 4, episode 3; originally aired 1992.10.08; written by George Meyer, directed by Jim Reardon)

1§154. After mentioning only two of the five senses in describing his contact with God—divine teeth to look at and a divine scent to smell—our Homer continues by rounding out his thought with these words: "a class act, all the way." The wording here seems at first imprecise, but this way of speaking is typical of metonymy. As I will now argue in my concluding remarks, metonymy can in fact be quite precise, accurate, in giving a sense of direction.

The Directional Power of Metonymy

1§155. Metonymy has a directional power. When you say what is connected to what, you do not have to say everything. You can just say a part of everything, a part of the whole. As we have seen earlier, this kind of metonymic expression is what can be called *synecdoche*. Whatever is highlighted as a part can help us get a sense of the whole. But, more than that, the metonymy of synecdoche can actually set the direction of our thinking. And here is where the sensory fusion of the divine, as expressed by Homer, is most telling: he homes in on the scent of

God. No need to say anything further. Everything after that is understandable: "a class act, all the way."

1§156. Homer's homing in on the sense of smell here is relevant to a point I am about to make, which is about the experience of smelling as a sign of accuracy in metonymic thinking. One last time here I pick up on the semantics of the French verb *sentir*, which as we have seen means 'to sense' in general but also 'to smell' in particular. This time, I consider also the corresponding French noun *sens*, which means not only 'sense' or even 'meaning' in general but also 'direction' in particular. The directionality of the French word *sens* is evident, for example, in French roadway signs saying *sens unique*. This French expression can become a "false friend," as teachers of the French language would describe it to speakers of English, if these speakers think it means *unique sense*. Rather, the sign saying *sens unique* is warning the driver that the direction of traffic is not two-way but one-way.

1§157. So, what is the connection between *smelling* and *a sense of direction*? Here is a simple answer: by following the scent of whatever given thing we are looking for, we are following along in a given direction.

1§158. Here is an example that shows what I mean. Some years, ago, as I was paging through the *New York Times*, something caught my eye that bothered me: it was the use of the word *epiphany* in the headline of a brief obituary article. Ancient epiphanies, I was saying to myself, were not the same thing that most people mean nowadays when they use this word *epiphany*. I noted a moment ago the fact that the ancient Greek word *epiphaneia*, which we translate as 'epiphany', refers to the experiencing of something superhuman that makes itself known primarily by way of a visual appearance. In modern usage, by contrast, this word *epiphany* can refer in general to any sudden thought that leads to the solution of a problem. Despite my initial reservations about the use of this word in the *New York Times*, however, I ended up appreciating the motivation for this use: what was being described in the story is in fact an experience that verges on the superhuman. Here is the text of the brief story, in its entirety:

Extract 1-V

> Serendipity led Dr. Hasler to explain how migrating salmon find their way back to their home streams to spawn. Hiking near his birthplace in Utah in 1946, he had a homing epiphany. | At a waterfall, the fragrances of mosses and columbine enveloped him, evoking forgotten memories. And he wondered whether salmon might have a similar experience. | In the late 1940's he translated that hypothesis of "olfactory imprinting" into science to demonstrate that salmon could journey thousands of

miles to spawn in the precise stream of their birth. The secret, he said, was a finely honed and ingrained sense of smell.

> Wolfgang Saxon, *New York Times* obituary, Saturday March 31, 2001, p. A 15. The headline reads: "Arthur D. Hasler, 93; Deciphered Salmon's Homing Instinct"; the sub-headline reads: "Scientist inspired by an epiphany at a waterfall."

1§159. Reading this story, I find myself drawn to the word *homing*, combined here with the word *epiphany*. It brings me back to my second working definition of *metonymy* as a mental process of *connecting* things that are *familiar* to the self. Familiar things are those kinds of things that make the self feel *at home*. So, the directional power of metonymy leads the self *back home* to familiarity. And the association of this homing instinct with the sense of smell leads me back to something I said near the beginning, that smell is almost as primal as sight, if it is fair to say that the olfactory nerve of humans is secondary only to the optic nerve as a pathway to the brain. By now we see that the *olfactory imprinting* of the familiar can give the self its sense of direction for finding its way back home. I cannot resist making a mental connection here between the reproductive drive that we see at work in the spawning of salmon coming back home where they had once been spawned and the sense of sexual attraction expressed by the names of perfumes such as *Je Reviens*, 'I am coming back'.[115]

[115] http://worthjereviens.com

Part Two

Interweaving Metonymy and Metaphor

2§01. I come back to the point in the Introduction where I started to argue that metonymy and metaphor interact with each other as mental processes—and that this interaction can be seen as a coordination of a *horizontal axis of combination* in the case of metonymy with a *vertical axis of selection* in the case of metaphor. So far, in both the Introduction and in all of Part One, I have confined myself to the basic idea that metonymy and metaphor are coordinated with each other, without yet explaining the rationale for thinking of metonymy as a horizontal coordinate and of metaphor as a vertical one. Now in Part Two, I will offer an explanation, focusing on a metaphorical system that actually operates on the idea of an interaction between horizontal and vertical coordinates. And this metaphorical system, as I will show, pictures metaphor itself in a special moment. It is the moment when metaphor is caught in the act of interacting with metonymy.

2§02. Such a picturing is at work in the word *interweaving*, which I use here already in the title of Part Two, "Interweaving Metonymy and Metaphor." This word *interweaving* is itself an example of the metaphorical system that I have in mind here. Given that the craft of *weaving* is a process of *coordination* between horizontal and vertical threads, the word *interweaving* is itself a suitable metaphor for the *coordination* of metonymy and metaphor. Moreover, as we will soon see, the meaning of this word *interweaving* is actually built into the word *coordination*, which is derived from Latin *ōrdō*, meaning 'a thread on a loom for weaving'.

2§03, But before we can delve into the metaphorical world of weaving, I need to step back and review the ancient Greek terms for describing metonymy and metaphor, since the meanings of these descriptive terms are themselves coordinated with each other.

Starting Over with the Relevant Greek Terms

2§1. Although we find no explicit statement in ancient Greek sources about the coordination of metonymy and metaphor, I have argued in the course of Part

One that we can build a model for such a coordination by analyzing the terminology developed by Dionysius of Thrace for describing metonymy together with the terminology developed by Aristotle for describing metaphor. As I have shown, the relevant Greek terms are *oikeio-* 'familiar' in the case of metonymy and *allotrio-* 'alien' in the case of metaphor. In Part One, I have already followed through on the concept of *tò oikeion*, 'the familiar', in analyzing examples of metonymy. Now in Part Two, I intend to follow through on the concept of *tò allotrion*, the 'alien'. In this case, the examples I analyze will involve not only *metaphor* but also another kind of comparison, *simile*. As we will see, a paired analysis of simile and metaphor together will help clarify the coordination of metonymy and metaphor.

A Further Rethinking of Metaphor as a Coordinate of Metonymy

2§2. In the Introduction (0§01), I initially defined metaphor as an expression of meaning by way of substituting something for something else. Then I rethought that definition in order to show more clearly the coordination of metaphor and metonymy. Given that metonymy is a mental process of connecting something that is familiar with something else that is familiar (0§3), I started thinking of metaphor as a mental process of substituting for something that is familiar something that is not familiar, alien (0§2). In such a process of substitution, one way of looking at things is replaced by another way that is alien to the previous way. But now I need to rethink even further this definition by readjusting the idea of the alien, *tò allotrion*.

2§3. Although the Greek word *allotrio-* 'alien' is the opposite of the word *oikeio-* 'familiar', it does not follow that the alien is completely different from the familiar. In some ways the alien is *different*, of course, but in other ways it can be *similar* to the familiar. And in fact *similarity* is the primary feature of metaphor, while *difference* is only secondary. To make a metaphor is to make a comparison, and similarity is what drives the making of comparison in the first place—while the differences we see in the process of making a comparison become the markers of what is alien in a metaphor.

2§4. So, to rethink even further my definition of metaphor, I start by highlighting a basic fact: that the making of metaphor depends primarily on an awareness of *what is similar to what*. With that awareness in place, we can become aware of *what is different from what*, and it is this difference that creates the sensing of what is alien as opposed to familiar.

2§5. In Greek, the word that conveys the meaning 'similar' is *homoio-*, and Aristotle actually uses this word is describing the essence of metaphor. I already quoted his description in Extract 1-A of Part One, and now I quote it here again in Extract 2-A of Part Two:

Extract 2-A (repeating Extract 1-A)

> But the greatest use of words is the use of metaphor [*tò metaphorikon* 'that which is transferable']. This is the only thing that cannot be learned from someone else; and it is also a sign [*sēmeion*] of a good quality that is inborn [*euphuia*], since the making of good metaphors [*eu metapherein* 'good transference'] is the same thing as the contemplation [*theōreîn*] of what is similar [*homoion*] to what.
>
> Aristotle *Poetics* 1459a5–8[1]

Models of Similarity and the Meaning of the Word *Simile*

2§6. This word *homoio-* meaning 'similar' indicates an act of comparison not only in the making of *metaphor* but also in the making of what we in English call the *simile*. This term *simile* is derived from the neuter form of the Latin adjective *similis* meaning 'similar', from which the English word *similar* is in turn derived. In English, a *simile* is signaled by expressions such as *like* or *as* or *similar to*. As for Greek, the primary word for signaling a simile is *homoio-* in the sense of 'similar to'. As we will now see, the meaning of *homoio-* 'similar' is essential for understanding how to make a simile—not only how to make a metaphor.

2§7. The etymology of *homoio-* shows that the meaning 'similar' derives from a more basic meaning, 'same as'.[2] From the standpoint of Indo-European linguistics, the Greek adjective *homoios* (ὁμοῖος) derives from a prototypical form **somo*, meaning 'same as'.[3] The English adjective *same* is derived from this prototypical form. Another derivative is the Latin adjective *similis*, meaning 'same as' or 'similar to'. In the usage of both Latin *similis* and Greek *homoios* (ὁμοῖος), the same semantic principle applies: for A_2 to be similar to A_1, it has to be the same as A_1 in some respect, which is X. Further, for A_2 to be the same as A_1, it has to be one with A_1 in respect to X. That is because the Indo-European root **som* of **somo* 'same as' means 'one', as we see in such forms as the Latin adverb *semel* 'one time'. And the idea of 'one' in words like English *same* has to do with *an act of comparing*. When we compare things, what is the 'same as' something else in

1 πολὺ δὲ μέγιστον τὸ μεταφορικὸν εἶναι. μόνον γὰρ τοῦτο οὔτε παρ' ἄλλου ἔστι λαβεῖν εὐφυΐας τε σημεῖόν ἐστι· τὸ γὰρ εὖ μεταφέρειν τὸ τὸ ὅμοιον θεωρεῖν ἐστιν.

2 The rest of this analysis derives from Nagy 2010c.

3 *DELG* s.v. ὁμός.

some respect becomes ‘one with’ that something in that respect. That is how a word like Latin *similis*, deriving from the concept of ‘one’, means ‘similar to’ in the sense of ‘one with’. What is *similis* ‘similar’ to something else in some respect is ‘one with’ that something in that respect. Similarly in the case of the Greek adjective *homoios* (ὁμοῖος), it refers to something that is ‘one with’ and therefore ‘the same as’ something else in some respect. And, as we will see later, if something else is not the same, then it is *alloios* (ἀλλοῖος) ‘a different kind’, which is the opposite of *homoios* (ὁμοῖος) or ‘the same kind’. As we will also see later, the extension *ios* (ιος) of the two adjectives *homoios* (ὁμοῖος) ‘the same kind’ and *alloios* (ἀλλοῖος) ‘a different kind’ is parallel to the extension *ios* (ιος) of the adjectives *hoios* (οἷος) ‘what kind’ and *toios* (τοῖος) ‘that kind’.[4]

2§8, For illustration, I will now analyze some contexts of *homoios* (ὁμοῖος) in Homeric and Hesiodic poetry. And, in analyzing these contexts, I start with a basic observation. When *homoios* (ὁμοῖος) as an adjective describing a noun A_2 is combined with the dative case of a noun A_1, then A_2 is ‘the same as’ A_1 with respect to X. Another way to say it is that A_2 is ‘equal to’ A_1 with respect to X. And the ‘X’ can be indicated in any one of three different grammatical ways: an accusative of respect, an epexegetical infinitive, or a prepositional phrase.[5]

2§9. So, I begin with three examples that match these three different ways of setting up a comparison (Extracts 2-Ba, 2-Bb, 2-Bc):

Extract 2-Ba

> Back then, there was nobody who would set himself up as *equal to* [homoios] him [= Odysseus] *in craft* [mētis], | no, nobody would be willing to do so, since radiant Odysseus was so much better.
>
> *Odyssey* iii 120–121[6]

Extract 2-Bb

> Never before had there been a mortal man who was *equal to* [homoios] him [= Menestheus] | *in marshaling* [kosmeîn] the horse-drawn chariot teams and the shield-bearing warriors.
>
> *Iliad* II 553–554[7]

4 This paragraph and the connected paragraphs that follow derive from Nagy 2010c:153–157.

5 These three categories have been noted by Heiden 2007:156.

6 ἔνθ’ οὔ τίς ποτε μῆτιν ὁμοιωθήμεναι ἄντην | ἤθελ’, ἐπεὶ μάλα πολλὸν ἐνίκα δῖος Ὀδυσσεύς.

7 τῷ δ’ οὔ πώ τις ὁμοῖος ἐπιχθόνιος γένετ’ ἀνὴρ | κοσμῆσαι ἵππους τε καὶ ἀνέρας ἀσπιδιώτας·

Extract 2-Bc

> My dear friends! You who are top-rank among the Argives, and you who are middle-rank, | and you who are of lower rank—I say this because it has never yet happened that all men are *equal* [*homoioi*] | as men *in war*—now is the time when everybody has work to do.
>
> *Iliad* XII 269–271[8]

2§10. As we see from each of the three examples I have just quoted, each occurrence of *homoios*, which I translated each time as 'equal', has to do with *an act of comparing*, where A_2 (and we may add A_3 and A_4 and so on) is compared to A_1 in respect to X. And, in each of these examples, the point that is being made is that someone is superior to all others, who therefore cannot be that someone's equal.

2§11. Claims of superiority can be contested, however, as we see in the following three examples (Extracts 2-Ca, 2-Cb, 2-Cc):

Extract 2-Ca

> ... so that any one else will draw back | from saying that he is *equal to* [*isos*] me [= Agamemnon] and from making himself *equal to* [*homoios*] me face to face.
>
> *Iliad* I 186–187[9]

Here we see Agamemnon in the act of showing off his political power to Achilles and threatening to show off that same power, which is based on his social status, to anyone else who dares to challenge him. The adjective *isos* (ἴσος) here, which means 'equal', is synonymous with *homoios* (ὁμοῖος), which I translate also as 'equal' here. The point being made by the figure of Agamemnon is that nobody is his equal, not even Achilles. To put it another way, we can say that Agamemnon is claiming that nobody is his peer, that he is peerless.

But this claim of Agamemnon can be contested, as we see from the next example, featuring words spoken by the figure of Nestor:

Extract 2-Cb

> Don't you, [Achilles] son of Peleus, be quarrelling with the king, | force against force, since it is never an *equal* [*homoiē*] thing, I mean, the rank

[8] ὦ φίλοι Ἀργείων ὅς τ' ἔξοχος ὅς τε μεσήεις | ὅς τε χερειότερος, ἐπεὶ οὔ πω πάντες ὁμοῖοι | ἀνέρες ἐν πολέμῳ, νῦν ἔπλετο ἔργον ἅπασι.

[9] στυγέῃ δὲ καὶ ἄλλος | ἶσον ἐμοὶ φάσθαι καὶ ὁμοιωθήμεναι ἄντην.

> inherited | by a king holding the scepter, to whom Zeus has given a luminous sign of sovereignty. | Even if you [= Achilles] are as mighty as you are, born of a goddess, | nevertheless, he [= Agamemnon] is superior in status, since he rules over more subjects.
>
> *Iliad* I 277–281[10]

By implication, Nestor here is recognizing that Agamemnon is actually inferior to Achilles in warfare, even though he is superior in social status. So Agamemnon is not peerless, as he claims to be.

Achilles himself questions Agamemnon's claim to be peerless. Speaking to his friend Patroklos, here is how Achilles lays claim to his own social status as a peer of Agamemnon:

Extract 2-Cc

> But I have this terrible sorrow that has come over my heart and spirit, | seeing as I do that the man [= Agamemnon] is trying to deprive a man who is *equal to* [<u>*homoios*</u>] him | and to take away the prize of this man [= Achilles], just because he [= Agamemnon] is ahead in power.
>
> *Iliad* XVI 52–54[11]

In this last example, equality in respect to social status is seen as an acceptable alternative to superiority.

2§12. Equality in most other respects, however, is merely a foil for the superiority of whatever or whoever is being highlighted. Here are two examples featuring the word *homoios* (Extracts 2-Da and 2-Db):

Extract 2-Da

> Of all these women, not one knew thoughts *equal to* [<u>*homoia*</u>] the thoughts that Penelope | knew.
>
> *Odyssey* ii 121–122[12]

[10] μήτε σὺ Πηλείδη 'θελ' ἐριζέμεναι βασιλῆϊ | ἀντιβίην, ἐπεὶ οὔ ποθ' <u>ὁμοίης</u> ἔμμορε τιμῆς | σκηπτοῦχος βασιλεύς, ᾧ τε Ζεὺς κῦδος ἔδωκεν. | εἰ δὲ σὺ καρτερός ἐσσι θεὰ δέ σε γείνατο μήτηρ, | ἀλλ' ὅ γε φέρτερός ἐστιν ἐπεὶ πλεόνεσσιν ἀνάσσει.

[11] ἀλλὰ τόδ' αἰνὸν ἄχος κραδίην καὶ θυμὸν ἱκάνει, | ὁππότε δὴ τὸν <u>ὁμοῖον</u> ἀνὴρ ἐθέλῃσιν ἀμέρσαι | καὶ γέρας ἂψ ἀφελέσθαι, ὅ τε κράτεϊ προβεβήκῃ.

[12] τάων οὔ τις <u>ὁμοῖα</u> νοήματα Πηνελοπείῃ | ᾔδη.

Extract 2-Db

> Then Zeus the father made a third generation of radiant humans, |
> making it a bronze one, not at all *equal to* [homoion] the silver one [that came before].
>
> Hesiodic *Works and Days* 143–144[13]

In the first of these two examples, Penelope is incontestably superior to the other women, and, in the second, the bronze generation is incontestably inferior to the silver.

Making Similes

2§13. Continuing my survey of examples where the adjective *homoios* is used in comparisons, I now turn to a distinct subset of examples that will prove to be basic for my argumentation.[14] In the examples that belong to this subset, the act of comparing by way of the word *homoios* takes the form of a *simile*. When X is said to be *homoios* to Y within the framework of a simile, the comparison allows for translating not only as 'A_2 is equal to A_1' but also as 'A_2 is similar to A_1' or as 'A_2 resembles A_1' or even as 'A_2 looks like A_1'. That is because, as we will now see, *the making of a simile is primarily the making of a visual comparison*. And what I have just said applies not only to *homoios* (ὁμοῖος) but also to other words used in the making of similes, such as *isos* (ἴσος) 'equal to' and *enalinkios* (ἐναλίγκιος) 'looking like'.

2§14. Before I show examples of *homoios* (ὁμοῖος) as used in the making of similes, I propose to show two comparable examples of *isos* (ἴσος) 'equal to'. I take these two examples from a study of mine that centers on the making of similes by way of this adjective *isos* in sacred contexts *where a comparison is being made between a human and a divinity*. The sacred context in both examples is a ritual. Specifically, it is a wedding. In the context of such a ritual, the comparison between the human and the divinity is visualized as a fusion of identities between the two.[15]

2§14a. In the first example, the *gambros* 'bridegroom' is envisioned as *isos Areui* (ἶσος Ἄρευι) 'equal to Ares':

13 Ζεὺς δὲ πατὴρ τρίτον ἄλλο γένος μερόπων ἀνθρώπων | χάλκειον ποίησ', οὐκ ἀργυρέῳ οὐδὲν ὁμοῖον.

14 What follows here derives from Nagy 2010c:157–167.

15 Nagy 2007c:28–29.

Extract 2-Ea

> Here comes the bridegroom, *equal to* [*isos*] *Ares*, | bigger than a big man, much bigger.
>
> Sappho F 111.5–6[16]

2§14b. In the second example, we see again a bridegroom, though the identity of the third-person 'he' in the wording that I quote is not explicitly identified as a bridegroom. In any case, the 'he' here is envisioned as *isos theoisin* (ἴσος θέοισιν) 'equal to the gods':

Extract 2-Eb

> He *appears* [*phainetai*] to me, that one, to be *equal to* [*isos*] *the gods*, | that man who ...
>
> Sappho F 31.1–2[17]

In this second example, the envisioning is expressed by the word *phainetai* (φαίνεται) 'he appears'. Appearances become realities here, since *phainetai* means not only 'he appears' but also 'he is manifested in an epiphany', and this epiphany is felt as real.[18]

2§15. Just as the bridegroom can be equated with the god Ares in the wedding songs of Sappho, the bride can be equated with the goddess Aphrodite.[19] Relevant to the second of these two equations is the Greek word that we translate as 'bride'—which is *numphē* in Homeric usage and *numpha* in the poetic dialect of Lesbos, as in Song 116 of Sappho. In my earlier study, I made the following relevant observations about *numphē*/*numpha*:

> This word, as we can see from its Homeric usage, means not only 'bride' but also 'goddess'—in the sense of *a local goddess as worshipped in the rituals of a given locale*. And, as we can see from the wedding songs of Sappho, the *numphē* is perceived as both a bride and a goddess at the actual moment of the wedding. Similarly, the bridegroom is perceived as a god at that same moment. These perceptions are mythologized in the description of Hector and Andromache at the moment of their wedding in Song 44 of Sappho: the wedded couple are called [*i*]*keloi*

16 γάμβρος ἔρχεται ἶσος Ἄρευι, | ἄνδρος μεγάλω πόλυ μέζων.

17 φαίνεταί μοι κῆνος ἴσος θέοισιν | ἔμμεν' ὤνηρ ὄττις ...

18 Nagy 2007c:28; further analysis in *H24H* 5§§36–48, where I argue that Song 31 of Sappho is morphologically a wedding song, and that the referent of the 'he' is the bridegroom' while the referent of the 'you' is the bride.

19 Nagy 2007c:27–28; further analysis in *H24H* 5§§36–48.

theoi[s] (line 21) and *theoeikeloi* (line 34), and both these words mean 'looking like the gods'.[20]

2§16. This idea of 'looking like the gods' in the context of a ritual is evident in the Homeric usages of *homoios* (ὁμοῖος) in situations where a hero emerges from a ritual bath in a sacred basin called the *asaminthos*. Here are two relevant passages:

Extract 2-Fa

> He [= Telemachus] emerged from the *asaminthos*, *looking like* [<u>*homoios*</u>] *the immortals* in size.
>
> *Odyssey* iii 468[21]

Extract 2-Fb

> He [= Odysseus] emerged from the *asaminthos*, *looking like* [<u>*homoios*</u>] *the immortals* in size.
>
> *Odyssey* xxiii 163[22]

And here is a parallel usage of the word *enalinkios* (ἐναλίγκιος) 'looking like':

Extract 2-Fc

> And he [= Odysseus] emerged from the *asaminthos*. His dear son [= Telemachus] marveled at him, | *when he saw him, face to face, looking like* [<u>*enalinkios*</u>] *the immortal gods*.
>
> *Odyssey* xxiv 370–371[23]

In the example that we have just seen (Extract 2-Fc), the visual aspect of the simile is made explicit with the phrasing ὡς ἴδεν ... ἄντην 'when he [= Telemachus] saw him [= Odysseus], face to face'. In this example, then, Odysseus is quite literally 'looking like' the gods, as expressed by the adjective *enalinkios*.

2§17. In the next example, which is far more complex than the other examples we have seen so far, it is the adjective *homoios* that expresses the idea that Odysseus is 'looking like' the gods when Telemachus sees him, face to face. In this case, the divine looks of Odysseus are caused not by a ritual bath in the *asaminthos* but by direct physical contact with the goddess Athena herself:

[20] Nagy 2007c:28; further analysis in *H24H* 4§§18–20.

[21] ἔκ ῥ' ἀσαμίνθου βῆ δέμας <u>ἀθανάτοισιν ὁμοῖος</u>.

[22] ἔκ ῥ' ἀσαμίνθου βῆ δέμας <u>ἀθανάτοισιν ὁμοῖος</u>.

[23] ἐκ δ' ἀσαμίνθου βῆ· θαύμαζε δέ μιν φίλος υἱός, | <u>ὡς ἴδεν ἀθανάτοισι θεοῖσ' ἐναλίγκιον ἄντην</u>.

Extract 2-Fd

|172 So spoke Athena, and she touched him [= Odysseus] with her golden wand. |173 First she made his mantle and his tunic to be cleanly washed, |174 she made it be that way, what he was wearing over his chest, and she augmented his size and his youthfulness. |175 His tan complexion came back, and his jaws got firmed up, |176 and dark again became the beard around his chin. |177 Then she [= Athena], having done her work, went back where she came from, while |178 Odysseus headed for the shelter. His dear son [= Telemachus] marveled at him, |179 and, in his amazement, *he [= Telemachus] cast his gaze away from him, in another direction, fearing that he [= Odysseus] might be a god.* |180 And he [= Telemachus] addressed him [= Odysseus], speaking winged words: |181 "As *a different kind of person* [alloios], stranger, *have you appeared* [phainesthai] to me just now, different than before. |182 You have different clothes and your complexion is no longer *the same kind* [homoios]. |183 You must be some god, one of those gods who hold the wide sky. |184 So be gracious, in order that we may give you pleasing sacrifices |185 and golden gifts of good workmanship. Have mercy on us." |186 And he [= Telemachus] was answered then by the one who suffered many things, the radiant Odysseus: |187 "I am not some god. Why do you *liken* [eïskein] me *to the immortals*? |188 But I am your father, for whom you mourn and |189 suffer many pains, enduring the violent acts of men." |190 Having said these things, he kissed his son and let fall from his cheeks |191 a tear, letting it fall to the ground. Until then he had persisted in showing no sign of pity. |192 And Telemachus, since he was not yet convinced that he [= Odysseus] was his father, |193 once again addressed him with words in reply: |194 "You are not Odysseus my father. Instead, some superhuman force |195 is enchanting me, and it makes me weep and mourn even more. |196 I say this because no mortal man could craft these things that are happening to me, |197 no mortal could do these things by way of his own devising, unless a god comes in person |198 and, *if he so wishes*, easily makes someone a young man or makes him an old man. |199 Why, just a little while ago you were an old man wearing unseemly clothes, |200 but now you *look like* [= perfect of eïskein] *the gods* who hold the wide sky." |201 He was answered by Odysseus, the one with many kinds of craft, who addressed him thus: |202 "Telemachus, it does not *seem right* [= perfect of eïskein] for you to be amazed at your father who is right here inside [the shelter], |203 for you to be amazed too much or to feel overwhelmed. |204 There will never again be some *different* [allos] person who comes

> here, some different Odysseus, |$_{205}$ but here I am *such* [*toiosde*] as I am. I have had many bad things happen to me. I have been detoured in many different ways. |$_{206}$ But now I am here, having come back in the twentieth year to the land of my ancestors. |$_{207}$ I tell you, this was the work of Athena, the giver of prizes, |$_{208}$ who has made me be *such* [*toios*] as she wants me to be, for she has the power. |$_{209}$ One moment, she has made me to be *looking like* [*enalinkios*] a beggar, and then, the next moment, |$_{210}$ *like* a young man who has beautiful clothes covering his complexion. |$_{211}$ It is easy for the gods, who hold the wide sky, |$_{212}$ to make a mortal man become exalted with radiance or to debase him.
>
> *Odyssey* xvi 172–212[24]

2§18. In this example (Extract 2-Fd), we see that Odysseus no longer looks the same when his complexion is changed by the goddess. His complexion is no longer *homoios* (ὁμοῖος) 'the same kind' (verse 182). That is why he no longer looks the same. Now he looks different. He is now a different kind of person. At the beginning of this analysis, I noted that *alloios* (ἀλλοῖος) 'a different kind' is the opposite of *homoios* (ὁμοῖος) 'the same kind'. In the example I have just quoted, we see this meaning of *alloios* 'a different kind' in action (verse 181). I also noted that the extension *ios* (ιος) of the adjectives *homoios* (ὁμοῖος) 'the same kind' and *alloios* (ἀλλοῖος) 'a different kind' is parallel to the extension *ios* (ιος) of the adjectives *hoios* (οἷος) 'what kind' and *toios* (τοῖος) 'that kind'. In the

24 |$_{172}$ ἦ, καὶ χρυσείῃ ῥάβδῳ ἐπεμάσσατ' Ἀθήνη. |$_{173}$ φᾶρος μέν οἱ πρῶτον ἐϋπλυνὲς ἠδὲ χιτῶνα |$_{174}$ θῆκ' ἀμφὶ στήθεσφι, δέμας δ' ὤφελλε καὶ ἥβην. |$_{175}$ ἂψ δὲ μελαγχροιὴς γένετο, γναθμοὶ δ' ἐτάνυσθεν, |$_{176}$ κυάνεαι δ' ἐγένοντο ἐθειράδες ἀμφὶ γένειον. |$_{177}$ ἡ μὲν ἄρ' ὣς ἔρξασα πάλιν κίεν· αὐτὰρ Ὀδυσσεὺς |$_{178}$ ἤϊεν ἐς κλισίην. θάμβησε δέ μιν φίλος υἱός, |$_{179}$ ταρβήσας δ' ἑτέρωσε βάλ' ὄμματα, μὴ θεὸς εἴη, |$_{180}$ καί μιν φωνήσας ἔπεα πτερόεντα προσηύδα· |$_{181}$ "ἀλλοῖός μοι, ξεῖνε, φάνης νέον ἠὲ πάροιθεν, |$_{182}$ ἄλλα δὲ εἵματ' ἔχεις καί τοι χρὼς οὐκέθ' ὁμοῖος. |$_{183}$ ἦ μάλα τις θεός ἐσσι, τοὶ οὐρανὸν εὐρὺν ἔχουσιν· |$_{184}$ ἀλλ' ἵληθ', ἵνα τοι κεχαρισμένα δώομεν ἱρὰ |$_{185}$ ἠδὲ χρύσεα δῶρα, τετυγμένα· φείδεο δ' ἡμέων." |$_{186}$ τὸν δ' ἠμείβετ' ἔπειτα πολύτλας δῖος Ὀδυσσεύς· |$_{187}$ "οὔ τίς τοι θεός εἰμι· τί μ' ἀθανάτοισιν ἐΐσκεις; |$_{188}$ ἀλλὰ πατὴρ τεός εἰμι, τοῦ εἵνεκα σὺ στεναχίζων |$_{189}$ πάσχεις ἄλγεα πολλά, βίας ὑποδέγμενος ἀνδρῶν." |$_{190}$ ὣς ἄρα φωνήσας υἱὸν κύσε, κὰδ δὲ παρειῶν |$_{191}$ δάκρυον ἧκε χαμᾶζε· πάρος δ' ἔχε νωλεμὲς αἰεί. |$_{192}$ Τηλέμαχος δ',—οὐ γάρ πω ἐπείθετο ὃν πατέρ' εἶναι,—|$_{193}$ ἐξαῦτίς μιν ἔπεσσιν ἀμειβόμενος προσέειπεν· |$_{194}$ "οὐ σύ γ' Ὀδυσσεύς ἐσσι πατὴρ ἐμός, ἀλλά με δαίμων |$_{195}$ θέλγει, ὄφρ' ἔτι μᾶλλον ὀδυρόμενος στεναχίζω. |$_{196}$ οὐ γάρ πως ἂν θνητὸς ἀνὴρ τάδε μηχανόῳτο |$_{197}$ ᾧ αὐτοῦ γε νόῳ, ὅτε μὴ θεὸς αὐτὸς ἐπελθὼν |$_{198}$ ῥηϊδίως ἐθέλων θείη νέον ἠδὲ γέροντα. |$_{199}$ ἦ γάρ τοι νέον ἦσθα γέρων καὶ ἀεικέα ἕσσο· |$_{200}$ νῦν δὲ θεοῖσιν ἔοικας, οἳ οὐρανὸν εὐρὺν ἔχουσι." |$_{201}$ τὸν δ' ἀπαμειβόμενος προσέφη πολύμητις Ὀδυσσεύς· |$_{202}$ "Τηλέμαχ', οὔ σε ἔοικε φίλον πατέρ' ἔνδον ἐόντα |$_{203}$ οὔτε τι θαυμάζειν περιώσιον οὔτ' ἀγάασθαι· |$_{204}$ οὐ μὲν γάρ τοι ἔτ' ἄλλος ἐλεύσεται ἐνθάδ' Ὀδυσσεύς, |$_{205}$ ἀλλ' ὅδ' ἐγὼ τοιόσδε, παθὼν κακά, πολλὰ δ' ἀληθείς, |$_{206}$ ἤλυθον εἰκοστῷ ἔτεϊ ἐς πατρίδα γαῖαν. |$_{207}$ αὐτάρ τοι τόδε ἔργον Ἀθηναίης ἀγελείης, |$_{208}$ ἥ τέ με τοῖον ἔθηκεν ὅπως ἐθέλει, δύναται γάρ, |$_{209}$ ἄλλοτε μὲν πτωχῷ ἐναλίγκιον, ἄλλοτε δ' αὖτε |$_{210}$ ἀνδρὶ νέῳ καὶ καλὰ περὶ χροῒ εἵματ' ἔχοντι. |$_{211}$ ῥηΐδιον δὲ θεοῖσι, τοὶ οὐρανὸν εὐρὺν ἔχουσιν, |$_{212}$ ἠμὲν κυδῆναι θνητὸν βροτὸν ἠδὲ κακῶσαι."

example I have just quoted, we also see this meaning of *toios* 'that kind' in action (verses 205, 208).

2§19, In this same example (Extract 2-Fd), it is said that Odysseus looks like an old man or looks like a young man, whatever a divinity may wish (verse 198). But when he looks like a young man for Telemachus to see, his son needs to avert his eyes because he sees what he sees (verse 179). What he sees is *that Odysseus at that moment looks not only like a young man but also like a divinity*. When Odysseus asks his son, 'Why do you *liken* [<u>eïskein</u>] me *to the immortals*' (verse 187), Telemachus can rightly answer: 'but now you *look like* [= perfect of <u>eïskein</u>] *the gods* who hold the wide sky' (verse 200). And, in terms of the ritual transformation of Odysseus by way of a sacred bath in an *asaminthos* or by way of a sacred contact with the wand of the goddess Athena herself, this mortal not only looks like one of the gods but he actually becomes a god in the ritual moment marked by the similes that liken him to the god.

2§20. I offer at this point this general formulation: for a mortal to appear like an immortal to other mortals is to become a divinity in a ritual moment of epiphany—as marked by the similes that make mortals equal to divinities in that ritual moment.

2§21. Similarly, when the divine Muses so wish, words that appear to be true can really be true, as we see from the words spoken by these goddesses in their dramatized encounter with Hesiod:

Extract 2-Ga

> Shepherds camping in the fields, base objects of reproach, mere bellies! | We know how to say many deceptive [*pseudea*] things *looking like* [<u>*homoia*</u>] genuine [*etuma*] things, | but we also know how, whenever we wish it, to proclaim things that are true [*alēthea*].
>
> Hesiodic *Theogony* 26–28[25]

2§22. In this example, what is deceptive is not that some things 'look like' other things. Rather, what is deceptive is that *pseudea* 'deceptive things' can look like *etuma* 'real things'. And even these deceptive things that look like real things can still be equal to real things, the same as real things. As we saw earlier, for example, Odysseus is really 'equal to the immortals' when he looks like an immortal in ritual contexts. If Telemachus is deceived by the looks of Odysseus in such contexts, then the deception is in the eyes of the uninitiated beholder who cannot yet distinguish between what is deceptive and what is

[25] ποιμένες ἄγραυλοι, κάκ' ἐλέγχεα, γαστέρες οἶον, | ἴδμεν ψεύδεα πολλὰ λέγειν ἐτύμοισιν <u>ὁμοῖα</u>, | ἴδμεν δ', εὖτ' ἐθέλωμεν, ἀληθέα γηρύσασθαι. For other translations, I single out Pucci 2007:27.

real. Similarly in the Hesiodic *Theogony*, the figure of Hesiod has been such an uninitiated beholder before his poetic initiation into the art of the Muses. After his initiation, however, he can now envision what is real even when he beholds things that can be deceptive.[26]

2§23. The same principle holds whenever Odysseus utters words to be envisioned only by those who have already been initiated into the art of the Muses of poetry:

Extract 2-Gb

> He *made likenesses* [*eïskein*], saying many deceptive [*pseudea*] things *looking like* [*homoia*] genuine [*etuma*] things.
>
> *Odyssey* xix 203[27]

2§24. In this example as well, what is deceptive is not that some things 'look like' other things. Rather, what is deceptive is that *pseudea* 'deceptive things' look like *etuma* 'real things'. And, once again, even these deceptive things that look like real things can still be equal to real things—the same as real things seen by those who are initiated into the art of the Muses.[28]

2§25. The art of the Muses is the art of poetic imagination, which can make even deceptive things look like real things, be equal to real things, be the same as real things.

2§26. Such is the art that is borrowed by the alluring figure of Helen when she makes her voice identical to the voice of any wife of any Homeric hero:

Extract 2-Gc

> She [= Helen] was *making* her voice *like* [*eïskein*] the voices of their wives.
>
> *Odyssey* iv 279[29]

2§27. Helen's voice, borrowed from the poetry of the Muses, has the power of conjuring the voices of the wives themselves. And, by extension, her poetic voice has the power of conjuring the very images of the wives.

2§28. True, Helen means to deceive, but her deceptive words in this narrative frame are the same as the real words of Homeric poetry in the overall

26 On the theme of Hesiod's poetic initiation, I have more to say, with further references, in Nagy 2009a.

27 ἴσκε ψεύδεα πολλὰ λέγων ἐτύμοισιν ὁμοῖα.

28 My interpretation of *Odyssey* xix 203 follows my analysis *GM* 44, 274. I consider my current translation, however, to be an improvement on the one I offered in that analysis: "He spoke, assimilating many falsehoods to make them look like genuine things."

29 φωνὴν ἴσκουσ' ἀλόχοισιν.

narrative frame of that poetry—real words that activate visions of the real things of Homeric poetry. These real things are whatever is real for this poetry, which is figured as true. For Homeric poetry, whatever is divinely true can contain deceptions and still be true.

2§29a. A salient example of such deception contained within the overall framework of divine truth is the moment when the goddess Aphrodite appears in an epiphany to the young hero Anchises, looking like a young girl:

Extract 2-Ha

> Like a virgin unwed, in size and in *looks* [*eidos*], that is what she [= Aphrodite] was *looking like* [*homoiē*]. | She did not want him to get alarmed when he *with his own eyes* perceived her.
>
> *Homeric Hymn to Aphrodite* 82–83[30]

2§29b, Later on in the same narrative, when Aphrodite reveals herself as a goddess to Anchises, she says:

Extract 2-Hb

> And now you should take note whether I *look like* [*indallesthai*] the *same kind of person* [*homoiē*] | *as the kind of person* [*hoiē*] you first saw when *with your own eyes* you perceived me.
>
> *Homeric Hymn to Aphrodite* 178–179[31]

2§29c. In response, Anchises claims that he knew all along that the beautiful young girl was Aphrodite:

Extract 2-Hc

> The moment I *saw* you, goddess, *with my own eyes* | I just knew that you were a goddess.
>
> *Homeric Hymn to Aphrodite* 185–186[32]

2§30. Whether or not Anchises knew all along that the girl was Aphrodite, it is all in the eyes of the mortal viewer, the sameness or the difference. But the divine vision, either way, is true in the long run, and this truth is mediated by the poetic art of the Muses.

30 παρθένῳ ἀδμήτῃ μέγεθος καὶ εἶδος ὁμοίη | μή μιν ταρβήσειεν ἐν ὀφθαλμοῖσι νοήσας.
31 καὶ φράσαι εἴ τοι ὁμοίη ἐγὼν ἰνδάλλομαι εἶναι | οἵην δή με τὸ πρῶτον ἐν ὀφθαλμοῖσι νόησας.
32 αὐτίκα σ’ ὡς τὰ πρῶτα θεὰ ἴδον ὀφθαλμοῖσιν | ἔγνων ὡς θεὸς ἦσθα.

2§31. Despite the seemingly easy equivalence of immortals and mortals in these last three examples (Extracts 2-Ha, 2-Hb, 2-Hc), there is a fundamental difference between gods and humans that proves to be a fatally serious difficulty, as we see elsewhere in the ominous words of Apollo when the god warns the reckless hero Diomedes:

Extract 2-I

> Take note, son of Tydeus, and draw back. Do not try, with regard to the gods, | to think thoughts *equal* [*isa*] to their thoughts, since our kind and your kind are not at all *the same* [*homoion*], | I mean, the lineage of the immortal gods and the lineage of humans who walk the earth.
>
> *Iliad* V 440–442[33]

2§32. I bring this analysis to a close by showing three more examples of similes activated by the adjective *homoios*:

Extract 2-Ja

> She [= the goddess Athena] came into the private chamber, with its many adornments, where the girl [= Nausikaa] | was sleeping. Like the immortal goddesses, in shape and in *looks* [*eidos*], she [= Nausikaa] was *looking like* [*homoiē*] them.
>
> *Odyssey* vi 15–16[34]

Extract 2-Jb

> And they [= the horses of Rhesus] were whiter than snow, and they were *like* [*homoioi*] the winds, the way they ran.
>
> *Iliad* X 437[35]

Extract 2-Jc

> And they [= the goddesses Hera and Athena] went along, *like* [*homoiai*] tremulous doves, the way they went.
>
> *Iliad* V 778[36]

[33] φράζεο Τυδεΐδη καὶ χάζεο, μηδὲ θεοῖσιν | ἶσ' ἔθελε φρονέειν, ἐπεὶ οὔ ποτε φῦλον ὁμοῖον | ἀθανάτων τε θεῶν χαμαὶ ἐρχομένων τ' ἀνθρώπων.

[34] βῆ δ' ἴμεν ἐς θάλαμον πολυδαίδαλον, ᾧ ἔνι κούρη | κοιμᾶτ' ἀθανάτῃσι φυὴν καὶ εἶδος ὁμοίη.

[35] λευκότεροι χιόνος, θείειν δ' ἀνέμοισιν ὁμοῖοι.

[36] αἳ δὲ βάτην τρήρωσι πελειάσιν ἴθμαθ' ὁμοῖαι.

2§33. All three of these examples (2-Ja, 2-Jb, 2-Jc) show the power of poetic visualization, even though only the first of the three is explicit in expressing the use of eyesight in the visualization. In a simile, when something is like something else, the likeness does not have to be a permanent resemblance that links one noun visually with another noun. The likeness can be a momentary resemblance between any overall visualization and any other overall visualization. For example, it is not that Hera and Athena always look like tremulous doves.[37] But there are moments when they can be envisioned that way. One such moment is when you see them in motion, when you see them fluttering like tremulous doves.

2§34. Concluding this survey, I propose to say more generally what I said earlier with specific reference to *Odyssey* xvi 172–212 (Extract 2-Fd). *When anyone in Homeric narrative is deceived by the looks of something or someone, such deception is in the eyes of the uninitiated beholder who cannot distinguish between what is deceptive and what is real.* Similarly in the Hesiodic *Theogony* (Extract 2-Ga), I argue, the figure of Hesiod is such an uninitiated beholder before his poetic initiation into the art of the Muses. After his initiation, Hesiod can envision what is real even when he beholds those things that may be deceptive. In translating *pseudea ... etumoisin homoia* (ψεύδεα ... ἐτύμοισιν ὁμοῖα) as 'deceptive things [*pseudea*] *looking like* [*homoia*] genuine [*etuma*] things' at verse 27 of the *Theogony*, I highlight the idea that whatever things look like *etuma* 'genuine things' in one given localized poetic version could look like *pseudea* 'deceptive things' in a rival localized poetic version; each locale could have its own poetic version, and all such local versions show relative truth values—in comparison to the absolutized truth that is signaled by the word *alēthea* 'true things' at verse 28.[38]

Back to Metaphor

2§35. From these examples of similes introduced by words like *homoio-*, the meaning of which is 'similar to' or, more basically, 'same as', we can see that the act of comparing by way of similes is *selective*. When A_2 is being compared to A_1 in a simile, this A_2 can be similar to or even the same as A_1 in some selective ways, but in other ways it can be different from A_1, even alien to A_1. For example, mortals may become the same as immortals in special sacred circumstances, but they are still mortals in other circumstances, since immortality in this life

[37] With reference to this example as well as to others I have already analyzed, my interpretation differs from that of Heiden 2007.

[38] *GM* 44–46; at p. 44 I compare the use of *pseudea* 'deceptive things' in the Homeric *Odyssey* with reference to localized poetic versions of a "Cretan odyssey" as narrated by the disguised Odysseus in the form of "Cretan lies."

does not belong to mortals: it is alien to them. Here I return to the word *allotrio-*, meaning 'alien to' or 'belonging to someone else', as opposed to *oikeio-*, meaning 'familiar to' or 'belonging to the self'. And I return also to Aristotle's working definition of metaphor.

2§36. At the beginning of Part Two, in Extract 2-A, I had started by repeating from Extract 1-A the formulation of Aristotle concerning the function of metaphor in selectively expressing what is 'similar', *homoio-*. Now, in Extract 2-K, I will repeat from Extract 0-A the formulation that Aristotle had devised to describe the function of metaphor in selectively expressing what is 'alien', *allotrio-*. Here again, then, is that formulation of Aristotle, embedded in his working definition of metaphor:

Extract 2-K (repeating Extract 0-A)

> Metaphor [*metaphorā*] is the application of a noun [*onoma*] that is *alien* [<u>*allotrion*</u>], by transference either from the general [*tò genos*] to the specific [*tò eidos*], or from the specific [*tò eidos*] to the general [*tò genos*], or from the specific [*tò eidos*] to the specific [*tò eidos*], or [it is a transference] by way of analogy [*tò analogon*].
>
> Aristotle *Poetics* 1457b5–9[39]

2§37. This formulation of Aristotle, as I quoted it again here in Extract 2-K, needs to be integrated with his other formulation, quoted earlier in Extract 2-A, where he says that metaphors, like similes, are *selective* about making *comparisons*—indicating what is similar to what. Complementing that observation, his formulation here in Extract 2K says that metaphors are also selective about making *distinctions*—indicating what is different from what. When A_2 is being compared to A_1 in a metaphor, A_2 can be similar to or even the same as A_1 in some ways, but in other ways it can be different from A_1, even alien to A_1. For example, when we say that the sky is weeping, the image of raindrops pouring from the sky is figured as similar to the pouring of teardrops from the eyes, but the sadness of weeping is selectively alien to the sky—unless we participate in a premodern system of thinking that connects the sky to a sky god who has eyes and who occasionally experiences feelings of sadness about mortality.

2§38. In the case of the *weeping sky* as a metaphor, the mental transference of what is alien to the sky, what does not belong to it, is achieved by way of analogy: if weeping is to the eyes as raining is to the sky, then weeping is alien to the sky. So here we have an example of metaphor as a mental transference by

[39] μεταφορὰ δέ ἐστιν ὀνόματος <u>ἀλλοτρίου</u> ἐπιφορὰ ἢ ἀπὸ τοῦ γένους ἐπὶ εἶδος ἢ ἀπὸ τοῦ εἴδους ἐπὶ τὸ γένος ἢ ἀπὸ τοῦ εἴδους ἐπὶ εἶδος ἢ κατὰ τὸ ἀνάλογον.

way of *analogy*—which was the last of the four criteria for metaphor as defined by Aristotle.

2§39. And now I offer three further examples of metaphor, showing mental transference corresponding to the first three criteria in the definition of Aristotle: (a) from the general to the specific, (b) from the specific to the general, and (c) from the specific to the specific:

Extract 2-La

> And he [= Achilles], addressing her [= Athena], spoke winged words.
>
> *Iliad* I 201[40]

Words can travel from one person to another in any general way imaginable, and so the picturing of words flying on wings is a more specific way of imagining how words travel. But the idea of flying on wings is alien to words.

Extract 2-Lb

> Then they went on board and started sailing along the watery pathways.
>
> *Iliad* I 312[41]

A pathway is a specific way to travel by land, and so the picturing of travelers sailing along the pathways of the sea is a more general way of imagining a pathway for traveling. But the idea of a pathway is alien to the sea.

Extract 2-Lc

> And the ship ran along the waves, on its pathway leading to its destination.
>
> *Iliad* I 483[42]

A specific way of imagining, say, a speeding woman is to picture her running, and so a comparably specific way to imagine a speeding ship is to picture it too as running. But the idea of running is alien to a ship.

2§40. In all such examples of metaphor, as we can see, the selective application of something that is *allotrio*- 'alien' is part of a broader and more inclusive mental process, which is the act of *comparing*—whether the comparison is a metaphor or a simile. And, in the mental process of comparing one thing to

[40] καί μιν φωνήσας ἔπεα πτερόεντα προσηύδα.
[41] οἳ μὲν ἔπειτ' ἀναβάντες ἐπέπλεον ὑγρὰ κέλευθα.
[42] ἣ δ' ἔθεεν κατὰ κῦμα διαπρήσσουσα κέλευθον.

another, the new thing that is being compared to the previous thing will be *allotrio-* 'alien' only in some ways but *oikeio-* 'familiar' in other ways. That is, when you compare a new thing that is A_2 to a previous thing that is A_1, some aspects of A_2 will be different from what we see in A_1 but other aspects can be the same as in A_1. In the case of similes involving the adjective *homoio-* 'same as', as we saw earlier, the differences between A_1 and A_2 are shaded over while the similarities or 'samenesses' are selectively highlighted. But it is the other way around, as we have just seen, in the case of metaphors: here it is the 'samenesses' between A_1 and A_2 that are shaded over, and that is why Aristotle in his working definition highlights instead the differences, concentrating on what is selectively alien about A_2 when you look back at A_1. So, the metaphors of the weeping sky and the winged words and the watery pathways and the running ship highlight what is alien, not what is familiar, in the overall mental process of comparison.

Revised Definitions of Metonymy and Metaphor

2§41. I come back to the point in the Introduction (0§04) where I started to argue that metonymy and metaphor interact with each other—and that this interaction can be seen as a coordination of a *horizontal axis of combination* in the case of metonymy with a *vertical axis of selection* in the case of metaphor. Having just reviewed the ancient Greek evidence for understanding how metaphors work, we can by now visualize more clearly the process of *selection* in the making of metaphors. As with the making of similes, *selection* is part of a broader and more inclusive mental process, which is the act of *comparing.* And the mental process of *comparison* requires primarily the perception of *similarities.* The perception of *differences* is only a secondary requirement.

2§42. That said, I am ready to rethink my earlier formulation by saying it in a new way: *metonymy* and *metaphor* are coordinated respectively along the lines of a horizontal axis of *combination* and a vertical axis of *comparison* involving a *selection* of similarities and differences.

The Craft of Weaving as a Metaphor

2§43. I am now ready to argue that such a *coordination* of metonymy and metaphor is analogous to the *interweaving* of horizontal and vertical threads in the craft of weaving. And, in making this argument, I will focus on metaphors that actually compare verbal art to weaving. Such metaphors will be essential for my argumentation, since metonymy and metaphor are aspects of verbal art—and of language in general.

2§44. Already in the title of Part Two here, I used the word *interweaving* with reference to the *coordination* of metonymy and metaphor. That is because, as I noted from the start, the word *interweaving* is itself an example of a metaphor for such *coordination*, given that the process of *weaving* is a process of *coordination* between horizontal and vertical threads.

2§45. In a book that goes by the title *Plato's Rhapsody and Homer's Music*, I argue that *weaving* is a process of *coordination* between a horizontal axis of combination and a vertical axis of selection.[43] In the first edition of that book, published in 2002, I did not say explicitly that the mechanical coordination of horizontal and vertical axes in the craft of weaving is analogous to the mental coordination of metonymy and metaphor in verbal art—that is, in the craft of making song, poetry, and prose. Back then, all I said was that the craft of weaving is analogous to verbal art—as also to language in general. Returning to my formulation as I had originally constructed it, I now intend to put together a restatement. Before I can do that, however, I have to produce an inventory of relevant terms.

An Inventory of Terms Relating to the Technology of Weaving

2§46. Here, then, is a brief inventory of basic terminology relating to the mechanical process of weaving as a technology. In this inventory, I draw heavily on my original wording as published in the first edition of *Plato's Rhapsody and Homer's Music*.[44]

2§46-A. *Weaving* is a specialized form of *interlacing* or *plaiting*. The Greek equivalent of the archaic English word *plait* is *plekein*. Whereas *plaiting* is basically the process of joining two lines of thread—or whatever other two sets of elements—in an over-under-over-under pattern, *weaving* superimposes a *frame* on this process. I quote the expert wording of Elizabeth Barber:

> Weaving, in the narrow, technical sense, involves two operationally different sets of elements: a pre-arranged and more-or-less fixed set, the *warp*, and a second set, the *weft* (or *woof*), interlaced into the first set. Weaving differs from plaiting and basketry partly in the differentiation of a weft from a warp, partly in the fixed nature of the warp, and partly in the extreme length and flexibility of the typical weft.[45]

43 *PR* 79.

44 *PR* [2002] 77–79, where I already emphasize my reliance on the expertise of Barber 1991.

45 Barber 1991:79.

2§46-B. The *frame* for the *warp* and the *weft* is the *loom*.[46] For reasons that I will explain at a later point in my inventory, I give here the equivalents of these three English words in French: *warp* = *chaîne*, *weft* = *trame*, and *loom* = *métier*.

2§46-C. I will focus on the single-beam warp-weighted loom,[47] not on the ground loom[48] or on the vertical two-beam loom.[49] That is because, as we will see, it is the single-beam warp-weighted loom that figures as the primary point of reference for the ancient Greek and Latin terminology related to the traditional process of weaving.

2§46-D. In terms of this single-beam warp-weighted loom, which I will hereafter call simply the *loom*, the set of threads called the warp is *vertical*, hanging from a single beam or crossbeam, and the set of threads called the weft is *horizontal*. The rod that separates, in an over-under-over-under pattern, the odd and the even threads of the warp is the *shed bar* (*shed* is cognate with German *scheiden*).[50] The shed bar guides the *shuttle*, the word for which in French is *navette*.[51] Besides the shed bar, there exists a differentiated type of rod known as the *heddle bar*.[52] As for the direction of the whole process, "the weaving started at the top, and the rows of weft had to be packed upwards, against gravity."[53]

2§46-E. Here is the pertinent terminology in ancient Greek: *histos* is the loom; *mitos* or *stēmōn* is the warp, while *krokē* or *rhodanē* is the *weft*; *kerkis* is in some situations the shuttle.[54] The *kanōn*, as in the description of a weaving woman in *Iliad* XXIII 760–763, is commonly interpreted as a shed bar,[55] though the word may be referring in this context to the more differentiated concept of a heddle bar.[56] The *pēnion* is the bobbin or spool that guides, by way of the *kanōn*, the horizontal threading as it travels over and under and over and under the vertical threading.[57]

46 Barber 1991:80.

47 Barber 1991: 91–113.

48 Barber 1991:83–91.

49 Barber 1991:113–116. The idiosyncrasies of loom traditions in Egypt are connected to the restrictions in raw material used for weaving: unlike elsewhere, the Egyptian tradition concentrates on linen, not wool. See Barber 1991:211.

50 Barber 1991:82.

51 See Barber 1991:85n3 on the metaphors inherent in the words *shuttle* and *navette*. These metaphors picture a ship bobbing over and under and over and under as it makes its way through the waves.

52 Barber 1991:110.

53 Barber 1991:92.

54 Scheid and Svenbro 1994:21. More generally, as Edmunds 2012 argues, *kerkis* is a 'pin-beater'.

55 For example, Richardson 1993:253.

56 Barber 1991:112, 267.

57 Barber 1991:267 refers to the *pēnion* as a weft bobbin, and she draws attention to the expression *kata miton* in the sense of 'in due order'. For a semantic parallel, I suggest Latin *ōrdō*, the meaning of which I will analyze later.

2§46-F. I must qualify what I just said in the last sentence. It is rarely the case, in the process of weaving as we see it described in ancient Greek contexts, that the weft is taken over and under and over and under the warp threads directly. The more usual procedure is that the warp threads are separated from each other to form a shed, which is the actual passage for the weft.[58]

2§46-G. Here is the pertinent terminology in Latin, with special reference to a passage in Ovid *Metamorphoses* 6.53–60 describing a primordial weaving contest between the two prototypical female weavers par excellence, the goddess Athena and her rival Arachne. The two rivals set up their looms or *tēlae*. The threads of the warp or *stāmen* (collective) are stretched vertically, attached from the single beam or crossbeam, that is, from the *iugum*. The shed or comb is the *harundō*. The transverse thread of the weft, or *subtemen*, is attached to the shuttle or *radius*.[59]

2§46-H. We may note some important semantic convergences and divergences in the Greek terminology for weaving. First of all, *huphainein* 'weave' is a specialized kind of *plekein* 'plait', but there are contexts where *plekein* can be used as a synonym of *huphainein*.[60] Also, the process of uniting, by way of weaving, the horizontal weft with the vertical warp is described as *sumplokē* in Plato *Politicus* 281a; the same word *sumplokē* describes sexual union in Plato *Symposium* 191c.[61]

2§47. I will now analyze some semantic convergences and divergences in English and other languages. In undertaking this analysis, I will apply the distinction between *marked* and *unmarked* members of an opposition—to use the terminology of Prague School linguistics.[62] Here is an admirable working definition of these terms:

> The "marked" member of a pair carries greater semantic weight, but can be used across a narrower range of situations, whereas the unmarked member—the more colorless member of the opposition—can be used to denote a broader range, *even that range covered by the marked member*: it is the more general term.[63]

58 Edmunds 2012.

59 I note that the woman described as weaving in *Iliad* XXIII 760–63 raises the *kanōn* to the same level as her breasts. This seemingly eroticized detail may be parallel to Ovid *Metamorphoses* 6.59–60: *utraque festinant cinctaeque ad pectora uestes | bracchia docta mouent studio fallente laborem* "Each one of the two of them went at it with speed, and, hitching their garments up toward their breasts | they set in motion their expert arms with an eagerness that gave no hint of any fatigue."

60 Scheid and Svenbro 1994:35, 126n26.

61 Scheid and Svenbro 1994:21n21.

62 There is an extended discussion of these terms in *PH* 0§§12–16 pp. 5–8. See also Waugh 1982 ("Marked and Unmarked: A Choice between Unequals in Semiotic Structure").

63 Martin 1989:29. See also *HQ* 119–120. Highlighting mine.

2§48. That said, I highlight the English word *web*, which can be used as a synonym for the words *weft* or *woof*. Such a use of *web* is restricted to the marked sense of this word. In an unmarked sense, on the other hand, *web* designates simply 'fabric' as an entirety, consisting of both warp and weft. Similarly in Latin, *tēla* in a marked sense means 'warp'; in an unmarked sense, however, *tēla* means 'loom' as an entirety, consisting of both warp and weft. French *trame*, as we have seen, is the *weft*. Metaphorically, however, *trame* in French means the *plot* of a narrative.

2§49. This metaphorical meaning of French *trame* as the *plot* of a narrative turns out to be my main reason for having highlighted this and other French words referring to the craft of weaving. It is because the meaning of *trame* as *plot* goes to the heart of the metaphorical world of weaving as applied to verbal art. In my other project on the craft of weaving, *Plato's Rhapsody and Homer's Music*, I offer this formulation:

> As the metaphor of *trame* implies, you cannot have a plot in a story, a horizontal weft, if you do not have a framework to begin with. That framework is the loom, which must start with a vertical warp, which in turn makes possible the horizontal weft. Further, from the standpoint of working at the loom, you cannot start the horizontal weft without first attaching the vertical warp from the cross-bar. The English word *web*, as we have seen, can mean the entire fabric by default, not just the horizontal weft, but that entirety still depends on the warp to start it off. Similarly, the Latin word *tēla* may mean the entire loom, not just the vertical warp, and the horizontal axis of the weft depends on the vertical axis of the warp to give it a frame.[64]

2§50. My reference, in this quoted formulation, to the *coordination* of vertical and horizontal threads is the centerpoint of my ongoing argument about the *coordination* of metonymy and metaphor. To highlight the centrality of this point, I now quote another formulation of mine that immediately follows what I have just quoted:

> Let us apply here the Prague School construct of a horizontal axis of combination interacting with a vertical axis of selection. From the standpoint of working at the loom, you cannot move horizontally from one point to the next unless each given oncoming point has already been set for you vertically.[65]

64 *PR* 79.

65 *PR* 79

2§51. In this follow-up formulation as quoted from my other project on weaving, I compare the technical coordination of horizontal and vertical threads used in weaving at the loom with the mental coordination of two kinds of thinking in language—and when I say *language* here, I include the various specialized languages of verbal art.

2§52. In that other project, I go on to analyze some ancient Greek and Latin metaphors that compare the mechanical process of actually *beginning and then continuing and then finishing* the work of weaving a fabric with the mental process of *beginning and then continuing and then finishing* a given string of words in language—especially in the various specialized languages of poetry.[66] Here I highlight one single detail in that analysis, since it concerns the centerpoint of my present argument. This detail is the fact that Latin *ōrdō*, from which the modern word *coordination* is derived, has the basic meaning of 'a thread on a loom'.[67] With this detail now in place, we can see, finally, that the idea of *interweaving* is actually built into the modern word *coordination*, which is derived from the idea of weaving a fabric by interweaving the vertical and the horizontal threads on a loom.

2§53. That said, I offer here a synthesis of the two formulations that I just quoted from my other project related to weaving:

> The mechanical coordination of *weft* and *warp* in the craft of weaving can be pictured as a metaphor for expressing the mental coordination of *metonymy* and *metaphor* in verbal art—that is, in the craft of making song, poetry, and prose—as also in the production of language in general.

Weaving a Song

2§54. The wording of the synthesis that I have just offered is designed to account for the existence of an ancient system of metaphors that compared the verbal art of song, poetry, and prose to the craft of weaving. As we are about to see, the most ancient way to make such a comparison was to focus on the making of song. In ancient Greek songmaking, for example, metaphors that compare the making of a song to the weaving of a web are in fact so old that we can trace them back in time to prehistoric Indo-European poetic traditions.[68] Here is an example:

66 *PR* 79–82.

67 *PR* 80.

68 *PP* 64. See also Schmitt 1967:298–300. As I argue at *PP* 64n22, it is not justified to claim, as do Scheid and Svenbro 1994:119–138, that the metaphor of singing as weaving was invented by

Extract 2-M

> I weave [*huphainein*] a patterned [*poikilos*] headband [of song] for the lineage of Amythaon.
>
> Pindar *Fragment* 179[69]

2§55. As we see from this wording, song is being visualized here as a web, a fabric, a textile. The modern word *textile*, I must emphasize, is derived from Latin *textilis*, meaning 'woven', which is derived in turn from *texere*, meaning 'weave'. Relevant here is another modern word, *text*, which is derived from Latin *textus*, meaning 'woven fabric', which is derived in turn from the same word *texere*, meaning 'weave': in this case, as we can see clearly, the modern word has lost its force as a metaphor.[70]

2§56. In Greek poetic traditions, a traditional epithet for the skillful handiwork of weaving is the adjective *poikilos* 'patterned, varied', as we see it applied to a most famous prototypical fabric in myth, the *peplos* or 'robe' that the goddess Athena herself wove with her own divine hands once upon a time, in a primordial moment narrated at *Iliad* V 734–735 (πέπλον … | ποικίλον).[71]

2§57. I am about to analyze in some detail the relevance of this robe, situated in the world of myth, to a set of rituals celebrating the goddess Athena in Athens. In this analysis, I will focus on the special meaning of the adjective that describes the fabric of this primordial robe. That adjective is *poikilos*, for which I have initially given the translation 'patterned, varied'. It is this same adjective that we saw a minute ago in the Pindaric reference to song as a fabric that is *poikilos*, 'patterned, varied'. As we will now see, *poikilos* refers to artistic variations achieved by way of a special kind of virtuoso weaving, the technical term for which is *pattern-weaving*.[72]

Metonymy and the Artistry of Pattern-Weaving

2§58. So far, we have seen how metonymy can be pictured metaphorically as the threading of horizontal threads, that is, as the threading of the weft, in the

poets like Pindar, who lived in the fifth century BCE. Nor, as I argue further at *PP* 64–65n23, is it justified for Scheid and Svenbro to claim that this metaphor is unknown in the poetics of the Homeric *Iliad* and *Odyssey*. In Part Three of my present project, I will go beyond these cited arguments of mine and argue further that Homeric poetry actually metaphorizes itself as a fabric that is in the process of being woven.

69 ὑφαίνω δ' Ἀμυθαονίδαισιν ποικίλον ἄνδημα (cited at Schmitt 1967:300).

70 *PP* 64–65; see also Schmitt 1967:14–15.

71 Commentary in *HC* 4§§185–210.

72 In Part Three, we will also consider the verb *poikillein*, which means 'pattern-weave' just as the adjective *poikilos* means 'pattern-woven'.

process of weaving at a loom. A case in point is the metaphorical meaning of the French word *trame* as the *plot* of a narrative, to be contrasted with the non-metaphorical meaning, which is *weft* or *transverse threading*. In this case, the plot of a story can be seen metaphorically as a metonymic process, since the making of a plot is a *combining* of a sequence of narrative elements ABC ... XYZ, "from A through Z," in a narrative. But now we will see how this metonymic process of *combination* along a horizontal axis can be *varied* by way of a metaphorical process of *selection* along a vertical axis, so that the elements ABC ... XYZ in a given metonymic sequence may become interchangeable with other elements that are *variants* of ABC ... XYZ. To say it another way: the elements of a given metonymic sequence ABC ... XYZ in a given story or description may allow substitutions, so that a variant A_0 or A_1 or A_2 or A_3 ... may be substituted for the element A, and a variant B_0 or B_1 or B_2 or B_3 ... may be substituted for B, and so on. Here I will argue that this kind of variation, as it operates in metonymic sequences found in verbal art, can be pictured metaphorically as a special process of artistic weaving, known as *pattern-weaving*.

2§59. To say it still another way: *pattern-weaving* is a metaphorical way of picturing virtuosity in the making of metonyms. Such virtuosity is perceived as an artistic ability to produce a *variety* of patterns, and such variety is conveyed by way of words like the Greek adjective *poikilos*, which I have so far been translating as 'patterned, varied'. As for the actual *patterning*, it results from the *varying* of patterns in the process of threading the horizontal threads.

A Brief History of the Author's Encounters with the Idea of Pattern-Weaving

2§60. My interest in this special technique known as *pattern-weaving* started when I was studying the word *poikillein* as we see this word deployed in two passages of Plato, *Euthyphro* 6b–c and *Republic* II 378c. For the moment, I will leave this word untranslated, noting only that it is a verb closely related to the adjective that I have just highlighted a moment ago, *poikilos*. In *Plato's Rhapsody and Homer's Music*, I published the results of a study centering on these two words, showing that both the verb *poikillein* and the adjective *poikilos* actually refer to pattern-weaving.[73] Here I will expand on that study, with special reference to the two passages from Plato.

2§61. Back when I was beginning to trace the meanings of the words *poikilos* and *poikillein*, I was also getting interested in pattern-weaving as a metaphor. Homeric poetry, I found, actually compares itself metaphorically as a verbal art

[73] *PR* 91–94.

to this special technique known as pattern-weaving. My interest in pattern-weaving as a metaphor that actually refers to Homeric poetry slowly developed into a general project of major proportions, one part of which made its way into the Sather Classical Lectures that I presented in the spring of 2002 at the University of California in Berkeley, under the title *Homer the Classic*, while another part got integrated into the Martin Classical Lectures that I presented in the spring of 2003 at Oberlin College, under the title *Masterpieces of Metonymy*. Eventually, the 2002 Sather Lectures were published as not one but two books, which I can describe metaphorically as "Siamese twins" separated at birth. One twin book, under the title *Homer the Preclassic*, was published in printed form by the University of California Press in 2010 and in online form by the Center for Hellenic Studies in 2009, while the other twin book, under the title *Homer the Classic*, was published in printed and in online forms by the Center in 2008 and 2009 respectively.

2§62. Those two twin books complement each other in presenting parts of the big picture, as it were, concerning pattern-weaving. But now, in my book here, I present a part that has up to now been missing from that picture. This new part of the big picture is what I had presented "live" as the second of my four Martin Classical Lectures of 2003.

2§63. So, here in Part Two of *Masterpieces of Metonymy*, my analysis of pattern-weaving completes the analysis that I started in *Plato's Rhapsody* and then continued in *Homer the Classic* together with *Homer the Preclassic*. There is some overlapping with the previous three books, but even the overlaps contribute to highlighting something new—something that I have just described as a new part of the big picture.

Words For Pattern-Weaving

2§64. My use of the expression *the big picture* in saying what I just said about pattern-weaving is in fact relevant to the technique required for the practice of this special form of weaving. That relevance comes alive in the Latin word *pictūra*, from which the modern word *picture* is derived: this word, as we will see, means not only 'painting, picture' but also 'pattern-weaving'. Moreover, the element *pic-* of the noun *pictūra* in Latin originates from the Indo-European root **peik-*, just as the element *poik-* of the adjective *poikilos* in Greek originates from that same root. And, as we will also see in due course, this Greek word *poikilos*, which I have been translating as 'patterned, varied', likewise refers to pattern-weaving.

2§65. An example of *pictūra* in the sense of 'pattern-weaving' comes from the use of the verb *pictūrāre* 'pattern-weave', derived from the noun *pictūra*, as used in a remarkable passage that I am about to quote from the *Aeneid* of Virgil. In this passage, we will see once again the sad figure of Andromache. By now she has broken free from the degrading captivity that had become her cruel destiny after the capture of Troy, and she has even emerged as the ruling queen of a "new Troy" situated near the coast of the Adriatic Sea, at Buthrotum in Epirus. The wandering hero Aeneas and his young son Ascanius have come to visit her there. We join the action at a moment when the visit has almost come to an end, and the visitors are in fact already about to depart from "new Troy"—but not before Andromache together with Helenos, another survivor from Troy, brings parting gifts to the youthful hero Ascanius:

Extract 2-N

> $|_{482}$ Next [= after Helenos had given parting gifts], Andromache, mournful over the final *parting of company*, $|_{483}$ brings *fabrics* [<u>*vestis*</u> plural] that are *pattern-woven* [<u>*pictūrātae*</u>] with *transverse threading* [<u>*subtemen*</u>] of gold $|_{484}$ to Ascanius, and also a Phrygian *chlamys*—she is second to none in honoring him [= Ascanius]— $|_{485}$ *weighing* him *down* [<u>*onerare*</u>] with a mass of *woven* [<u>*textilis*</u> neuter plural] gifts.
>
> Virgil *Aeneid* 3.482–485[74]

2§66. The participle *pictūrātae* 'pattern-woven', applied to the plural form of the noun *vestis* 'fabric' here at verse 483 of *Aeneid* 3, highlights the artistic virtuosity of *patterning* in the process of weaving. We see another example of such *patterning* in the text of Apuleius *Florida* 15, where we read the wording <u>*tunicam picturis variegatam*</u> 'a tunic *variegated* with *pattern-weavings*' [<u>*pictūrae*</u>].[75]

2§67. This kind of pattern-weaving is achieved by way of a *subtemen*, and we have just seen this word being used at verse 483 of Virgil's *Aeneid* 3. This noun *subtemen* (/*subtegmen*), which means 'transverse threading', is derived from the verb *texere* 'weave' and refers to a process of interweaving the horizontal threading or weft with the vertical threading or warp, thus creating the ongoing foregrounded narrative of the pattern-weaving. In this case the foregrounding is golden in color, while in other cases it can be purple. For a case of foregrounding in purple, I cite the wording we see in Tibullus 3.7.121, *fulgentem Tyrio subtemine vestem* 'fabric gleaming with Tyrian transverse threading [*subtemen*]'.[76]

74 $|_{482}$ *nec minus Andromache* <u>*digressu*</u> *maesta supremo* $|_{483}$ *fert* <u>*picturatas*</u> *auri* <u>*subtemine vestis*</u> $|_{484}$ *et Phrygiam Ascanio chlamydem (nec cedit honore)* $|_{485}$ <u>*textilibusque*</u> <u>*onerat*</u> *donis.*

75 *HC* 1§201, following Barber 1991:359n2.

76 *HC* 1§201.

2§68. As we learn from the context of the wording I quoted from Virgil, the *vestēs* 'fabrics' that had been *pictūrātae* 'pattern-woven' by Andromache were originally meant as tokens of love for her husband Hector—and then, once Hector was killed by Achilles, for her son Astyanax. But now, since Astyanax too is dead, Andromache gives the pattern-woven fabrics to young Ascanius, who will take the place of Astyanax by receiving tokens of love that connect with the epic past of Troy.[77]

2§69. Virgil's use of the wording *pictūrātae vestēs* 'pattern-woven fabrics' in the *Aeneid* connects with the Homeric use of the word *poikilos* in describing the fabric that Andromache was pattern-weaving in the *Iliad*. And Virgil's wording highlights this connection, as we will now see, by way of directly evoking the relevant passage from Homeric poetry—from *Iliad* XXII, to be precise. I quote here a portion of that Homeric passage, starting with a span of time that elapses just before the terrible moment when Andromache learns the piteous news that her husband Hector has been killed by Achilles. Within this span of time, Homeric narrative catches Andromache in the act of weaving a fabric, a web:

Extract 2-O

> $|_{440}$ She [= Andromache] *was weaving* [*huphainein*] a web in the inner room of the lofty palace, $|_{441}$ a *purple* [*porphureē*][78] *fabric that folds in two* [= *diplax*], and she *was inworking* [*en-passein*] *patterns of flowers* [*throna*] that were *varied* [*poikila*].
>
> *Iliad* XXII 440–441[79]

2§70. As archaeological research has shown, the artistic technique that we see represented here is not *embroidery*, which is commonly assumed, but *pattern-weaving*.[80] A narrative sequence is being pattern-woven, by way of transverse threading, into the web. In this case, the dominant color of this transverse threading, as we read at verse 441 of *Iliad* XXII here, is *porphureē* 'purple'. We may compare the wording I already cited in Tibullus 3.7.12, where the color of a weaver's *subtemen* or 'transverse threading' is purple. I should add that, according to a variant reading found in the medieval manuscript tradition of Homeric poetry, the transverse threading at verse 441 of *Iliad* XXII is not specifically purple but

77 *HC* 1§202.

78 The medieval manuscript tradition of Homeric poetry shows a variant reading at verse 441 for *porphureē* 'purple', which is *marmareē* 'gleaming'.

79 $|_{440}$ ἀλλ' ἥ γ' ἱστὸν ὕφαινε μυχῷ δόμου ὑψηλοῖο $|_{441}$ δίπλακα πορφυρέην, ἐν δὲ θρόνα ποικίλ' ἔπασσε.

80 On pattern-weaving as opposed to embroidery, see *HPC* II§374 p. 274, with reference to *PR* 93, following Wace 1948. Also following Wace is Kirk 1985:280 and 1990:199.

simply *marmareē* 'gleaming' in general.[81] As an epithet, *marmareē* refers to the luminosity of a color like purple, not to the color itself.[82] In making this point, I am guided by the observations of my friend Susan Edmunds, a master weaver as well as a master classicist, and I quote what she wrote to me about the visual effect of luminosity:

> Luminosity in weaving is the illusion of light created by judicious placement of light, medium, and dark colors. Luster is another quality that thread can have (like fine silk, or wool prepared to preserve that quality in it). The luster in the thread will appear or not depending on how the fabric is woven (think of damask in white linen, for instance, where pattern is made by contrasting shinier weave with more matt weave). [The epithet *marmareē* 'gleaming'] may describe one or another of these effects or, perhaps, the 'brilliance' of the overall effect of beautifully chosen colors and patterns.
>
> Susan Edmunds *per litteras* 2007.02.27[83]

2§71. There are three words referring specifically to the process of pattern-weaving in the Homeric passage we have just read about the web of Andromache. The first is *en-passein*, at verse 441 of *Iliad* XXII, which means that Andromache is 'inworking' or literally 'sprinkling' various different patterns into her web by way of pattern-weaving.[84] These varied patterns are called *throna*, again at verse 441, which I have translated as 'patterns of flowers'. So, now we have just seen the second word used here for pattern-weaving, since this word *throna* can refer to floral patterns that are woven into the fabric.[85] Finally, we come to the third word for pattern-weaving in this same context, which is *poikilos*. As I have emphasized already, this Greek adjective *poikilos*, which I have been translating as 'patterned, varied', is cognate with the Latin noun *pictūra* in the sense of 'pattern-weaving'. And, here at verse 441 of *Iliad* XXII, the *throna* or 'floral patterns' woven by Andromache are described as *poikila*, which I translate as 'varied'. So, Andromache is weaving varied or variegated floral patterns into her web.

81 Again, *HPC* II§374 p. 274.

82 For a general discussion of the color purple, see Lepschy 1998, especially at p. 54.

83 First quoted in *HPC* II§394 p. 284n39.

84 *PR* 93, with further references, including Kirk 1985:280, who relies (as I do) especially on Wace 1948.

85 *HPC* II§§376–377 pp. 274–275, with references.

Artistic Variation in Pattern-Weaving

2§72. In this picture of a weaving Andromache, I see a pointed display of *artistic variation* as a driving force in the patterning of flowers that are literally 'sprinkled' into the weaver's variegated web. To make this display more visible, I need to explore here in more detail the meaning of the word *throna*. So far, I have limited myself to the translation 'floral patterns', but *throna* can mean also 'love charms' or 'enchantments of love' or even 'erotic incantations'.

2§73. In the wording of Theocritus 2.59, for example, *throna* refers to some mysterious kind of floral substance that helps you create a magical effect if you sprinkle it secretively while chanting erotic incantations. Such magical *throna* have the power of attracting the love of an intended lover. That is, they have the power to enchant.

2§74. This magical power of erotic enchantment is visualized in the combination of the verb *en-passein* with the noun *throna* as its direct object. Here I repeat my translation of *Iliad* XXII 441: 'and she [Andromache] she was inworking [*en-passein*] patterns of flowers [*throna*] that were varied [*poikila*]'. Literally, the element *-passein* of *en-passein* means 'sprinkle'. Metaphorically, then, the weaver is 'sprinkling' flowers into her web. Relevant here is a technical term for this kind of weaving, which is, *scattered flower style.*[86]

2§75. The erotic connotations of such a *sprinkling style* are still visible in the meanings of two nouns derived from the verb *passein*, which as we have seen means 'sprinkle'. The masculine noun *pastós* and its feminine counterpart *pastás* both mean 'bridal chamber' or 'bridal bed', while *pastós* also means specifically 'bridal bed curtain' (Pollux 3.37).[87]

2§76. So, there is an erotic as well as a magical effect created by the artistic variation of the *throna* 'flowers', described as *poikila* 'varied, variegated', which Andromache *en-passei* 'sprinkles' into her web. And such an aphrodisiac effect comes to life in the epithet *poikilo-thronos*, applied to the goddess Aphrodite herself.[88] This epithet appears as the first word of the first line of the first song of the ancient collection of songs attributed to Sappho, where the goddess is invoked as *poikilo-thronos* (Sappho *Song* 1.1). Translated literally, *poikilo-thronos* means 'having love charms [*throna*] that are varied [*poikila*]'. Interpreted more fancifully, *poikilo-thronos* would mean 'Our Lady of the varied pattern-woven floral love charms'.[89] In terms of this epithet, the love charms or erotic enchantments conveyed in love songs are exteriorized as variegated

[86] On this style of weaving, see Barber 1991:366n7.

[87] *HPC* II§377 p. 275n12.

[88] Petropoulos 1993.

[89] *HPC* II§381 p. 276. Details in *PR* 93; see also *PP* 101.

floral patterns that are woven into a fabric. And it is the song itself—in this case, Song 1 of Sappho—that weaves these variegated floral patterns into the enchanted fabric. Once the singing begins, this fabric is ready to wear for the enchanting Aphrodite. Conversely, the variegated floral patterns or *throna* that Andromache weaves into her own enchanted fabric as described at verse 441 of *Iliad* XXII are interiorized as intimate love songs that are meant to attract the love of her beloved husband. And what we see at work in the creation of such enchanted fabrics, I maintain, is a kind of virtuosity that I describe here as *artistic variation.*

2§77. In *Homer the Preclassic*, I attempted an analysis of such artistry as it comes to life in the pattern-weaving of Andromache. Focusing on verse 441 of *Iliad* XXII, where the narrative catches Andromache in the act of sprinkling the patterned flowers or *throna* into her variegated web, I described in the following words the enchanting display of her artistry as a master weaver:

> Each flower in the sequence of flowers woven into the web is a love charm, an incantation that sings its own love song. Each flower is different from the next, and the sequence of flowers becomes a variety of love songs within a single sustained narrative, a single love story, which is the pattern-woven web in its entirety.[90]

2§78. As I went on to argue in *Homer the Preclassic*, the sequence of *throna* or 'floral patterns' as pattern-woven by Andromache is telling its own love story, but this story is overtaken by the overall story of the *Iliad*, which is far more than a love story: it is a story of terror and pity, a story of war, an Iliadic story in the making.[91]

2§79. This overall story is already in the making when another major figure in the *Iliad*, Helen herself, appears for the first time in the narrative. I have in mind the passage in *Iliad* III 125–128 where we find Helen in the act of weaving her own web. Here I return to what I argued in *Homer the Classic* about this passage. I said there that Helen too, like Andromache, is pattern-weaving in this scene. But the difference is, the patterns that Helen weaves into her own fabric are not *throna* or 'love charms' that thread a story of love. In the web of Helen, the varied patterns are most tellingly pictured as *athloi* 'ordeals'. In other words, the transverse threading here is telling a tale of war. It is the tale of the Trojan War.[92] Here, then, is wording of the passage:

90 *HPC* II§376 p. 275 .

91 *HPC* II§382 p. 276.

92 *HPC* II§382 p. 276. See also Clader 1976:7n8 and Collins 1988:42–43.

Extract 2-P

> $|_{125}$ She [= the divine messenger Iris] found her [= Helen] in the palace. She was *weaving* [*huphainein*] a great web, $|_{126}$ a *purple* [*porphureē*][93] *fabric that folds in two* [= *diplax*], and she *was inworking* [*en-passein*][94] many *ordeals* [*athloi*] $|_{127}$ of Trojans, tamers of horses, and of Achaeans, wearers of bronze tunics [*khitōnes*], $|_{128}$ —ordeals that they suffered at the hands of Ares all because of her.
>
> *Iliad* III 125–128[95]

2§80. As with the web of Andromache, the narrative sequence woven into the web of Helen is created by way of the transverse threading, described here as either *porphureē* 'purple' or, according to a variant reading also found in the medieval manuscript tradition, *marmareē* 'gleaming'.[96] But Helen's transverse threading, unlike Andromache's, is telling not only her own tale but also the tale of the whole *Iliad*, which centers on all the ordeals suffered by all the heroes of the Trojan War.

2§81. At this point, I find it most relevant to compare the two meaning of the French word *trame*, which as we saw refers literally to the transverse threading or 'weft' of a loom and, metaphorically, to the 'plot' that drives a story or a description. From a comparative standpoint, these meanings fit the description of Helen's web in *Iliad* III 125–128, in that her weaving can be seen as a metaphor for creating the overall plot of the *Iliad*. This plot moves along a horizontal axis of transverse threading, which is the weft of the loom. Meanwhile, the vertical axis of threading, which is the warp, gives variety to the plot. And the variations produced by this variety make it possible to show the many different ordeals suffered by the many different heroes of the Trojan War.

2§82. The one thing that all these sufferings have in common is encoded in the transverse threading. When this threading is suffused with purple dye, as overtly signaled by the variant reading *porphureē* at verse 126 of *Iliad* III, the color itself can track all the blood that was being shed by all who were killed or wounded in the war they fought for the sake of Helen. At a later point, when we consider the traditional pattern-weaving of another tale—about a primordial battle between Olympian gods and Earth-born Giants—we will see a comparable use of the color purple, signaling in that case the blood that is shed by the Giants in the course of their disastrous defeat by the Olympians.

[93] There is a variant reading at verse 126 for *porphureē* 'purple', which is *marmareē* 'gleaming'.

[94] To repeat, *en-passein* is to 'sprinkle': *PR* 93.

[95] $|_{125}$ τὴν δ' εὗρ' ἐν μεγάρῳ· ἣ δὲ μέγαν ἱστὸν ὕφαινε $|_{126}$ δίπλακα πορφυρέην, πολέας δ' ἐνέπασσεν ἀέθλους $|_{127}$ Τρώων θ' ἱπποδάμων καὶ Ἀχαιῶν χαλκοχιτώνων, $|_{128}$ οὓς ἕθεν εἵνεκ' ἔπασχον ὑπ' Ἄρηος παλαμάων.

[96] *HPC* II§383 p. 277.

Pattern-Weaving as a Metaphor for Homeric Poetry

2§83. The web of Helen is not just a metaphor for the overall plot of the *Iliad*. By extension, this web is also a metaphor for Homeric poetry itself. To make this point, I start with the idea of the *Iliad* itself as 'the tale of Troy'—which is in fact what the name *Iliad* means. Given this fact, we can think of the web of Helen as a metaphor for the telling of the tale. Similarly, the web of Andromache is a metaphor for telling a part of this tale, focusing on those precious few moments when the pleasure and the beauty of love are temporarily dominant. And then, once the weaving of Andromache is interrupted when she hears from outside her private chamber the wailing of women who already know the news about the death of Hector—news still unknown to Andromache—this part of the tale is rapidly overtaken by the overall plot of the *Iliad*. Now the dominance of war can once again be asserted.

2§84. Here is another way to say what I just said about these two webs pattern-woven by these two main characters of the *Iliad*: the web of Helen is a fully-formed metaphor for the Homeric narrative that draws attention to it, while the web of Andromache is at least a partial metaphor for this same narrative. But there is more to it. The pattern-weaving that creates these webs is a metaphor for the verbal art that creates Homeric poetry. In other words, Homeric poetry can actually refer to its own creation by way of this metaphor.

Artistry as Variation

2§85. Such a Homeric self-reference, then, is defining a special kind of verbal art that is modeled on the art of pattern-weaving. Before we consider further this verbal art in terms of such modeling, however, I first need to concentrate on the artistry of the actual pattern-weaving. In particular, I need to consider how this artistry depends on the weaver's ability to create variation.

2§86. In the previous section, I referred to "a single sustained narrative" in describing the sequence of *throna* or 'floral patterns' woven into the web of Andromache. And I showed that a comparable description applies to the web of Helen, where the sequencing of *athloi* or 'ordeals' is likewise a sustained narrative. Each one of these two narratives, as we will now see, is actually *created* by the sequences of patterns woven into the fabric, and such sequencing is the metonymic logic that drives the narration. Here is what I mean when I say *metonymic logic*: the entire process of narration in each case of weaving is a metonymic sequence ABC ... XYZ, which is a story that runs "from A to Z." But the process is more complicated. In the case of each one of these two webs, what makes the whole sequence a work of art is not only the sequence itself but also the *variation* that is added to the sequence by way of pattern-weaving. The artistry depends on this variation.

2§87. Here is how the variation works: the metonymic sequence of elements ABC ... XYZ allows for substitutions, so that a variant A_0 or A_1 or A_2 or A_3 ... may be substituted for the element A, and a variant B_0 or B_1 or B_2 or B_3 ... may be substituted for B, and so on, from A through Z. Such substitutions are guided by the vertical threading of metaphorical selection, meshing with the horizontal threading of metonymic combination. And it is this kind of variation in pattern-weaving that makes the whole metonymic sequence ABC ... XYZ a work of art. Such a work of art, in terms of my overall argument, is a *masterpiece of metonymy*.

A New Way of Looking at Masterpieces of Metonymy

2§88. For the very first time, I have applied here this term *masterpiece of metonymy* to works of art produced not by way of song, poetry, or prose. Instead, the masterpieces of Helen and Andromache are produced by way of weaving—specifically, pattern-weaving. And, by taking a closer look at this medium of pattern-weaving, we can see for the first time that a masterpiece of metonymy requires a kind of artistry that is not—and cannot be—restricted to metonymy. Instead, the artistry coordinates metonymy with metaphor. That is, a masterpiece of metonymy in pattern-weaving actually coordinates the process of making metonymic combinations on a horizontal axis, which is the primary process, with the secondary process of making metaphoric selections on a vertical axis. The actual coordination of a horizontal axis of combination and a vertical axis of selection is what produces the kind of variation that is so prized in the art of pattern-weaving. In terms of this medium of art, then, *a masterpiece of metonymy* is really *a masterpiece of metonymy coordinated with metaphor*.

2§89. This formulation brings me all the way back to the Introduction to the book (0§04), where I had already described in terms of *variation* the coordination that we see at work between an axis of combination and an axis of selection:

> The axis of combination in meaning can be seen as a horizontal movement connecting elements A and B and C ... to each other in a sequence that proceeds all the way to ... X and Y and Z; correspondingly, the axis of selection in meaning can be seen as a vertical movement that varies the elements in the same sequence by allowing substitutions of one variant for another, so that the element A can become A_0 or A_1 or A_2 or A_3 ..., or the element B can become B_0 or B_1 or B_2 or B_3 ..., and so on.

2§90. By now we see that the poetics of variation, as initially formulated in the wording I have just repeated here, can be metaphorically modeled on the mechanical process of pattern-weaving.

On the Meaning of the Greek Adjective *poikilos*

2§91. In my analysis of the Homeric reference in *Iliad* XXII 440–441 to the web of Andromache, which is poetically displayed as a masterpiece of pattern-weaving, I have already shown that the adjective *poikilos*, when it applies to the floral patterns that are worked into such a web, means not only 'patterned, varied' but also 'pattern-woven'.[97] What I have not yet shown, however, is that this meaning applies not only to masterpieces of pattern-weaving but also to the virtuosity of the verbal art that compares itself to such masterpieces. To make this point, I return to a passage that I quoted when I gave my first example of the word *poikilos*:

Extract 2-Q (repeating Extract 2-M)

> I weave [*huphainein*] a patterned [*poikilos*] headband [of song] for the lineage of Amythaon.
>
> Pindar *Fragment* 179[98]

2§92. Already when I first quoted this passage, I translated *poikilos* as 'patterned'. But by now we see that this word means, more specifically, 'pattern-woven'. In other words, the metaphor for song here is expressed not generally in terms of *weaving* but instead, more specifically, in terms of the specialized technique that I have by now identified as *pattern-weaving*. That said, I can proceed to reword my ongoing argument in terms of this word *poikilos*, and my new wording goes like this: just as the virtuosity of pattern-weaving produces a web that is *poikilos* 'patterned, varied', so also the verbal art of a virtuoso singer is *poikilos*, that is 'pattern-woven' as well as 'patterned, varied'. And such verbal art, as we will see, can be treasured as a masterpiece of metonymy, just as the ancient world treasured the artistry that went into the making of a pattern-woven web.

A Prototype of Pattern-Weaving

2§93. In the passage I just quoted again from Pindar, we saw a form of verbal art compared metaphorically to the craft of pattern-weaving. Later on, in passages still to be quoted, we will see a number of other such comparisons to

[97] See also *HPC* II§392 p. 283, following Barber 1991:359n2.
[98] ὑφαίνω δ' Ἀμυθαονίδαισιν ποικίλον ἄνδημα.

pattern-weaving. But now I highlight another kind of comparing, where pattern-weaving is actually a *model* for comparison. And when I say *model* here, I mean an absolute model, a *prototype*. As we will see, the idea of such a prototype actually existed in the world of ancient Greek myth and ritual.

2§94. The prototype I have in mind is signaled in lines 734–735 of *Iliad* V: in these two lines, we catch a glimpse of a *peplos* or 'robe' worn by the goddess Athena herself, which is described as *poikilos* 'pattern-woven' (πέπλον ... | ποικίλον)—and which she is said to have woven with her own divine hands in a primordial moment. It is this *peplos*, as the narrative of *Iliad* V indicates in the context of these two lines, that Athena wore before she started to arm herself in preparation for fighting against the Trojans in the Trojan War. In Part Three, I will examine the entire Homeric passage that includes the full text of the two lines that I am now highlighting, but for now I quote only the relevant wording in these lines:

Extract 2-R

> $|_{734}$ the robe [*peplos*] ... $|_{735}$ [the] pattern-woven [*poikilos*] robe, the one that she herself [= Athena] made and worked on with her own hands.
>
> *Iliad* V 734–735[99]

The Robe of Athena as a Perfect Masterpiece of Metonymy

2§95. Viewed from the perspective of ancient Greek myth and ritual, this robe that was pattern-woven by Athena herself in *Iliad* V 734–735 must surely be a masterpiece. In the logic of myth, a piece of art produced by a divinity is absolutely the best piece of art—the perfect masterpiece. So, the robe produced by Athena is a perfect masterpiece of pattern-weaving. And, by extension, this robe of Athena is also a perfect masterpiece of metonymy. I say this because we have already seen how the process of pattern-weaving is actually driven by a metonymic way of thinking.

2§96. I add here a qualification. In the art of pattern-weaving, the artistry actually coordinates the process of making metonymic combinations on a horizontal axis, which is the primary process, with the secondary process of making metaphoric selections on a vertical axis. So, in terms of pattern-weaving, *a masterpiece of metonymy* is to be understood more fully as *a masterpiece of metonymy coordinated with metaphor.*

99 $|_{734}$ πέπλον ... $|_{735}$ ποικίλον, ὅν ῥ' αὐτὴ ποιήσατο καὶ κάμε χερσίν.

2§97. With this qualification in place, I can continue to describe the robe woven by Athena as perfect masterpiece of metonymy, not only as a perfect masterpiece of pattern-weaving. And both these descriptions merit the addition of the adjective *perfect* because, as we will see, the masterpiece that Athena created by way of pattern-weaving her robe was understood to be not only a model but also an absolutizing prototype for any and all other such masterpieces.

Re-Enacting in Ritual a Prototype in Myth

2§98. Once again I am making a distinction here between *model* and *prototype*. And that is because, to repeat, a *prototype* is understood to be an *absolute model* in the world of myth and ritual. By contrast, non-prototypical models are not necessarily absolute. A *model* is meant to be *imitated*, but a *prototype* is meant to be *ritually re-enacted*, not just imitated. As we will now see, the pattern-woven *peplos* or 'robe' of Athena in *Iliad* V 734–735 is a perfect example of a prototype in myth that is meant to be re-enacted in ritual. And, as we will also see, such re-enactment takes place by way of rituals involving the process of pattern-weaving.

2§99. Already when I first drew attention to this *poikilos peplos* or 'pattern-woven robe' of Athena in *Iliad* V 734–735 (πέπλον ... | ποικίλον), I noted that I will analyze in detail the relevance of this robe, situated in the world of myth, to a set of rituals celebrating the goddess Athena in Athens. Now I am ready to present such an analysis.

The Relevance of Athena's Robe to Rituals of Re-Enactment

2§100. I start, then, with the wording of the passage in *Iliad* V 734–735 describing the primordial act of pattern-weaving performed by Athena. As we know from the words I already quoted from that passage in Extract 2-R, Athena produced a primordial robe that was ready to wear. It was *prêt-à-porter*. This detail about divine wear has a direct bearing, as we will now see, on a set of rituals that I am about to analyze. These rituals will show how Athena's primordial act of weaving a robe for herself to wear was seen as a prototype, in the world of myth, for the re-enacting of this act in the world of ritual.

2§101. The historical setting for this re-enactment was the city of Athens, where the goddess Athena was worshipped by the Athenians as their all-important deity. In this city, there were seasonally recurring rituals that re-enacted the primordial weaving of the robe that the goddess wove for herself to wear. And these rituals were connected to an Athenian myth that explained why the goddess Athena was all-important to the Athenians. To understand the meaning of this myth, as we will see, we need to understand the meaning of Athenian rituals related to the robe worn by Athena.

A Charter Myth for the Athenians

2§102. This Athenian myth about Athena as the all-important divinity of the Athenians is a *charter myth*. In anthropological terms, a charter myth is a myth that is so central, from the standpoint of a given society, that it becomes the foundational statement about the identity of that society.[100] I give here a brief synopsis of this Athenian charter myth, tracing its evolution from prehistoric times all the way into the historical era of the sixth and the fifth centuries BCE and later.

2§103. This myth, as we know from ancient sources, was about a primordial battle of the *gigantes* 'Giants' against the celestial gods, who were led by Zeus and by his daughter Athena. That battle was called the *gigantomakhiā* or Gigantomachy.[101] The myth, as it took shape in the historical era of Athens, told how the Giants, generated from and by the primal goddess Earth, rebelled against Zeus and Athena and all the other divinities who dwell on Mount Olympus. The Giants attempted to overthrow the gods of Olympus by piling up a mass of rocks, or even mountains on top of mountains, in order to reach the celestial heights. But the Olympian gods defeated the Giants in battle, thrusting them back down into the Earth. After their divine victory, Zeus and Athena and the other Olympians could finally re-establish cosmic order.[102]

2§104. In the narrative of this charter myth, the goddess Athena was born on the same day when she joined the other Olympian gods in the battle against the Giants. On that primordial day, the goddess was born fully formed—and armed—from the head of her father Zeus. The primary sources for this event are Hesiod *Theogony* 886–900, 924–926 and the *Homeric Hymn* [28] *to Athena* 4–6. It is important for me to emphasize here, in the context of my mentioning Hesiod, that Hesiodic poetry—not just Homeric poetry—was an integral part of the repertoire in the performance traditions of the Panathenaia in Athens during the preclassical era of the sixth century BCE.[103]

2§105. Athena's birthday, then, was understood to be simultaneous with the primordial day of the Gigantomachy.[104] It is vitally important for my ongoing

100 *PR* 90–93.

101 Details and citations in *HC* 1§130.

102 On the central role of Athena in the Athenian version of this myth, see especially Pinney 1988.

103 *HPC* I §§171–177 pp. 70–73; E§71 p. 333; E§§83–94 pp. 336–340, E§§111–113 pp. 345–346.

104 Details in *HC* 1§131, 4§217.

argument to stress here the mythological synchronicity linking the sacred day of Athena's birth and the primordial day when she and the other Olympians defeated the Giants.[105]

A Charter Ritual for the Athenians

2§106. The same primordial day when the goddess Athena was born, proceeding immediately to join her father Zeus in defeating the Giants, was equated with the climactic last day of a festival cherished by the Athenians as the greatest of all festivals. Known as the Panathenaia, this festival was celebrated every year in the late summer on the 28th of Hekatombaion, which was the last day of the first month of the Athenian year.[106] In terms of my ongoing argumentation, this date marked not only the victory of the goddess Athena in the Gigantomachy but also her birth from the head of Zeus, since the victory and the birth were synchronized by the myth.[107] So, this day was the sacred annual birthday of Athena.[108] And there was a most special event that marked this most special day: it was the Panathenaic Procession, a spectacular parade that culminated in the presentation of a newly woven *peplos* or 'robe' to the goddess. This procession, culminating in the presentation of the robe, was a ritual that matched the charter myth of the Athenians, that is, the Gigantomachy. In referring to this ritual here, I coin the term *charter ritual.*

2§107. Here is what I mean. What happened on the primordial day of Athena's birth in the world of Athenian myth was re-enacted on that same day, as it were, in the world of Athenian ritual. And, just as this ritual of re-enactment was thought to be sacred, so also was the birthday of Athena.

2§108. I draw attention here to my use of the word *sacred* in describing ritual. In saying that such a charter ritual of celebrating the birthday of Athena was

[105] Details in *HC* 1§131, 4§217. See also *HPC* I§201 p. 84n11.

[106] See Rhodes 1981:693, who also considers surviving traces of fluctuation between the 28th and the 27th of Hekatombaiōn as the main day of celebration.

[107] What I argue here is not incompatible with the argumentation of Pinney 1988 about the aetiological link between the mythical victory of the goddess and the ritual celebration of this victory on the 28th day of the month Hekatombaiōn at the festival of the Panathenaia. But I have added to Pinney's argumentation the idea that the victory of the goddess is synchronized with her birth.

[108] I am making a distinction here between one yearly birthday and twelve monthly birthdays for the goddess, since these distinct birthdays were apparently dated at different days of the month. It is reported that the monthly birthday was celebrated on the third day of every month in the year: see Harpocration s.v. τριτομηνίς and the commentary of Shear 2001:37n30. I disagree, however, with Shear's argument (especially pp. 3, 29–30, 37, with bibliography) for discounting the rival testimony about the 28th day of the month as the monthly birthday, as reported for example in the Suda s.v. τριτογενής. Such testimony, I argue, stems from a misreading of earlier traditions about the 28th day of the month Hekatombaiōn as the yearly birthday of Athena.

sacred, I do not mean to imply that whatever happened at the celebration was exclusively solemn. As we will see in Part Four, a festival like the Panathenaia was also the occasion of festive merriment. Nor do I mean to say, I should add, that anything we may describe as *sacred* cannot be at the same time *practical*, *ideological*, and even *political*.

2§109. That said, I repeat the essentials of the sacred charter ritual of the Panathenaic Procession. Every year in Athens, a new *peplos* or 'robe' was to be woven for Athena to celebrate the occasion of her cosmic birthday, which as I said was the climactic day of the festival of the Panathenaia. This day was marked by a spectacular *pompē* or 'procession' that culminated in the presentation of the newly woven *peplos* or 'robe' to Athena in her role as *Polias*, meaning 'goddess of the city'.[109] Here is a prosaic but accurately programmatic description that survives from the ancient world:

Extract 2-S

> For Athena the city-goddess [Polias] there was a robe [*peplos*] made. It was completely pattern-woven [*pan-poikilos*]. And it was ritually carried and presented to her in the procession [*pompē*] of the Panathenaia.
>
> Scholia for Aristophanes *Birds* 827[110]

2§110. I highlight in this programmatic statement the epithet *pan-poikilos*, which describes the *peplos* or 'robe' presented to Athena Polias. Earlier, I had highlighted the epithet *poikilos* 'pattern-woven' describing the *peplos* made by Athena herself in the passage I cited from *Iliad* V 735. I interpret *pan-poikilos* as 'completely pattern-woven', just as I interpreted *poikilos* as 'pattern-woven'. These two words, as we will see, are germane to the identity of the goddess Athena as an ideal pattern-weaver—a model for all other pattern-weavers.[111]

2§111. To these two words *poikilos* 'pattern-woven' and *pan-poikilos* 'completely pattern-woven' I now add two more, *poikillein* 'pattern-weave' and *poikiltēs* 'pattern-weaver'. The verb *poikillein*, which I have not translated till now, is a synonym of *en-huphainein*, meaning 'weave patterns [into the fabric]'.[112] As for *poikiltēs*, it is an agent-noun derived from this verb *poikillein*. So, from here on, I will translate *poikillein* as 'pattern-weave' and *poikiltēs* as 'pattern-weaver'. I must add that the plural form of *poikiltēs*, which is *poikiltai*, refers to a special category of professional male weavers in Plutarch *Pericles* 12.6.[113] The signifi-

[109] Details and references in *HC* 4§§189, 194.

[110] Τῇ Ἀθηνᾷ πολιάδι οὔσῃ πέπλος ἐγίνετο παμποίκιλος, ὃν ἀνέφερον ἐν τῇ πομπῇ τῶν Παναθηναίων.

[111] *HC* 4§195.

[112] Barber 1991:359n2.

[113] *HC* 4§199, with further analysis.

cance of this word *poikiltai* will soon become clear in the course of the argumentation that follows.

The Weaving of Athena's Robe for the Quadrennial and the Annual Panathenaia

2§112. In the previous section, I said that the robe for Athena was woven every year to celebrate the festival of the Panathenaia. But now I need to make a distinction between two kinds of Panathenaia. In 566/5 BCE, a large-scale version of this festival started operating in the late summer of every fourth year, while the smaller-scale version of the Panathenaia continued to be celebrated in the late summer of the three other years. The large-scale version of the Panathenaia was the quadrennial or Great Panathenaia, while the smaller-scale and far older version of the festival was the annual or Lesser Panathenaia.

2§113. There were two kinds of weavers weaving the robe of Athena for these two kinds of Panathenaia:

> On the occasion of the quadrennial Great Panathenaia, professional male weavers were hired to weave a spectacularly elaborate and oversized *peplos* destined for formal presentation to the goddess Athena. These workers can be equated with the *poikiltai* 'pattern-weavers' mentioned in Plutarch *Pericles* 12.6. As my argumentation proceeds, I will show evidence that backs up the formulation that I have just given here.
>
> By contrast, on the occasion of the annual Lesser Panathenaia, specially selected non-professional female weavers performed the ritual procedure of weaving a *peplos* for Athena; in this case, the fabric was considerably less elaborate in its specifications and perhaps smaller.[114] There are surviving ancient references to these non-professional female weavers of the annual *peplos*, who were known as the *Ergastīnai*, and to their primary representatives, who were specially selected young girls known as the *Arrhēphoroi*.[115]

2§114. How, then, are we to visualize the *peplos* of Athena? On the basis of the few surviving references from the ancient world, I offer a brief inventory of details about the quadrennial *peplos*, and then a comparably brief inventory of further details about the annual *peplos*.

[114] *HC* 4§206

[115] Overview by Barber 1991:362, 377. I rely especially on the relevant work of B. Nagy 1972. I will have more to say later about both the *Arrhēphoroi* and the *Ergastīnai*.

2§115. In the case of the *peplos* featured at the quadrennial Panathenaia, we know that it was a web of truly gigantic proportions. On the occasion of the spectacular quadrennial parade known as the Panathenaic Procession, this *peplos* was displayed as an archetypal Sail rigged to the mast of a float that re-enacted the archetypal Athenian Ship of State; this float was rolled on wheels along the Sacred Way, from the Kerameikos through the Agora, all the way to a sacred space known as the Eleusinion (scholia for Aristophanes *Knights* 566).[116]

2§116. As for the *peplos* featured at the annual Panathenaia, it was displayed as a robe or dress to be worn—or, at least, notionally "worn"—by an old wooden cult statue or *xoanon* of Athena Polias, which resided in the old temple of Athena on top of the Acropolis.[117] This old temple, containing the old statue, must not be confused with the new temple of the goddess, known as the Parthenon, which was the residence of a colossal new gold-and-ivory statue of Athena. This statue was created by the sculptor Pheidias and inaugurated in 438/7 BCE under the supervision of the statesman Pericles.[118] I have already highlighted in Part One what I described there as the theo-eroticism of this spectacular simulacrum of Athena in the Parthenon.[119]

2§117. I will not delve here into debates about distinguishing between the "dress-peplos" presented to Athena at the annual Panathenaia and the "sail-peplos" presented to her at the climax of the Panathenaic Procession that took place on the last day of the quadrennial Panathenaia.[120] Instead, I assert one general observation that is relevant to such debates: I find it less than useful to make distinctions between "sail" and "dress" in considering any ancient references to any fabric that qualified as a *peplos*. In general, this word *peplos* was appropriate for designating masterpieces of weaving that were meant primarily for display, distinguished by the patterns of images woven into them. To say it another way: *peplos* was a specialized term having little to do with everyday wear in the ancient Greek world. And the relevant terminology focused on the art of weaving, not on any utilitarian aspect of the fabric that was woven.[121]

[116] Further details and documentation are provided by Barber 1992:114, especially with reference to Plutarch *Demetrius* 10.5, 12.3.

[117] Ridgway 1992:120–123.

[118] The source for the dating is Philochorus *FGH* 328 F 121, who lived in the fourth/third centuries BCE.

[119] In *HC* 490–507 = 4§§97–124, I analyze the rationale that led to the commissioning of Pheidias to make the gold-and-ivory statue of Athena.

[120] *HC* 4§207, following *PR* 90.

[121] This paragraph is a rewording of an earlier formulation in *HC* 4§102, following Lee 2004.

The Eternal Sameness of an Eternally Rewoven Picture

2§118. Essential for my overall argumentation is the detail I just highlighted about patterns of images that were woven into fabrics. Technically speaking, I prefer to call these images *pictures*, in the sense of Latin *pictūrae* or 'pattern-weavings', as we saw them described in Virgil's reference to the sumptuous fabrics woven by Andromache. Here, then, we have finally reached the point where we are ready to consider the actual picture that was pattern-woven into the seasonally recurring versions of the *peplos* presented to the goddess Athena at the climax of the Panathenaia. This picture, as we will see, was notionally always the same picture, just as the *peplos* of Athena, as rewoven year after year for the festival of the Panathenaia, was notionally always the same *peplos*.

2§119. To highlight this notional sameness, I will now introduce a special format for referring to the Panathenaic *peplos*. I will hereafter spell the word for this special *peplos* simply as Peplos, with a capital P and showing no italics, to distinguish it from other *peploi*. In Part Four, we will consider a notable example of another such *peplos* as it figured in myths and rituals involving a goddess other than Athena, Hera.

2§120. That said, we are ready to consider the picture that was eternally rewoven, year after year, into the Panathenaic Peplos. *On the occasion of each and every yearly recurrence of the Panathenaia, the picture that was eternally rewoven into the Panathenaic Peplos was supposedly retelling, for all eternity, the myth of the Gigantomachy*. In terms of this formulation, each new reweaving of each new Peplos on the occasion of each new seasonal recurrence of the Panathenaia was not only a ritual celebration of the victory of the Olympian gods over the Giants: more than that, each and every seasonally recurring version of the rewoven Peplos was also a ritualized retelling, by way of pattern-weaving, that enfolded the entire myth about this cosmic victory.[122]

A Reference by Plato to the Pattern-Woven Robe of Athena

2§121. As we have already seen, the myth of the Gigantomachy was the equivalent of a *charter myth* for Athens. That is, the narration of the Gigantomachy

[122] In what follows, I collect some of the most telling pieces of evidence concerning the myth of the Gigantomachy as pattern-woven into the Panathenaic Peplos. From this evidence, we can see that this myth was pattern-woven into the annual as well as the quadrennial versions of the Peplos. Accordingly, I note my disagreement with Mansfield 1985, who questions whether the myth of the Gigantomachy could have been woven into the smaller web of the Lesser Panathenaia.

was considered to be a foundational statement about Athenian identity—the ultimate statement.[123] And, as we will now see, the ritualized process of pattern-weaving the robe or Peplos of Athena was the equivalent of actually narrating this charter myth.[124] That is to say, the narration of the Gigantomachy as a charter myth was literally woven into the Peplos of Athena. A vital piece of evidence comes from a passage I am about to quote from Plato, whose wording refers specifically to the weaving of the quadrennial Peplos. I quote here that passage, joining the dialogue at a moment when Socrates has this to say to Euthyphro:

Extract 2-T

> |b So, do you think that there really was a war among the gods with each other, and that there were terrible hostilities and battles and many other such things as are narrated by poets—sacred things [*hiera*] that have been patterned [*kata-poikillein*] for us by noble |c masters of visual arts [= *grapheus* plural], in particular the Peplos at the Great [= quadrennial] Panathenaia, which is paraded up to the Acropolis, and which is full of such pattern-weavings [*poikilmata*]? Shall we say that these things are true, Euthyphro?
>
> Plato *Euthyphro* 6b–c[125]

2§122. We see here an explicit reference to the pattern-weaving of the Gigantomachy, as a sacred myth, into the Peplos rewoven for the quadrennial or Great Panathenaia. And we also see that the weaving was done by male professionals.

2§123. In my initial formulation about the weaving of the quadrennial Panathenaic Peplos, I had already asserted that its weavers were male professionals. And now the evidence of Plato's wording here backs up that assertion, since the word he uses with reference to the weavers of the Peplos is the masculine plural noun *grapheis*, meaning 'masters of the visual arts'. This noun, which is *grapheus* in the singular, is relevant in other ways as well. For example, *grapheus* can mean not only 'visual artist' in general but also 'painter' in particular, as in Plato *Phaedo* 110b. Further, we have already seen the related noun *graphē* used in the sense of 'painting' when we were reading a passage about

[123] See also again *PR* 90–93.

[124] *PR* 90–91. See also Barber 1992:114.

[125] |b Καὶ πόλεμον ἆρα ἡγῇ σὺ εἶναι τῷ ὄντι ἐν τοῖς θεοῖς πρὸς ἀλλήλους, καὶ ἔχθρας γε δεινὰς καὶ μάχας καὶ ἄλλα τοιαῦτα πολλά, οἷα λέγεταί τε ὑπὸ τῶν ποιητῶν, καὶ ὑπὸ τῶν |c ἀγαθῶν γραφέων τά τε ἄλλα ἱερὰ ἡμῖν καταπεποίκιλται, καὶ δὴ καὶ τοῖς μεγάλοις Παναθηναίοις ὁ πέπλος μεστὸς τῶν τοιούτων ποικιλμάτων ἀνάγεται εἰς τὴν ἀκρόπολιν; ταῦτα ἀληθῆ φῶμεν εἶναι, ὦ Εὐθύφρων;

Pheidias in Strabo 8.3.30 C354, as already quoted in Extract 1-M. The meanings of these words *grapheus* and *graphē* as 'painter' and 'painting' are also relevant to pattern-weaving, since we already know that the idea of painting can overlap with the idea of pattern-weaving, as in the case of the Latin noun *pictūra*. Even more telling is the Greek verb *en-graphein*, which is actually attested in a context that refers specifically to the weaving of patterns into the fabric of the quadrennial Peplos (scholia for Aristophanes *Knights* 566).[126]

2§124. Here I draw special attention to a word used in the passage I just quoted here from Plato with reference to the Peplos of the goddess: it is the noun *poikilma*, derived from the verb *poikillein* in the specific sense of 'pattern-weave'. So *poikilma* in this context means 'pattern-woven web'. A perfect match for the meaning of this form is the form *poikiltēs*, which as we have seen means 'pattern-weaver' in Plutarch *Pericles* 12.6.[127] So, by now I have evidence to back up my assertion that the web of the quadrennial Peplos was woven by professional male weavers who were actually known as *poikiltai* 'pattern-weavers'. And, in a minute, we will see further evidence.

2§125. Now I can highlight the overall significance of the passage I have just quoted from Plato.[128] What Socrates is staged as saying here is significant politically as well as philosophically. By disparaging the narrative of the Gigantomachy as a quaint invention that cannot be true for a philosopher, Plato's Socrates is subverting the charter myth of the Athenians and, by extension, he is subverting the state of Athens itself.[129]

2§126. The subversion is all the more telling because the wording of Socrates as staged by Plato is most accurate in conveying the central importance of this myth of the Gigantomachy to the Athenians. As Socrates himself admits in the passage I quoted, the things that happened in the course of the battle of the Olympians and Giants were *hiera* 'sacred' (Plato *Euthyphro* 6b). Not only was the content of this myth sacred for the Athenians: so also, by extension, was the form of telling the myth.

2§127. As we see from Plato's wording, then, the primary form of narrating the Gigantomachy was to pattern-weave the sacred myth into the Peplos of Athena, which was then carried up to the sacred space of the goddess on top of the Acropolis at the ritual climax of the Panathenaic Procession.[130]

[126] *HC* 4§204.
[127] I cite again *PR* 92–93.
[128] The observations that follow are based on my analysis of Plato *Euthyphro* 6b–c in *HC* 4§203, following *PR* 92–93.
[129] *PR* 92.
[130] *HC* 4§203, following *PR* 92–93.

Another Reference by Plato to the Pattern-Woven Robe of Athena

2§128. Elsewhere as well in the works of Plato, the verb *poikillein* in the sense of 'pattern-weave' refers specifically to the act of weaving the narrative of the Gigantomachy into the robe or Peplos of Athena. In Plato's *Republic* 2.378c, the expression *muthologēteon* 'to be mythologized' is made parallel to *poikilteon* 'to be pattern-woven', and the subject that is being simultaneously mythologized and pattern-woven is none other than the Gigantomachy (here Plato explicitly uses the noun *gigantomakhiai*, in the plural: 'gigantomachies').[131]

2§129. The evidence of this wording provides further support for the argument that the *poikiltai* 'pattern-weavers' mentioned in Plutarch *Pericles* 12.6 can be equated with professional male weavers who were hired every four years to weave the elaborate and oversized robe or Peplos destined for formal presentation to the goddess Athena on the occasion of the quadrennial Great Panathenaia.[132]

A Spectacular Picturing of Athena's Robe

2§130. I will now quote the most detailed surviving description of the actual narrative of the Gigantomachy *as it was woven into the Panathenaic Peplos*, that is, into the quadrennial robe of the goddess Athena. This description comes from a poem entitled *Ciris*, preserved in the *Appendix Vergiliana*, a collection of anonymous Latin poems that were eventually attributed to Virgil. On the basis of the details that we find in this poem, we can be sure that the composition of the *Ciris* is referring to a celebration of the quadrennial or Great Panathenaia, instead of the smaller-scale annual Panathenaia. And, again on the basis of the details, the historical occasion of this celebration can be dated to the first century BCE; in particular, the details can be matched with the historical realia of any one of the following years when the festival of the quadrennial Panathenaia was actually celebrated in Athens: BCE 74/3 or 70/69 or 66/5 or 62/1 or 58/7 or 54/3 or 50/49.[133]

2§131. I proceed, then, to quote from the *Ciris* a description of the Gigantomachy *as a myth that was actually pattern-woven into the Panathenaic Peplos*. I start the quotation at a special moment in the poem when the poet, who cannot be

[131] *HC* 4§205, following *PR* 93. On the *peplos* of Athena and the *gigantomakhiai* or Gigantomachy woven into it, I find the discussion of Pinney 1988 indispensable (especially p. 471). I interpret the plural of *gigantomakhiā* as designating specific "close-ups" of the overall battle of the gods and giants.

[132] *HC* 4§206

[133] Shear 2001:629.

identified for certain, creates a metaphor for the words that he addresses to his patron, who likewise cannot be identified. The creation of these words, the poet says, is like the creation of the pictures that are pattern-woven into the Panathenaic Peplos:

Extract 2-U

> $|_{21}$ But (I am) weaving (you) into [*in-texere*] the great—if it is sanctioned to say it—Peplos $|_{22}$—the kind of *peplos* that is carried in the city of Erekhtheus, in Athens, on the ancient occasion $|_{23}$ when vows are kept by offering gifts that are owed to virginal Minerva [= Athena], $|_{24}$ when the period of four years comes full circle as it slowly nears the oncoming fifth year, $|_{25}$ when the light Zephyrus wind accelerates in its rivalry with the alternating Eurus wind $|_{26}$ and drives forward the Vehicle, weighted down with its buckling load. $|_{27}$ Blessèd is that day. That is what it is to be called. And blessèd is that year. $|_{28}$ Blessèd as well are they who have seen such a year, such a day. $|_{29}$ Thus does the weaving [*texere*] take place, the weaving that narrates in their proper order [*ōrdō*] the battles of Pallas [= Athena], $|_{30}$ and the great folds of the Peplos are adorned with signs that signal the moment when the Giants were turned back, $|_{31}$ and terrifying battles are rendered in color [*pingere*], with the color of a dye that is blood-red, $|_{32}$ and added to that is the picturing of the Typhon repulsed by the golden tip of the spear. $|_{33}$ He is the one who made the aether concrete by using the rocks of Mount Ossa, $|_{34}$ piling them on top of the peak of Emathia [= Pelion] to double the height of Olympus $|_{35}$—such is the Sail [= the Peplos] that they [= the Athenians] carry for the goddess on that solemn occasion, $|_{36}$ and it is by way of such a ritual that I would want (to weave) you (in), O most learned of young men, yes, exactly such a ritual, $|_{37}$ so that you may be enveloped by the purple flashes of the sun and by the incandescent beams of the moon $|_{38}$—beams that pulsate against the orb of the world with the galloping feet of the two blue horses drawing the moon's chariot. $|_{39}$ Yes, I would want to weave (you) in [*in-texere*], into the great papyrus rolls of the Nature of the Universe, $|_{40}$ so that a name conjoined with the ever recycling song of personified Wisdom $|_{41}$—your name—may be spoken by my page through the ages as they grow ancient.
>
> From the *Appendix Vergiliana*, *Ciris* 21–41[134]

[134] $|_{21}$ *sed magno intexens, si fas est dicere, peplo,* $|_{22}$ *qualis Erechtheis olim portatur Athenis,* $|_{23}$ *debita cum castae solvuntur vota Minervae* $|_{24}$ *tardaque confecto redeunt quinquennia lustro,* $|_{25}$ *cum levis alterno*

2§132. I will now weave into my analysis a line-by-line commentary on the complex wording of this poem.[135]

$|_{21a}$ **weaving in [*in-texere*]**: The Latin word *in-texere* expresses explicitly and accurately the technique of pattern-weaving, which refers here metaphorically to the process of narration as performed by the poet.

$|_{21b}$ **Peplos**: In this line, the Peplos refers metaphorically to the piece of narrative that is being narrated by the poet, who is dedicating his poem to his youthful patron. In the next line, we see that the metaphor for this poetic process of narration is the technical process of narrating what is pattern-woven into the Panathenaic Peplos. Evidently, there were poetic precedents for the use of such a metaphor as we see it at work here in this anonymous poem, the *Ciris*. The poet's reference to the Peplos of the goddess Athena as displayed at the festival of the Panathenaia in the city of Athens was probably influenced by an earlier poem featuring references to the *peplos* of the goddess Hera as displayed at the festival of the Heraia in the city of Argos. Such references to the *peplos* of Hera were featured in a lost work of the poet Calvus, the *Io*.[136] I will have more to say about the *peplos* of Hera when we reach Part Four.

$|_{22}$ **Erekhtheus**: In the historical phases of Athenian myth, this hero was said to be a prototypical king of Athens. So the city of Erekhtheus is Athens. In a prehistoric phase of Athenian myth, as we will see when we reach Part Three, the hero Erekhtheus was both the son and the sexual partner of the goddess of Athens, Athena.

$|_{23}$ **virginal Athena**: In the historical phases of Athenian myth, the goddess Athena was of course a permanent virgin. As we will see when we reach Part Three, however, Athena was a mother goddess in prehistoric Athenian myth.

$|_{24}$ **when the period of four years comes full circle**: Highlighted here is the seasonal recurrence of the festival of the Panathenaia, notionally

Zephyrus concrebuit Euro $|_{26}$ *et prono gravidum provexit pondere currum.* $|_{27}$ *felix illa dies, felix et dicitur annus,* $|_{28}$ *felices qui talem annum videre diemque.* $|_{29}$ *ergo Palladiae texuntur in ordine pugnae,* $|_{30}$ *magna Giganteis ornantur pepla tropaeis,* $|_{31}$ *horrida sanguineo pinguntur proelia cocco,* $|_{32}$ *additur aurata deiectus cuspide Typhon,* $|_{33}$ *qui prius Ossaeis consternens aethera saxis* $|_{34}$ *Emathio celsum duplicabat vertice Olympum.* $|_{35}$ *tale deae velum sollemni tempore portant,* $|_{36}$ *tali te vellem, iuvenum doctissime, ritu* $|_{37}$ *purpureos inter soles et candida lunae* $|_{38}$ *sidera, caeruleis orbem pulsantia bigis,* $|_{39}$ *naturae rerum magnis intexere chartis,* $|_{40}$ *aeterno ut sophiae coniunctum carmine nomen* $|_{41}$ *nostra tuum senibus loqueretur pagina saeclis.*

135 Much of this commentary derives from *HPC* II§§390–394 pp. 281–284.

136 See Lyne 1978:109–110.

ongoing for eternity. The reference to the fifth year, in terms of the inclusive numbering used here (which is typical of a way of thinking that has no concept of zero), signals explicitly the celebration of a quadrennial form of the Panathenaia.

$|_{26a}$ **the Vehicle:** The *currus* or 'vehicle' in this description of the Panathenaic Festival is the Athenian Ship of State, which as I noted earlier was paraded on wheels along the Sacred Way during the Panathenaic Procession that culminated in the presentation of the Peplos to the goddess Athena. That presentation, as I also noted earlier, was the ritual climax of the whole festival of the quadrennial Panathenaia. Rigged to the mast of this Ship of State, as described here at line 26, was a Sail, described later at line 35. This *velum* 'sail' at line 35 was the gigantic pattern-woven Peplos of Athena.[137] In the ritual context of the Panathenaic Procession, the Vehicle and the Sail must have been viewed as prototypical, just as the Peplos was supposedly prototypical.

$|_{26b}$ **weighted down with its buckling load:** This "load" was the massive *velum* or 'Sail' that was hanging down so heavily from the mast of the Ship of State. We have already seen a reference to the heaviness of pattern-woven fabric in Virgil *Aeneid* 3.485, quoted in Extract 2-N, describing the ritual act of Andromache in presenting to the youthful hero Ascanius a set of folded fabrics that she herself had originally pattern-woven in Troy.

$|_{29}$ **Thus does the weaving [*texere*] take place, the weaving that narrates in their proper order [*ōrdō*] the battles of Pallas [= Athena]:** The process of narrating is equated here with the process of weaving, *texere*. So, in terms of this equation, the battles of Pallas [= Athena] are being literally woven [*texere*]. Enhancing the equation is the use here of the word *ōrdō*, which I translated as 'order'. The modern term *coordination*, as I noted earlier, is derived from Latin *ōrdō*, which has the basic meaning of 'a thread on a loom'. So, here at line 29 is where the poem actually begins to narrate the narration that is woven into the Peplos. And the poem 'weaves' the narration just as the pattern-weaving weaves the narration.

$|_{30}$ **and the great folds of the Peplos:** The Latin plural *pepla* is a metonymic reference to the 'foldings' of the Peplos.[138] Given that the basic meaning of the Greek noun *peplos* is 'fold' or 'folding', we can see that

137 Barber 1991:361–365.

138 *HPC* II§386 pp. 278–279.

the idea of folding a *peplos* is a metonymic way of thinking of the fabric itself as *an object that is folded*. For example, a *peplos* is traditionally *folded* in ritual situations of giving or receiving such a fabric. A most striking example is a *peplos* that is pictured in the relief sculpture of Block 5 of the East Frieze of the Parthenon Frieze. Later on in Part Two here, I will argue that this sculpted image of a *peplos* is in fact a representation of the Panathenaic Peplos itself. For now, however, I will simply focus on the fact that the *peplos* in this sculpted image is shown *folded*—and on the fact that the folding is multiple, as we can see by viewing the edge of the web, showing manifold layers of foldings. Correspondingly, the Latin plural *pepla* may convey the idea of multiple foldings—or perhaps the idea of a seasonal recurrence of foldings.

|30b **the moment when the Giants were turned back**: The narrative of the pattern-weaving is a freeze-frame picture that signals the turning point or *tropaion* of the Gigantomachy—and the poetic narrative here is imitating the visual effect of such a freeze-frame.

|31 **and terrifying battles are rendered in color [*pingere*], with the color of a dye that is blood-red**: I translate *coccum* here as 'dye', since this noun means not just 'berry': it can refer also to any organic substance that stains, like berries, and such substances include the purple dye that is extracted from the mollusk that inhabits the murex shell (Pliny the Elder *Natural History* 9.140).[139] The verb *pingere* can mean not only 'render in color' but also 'pattern-weave'—a meaning that we have already seen in uses of the derivative noun *pictūra* 'pattern-weave', as in Virgil *Aeneid* 3.483, quoted in Extract 2-N, referring to the fabrics pattern-woven by Andromache.

|32 **the golden tip of the spear**: In the pattern-weaving of the Peplos, there is a visual interaction of the color yellow, whether it is gold as here or saffron as elsewhere, with the color purple. Depending on the mode of combining purple with yellow, the color purple is perceived as *red* in some combinations and *blue* in others.[140] In the present case, the combination of the yellow color of the golden tip of Athena's spear here at line 32 with the purple color that dominates the entire battle with the Giants at line 31 creates the dominant visual effect of red—blood red—for viewing that battle. Here the purple that visualizes the blood that is shed by the Giants in the Gigantomachy corresponds to

[139] Lyne 1978:114.

[140] A distinction between red and blue as two different kinds of purple dye for wool is evident in Akkadian (*argamannu* and *takiltu*) and Hebrew (*argaman* and *tekelet*): see Lepschy 1998:54.

the variant reading *porphureē* 'purple' visualizing the dominant color of Helen's web at verse 126 of *Iliad* III, as quoted in Extract 2-P, where the color itself can track all the blood that was being shed by all the Achaeans and Trojans who were killed or wounded in the war they fought for the sake of Helen.

|33 **He is the one who made the aether concrete:** The aether, which is conventionally imagined as a non-solid space separating the celestial and terrestrial realms, is here made solid in the Gigantomachy, since the gigantic enemies of the Olympians are piling up massive rock formations, one on top of another, in their quest to exceed the heights of Olympus.

|36 **I would want (to weave) you (in):** In my working translation, I have used parentheses to indicate a syntactical link that extends from verse 21, *But (I am) weaving (you) into [in-texere] the great ... Peplos*, all the way to here at verse 36, *I would want (to weave) you (in)*. Verse 21 already signals that the cosmic picturing of the Gigantomachy, which weavers weave into the Peplos of Athena as featured at the festival of the quadrennial Panathenaia, will be 'woven' into the papyrus rolls indicated here at verse 36.

|37 **enveloped by the purple flashes of the sun and by the incandescent beams of the moon:** Again we see an interaction between yellow and purple here. The visual effect of this interaction is a red look for the sun, shown in purple threading, by contrast with the 'incandescent' moon, shown in yellow threading.

|38 **the two blue horses drawing the moon's chariot:** In this case, the interaction between yellow and purple creates the visual effect of a blue look for the horses shown in the purple threading, by contrast with the yellow threading that shows the lunar chariot pulled along by these horses.

2§133. I stop here to contemplate the dominant color scheme of this masterpiece of pattern-weaving. The narrative thread or *fil conducteur* of the pattern-weaving is purple, which as we have seen is perceived as the color of blood (31 *sanguineo ... cocco*). This color is associated with the theme of war (31 *horrida ... proelia*) in the context of the narrative that is pattern-woven into the fabric, and this narrative is the central myth about the victory of Athena and the other Olympians over the Giants (30 *Giganteis ... tropaeis*).[141] I find it relevant

[141] *HPC* II§392 p. 283.

that the primary opponent of Athena in the myth of the Gigantomachy, as narrated on the occasion of the quadrennial Panathenaia, is *Porphuriōn*, king of the Giants (Pindar *Pythian* 8.12–13, Aristophanes *Birds* 1251, "Apollodorus" *Library* 1.6.1–2).[142] Thus the cosmic figure who shares with Athena a central place in the narrative of the Gigantomachy is the very embodiment of purple—as pattern-woven into the Peplos of Athena on the occasion of the quadrennial Panathenaia.[143]

Variations on a Theme of a Colored Robe for Athena

2§134. So far, then, we have seen that the purple threading that dominates the pattern-weaving of the quadrennial Panathenaic Peplos is a visual foregrounding of the bloodshed of war as a dominant theme in the myth of the Gigantomachy. And we have also seen a parallel visual foregrounding when we considered the purple threading that dominates the pattern-weaving of Helen at verse 126 of *Iliad* III, as quoted in Extract 2-P: there too, the dominant theme is the bloodshed of war. But the color scheme was different in the pattern-weaving of the Peplos of Athena for the festival of the annual or Lesser Panathenaia that was held on every year other than the year of the quadrennial or Great Panathenaia. In this case, the dominant color of the threading was yellow, not purple.

2§135. To show this difference, I start with the name given to the king of the Giants as represented in the annual Panathenaic Peplos. Unlike *Porphuriōn*, the name of the purple king of the Giants in the quadrennial Panathenaic Peplos, the name of the corresponding Giant in the annual Panathenaic Peplos shows that he was threaded in yellow, not in purple.

2§136. We learn from Aristotle (F 637 ed. Rose)[144] that the festival of the annual or Lesser Panathenaia was aetiologized by way of a specialized myth that told of the primal killing of a Giant named *Asterios* or *Astēr* by the goddess Athena.[145] These two names *Asterios* or *Astēr* are most revealing, since both forms derive from the noun *astēr* meaning 'star': so the Giant is a 'Star'.[146] The proper threading, then, for this shining Giant is not purple but yellow.[147]

[142] *HPC* II§393 pp. 283–284n38.

[143] *HPC* II§393 pp. 283–284.

[144] The information comes from the scholia for Aristides p. 323 ed. Dindorf.

[145] *Asterios* according to one set of scholia for Aristides (Aristotle F 637 ed. Rose p. 395.20). *Astēr* according to another set of scholia (ed. Rose p. 395.5).

[146] The wording of the second set of scholia is of special interest: ἐπὶ Ἀστέρι τῷ γίγαντι ὑπὸ Ἀθηνᾶς ἀναιρεθέντι "to commemorate *Astēr* the Giant, killed by Athena." On the semantics of *epi* plus dative in contexts of aetiologizing various festivals, see *PH* 4§7 pp. 120–121; also 4§6n15 p. 119 and 5§12n38 p. 142.

[147] *HPC* II§403 p. 287.

2§137. Such a difference in the color schemes of the annual and the quadrennial Peplos can be correlated with another difference that I have already highlighted. Whereas the quadrennial Peplos, as I have argued, was pattern-woven by professional male weavers, the annual Peplos was the work of specially selected non-professional female weavers.[148]

2§138. Here I find it relevant to recall the fact that the *peplos* presented as an offering to the goddess Athena by the women of Troy at *Iliad* VI 295 is said to shine like an *astēr* 'star'. According to one theory, this Iliadic simile was the inspiration for the naming of the Giant known as *Astēr* or *Asterios*.[149] I argue instead that the simile and the name are both cognate with a traditional iconographic narratology of star patterns woven into the Peplos of Athena at the Panathenaia.[150] These stars, as I once observed, are telling their own story.[151] And it is a story told primarily in yellow.

2§139. The mark of femininity in the accentuation of yellow rather than purple threading can be seen in references to the color of saffron in descriptions of the annual Panathenaic Peplos. I am about to show one such description, which I have extracted from the *Hecuba* of Euripides. And, as we will see in this example, there is reason to think that the dominant yellow threading of the annual Peplos was correlated with a feminized pattern of avoiding the grim theme of bloodshed in war, by contrast with the dominant purple threading of the quadrennial Peplos.

2§140. The example I have in mind here comes from a choral lyric passage in the *Hecuba* of Euripides. The dramatic time of this drama focuses on the grim aftermath of the Trojan War, and we are about to read words sung-and-danced by a chorus of captive Trojan women who are imagining their future as slaves living in the foreign lands of their Hellenic captors.[152] If they are to be taken to Athens, they imagine, their work there will be the weaving of the Peplos of Athena. Such an act of imagination, as I have argued before, is typical of the aristocratic ethos that characterizes Trojan captive women in both epic and tragedy.[153] Although their bad fortune has transformed them into slaves, these Trojan women still think and behave like aristocrats.[154] Even though they will be slaves of the Hellenes, these Trojan women retain their aristocratic charisma by

[148] Again, *HC* 4§206

[149] Scheid and Svenbro 1994:28n48.

[150] *HPC* II§403 p. 288.

[151] *PR* 93–94.

[152] Here and elsewhere, I use hypenations in referring to the *song-and-dance* of choral performance.

[153] *HPC* II§396 pp. 284–285, following Dué 2006:114, who says: "The sympathetic Trojans of Euripides are not a new phenomenon, but rather represent a continuity of treatment from the earliest Greek epic poetry onward."

[154] Dué 2006:27, 109.

pathetically imagining themselves in the act of performing a task traditionally performed by the aristocratic daughters of Athens. And that task is the weaving of the Peplos of Athena.[155] Here is the women's description of the Peplos—and of the colors to be pattern-woven into it:

Extract 2-V

> Or, in the city of Pallas [Athena], into [the texture of] the *saffron-colored Peplos* of Athena, shall I yoke beautiful horses to her chariot [*harma*],[156] matching the beautiful vehicle,[157] as I *pattern-weave* [*poikillein*] them [= the horses and the chariot] with *threads colored by the blossoms of saffron*, or [as I pattern-weave] the generation of Titans[158] who were put to sleep [*koimizein*] by Zeus the son of Kronos with a lightning stroke that had fire flashing all around it?
>
> Euripides *Hecuba* 466–474[159]

2§141. In this pattern-woven picture of Athena riding on a chariot drawn by horses, I argue, the dominant color of the horses together with their chariot is yellow. If this argument holds, then the flashing thunderbolt of Zeus would be yellow. And here the destruction of the Giants seems to be taking place without bloodshed, since they are 'put to sleep' by the radiant weapon of Zeus. If in fact the foregrounding of the luminous gods is pattern-woven in yellow, that is, in the color of saffron, then any purple in the background can now default to blue, matching the blue skies of a most successful cosmic outcome.

A Tension between Sacred Sameness and Real Differences

2§142. By now we have seen a variety of differences in descriptions of the patterning that was woven, year after year, into each annual and each

[155] *HPC* II§396 p. 285, where I note the relevance of the *peplos* presented to Athena by the Trojan women in *Iliad* VI.

[156] In *HPC* II§396 p. 285n46, I offer arguments in support of the manuscript reading ἅρματι 'to her chariot [*harma*]'.

[157] I translate καλλιδίφρους, the epithet of the horses yoked to the chariot of Athena, as 'matching the beautiful vehicle' in order to convey a link between this epithet and the noun ἅρματι. I see a metonymic effect here. Further argumentation in *HPC* II§396 p. 285n47.

[158] I interpret the reference here to *Titans* as a Panhellenic way of referring to the Athenian myth about the *Giants* who battle the gods for cosmic supremacy.

[159] |$_{466}$ ἢ Παλλάδος ἐν πόλει |$_{467}$ τὰς καλλιδίφρους Ἀθα|$_{468}$ναίας ἐν κροκέωι πέπλωι |$_{469}$ ζεύξομαι ἅρματι πώ|$_{470}$λους ἐν δαιδαλέαισι ποι|$_{471}$ κίλλουσ᾽ ἀνθοκρόκοισι πή|$_{472}$ναις ἢ Τιτάνων γενεάν, |$_{473}$ τὰν Ζεὺς ἀμφιπύρωι κοιμί |$_{474}$ζει φλογμῶι Κρονίδας;

quadrennial Peplos of Athena. But we have also seen that such patterning, which narrated the Gigantomachy as a charter myth for the Athenians, was nevertheless supposed to be one and the same narrative. There is an ideology of sacred sameness at work here. Notionally, the recurring picture that was seasonally rewoven into the Panathenaic Peplos was telling one and the same charter myth, which was considered to be sacred, as we have seen from the explicit wording of Plato *Euthyphro* 6b. So, we find a tension here between the notional sameness of the Gigantomachy as a sacred charter myth and the historical reality of differences that emerge in the seasonal reweavings of this myth into the Panathenaic Peplos.

2§143. But it is surely to be expected that the narration of the Gigantomachy as a charter myth for the Athenians kept on changing every year throughout the lengthy history of seasonally recurring pattern-weavings for each annual and each quadrennial occasion of celebrating the Panathenaia. We must reckon, I argue, with the historical reality of an ever-changing picture that counterbalances, by way of its ever-new differences, the notional sameness of the sacred Peplos.

2§144. In fact, as we see from the Aristotelian *Constitution of the Athenians* (60.1–3), dating from the fourth century BCE, the State of Athens actually regulated the form and the content of the pattern-weaving that narrated the myth of the Gigantomachy. The regulators were elected officials known as the *athlothetai*, meaning 'ordainers of the competitions [*athloi*]', who were directly in charge of all activities concerning the quadrennial Panathenaia, including the task of supervising the design for the quadrennial making of the Peplos. To quote from the Aristotelian *Constitution* (60.1): *kai ton peplon poiountai* 'and they [= the *athlothetai*] are in charge of having the Peplos made'. Further, these *athlothetai* were in charge of approving the *paradeigmata* or 'models' of the patterns to be woven into each quadrennial Peplos (49.3).[160] Those woven patterns, to return to the wording of Plato *Euthyphro* 6b, were the *hiera* 'sacred things' that were narrated in the process of reweaving the charter myth of the Gigantomachy. The technique of narration by way of weaving such patterns has aptly been described by one expert as a *story-frieze* style of weaving.[161]

2§145. In the book *Homer the Classic*, I asked the question: why would such important elected state officials be held responsible for the narrative agenda of the story-frieze patterns woven into the Peplos of Athena? My answer then and

[160] *HC* 4§208, following Rhodes 1981:671–672. For more on the interpretation of *paradeigmata* here as referring specifically to the patterns woven into the fabric, see Rhodes 1981:568.

[161] *HC* 4§208, following Barber 1992:114–116.

now is the same: such explicit narrative agenda must have matched in importance the implicit political agenda of the State.[162]

2§146. That said, I am ready to put together a formulation that sums up my assessment of the tension between notional sameness and real differences in the seasonally recurring narration of the Gigantomachy—a narration achieved by way of reweaving this myth into the Panathenaic Peplos. Each time when this myth was rewoven, it had to be notionally the same, since it was after all a sacred charter myth, but it could also be different each time in its variations, which were conditioned by the vicissitudes of history.

2§147. Here, then, is my concluding formulation: despite an ideology of sacred unchangeability, there were in fact changes over time both in the telling of the charter myth of the Gigantomachy and in the weaving of this myth into the Peplos. And this formulation applies, I maintain, not only to the great Peplos of the quadrennial or Great Panathenaia but also to the smaller Peplos of the annual Lesser Panathenaia.

[162] *HC* 4§209. There are also some isolated historical occasions when the political agenda must have been featured explicitly, not just implicitly, in the narrative that was woven into the Peplos itself: I cite again Plutarch *Demetrius* 12.3; also Diodorus 20.46.2.

Part Three

Masterpieces of Metonymy on the Acropolis

3§01. By now we have seen many times and in many ways how the act of narrating the myth of the cosmic battle between the Olympians and the Giants was intrinsic to and inextricable from the seasonally recurring ritual of pattern-weaving the sacred robe or Peplos of Athena in Athens. To narrate the sacred myth was to pattern-weave it into the sacred Peplos.[1] This seasonally rewoven Peplos, as I will argue here in Part Three, was meant to be the re-enactment of a perfect sacred model, which was the original work of pattern-weaving performed by the goddess Athena herself. The myth about that original pattern-weaving is highlighted in *Iliad* V 734–735, which I already quoted in Extract 2-R of Part Two. In that context, I described Athena's masterpiece of pattern-weaving as a perfect masterpiece of metonymy, and I must review here why I said it that way. It is because, as I argued in Part Two, the mechanical process of pattern-weaving a *peplos* was actually driven by a metonymic way of thinking, and so the pattern-weaving of the Peplos of Athena by Athena would surely have resulted in something that is considered to be absolutely perfect—a perfect masterpiece of metonymy.

3§02. Here in Part Three, I will argue further that this original Peplos of Athenian myth, this masterpiece of metonymy, actually became a model for the marvels of visual art that honored the goddess Athena in her sacred space situated on top of the Acropolis in Athens. In making this argument, I will correlate the physical evidence of such marvels with the actual myth about the making of the Peplos of Athena by Athena. What will stand out, I say already now, is the visual testimony of the sculptures adorning that ultimate marvel of the Athenian Acropolis, the Parthenon. On the basis of that visual testimony, I will argue that the Parthenon itself is in its own right another ultimate marvel—a perfect masterpiece of metonymy.

[1] This formulation goes back to *HC* 4§210. See also Barber 1992:114.

Starting Over with the Robe Woven by Athena

3§1. I return here to the two lines of *Iliad* V 734–735 that I quoted in Extract 2-R of Part Two. As we learned when we first looked at those two Homeric lines, the wording there says explicitly that the goddess Athena herself pattern-wove with her own hands the Peplos that she herself was wearing at the exact moment when she entered the war between the Achaeans and the Trojans in the *Iliad*.

3§2. Now the time has come for me to consider the larger context of the Homeric passage that frames these two lines, and I will argue that this framing passage, extending from verse 733 to verse 747 in *Iliad* V, combines the fundamental idea that Athena wove her own *peplos* with a further fundamental idea, that she actually narrated the Gigantomachy by way of pattern-weaving her narration into her *peplos*. And, as I will also argue, the poetic combination of these two fundamental ideas leads to the artistic creation of a Homeric masterpiece of metonymy that matches the Peplos itself as a metonymic masterpiece in its own right.

3§3. I now quote, in its entirety, the Homeric passage:

Extract 3-A (including the full text of the two lines 734–735 quoted in Extract 2-R)

> |$_{733}$ As for Athena, daughter of Zeus who has the aegis, |$_{734}$ she let her woven *robe* [<u>*peplos*</u>] slip off at the threshold of her father, |$_{735}$ her pattern-woven [*poikilos*] robe, the one that she herself made and worked on with her own hands. |$_{736}$ And, slipping into the tunic [*khitōn*] of Zeus the gatherer of clouds, |$_{737}$ with armor she armed herself to go to war, which brings tears. |$_{738}$ Over her shoulders she threw the aegis, with fringes on it, |$_{739}$ —terrifying—garlanded all around by Fear personified. |$_{740}$ On it [= the aegis] are Strife [Eris], Resistance [Alkē], and the chilling Shout [Iōkē, as shouted by victorious pursuers]. |$_{741}$ On it also is the head of the Gorgon, the terrible monster, |$_{742}$ a thing of terror and horror, the portent of Zeus who has the aegis. |$_{743}$ On her head she put the helmet, with a horn on each side and with four bosses, |$_{744}$ golden, adorned with pictures showing the warriors [*pruleis*] of a hundred cities. |$_{745}$ Into the fiery chariot with her feet she stepped, and she took hold of the spear, |$_{746}$ heavy, huge, massive. With it she subdues the battle-rows of men— |$_{747}$ heroes against whom she is angry, she of the mighty father.
>
> *Iliad* V 733–747[2]

[2] |$_{733}$ Αὐτὰρ Ἀθηναίη κούρη Διὸς αἰγιόχοιο |$_{734}$ <u>πέπλον</u> μὲν κατέχευεν ἑανὸν πατρὸς ἐπ' οὔδει |$_{735}$ ποικίλον, ὅν ῥ' αὐτὴ ποιήσατο καὶ κάμε χερσίν· |$_{736}$ ἣ δὲ χιτῶν' ἐνδῦσα Διὸς νεφεληγερέταο |$_{737}$

3§4. I begin my analysis of this Homeric passage by highlighting two moments. One of these moments is when Athena is seen slipping out of her *peplos* or 'robe', and the other moment is when she is then seen slipping into a *khitōn* or 'tunic', which now becomes the undergarment for the suit of armor that she proceeds to put on her divine body.[3] But there is yet another moment, and it comes between these two delimiting moments. In that intervening moment, as I observed in an earlier analysis of this passage featuring Athena's arming scene, "there is room for the thought—if not the image—of the goddess in the nude."[4] In that analysis, I went on to compare the thinking of Friedrich Nietzsche when he speaks "about that one nude goddess," *um jene eine nackte Göttin*, who is somehow the essence of *Wissenschaft* or 'learning, knowledge'.[5] Even if Nietzsche may not have in mind the Homeric context that I am analyzing here, it seems to me that his wording is a perfect fit for the goddess Athena as we see her in this one truly singular moment.

3§5. That fleeting thought about the goddess in the nude can be connected, as we will see later, to a detail we find embedded in Athenian myths and rituals linked with Athena—a detail that I will introduce at a later point here in Part Three. For now, however, I focus on the actual moment that intervenes between the earlier moment when the goddess slips out of her *peplos* and the later moment when she slips into her *khitōn*—into that divine tunic that now becomes the undergarment for her suit of armor. In my earlier analysis, I had this to say about that singular intervening moment:

> Even as the thought [of a nude goddess] flashes by, the Homeric picturing of Athena in motion moves on, without a blink, from a vision of the goddess in a *peplos* to a vision of the goddess in a *khitōn*. So there is a complementarity in Athena's wearing a *peplos* at one moment and in her wearing a *khitōn* at the next moment.[6]

3§6. The *peplos* that Athena takes off in *Iliad* V 734 "at the threshold of her father" connects her to her identity as a model weaver, since the wording here

---

τεύχεσιν ἐς πόλεμον θωρήσσετο δακρυόεντα. $|_{738}$ ἀμφὶ δ' ἄρ' ὤμοισιν βάλετ' αἰγίδα θυσσανόεσσαν $|_{739}$ δεινήν, ἣν περὶ μὲν πάντῃ Φόβος ἐστεφάνωται, $|_{740}$ ἐν δ' Ἔρις, ἐν δ' Ἀλκή, ἐν δὲ κρυόεσσα Ἰωκή, $|_{741}$ ἐν δέ τε Γοργείη κεφαλὴ δεινοῖο πελώρου $|_{742}$ δεινή τε σμερδνή τε, Διὸς τέρας αἰγιόχοιο. $|_{743}$ κρατὶ δ' ἐπ' ἀμφίφαλον κυνέην θέτο τετραφάληρον $|_{744}$ χρυσείην, ἑκατὸν πολίων πρυλέεσσ' ἀραρυῖαν· $|_{745}$ ἐς δ' ὄχεα φλόγεα ποσὶ βήσετο, λάζετο δ' ἔγχος $|_{746}$ βριθὺ μέγα στιβαρόν, τῷ δάμνησι στίχας ἀνδρῶν $|_{747}$ ἡρώων, οἷσίν τε κοτέσσεται ὀβριμοπάτρη. In *HC* 4§184, I comment on several of the words used in this passage.

3 *HC* 4§102.

4 *HC* 4§187.

5 Nietzsche 1872, *Die Geburt der Tragödie*, Section 15.

6 *HC* 4§187.

says explicitly that she wove this robe herself, while the *khitōn* that she puts on her divine body as she readies herself to engage in war at V 736–737—a *khitōn* that belongs to her father Zeus, as the Homeric wording says explicitly—connects her to her identity as a model warrior.[7] As we will now see, this complementarity of the *peplos* and the *khitōn* worn by Athena from one moment to another in Athena's arming scene at *Iliad* V 733–747 is matched by the complementarity of her two roles in the myths and rituals of the city of Athens. And these two roles are linked with the two primary statues of Athena that were housed on top of the Acropolis of Athens in the classical period of the mid-fifth century BCE, that is, in the age of Pheidias the sculptor. I now offer a brief description of these two statues of the goddess.

3§7. On the one hand, there was the classical statue of Athena the Virgin, the Parthénos, sculpted by Pheidias himself, which was housed in the classical temple known as the Parthenon. We have an eyewitness description of the statue, dating back to the second century CE, from the traveler Pausanias. As we will see from his wording, which I am about to quote, the appearance of this statue corresponds closely to the Homeric vision of Athena as a model warrior. As we saw in *Iliad* V 733–747, quoted in Extract 2-A, Athena at line 736 wears the *khitōn* or 'tunic' of her father as an undergarment for her suit of armor. So also, as we are about to see, the statue of Athena in the Parthenon was wearing her armor over an ankle-length *khitōn*. And, likewise corresponding to the Homeric description of Athena's arming scene, the statue as described by Pausanias showed Athena carrying a spear and wearing both a helmet and the feared aegis, which featured the head of the Gorgon Medusa. I quote here the description of Pausanias:

Extract 3-B

> The statue [*agalma*] itself is made of gold and ivory. In the middle of the helmet is placed a likeness of the Sphinx. [Pausanias here gives a cross-reference to an excursus of his, deployed at a later point in his work, about the Sphinx.] On each side of the helmet there are griffins worked in. [...] $|_7$ [...] The statue [*agalma*] of Athena is standing, wearing a tunic [*khitōn*] that extends to her feet. On her chest is the head of Medusa, made of ivory. She has [in one hand] a [figure of] Nike, around four cubits in height, and she holds in her [other] hand a spear. A shield [*aspis*] is positioned at her feet. And near the spear is a serpent [*drakōn*]. Now this serpent [*drakōn*] would be Erikhthonios. And on the surface of the base of the statue is a relief of the genesis of Pandora. The story of

[7] *HC* 4§197.

> the genesis of this first woman Pandora is told by Hesiod in his poetry as well as by others.
>
> Pausanias 1.24.5–7[8]

3§8. So much for the statue of Athena Parthénos, housed in the Parthenon. On the other hand, there was the preclassical statue of Athena Polias, the 'goddess of the city', which was housed in the old temple of the goddess. Whereas the statue of Athena Parthénos in the Parthenon was shown wearing a *khitōn*, the statue of Athena Polias was associated with a *peplos*. But the *peplos* of this preclassical Athena Polias residing in the old temple, unlike the *khitōn* of the classical Athena Parthénos residing in the Parthenon, was not sculpted into her own statue. As we have already seen, the *peplos* of Athena Polias was instead pattern-woven for her, year after year,[9] and the pattern that was woven into this *peplos* of the goddess was a narration of the Gigantomachy, which was a charter myth for the Athenians.[10]

3§9. Here I return to the complementarity of the *peplos* and the *khitōn* worn by Athena from one moment to the next in Athena's arming scene at *Iliad* V 733–747, as quoted in Extract 3-A. As we can see by now, this complementarity is matched by the complementarity of Athena's two roles in the myths and rituals of the city of Athens. As the resident of the old temple, on the one hand, the goddess was connected with the weaving of the *peplos*—for her to wear. As the resident of the new temple, on the other hand, she was connected with the wearing of a *khitōn* under her divine armor.

3§10. This match in complementarity does not mean, of course, that the Homeric passage we have read was somehow based on the myths and rituals of Athens as they existed in the classical era, that is, in the fifth century BCE, when the new temple of the Parthenon and the new statue of Athena Parthénos as its resident virgin warrior goddess were inaugurated. After all, the very idea of Athena as a warrior goddess was clearly preclassical: it was older, far older, than the classical statue that became the definitive visual realization of the goddess housed in the Parthenon. And the idea of Athena Polias was likewise preclassical, just as the statue of Athena Polias housed in the old temple was preclassical.

8 αὐτὸ δὲ ἔκ τε ἐλέφαντος τὸ ἄγαλμα καὶ χρυσοῦ πεποίηται. μέσῳ μὲν οὖν ἐπίκειταί οἱ τῷ κράνει Σφιγγὸς εἰκών [...] καθ' ἑκάτερον δὲ τοῦ κράνους {6} γρῦπές εἰσιν ἐπειργασμένοι. [...] |$_7$ [...] τὸ δὲ ἄγαλμα τῆς Ἀθηνᾶς ὀρθόν ἐστιν ἐν χιτῶνι ποδήρει καί οἱ κατὰ τὸ στέρνον ἡ κεφαλὴ Μεδούσης ἐλέφαντός ἐστιν ἐμπεποιημένη· καὶ Νίκην τε ὅσον τεσσάρων πηχῶν, ἐν δὲ τῇ χειρὶ δόρυ ἔχει, καί οἱ πρὸς τοῖς ποσὶν ἀσπίς τε κεῖται καὶ πλησίον τοῦ δόρατος δράκων ἐστίν· εἴη δ' ἂν Ἐριχθόνιος οὗτος ὁ δράκων. ἔστι δὲ τῷ βάθρῳ τοῦ ἀγάλματος ἐπειργασμένη Πανδώρας γένεσις. πεποίηται δὲ Ἡσιόδῳ τε καὶ ἄλλοις ὡς ἡ Πανδώρα γένοιτο αὕτη γυνὴ πρώτη.

9 My formulation here goes back to *HC* 4§188.

10 See also *PR* 90–93.

3§11. On the other hand, the match in complementarity between *Iliad* V 733–747 and the realia of Athenian myths and rituals does in fact indicate that this Homeric passage reflects at least a preclassical Athenian phase in the evolution of Homeric poetry. The argument for the existence of such an earlier phase, dating back to the sixth century BCE, has been laid out in my twin books *Homer the Classic* and *Homer the Preclassic*. Already during the preclassical phase of Homeric poetry, in terms of my argumentation, Athenians would be attending performances of the *Iliad* and the *Odyssey* at the festival of the quadrennial Panathenaia, and a Homeric reference to the charter myth of the Panathenaia in *Iliad* V 733–747 would be seen by them as a ringing validation of their all-important festival.

A Homeric Masterpiece of Metonymy

3§12. Having noted the preclassical Athenian agenda at work in the Homeric passage I quoted from *Iliad* V 733–747 in Extract 3-A, I return to my focus on the complementarity of the two aspects of Athena in classical as well as preclassical Athens: on the one hand, we have seen the goddess as the recipient of the Panathenaic Peplos for her to wear, and, on the other hand, we have seen her as the model warrior wearing her suit of armor. Such a complementarity, I will now argue, is accurately re-enacted in *Iliad* V 733–747. And the re-enactment, in terms of my present argumentation, is not only accurate but also artistic—so artistic, in fact, that it qualifies as a masterpiece. In what follows, I will analyze the artistry as well as the accuracy of this Homeric passage. And the artistry, as we are about to see, has produced here a Homeric masterpiece of metonymy.

3§13. Before I proceed, however, I need to highlight a heretofore missing piece in my analysis of the Athenian ritual of reweaving the Peplos of Athena every year for the occasion of celebrating her birthday at the festival of the Panathenaia. In the logic of that ritual, someone in the world of myth must have woven a *peplos* as a model, an absolute model, and it was this prototypical Peplos that was destined to be ritually rewoven forever, year after year, by the Athenians on each seasonally recurring occasion of the Panathenaia. In the logic of the charter ritual, that prototypical someone who wove the prototypical Peplos in the world of myth must surely have been the goddess Athena herself, and she must surely have woven the Peplos for herself to wear.

3§14. This logic, as I have called it, is an example of a theological way of thinking that is well known to researchers in comparative religion. On the basis of comparative studies centering on the interactions of myth and ritual in a wide variety of cultures, I can formulate in the following words such a theological construct: *A divinity in the world of myth can be seen as the prototypical performer of the rituals that mortals perform to worship that divinity.*[11] This way, a divinity can be seen as a prototypical performer of worship or sacrifice or prayer, so that human performers of worship or sacrifice or prayer may follow the lead of the divinity, *do as I do.*[12] In terms of this formulation, then, the charter ritual of the Athenians in reweaving, year after year, the prototypical Peplos of Athena for her to wear all over again, year after year, is motivated by a prototypical act of weaving performed by the goddess herself in the world of myth.

3§15. That said, the missing piece in my analysis is now in place. *The goddess Athena herself must have woven the prototypical Peplos that the Athenians rewove every year to worship her.*

3§16. Such a prototypical Peplos, made by Athena in the world of myth, makes sense only if we keep in mind the historical context, which is the seasonal reweaving of the Peplos by the Athenians in the world of ritual. The setting for such a reweaving was the Panathenaia, that all-important festival celebrating not only the victory of Athena over the Giants but also the day of her birth—which as we have seen was the same sacred day as the day of her cosmic victory. And this prototypical act of weaving performed by Athena, just like the recurrent acts of weaving performed by the Athenians, would have included not only the pattern-weaving of the Peplos as a web but also the pattern-weaving of the story that was woven into that web.

3§17. In further analyzing the Athenian charter ritual of weaving a yearly Panathenaic Peplos for Athena, I have by now reconstructed a piece of the picture that was missing in my earlier analysis. That missing piece, as we have already seen, is the mythological detail about the weaving of the Peplos by the goddess Athena herself. And now we will see that this same piece fits perfectly into the overall picture that is being narrated in *Iliad* V 733–747, quoted in Extract 3-A. After the first mention of the *peplos*, at line 734, the wording at line 735 goes on to say that Athena herself had once upon a time woven this robe with her own hands. This *peplos*, woven by Athena in the world of myth, could be seen as the prototype of the Panathenaic Peplos, rewoven every year by the Athenians in their seasonally recurring world of ritual. The prototypical Peplos, as made by Athena herself in *Iliad* V 734–735, and the recurrent Peplos, as made by the Athenians for the Panathenaia, could be seen *as one and the same sacred thing* from the standpoint of the Athenians. Further, this prototype and all its recurrences were *the same sacred thing not only in form but also in content*. In other words, just as the pattern-weaving of each new Peplos for each new celebration of the Panathenaia was a seasonally recurring narration of the Gigantomachy,

[11] I offer a prototype of this formulation in *PP* 57. A definitive work on the figuring of divinities as model worshippers is Patton 2009. A pioneer in the study of such figuring is Simon 1953.

[12] Again I cite especially Patton 2009.

so also the pattern-weaving of the prototypical Peplos made by the goddess Athena herself was a prototypical narration of the same Gigantomachy.

3§18. Here we encounter an internal contradiction that seems at first to be unfathomable. The myth that is retold here in *Iliad* V 734–735 about the prototypical pattern-weaving by and for Athena contradicts the world of time. The contradiction is built into the very core of the myth, which says explicitly that Athena wove the Peplos—while saying implicitly that she narrated the Gigantomachy by way of pattern-weaving the myth into the fabric. If this were so, of course, it should also be said that the Gigantomachy must have happened before the weaving—in the world of time. But the opposite could also be said: in the same world of time, the Gigantomachy must have happened after the weaving. That is because Athena was born fully-armed on the day of the Gigantomachy, and so the goddess could not have woven the Peplos before she was born.

3§19. Such contradictions in temporality, however, are neutralized by the myth. And that is because this myth is timeless. It operates on a principle of metonymical combinations that are sequenced in a timeless circle, not along a timeline. In this sequence, the Gigantomachy is followed by the weaving is followed by the Gigantomachy and so on, in an endless circle. In the circular timelessness of such a rewoven story, a poetic picturing of the Gigantomachy could be followed by a signal indicating that the ring-composition has come full circle, *this is what happened in the Gigantomachy*, followed by a signal that indicates a recircling, *this is the story that Athena wove into her Peplos*, followed again by *this is what happened in the Gigantomachy*, and so on.

3§20. But the Homeric reference to the Peplos made by Athena replaces such circularity with a linearity. From the standpoint of Athenians attending the quadrennial Panathenaic performances of Homeric poetry in the preclassical period and hearing the narration of *Iliad* V 733–747 about Athena and how she waged war against the Trojans, the sequence of events in this mythological narrative is linear, veering from the circular sequence of their charter myth about Athena and how she waged war against the Giants. And that is because Homeric poetry has replaced the circularity of timeless sequencing as we saw it at work in the myth of the Gigantomachy, substituting a linearity that follows a sequence controlled by time.

3§21. Here is how the substitution works in the narration of *Iliad* V 733–747. We see here a metonymic series of moments that combine with each other in a temporal sequence. But the first moment of this series of moments is not even mentioned in the narrative. That moment is when Athena is born wearing a suit of armor and getting ready to wage war on the Giants. Then, at that moment, after the war is won, Athena weaves her Peplos. And here is the first moment that is actually noted in the metonymic series of moments narrated in *Iliad* V 733–747. After that, Athena puts on the Peplos and wears it. But this moment in the narration, when Athena actually puts on the Peplos, is not noted. After that, sometime after Athena puts on the Peplos, she takes it off and puts on her suit of armor as she gets ready to wage war on the Trojans. This later sequence of moments, as we have seen, is closely tracked in the narration of *Iliad* V 733–747.

3§22. So, in the linear logic of the timeline in this myth as retold in the narration of *Iliad* V 733–747—and as understood by the Athenians in the preclassical period and thereafter—the Gigantomachy happens before Athena's weaving of the Gigantomachy into her Peplos. Then, since the weaving of the Peplos is a narration of the Gigantomachy, the goddess gets into her own story. But, once she is already inside her story, she can no longer wear the Peplos, since the story that is woven into her Peplos shows her wearing her armor, which is what she wore on that primal day when she was born and defeated the Giants. So, in the transition from the outer story, which is about the weaving, into the inner story, which is about the Gigantomachy, Athena takes off the Peplos she was wearing in the outer story and puts on the armor she will be wearing in the inner story told by way of weaving the Peplos.

3§23. Of course, those who heard the words of *Iliad* V 733–747 performed at the festival of the quadrennial Panathenaia in the preclassical and the classical eras of Athens would not get to hear the inner story of the Gigantomachy that was pattern-woven into the Panathenaic Peplos. That story, which Athena wove with her own hands, would have shown Athena at the timeless moment of her birth, fully armed and preparing to fight the Giants. That story would have visualized what had once been a timeless stop-motion picture of a fully-armed Athena stepping into her fiery chariot. Instead, after mentioning the Peplos that Athena has woven for herself to wear, Homeric poetry proceeds to show a woven picture in motion. The poetry now sets in motion what had once been that timeless stop-motion picture of a fully-armed Athena stepping into her fiery chariot. Unlike the metonymic sequence of the Gigantomachy that the goddess herself has woven into her Peplos, which circles back eternally, back to the re-weaving of the stop-motion picture, the motion picture of Homeric narrative moves the action forward in the linearity of time, so that the fiery chariot of the goddess will now move forward in time. So, in this motion picture, Athena will be attacking not the Giants in the Gigantomachy but the Trojans in the Trojan War that is being narrated by the Homeric *Iliad*. And that is because the metonymic sequence here is no longer circular. The sequencing has now become linear. And, in its new linearity, the metonymic sequence can now move forward in time. No longer does it have to circle back into the reweaving of the Gigantomachy.

3§24. For Athena to join the Achaeans in their war against the Trojans in *Iliad* V 733–747, she must wear her armor. So, if we continue to follow the logic of the myth as retold here in the *Iliad*—and as understood by the Athenians—Athena must take off her Peplos—and then she must put on the armor that she wore once upon a time when she was born fully-armed from the head of Zeus.

3§25. The actual weaving of the Peplos, as a performance of a narrative, can be seen metonymically as the primordial act that arms the body of Athena in the newer myth about her joining the war against the Trojans, just as the older myth about her joining the war against the Giants—a war that is woven into the Peplos—arms her divine body from the very start.

3§26. To narrate the arming of Athena is to arm Athena. In other words, the narration about the arming is the same act as the arming itself. And, to take it further, the process of weaving the narration into the Peplos that Athena wears is the same thing as the process of arming Athena.

3§27. Viewed in this light, the transition that we see taking place in Homeric poetry from the moment when Athena weaves her Peplos to the moment when she arms herself is achieved by way of coordinating metonymy with metaphor. Here is what I mean. There is a sequence of metonymic combinations that drives the narration of *Iliad* V 733–747 from the moment when Athena weaves her Peplos to the moment when she puts it on, and from there to the moment when she takes it off, and from there to the moment when she puts on her armor. At the final moment of this metonymic sequence, there is a metaphoric substitution. A new moment, when the goddess puts on her armor to fight the Trojans in the Trojan War, is being substituted here for the old moment when she is already wearing this armor to fight the Giants in the Gigantomachy. And this substitution moves the action forward in the story of the Trojan War, thus preventing the arming scene from circling back to the reweaving of the story of the Gigantomachy.

3§28. In the circular timelessness of such a rewoven story, to repeat what I said before, a poetic picturing of the Gigantomachy could be followed by a signal indicating that the ring-composition has come full circle, *this is what happened in the Gigantomachy*, followed by a signal that indicates a recircling, *this is the story that Athena wove into her Peplos*, followed by *this is what happened in the Gigantomachy*, and so on. In this kind of endless circle, Athena would be seen weaving again and again the Peplos that she weaves for herself when she weaves the story of the Gigantomachy into her robe. But she does not have to wear this Peplos, since she is wearing the armor in the arming scene while she is telling the story of that arming scene. By contrast, in the linear timeline of the story as retold in the Homeric narrative of *Iliad* V 733–747, Athena must stop wearing the Peplos in order to start wearing the armor in her own story. And here is where we see that moment of nakedness between the moment when the goddess slips out of her robe and the moment when she slips into the tunic that becomes the undergarment for the armor she will now wear in a new war. So, in the linear logic of Homeric narrative, the goddess must have already worn the Peplos that she once made when she pattern-wove her own story about the Gigantomachy, and it is this story that Homeric poetry now recombines by way of its own pattern-weaving. This recombining of the metonymic sequence by way of metaphorically substituting the Trojan War for the Gigantomachy is what leads here to the creation of a masterpiece of metonymy.

3§29. Such a coordination of metonymy with metaphor, achieved by way of recombination, brings me back to my initial formulation about masterpieces of metonymy in pattern-weaving. I will now repeat it here in the context of arriving at the core of my argumentation for Part Three:

> *A masterpiece of metonymy requires a kind of artistry that is not—and cannot be—restricted to metonymy. Instead, the artistry coordinates metonymy with metaphor.*

3§30. To say it another way, a masterpiece of metonymy in pattern-weaving actually coordinates the process of making metonymic combinations on a horizontal axis, which is the primary process, with the secondary process of making metaphoric selections on a vertical axis. The actual coordination of a horizontal axis of combination and a vertical axis of selection is what produces the kind of variation that is so prized in the art of pattern-weaving. In terms of this medium of art, then, *a masterpiece of metonymy* is really *a masterpiece of metonymy coordinated with metaphor.*

3§31. In the luminous Homeric passage that we have just finished studying, *Iliad* V 733–747, we can see in action such a masterpiece of metonymy. And I now add the word *perfect* in describing this masterpiece, since the poetic virtuosity of Homeric poetry itself in picturing the robe of Athena is in its own turn pictured here as an absolutely perfect work of art, created by the divine hands of the immortal goddess herself, who is the all-powerful embodiment of Athens. Such absolute perfection is truly a perfect masterpiece.

A Vision of Athena's Robe Sculpted into the Parthenon Frieze

3§32. In my commentary on the text of Extract 2-U, where I quoted from the poem *Ciris* a lengthy description of Athena's sacred robe, the Peplos, as it was paraded along the Sacred Way for all to see at the Panathenaic Procession, I briefly expressed a view about a folded robe that we see pictured in the relief sculptures of Block 5 of the east side of the Parthenon Frieze. In my view, this robe is the same sacred Peplos of Athena. To back up this view, I start by showing what is being pictured. Here is a line drawing:

Extract 3-C

Relief sculpture: Folding of the Peplos of Athena. Block 5, east side of the Parthenon Frieze, Athens. Now in the British Museum. Drawing by Valerie Woelfel.

3§33. This relief sculpture is carved into a block (often called instead a "slab") occupying the most prominent space of the Parthenon Frieze. This block, "Block 5," features a sculpted scene picturing five human figures in all. The two figures that I show in the line drawing are situated on the right side of Block 5, and there are also three other figures on the left side—to be described at a later point. Framing both sides of Block 5 are the sculpted figures of seated gods, larger in size than the five humans. On our left, in Block 4, the gods Zeus and Hera frame these humans, while in Block 6, on our right, the framing gods are Athena and Hephaistos. At a later point, I will have more to say about these larger-sized divine figures framing the five smaller-sized human figures.

3§34. One expert, Jennifer Neils, has aptly described the scene picturing the five human figures in Block 5 as "the high point" of the overall narrative of the Parthenon Frieze, "framed between the central columns of the temple façade,"[13] and "[i]t was here that the design [of the frieze] must have begun and for which an exceptionally long block [= Block 5] was ordered, quarried, and set into place."[14] The expert whom I have just quoted about Block 5 goes on to describe the narrative sculpted into this "exceptionally long block" as "important enough to dictate the layout of the entire frieze" into "two processional files" that converge on this narrative. When she says "two processional files" in her description, she makes it clear that she has in mind the overall narrative of the Parthenon Frieze, which she sees as a representation of the Panathenaic Procession at the festival of the Panathenaia.

3§35. Earlier in my argumentation, I have already noted the importance of this procession as the setting for the ritual presentation of the Peplos. I will soon have more to say about the ritual presentation, as experts call it, but for now I concentrate on the Panathenaic Procession itself, as represented on the Parthenon Frieze.

3§36. In emphasizing the importance of the narrative carved into Block 5 at the east side of the Frieze, Neils is saying that the overall representation of the Panathenaic Procession converges on this one single narrative. In her wording, as we just saw, the Procession splits into "two processional files" proceeding eastward from the north and from the south sides of the Parthenon Frieze and then converging at the "high point" featuring the five human figures carved into Block 5 of the east side.

3§37. But the narrative of this "high point" is problematic, since experts have till now been unable to shape a consensus about what it all means. From the standpoint of a casual viewer's first impression, the five human figures of Block 5 could understandably be described as "this unimpressive quintet."[15] But I think that all five of these human figures are in fact all-important.

13 Neils 2001:166.

14 Neils 2001:67.

15 Again, Neils 2001:67.

3§38. To back up this line of thinking, I start by concentrating on the two human figures positioned on the right side of Block 5, as shown in the line drawing. These two figures are pictured here in the act of holding on to a fabric as they face one another, and I agree with those who think that the two of them are participating in a ritualized act[16]—an act that I have been describing up to now as *the presentation of the Peplos.*[17] In comments that I have published in the past about this "Peplos Scene," however, I have consistently avoided asking myself this fundamental question: who is "presenting" the Peplos to whom?[18] In what follows, I will formulate an answer.

3§39. As we can see from the line drawing that I just showed, the figure on our left is a male adult, and the figure on our right is an adolescent, shorter than the corresponding adult by well over a head's length. The gender of the adolescent is no longer clearly distinguishable, partly because the surface of the relief sculpture has been so massively eroded. While I agree, as I said previously, with those who think that this scene, as sculpted into Block 5 of the east side of the Parthenon Frieze, is picturing some kind of ritual presentation involving a *peplos*, I also agree with Joan Connelly's interpretation of the male figure as the prototypical Athenian king Erekhtheus and of the adolescent figure as the king's youngest daughter.[19] Here we come to a point of controversy, since some experts do not accept Connelly's interpretation—even if there is general agreement about what we see being depicted in this scene, which is some kind of a ritualized presentation.[20] In my case, I do accept Connelly's argument for identifying the figures in question as Erekhtheus and his youngest daughter, and I will now explain why.

3§40. In terms of Connelly's argumentation, the stop-motion picture of the narrative we see recorded here in the relief sculpture corresponds to a climactic moment that takes place in another charter myth of the Athenians. Traces of this charter myth have been preserved primarily in the fragmentary tragedy *Erekhtheus*, composed by Euripides and initially staged sometime in the late fifth century BCE, as also in a scattering of other ancient sources. The myth, which is evidently older than the tragedy derived from it, told about the victory of the people of Athens, led by their king, Erekhtheus, over an invading horde of Thracians led by the king of Eleusis, Eumolpos, in a war that almost resulted in

16 For a survey of interpretations concerning the ritualized act itself, see Neils 2001:61–66, who also offers her own interpretation.

17 For an expert description of the fabric that is being presented and represented here, I cite Barber 1992:113. See also Barber 1991:361; see also p. 272, with further illustrations of selvedges as represented in the sculpture of the Parthenon Frieze.

18 *PR* 89–90, *HC* 4§220, *HPC* II§386 pp. 278–279.

19 Connelly 1993, 1996, 2014, especially 2014:169–171.

20 A case in point is the disagreement expressed by Neils 2001:178.

the capture of Athens.[21] The historian Thucydides (2.15.2) makes an overt reference to the myth, treating it as if the war between Erekhtheus and Eumolpos had really taken place in prehistoric times.

3§41. This particular charter myth about Erekhtheus, even if it is older than the tragedy named after this hero, may not have been as old as another charter myth we have already considered, which centered on the victory of the goddess Athena and the other Olympians over the Giants, but it was still old enough to be integrated into the overall mythological narrative conveyed by the vast array of sculpted images built into the Parthenon—specifically, into the continuum of relief sculptures that we know today as the Parthenon Frieze. Angelos Chaniotis has argued most effectively for the historical reality of such an integration of this charter myth into the Parthenon Frieze.[22]

3§42. According to the myth, it had been divinely ordained that Eumolpos and his horde would succeed in capturing the city of Athens and its inhabitants unless the Athenian king Erekhtheus slaughtered a daughter of his as the virginal victim of a human sacrifice. One of the daughters responded to the crisis by volunteering to serve as the victim, and so she was the first to die, though in the end two other daughters also gave up their lives. In Apollodorus *Library* 3.15.4, it is said that Erekhtheus slaughtered the youngest daughter first, and that the older daughters responded to this death by killing themselves in their own turns.[23] In the wording of the drama *Erekhtheus*, it is clear that there were three virginal daughters in all, *zeugos triparthenon* 'the yoking of three virgins' (Euripides F 47.1 ed. Austin).[24] In the Athenian charter myth about this set of three daughters, as we know from ancient lexicographical sources, no names were given to the girls, and, in line with sacred protocol, the Athenians referred to them simply as the *Parthénoi* or 'Virgins':

Extract 3-D

> *Parthénoi*: this is how they [= the Athenians] called the daughters of Erekhtheus, and this is how they worshipped them [= gave them *tīmē* 'honor'].[25]
>
> Hesychius s.v. Παρθένοι[26]

[21] Connelly 2014:122, 146.

[22] Chaniotis 2009:43 gives a formulation that summarizes his view of the charter myth about the victory of Erekhtheus over Eumolpos as memorialized in the relief sculptures of the Parthenon Frieze. His formulation is quoted and endorsed by Connelly 2014:202–203,

[23] Frame 2009:448n199 surveys the vast variety of myths about the daughters of Erekhtheus.

[24] ζεῦγος τριπάρθενον.

[25] On *tīmē* 'honor' in the sense of 'worship', see *H24H* 8§21, 12§21, 17§1.

[26] Παρθένοι· τὰς Ἐρεχθέως θυγατέρας οὕτως ἔλεγον καὶ ἐτίμων.

3§43. There is a parallel pattern in a Theban myth, as reported by Pausanias (9.17.1), about two female heroes named Androkleia and Alkis, who killed themselves as ritual substitutes for their father Antipoinos, whose death, as ordained by an oracle, was a precondition for making his people victorious over the people of Orkhomenos (the name *Anti-poinos* means, aptly, 'the one who is connected with a substitute ransom'): in compensation for their self-sacrifice, the bodies of the girls were buried within the sacred precinct of Artemis Eukleia, where they received *tīmai* 'honors' from their worshippers.[27]

3§44. There is yet a parallel pattern in an Athenian myth about a female hero called *Makaríā*, virgin daughter of Herakles who willingly offered herself as a human sacrifice to save Athens and her own siblings. The myth about these children of Herakles, taking refuge in Athens after fleeing from their persecutor, Eurystheus, is attested in a drama by Euripides, *The Sons of Herakles*, featuring explicit references to the sacrifice of the virgin sister, daughter of Herakles (especially at lines 502, 550–551, 558–562, 574–596). The euphemistic title of the virgin, *Makaríā*, meaning 'the Holy One', is not even spoken in this drama as we have it: instead, she is simply the *parthénos* (as at lines 489, 535, 567, 592), and we know of her title *Makaríā* only from the testimony of later sources.[28]

3§45. That said, I return to the myth about the *Parthénos* who was the daughter of Erekhtheus. In terms of Connelly's interpretation, the moment that is sculpted into Block 5 of the east side of the Parthenon Frieze shows Erekhtheus in the act of preparing for the sacrificial slaughter of this Parthénos, and that is why he is dressed as a priest, wearing an ankle-length short-sleeved beltless *khitōn* or tunic.[29] At this precise moment of preparation, according to Connelly, the father is handing over to his virginal daughter a *peplos*.

3§46. In terms of my own interpretation, the Parthénos herself would have originally woven the *peplos*, and, after the original weaving, this precious heirloom would have been stored in her father's residence until the daughter was ready to wear it as her wedding gown. But now—here I return to my tracking of Connelly's interpretation—the father is handing over the *peplos* to the Parthénos in preparation for a different occasion. The Parthénos will now be wearing this *peplos* not for her wedding but instead for her ritual slaughter as a willing virginal sacrifice.

3§47. As Connelly observes, there are myths about virginal sacrifices that actually show the victim wearing a *peplos* for the occasion of her ritual slaughter.[30] A shining example is the virgin heroine known euphemistically as *Makariā*.

27 Again I note the use of *tīmē* 'honor' in the sense of 'worship'.

28 Suda β 74, under the entry βάλλ' ἐς Μακαρίαν (also Zenobius 2.61).

29 Connelly 2014:168, 172.

30 Connelly 2014:172–174.

I have already noted the references to this *parthénos*, this virgin daughter of Herakles, in the drama by Euripides, *The Sons of Herakles*. In the wording of this drama, the doomed girl herself declares that her sacrificer must cover her, at the moment of the sacrificial slaughter, within the folds of a *peplos*, as we see at line 561 (πέπλοις). Another example is the heroine Iphigeneia, as we see from wording that refers to her virginal sacrifice in the *Agamemnon* of Aeschylus: at line 233, it is said explicitly that Iphigeneia is covered within the folds of a *peplos* at the moment when she is ritually slaughtered (πέπλοισι).[31] In both these two contexts, the use of the plural form of the word, *peploi*, is apt. As we saw earlier in Extract 2-U (*Ciris* 30), which shows another context involving a plural form of *peplos* (Latin *pepla*), the basic idea of 'foldings' is actually built into the meaning of this word. This emphasis on the multiple folds of the *peplos* leads me to think that my use of the word *wear* is not suitable for describing the function of the *peplos*: as we will see later, the word *wrap* is a better fit.

3§48. I must add, in the case of Iphigeneia, that this virginal heroine is a surrogate of the virginal goddess Artemis. Surveying the traditional myths and rituals connected with Iphigeneia, I have found a version of the myth, as retold in the epic Cycle (plot-summary by Proclus of the *Cypria* by Stasinus p. 104 lines 12–30), where the goddess Artemis miraculously substitutes a deer for Iphigeneia at the sacrificial altar, and this substitution takes place at the exact moment when Iphigeneia is about to be slaughtered (lines 19–20). So, in this version of the myth, a deer is killed instead of Iphigeneia, and, in the meantime, Artemis transports the girl to a remote place named Tauris, where Iphigeneia is immortalized as a *theos* or 'goddess' in her own right (lines 18–19). So, the virgin Iphigeneia as the mortal surrogate of Artemis is transformed into the goddess Artemis herself, who can now be seen in her own specialized role as an immortal virgin.

3§49. In the myth as retold in the *Agamemnon* of Aeschylus, by contrast, this salvation of Iphigeneia is not made explicit, and her story stops when she dies—not when she is rescued from death and becomes the goddess Artemis in her divine role as an immortal virgin.

3§50. It is relevant here, as I have argued in another project, that the drama of Aeschylus highlights the anger vicariously felt by Artemis on behalf of her surrogate—anger against Agamemnon and Menelaos for their willingness to sacrifice Iphigeneia. Artemis is angry at them even though it was she who ordained the sacrifice of her own surrogate as a precondition for her releasing the winds that blew eastward and made it possible for the Achaeans to sail off to Troy.[32] In the epic Cycle as well, the anger of Artemis is highlighted, and the

[31] Connelly 2014:172.

[32] *H24H* 16§22.

word for this anger is *mēnis* (*Cypria* p. 104 lines 14, 16); in that context, the word refers to the anger of the goddess at Agamemnon for boasting that he is a better hunter after he shoots down a deer. It is no coincidence that the sacrificial substitute for Iphigeneia is likewise a deer, as we just saw (*Cypria* p. 104 lines 19–20).[33]

3§51. Similarly, I will now argue that the virginal heroine known simply as the Parthénos is a surrogate of the virginal goddess Athena in the myths and rituals pictured on the Parthenon Frieze.

3§52. Here I return to my starting point concerning the scene that we see sculpted into Block 5 on the east side of the Parthenon Frieze. In terms of my interpretation, as I noted from the start, this scene refers to the moment when the presentation of the Peplos is performed at the Panathenaia. But now I need to make a distinction between the Peplos that was seasonally rewoven in the world of ritual and the *peplos* that was originally woven in the world of myth. In the world of ritual, as we saw many times already, the Peplos was seasonally rewoven by the Athenians and presented by them to the goddess Athena on the occasion of the Panathenaic Procession, which took place at the seasonally recurring festival of the Panathenaia. In the world of myth, on the other hand, there was a *peplos* originally woven by the Parthénos or 'Virgin', and this *peplos* was later presented to her by her own father—for her to wear in preparation for her ritual slaughter on the occasion of the original Panathenaic Procession, which was the climax of the original festival of the Panathenaia.

3§53. But I stop myself when I say *wear* here. As in the case of other virginal sacrifices that we have already noted, the word *wrap* would be a better fit. I will now explain why.

3§54. The multiple folds that are featured in the sculpted representation of the *peplos* indicate a fabric of relatively huge proportions, evoking the image of the gigantic *peplos* that used to be presented to the goddess herself at the climax of the Panathenaic Procession. The gigantic proportions of the *peplos* in the ritual of this procession seem at first ill suited for the small girl in the myth as represented in the sculpted image. Seen through the bifocal lenses of myth and ritual combined, however, the image is smoothed out: the sacrificial death of the mortal little girl in the myth points to her role as the sacred surrogate of the biggest of all girls, the immortal Parthénos, in the ritual of the Panathenaic Procession.

3§55. I will have more to say in a minute about the corresponding myth of an original Panathenaic Procession, which supposedly took place at an original festival of the Panathenaia. For now, however, I will simply continue to focus on the idea that the little mortal Parthénos, in weaving her *peplos*, is a surrogate

[33] Again, *H24H* 16§22.

of the great immortal Parthénos, the goddess Athena herself. And this idea is correlated with the further idea that Erekhtheus, figured as both king and chief priest of the Athenians, is a surrogate of Zeus himself.

3§56. To back up these two correlated ideas, I return to lines 734 and 736 of *Iliad* V, quoted in Extract 3-A. At line 734, we saw the goddess Athena in a primal moment, when she takes off the *peplos* that she had woven for herself with her own hands, and, at line 736, we saw her in another primal moment that happens seconds later, when she puts on a *khitōn* or 'tunic' as an undergarment for the armor she will wear in war. When I analyzed these two lines, I highlighted a third primal moment that comes between the two moments when the goddess slips out of the *peplos* and when she slips into the *khitōn*. In this intervening moment, I noted, the goddess must be in the nude. Now I highlight two details that I have not yet noted in these same two lines.

- At the moment in line 734 when the goddess takes off her *peplos*, it is said that she does so "at the threshold of her father."
- At the following moment in line 736 when she puts on the *khitōn*, it is said that this tunic actually belongs to her divine father.

3§57. In the myth of the Gigantomachy, as viewed in the temporal linearity of Homeric poetry, it would have been this same *khitōn* that the goddess was already wearing underneath her armor when she was born fully formed and fully armed from the head of Zeus. That is why Homeric poetry can refer to this *khitōn* as belonging not to the goddess but instead to her divine father. As for the *peplos* that Athena leaves "at the threshold of her father," it now appears that this *peplos* too belongs to the divine father, to be left behind in his residence, *as if Zeus were the father of a future bride.*

3§58. I see comparable details in the relief sculpture of Block 5. Here too, the Parthénos is about to leave the residence of her father. And, although she is about to put on her *peplos* instead of taking it off, she is seen in an intervening moment of changing her dress, just as the goddess Athena is changing her dress in *Iliad* V 734–735. In this intervening moment, as sculpted into Block 5 at the east side of the Parthenon Frieze, the Parthénos is practically in the nude. Connelly gives a lively description:

> She is about to be sacrificed at the hand of her father, who is dressed as a priest for the event. [...] The girl's dress is, very conspicuously, opened at the side, revealing her nude buttocks. It would be unthinkable for a historical girl, an *arrhēphoros* from an elite family, to be portrayed with backside casually exposed during the most sacred moment of the Panathenaic ritual. [...] I would argue that the girl's nudity is not

accidental. Her garment is open to communicate that she is in the process of changing clothes.[34]

3§59. I agree with Connelly's argument that this scene, as represented in the relief sculptures of the Parthenon Frieze, is happening not in the world of ritual as current in Athens at the time of the building of the Parthenon in the middle of the fifth century BCE.[35] Granted, in terms of the ritual world as it existed in that historical period, we might expect elite girls known as the *Arrhēphoroi* to be the chosen handlers of the Peplos. But the scene sculpted into Block 5 of the east side of the Parthenon Frieze is happening not in the historical world of Athenian ritual but in the prehistorical world of a charter myth telling about the time when Eumolpos and his horde of Thracians were attacking Erekhtheus and his fellow Athenians.

3§60. So, in terms of Connelly's argument, the *peplos* that is pictured in this scene was woven not by the young girls known as the *Arrhēphoroi* in the world of Athenian ritual in historical times. Instead, the weaving of the *peplos* as shown in Block 5 happened in the world of Athenian myth, and the weaver was a virgin known simply as the Parthénos, the Virgin. After the Parthénos wove her *peplos*, this most precious heirloom would have been stored in the residence of her father until it was time for her to become a bride, ready to be given away in marriage. At the time of the wedding, the father would have handed over to the Parthénos this *peplos* that she herself had pattern-woven with her own hands while residing in her father's residence. Then, taking this *peplos* off her father's hands, the Parthénos would now slip into it and wear it for her wedding.[36] But, tragically, the presentation of the *peplos* in this special case would be followed not by a wedding. Instead, what awaits the Parthénos is an act of ritual slaughter. So, the *peplos* that she receives in this scene of presentation is not exactly the kind of pretty dress that is made ready for a pretty girl to wear, tailor-made, fitting perfectly the contours of her beautiful body. She would not be wearing a peplos that fits her that way. Rather, she would be wrapped into the many folds of the massive *peplos* that we see represented in the sculpture.

3§61. For a parallel, I cite the picturing of the Trojan princess Polyxena in a vase painting that shows how the Achaeans slaughter this virgin after they capture Troy, sacrificing her at the tomb of Achilles. The picture captures

[34] Connelly 2014:172.

[35] Connelly 2014:171, following Connelly 2007:39.

[36] For a radically different interpretation of this scene in Block 5, see Neils 2001:68 (also p. 178), who supports an alternative argument: that the two figures who are represented as handling the fabric are getting it ready for storage, and thus they would be folding up rather than unfolding that fabric; also, she thinks that the figure of the adolescent here is a boy, not a girl (pp. 166–171, 178).

the moment when the girl's throat is slit and her blood gushes forth, pouring down upon a sacrificial altar positioned on top of the hero's tomb. And, at that moment of sacrificial slaughter, the girl is all wrapped up inside the folds of a massive *peplos*. Here is the picture:

Extract 3-E

Attic black-figure amphora: Side A, sacrifice of Polyxena. Attributed variously to the Tyrrhenian Group or the Timiades Painter, ca. 570–560 BCE. London, British Museum, 1897.0727.2. Line drawing from Walters 1898: Plate XV.

3§62. Using the comparative evidence of this picture, Connelly reasons that the *peplos* presented by the father to the Parthénos in the scene of presentation sculpted into the Parthenon Frieze could be seen as a shroud.[37] As I have been arguing here, however, this *peplos* could just as easily be seen as a wedding dress—even if the many folds of this massive fabric will cover the girl's body not for a wedding but for a human sacrifice.

3§63. The Parthénos, as she leaves the residence of her priestly father, could be getting dressed in her *peplos* as a bride who is getting married to a bridegroom. In a sense, the father is giving away the bride. But the destiny of this virgin is not to be married off but rather to be killed off. And, just as the bride is for the father to give away, the *peplos* that the Parthénos had woven is now for *him* to give to *her* to wear as she prepares to leave his residence. There is a comparable situation in

[37] Connelly 2014:172–173.

Iliad V 734–735, where Athena is pictured as leaving the residence of her father when she slips out of her *peplos* and slips into the *khitōn* that she wears as an undergarment for her suit of armor. In this case, however, the change of clothes is in reverse: she is slipping out of the *peplos* and slipping into the *khitōn*.

3§64. Viewing the scene sculpted into Block 5 on the east side of the Parthenon Frieze as a ritual where the father is giving away the bride, I find it most useful to paraphrase the anthropological perspective of James Redfield in analyzing the myths and rituals concerning the Locrian Maidens.[38] The basic details of these myths and rituals, originating from a variety of populations who described themselves as Locrians, are attested primarily in Lycophron's *Alexandra* (1141–1173) together with the accompanying scholia, where we see that the idea of killing the Locrian Maidens on the level of myth is correlated with the idea of marrying them off on the level of ritual. According to one particular Locrian tradition, reported by Polybius (12.5.7), only those girls who were descended from the most prestigious families of Locris, known as the Hundred Houses, were eligible for participating in the ritual of surrogacy that re-enacted the experiences of the prototypical Locrian Maidens.[39] Redfield has this to say about the sacrifice experienced by the Locrian Maidens in myth as correlated with ritual:

> Only in the mythical version of the ritual were they [= the Locrian Maidens] actually sacrificed; in the actual version they went through *an experience of sacrifice* [emphasis mine] and came out the other side enriched. The two versions, in fact, represent the doubleness of the Greek wedding, as transfer (by and for males) and as transformation (of and for women), as sacrifice and initiation.[40]

3§65. So, to sum it all up, my interpretation of the scene that is sculpted into Block 5 on the east side of the Parthenon Frieze supports the central theory of Connelly, who argues that this scene features Erekhtheus in the act of preparing his virginal daughter—known to Athenians simply as the Parthénos—for a human sacrifice. I find it apt to quote here the anthropological perspective of Redfield on ancient Greek wedding rituals in general: he speaks of "the wedding as the father's sacrifice of his daughter, and as requiring the bride's consent."[41]

38 Redfield 2003:90.

39 Redfield 2003:87, 89.

40 Redfield 2003:90.

41 Again, Redfield 2003:90.

A Prototypical Panathenaic Procession

3§66. So far, I have focused on one single scene that is pictured in the relief sculptures of the Parthenon Frieze. And I have interpreted this scene, sculpted into Block 5 on the east side of the Parthenon Frieze, as the climactic moment of a charter myth that centers on a prototypical presentation of a prototypical *peplos* to the Parthénos, the virgin daughter of Erekhtheus. But now I propose to consider the Frieze in its entirety, ready to embrace the idea that the visual narrative of the Frieze is picturing a prototype of the entire ritual that is aetiologized by the charter myth. And this ritual is the Panathenaic Procession. The idea, then, is that the Parthenon Frieze, considered in its entirety, pictures a prototypical Panathenaic Procession.

3§67. I start by quoting Joan Connelly's description of the Parthenon Frieze as it fits into the overall structure of the Parthenon:

> [It is] a band of sculptured relief showing 378 human and 245 animal figures and running some 160 meters (525 feet) around the top of the cella wall within the colonnade. Set at a height of 14 meters, or about 46 feet, and deeply shaded under the ceiling of the peristyle for most of the day, the frieze measures just over 1 meter from top to bottom, or roughly 3 feet 4 inches in height. [...] Truth be told, the frieze would have been difficult to see from ground level. The earth-bound Athenian would, of course, have made out the profiles of figures set against the frieze's deep blue painted background. Skin pigments of reddish brown for men and white for women would have made the sexes distinguishable at a distance. [...] But viewers would have already known the subject matter, thus easily recognizing the figures glimpsed between the columns. Still, to peer straight up at the frieze from thirty to forty feet below would have required an inordinate amount of squinting and neck craning.[42]

3§68. I agree with Connelly when she concludes:

> In fact, the primary intended viewers of the Parthenon frieze were not mortal visitors to the Acropolis but the gods eternally gazing down upon it.[43]

3§69. So, in terms of this argument, we can say that the story of the Parthenon Frieze, presented here as an ultimate spectacle for the divine gaze, is the story of the Panathenaic Procession. But the story depicts not the current

42 Connelly 2014:153.

43 Again, Connelly 2014:153.

version of the procession, as it took place at the seasonally recurring festival of the Panathenaia in the era when the Parthenon was built. Rather, the story depicts the supposedly original version. That is what Connelly argues, and what I argue as well.

3§70. In order to grasp the narrative logic of the Parthenon Frieze in picturing this supposedly original procession, I start again with that singular picture that has been the focus of attention up to now. In that picture, replicated in the line drawing that I showed when I started my analysis, we see the climactic moment when Erekhtheus is presenting to the Parthénos the *peplos* that this virginal girl had once woven—and that she will now be wearing for her virginal sacrifice.

3§71. That picture, as I indicated from the start, is situated on the right side of Block 5 on the east side of the Parthenon Frieze. Zooming out from that picture, we now see on the left side of Block 5 three other human figures. Moving our view from right to left, we start with the first of these three figures. She is a grown woman, to be identified with Praxithea, the wife of Erekhtheus, and we know her name from a variety of ancient sources (including Lycurgus *Against Leokrates* 99).[44] Moving further to the left, we see sculpted into the same Block 5 the other two Parthénoi who will be killed in the virginal sacrifice. They are taller than the Parthénos who is receiving the *peplos* on the right side of Block 5, and this detail on the corresponding left side matches those versions of the myth that describe the sacrificed virgin as the youngest of the three daughters of Erekhtheus. Moving our view further to our left, we see sculpted into Block 4 of the east side of the Parthenon Frieze two seated figures, larger in size than the five human figures representing the holy family of Erekhtheus and Praxithea and their three daughters. These two larger figures are the gods Zeus and Hera. Symmetrically, in Block 6 all the way across to our right, we see two other seated figures, again larger in size than the human figures, and these larger figures are the gods Athena and Hephaistos.

3§72. Having by now seen four of the twelve Olympian gods, we are ready to look at the other eight. Zooming further out, we get to see these gods as well. Their outer positioning frames the inner positions of Zeus and Hera on our left and of Athena and Hephaistos on our right—while the inner positioning of these four Olympian gods frames the innermost positions of the Parthénos and Erekhtheus and Praxithea and the two other Parthénoi.[45]

[44] On Praxithea as a prototypical priestess of Athena, I cite the argumentation of Connelly 2014:138–140.

[45] In this regard, I find myself attracted to an interpretation proposed by Neils 2001:61–66: she thinks that the twelve Olympian gods, seated on either side of the five standing humans, are imagined as sitting in a semicircle that surrounds the central scene featuring those humans.

3§73. And, zooming still further out, we see figures of humans and sacrificial animals processing toward the assembly of gods from the other three sides of the Frieze. These figures, Connelly argues, are processing in a prototypical Panathenaic Procession, which marks the victory of the Athenians in their battle against the invading horde led by Eumolpos:

> This procession brings animal offerings for the post-battle, thanksgiving sacrifice that follows the Athenian victory. The Parthenon frieze can thus be understood to show not just some historical Panathenaia but the very first Panathenaia, the foundational sacrifice upon which Acropolis ritual was based ever after. The offerings of cattle and sheep, of honey and water, as shown on the north and south friezes, are all made in honor of the king and his daughters as described in Euripides's *Erekhtheus*. The cavalcade of horsemen is the king's returning army, back from the war just in time to join the procession celebrating their victory.[46]

3§74. Such a picturing of a prototypical Panathenaic Procession seems to include details that go beyond the context of a formal procession—as we would expect such a procession to occur in the historical era of the Panathenaia. For example, in the formulation I have just quoted from Connelly, the cavalcade could be seen as part of the military action in the charter myth about the war waged by the Athenians against Eumolpos and his Thracians—not only as part of the procession itself. I would add that the picturing of men riding on horses in the relief sculptures of the Frieze could also be referring to aspects of the overall festival of the Panathenaia, which featured athletic competitions in equestrian events.[47] And the picturing of such equestrian competitions in the Parthenon Frieze could merge with the picturing of a parade of participants in these competitions. This way, the equestrian competitions could be seen as part of the Panathenaic Procession. In other words, the procession could include metonymically the athletic competitions that culminated in the procession.

3§75. Most experts think that the equestrian scenes of the Parthenon Frieze are in fact representations of horse-riders parading in the Panathenaic Procession.[48] I argue, however, for a combined perspective. In terms of my argument, the cavalcade pictured on the Frieze could be seen as a set of events that are simultaneously processional and athletic. And the athletic events, from the

46 Connelly 2014:186.

47 On the equestrian events at the Panathenaia, see Shear 2001:343, 546.

48 Shear 2001:744–745.

standpoint of the corresponding charter myth, could be re-enacting wartime events that happened in the mythologized age of heroes.

3§76. A related set of events that we see pictured in the relief sculptures of the Frieze involves charioteering. There are twenty-one chariot teams represented on the Frieze, with eleven chariots featured on the north side and ten on the south side; in each case, the chariot is shown with four horses, a driver, and an armed rider, who is wearing a helmet and a shield.[49] In the case of the armed rider, as we know from a variety of ancient sources, the word for such a figure standing on a chariot was *apobatēs*, which means literally 'he who steps off'.[50] The Parthenon Frieze shows these armed riders in a variety of maneuvers directly involved with the chariots in which they are riding: the riders are shown *stepping into the chariot*, *riding in the chariot*, *stepping out of the chariot*, and *running alongside the chariot*; in two cases, the *apobatai* are evidently wearing a full set of armor.[51]

3§77. In another project, I have studied at length the bits and pieces of surviving evidence about a most prestigious athletic event, held at the festival of the Panathenaia, involving a competition in apobatic charioteering.[52] In that project, I already argued that the chariot scenes of the Parthenon Frieze are picturing not only a parade of participants competing in the apobatic chariot races held at the festival of the Panathenaia. More than that, much more, these same scenes are simultaneously picturing some of the greatest imaginable moments that could ever be experienced in the course of actually competing in these apobatic chariot races. In addition, just as the cavalcade that is pictured on the Frieze could refer to the mythological war waged by the Athenians against Eumolpos and his horde of Thracians, so also the chariot scenes could refer in part to that same war. In other words, the stop-motion picturing of apobatic chariot scenes in the Parthenon Frieze captures not only moments of participation in the Panathenaic Procession but also moments of actual engagement in apobatic chariot racing—and even in the warfare of chariot fighting. That kind of warfare, of course, would be happening in a heroic era, not in the era when the Parthenon was built.

3§78. So, as in the case of the cavalcade that is pictured on the Frieze, the chariot scenes could be seen as referring to events that are simultaneously processional and athletic. And the formulation that I applied in the case of the

49 Shear 2001:304–305.

50 Photius *Lexicon* α 2449, 2450; *Suda* α 3250; Harpocration s.v. ἀποβάτης, with reference to Theophrastus *Laws* F 15 (ed. Szegedy-Maszák 1981); [Eratosthenes] *Katasterismoi* 1.13; Dionysius of Halicarnassus *Roman Antiquities* 7.73.2–3.

51 Shear 2001:746.

52 *H24H* 7b§3, following Shear 2001:304–305. For an inventory of inscriptions commemorating the victories of *apobatai* in competitions at the Panathenaia, see Shear 2001:305n341.

cavalcade can apply here as well: the athletic events of apobatic charioteering, from the standpoint of the corresponding charter myth, could be re-enacting wartime events that happened in the mythologized era of heroes.

3§79. I highlight here a contrast between the perspectives of ritual and myth in Athenian traditions. In the world of ritual, the Panathenaic Procession is followed by the presentation of the Peplos at the seasonally recurring festival of the Panathenaia. In the world of myth, by contrast, we cannot say that the procession happens *before* or *after* the presentation of the *peplos*. We see here once again a theological way of thinking about prototypical events, comparable to what we saw earlier when we considered the metonymic sequence of the myth about the Gigantomachy, which is followed by the narrating of the Gigantomachy by way of weaving the narration into the Peplos woven by Athena: in that case, the Gigantomachy is followed by the weaving is followed by the Gigantomachy and so on, in an endless circle. So also in the myth about the presentation of a *peplos* to be worn by the Parthénos, we can say that the original presentation is followed by the original Panathenaic Procession is followed by the presentation and so on, in an endless circle. Such is the logic of the prototypical Panathenaic Procession.

The Defining Moment in the Panathenaic Procession

3§80. Before I proceed, I stop here to take a closer look at the defining moment of the Panathenaic Procession as sculpted into the Parthenon Frieze—the moment that I have been describing as the presentation of the Peplos. In the book *Homer the Classic*, I had this to say about the Panathenaic Frieze as the defining context of that all-important moment:

> The ritual drama of the Panathenaic Procession, as represented on the Parthenon Frieze, is central to the whole Panathenaic Festival, central to Athena, central to Athens. It is an ultimate exercise in Athenian self-definition, an ultimate point of contact between myth and ritual. The dialectic of such a Classical Moment has us under its spell even to this day. And it is precisely the anxiety of contemplating such a spellbinding moment that calls for the remedy of objective observation, from diachronic as well as synchronic points of view.[53]

3§81. In using the terms *synchronic* and *diachronic* in this formulation, I was following a linguistic distinction made by Ferdinand de Saussure.[54] For Saussure,

53 *HC* 4§219, repeating what I said even earlier in *PR* 90.

54 Saussure 1916:117.

synchrony and *diachrony* designate respectively a current state of a language and a phase in its evolution.[55] Applying this terminology to the language, as it were, of the Parthenon Frieze, I was arguing that the visual narrative of the Frieze show shifts in meaning—once we view it not only synchronically but also diachronically.

3§82. That said, I focus here again on that Classical Moment. This is the moment, as I just said, when the Peplos is presented. But whose *peplos* is it? From a diachronic point of view, as we will now see, it is the Peplos of Athena, and that is why I just formatted the word as "the Peplos," not "a *peplos*." From a synchronic point of view, however, the referent here is not the Peplos of the goddess Athena but a *peplos* woven by a heroine known simply as the Parthénos or 'Virgin', who is the youngest daughter of the hero Erekhtheus, king and high priest of Athens. This moment, as I just narrated it, is a reconstruction, painstakingly put together on the basis of synchronic analysis. From this synchronic point of view, then, Erekhtheus and the Parthénos are father and daughter. From a diachronic point of view, however, the relationship is different—and far more complex.

Diachronic Athena

3§83. As Douglas Frame has argued at length—and most persuasively so—a prehistoric phase of Athenian mythmaking pictured the hero Erekhtheus as both the son and the consort of Athena herself, who was formerly not a divine virgin but a mother goddess, and who became an exclusively virgin goddess only in the era of Solon, around 600 BCE.[56] At a later point, we will consider a further argument, that an older form of the goddess Athena was formerly both a virgin and a mother, like the goddess Hera, recycling from mother to virgin to mother in an endless cycle. For now, however, I simply offer a working formulation about the theological essence of the goddess Athena as she was worshipped by the Athenians in the classical era when the Parthenon Frieze was created. My formulation is shaped by a diachronic point of view that links the goddess Athena, as a former mother, to the mortal Parthénos as a permanent virgin. From this point of view, the Parthénos who died a virgin is the daughter that Athena never had, making it possible for Athena to become an immortal virgin who forever replaces her mortal surrogate. Similarly, as I have already argued, Artemis is the immortal virgin who forever replaces her own mortal surrogate, who is Iphigeneia in some versions of the myth.

55 Again, Saussure 1916:117: "De même synchronie et diachronie désigneront respectivement un état de langage et une phase d'évolution."

56 Frame 2009 Part 3, especially pp. 458–486, with special reference to the doubling of Erekhtheus as Erikhthonios.

Back to the Defining Moment in the Panathenaic Procession

3§84. I return to the moment when the Peplos is presented in the scene sculpted into Block 5 on the east side of the Parthenon Frieze. By now we see that the recipient of this presentation is really the goddess Athena from a diachronic point of view, though she seems to be the mortal Parthénos from a purely synchronic point of view. Either way, what strikes the eye at this defining moment is the artistry of the sculpture in representing the Peplos itself, with its folds and its selvedge still clearly visible despite the massive erosion in the stonework.[57] The sculpting of this Peplos, I will now argue, is a shining example of a special kind of *metonym*—what we have been calling a *synecdoche*—for the sculpting of the Panathenaic Frieze in its entirety.

3§85. In making this argument, I find it relevant here to repeat the term *story-frieze*, as we saw it used before with reference to the narrative technique of pattern-weaving in the process of narrating myths, including the myth of the Gigantomachy as woven into the Peplos presented to Athena at the festival of the Panathenaia.[58] This term *story-frieze*, as a metaphor, is good to think with, provided we keep in mind that the creation of notional "friezes" in weaving cannot be derived from the creation of real friezes in sculpting. The direction of derivation was actually the reverse, as we can see from the fact that the pattern-weaving of stories like the myth of the Gigantomachy was an old tradition going back to prehistoric times, whereas the sculpting of a continuous narrative sequence like the Parthenon Frieze was an innovation of the classical period, concurrent with the time when the Parthenon was built. That said, I stress the intuitive appeal of comparing the artistry of sculpting a story into a frieze with the artistry of pattern-weaving a story into a fabric.

3§86. Returning to the argument, then, I find it relevant to apply this term *story-frieze* in the context of the Parthenon Frieze, since the artistry of this frieze exemplifies a cross-over from the craft of weaving to the craft of sculpture. And a signature of this cross-over, I argue, is the sculpting of the Peplos of Athena at the defining moment of its presentation to the goddess. In other words, the sculpting of the Peplos—and, by extension, the sculpting of the Panathenaic Procession in its entirety—is inspired by the pattern-weaving of the Peplos of Athena.[59]

57 Barber 1992:113. See also Barber 1991:361: "the ribbing of the heading-band—the trademark of the warp-weighted loom—was sculpted into the marble and shows quite clearly." At p. 272, she gives further illustrations of selvedges as represented in the sculpture of the Parthenon Frieze.

58 Barber 1992:114–116.

59 *HC* 4§221.

Linking the Robe of Athena to her Bronze Shield in the Interior of the Parthenon

3§87. The cross-over extends further.[60] The artistry of the craft of pattern-weaving crosses over also into the craft of metalworking. A prime example is a masterpiece of metalwork that was once housed in the interior of the Parthenon, abode of the statue of Athena Parthénos, made by Pheidias. Positioned next to this colossal gold-and-ivory statue of Athena Parthénos was the colossal bronze shield of the goddess, likewise made by Pheidias—and this sacred shield showed a complex metalworked narrative on its concave interior as also on its convex exterior.[61]

3§88. We find the essential facts about this bronze shield of Athena in a description by Pliny the Elder, which I am about to quote. As we will see, the convex exterior of the Shield featured a metalworked narrative of the Amazonomachy (*Amazonomakhiā*), that is, the primal conflict between the Athenians and the Amazons (*Amazones*); as for the concave interior, it featured a likewise metalworked narrative of a corresponding primal conflict. In this case, the narrative was none other than the Gigantomachy (*Gigantomakhiā*), that primal conflict between the gods and the giants (*gigantes*). Here, then, is the exact wording of Pliny's description:

Extract 3-F

> On her [= Athena's] Shield he [= Pheidias] chased [*caelāre*] the Battle of the Amazons in the convex part, while he chased in the concave part of the same shield the Conflicts of Gods and Giants.
>
> Pliny *Natural History* 36.18[62]

3§89. The wording of Pliny here makes it explicit that Pheidias was metal-working (verb *caelāre* 'chase') this visual narrative, not painting it.[63] And we see metalworked into the interior of this bronze shield the selfsame narrative that was pattern-woven into the fabric of the Peplos, namely, the myth of the Gigantomachy. From the evidence of ancient imitations of this metalworked narrative, one expert has pieced together a most vivid description:

60 In what follows, I reuse the argumentation I had used, for different purposes, in *HC* 4§§222–224.

61 Leipen 1971:49. She emphasizes that the interior as well as the exterior of Athena's Shield was *metalworked*, not *painted*.

62 *In scuto eius Amazonum proelium caelavit intumescente ambitu, ‹in› parmae eiusdem concava parte deorum et Gigantum dimicationes.*

63 And the metalwork was in bronze, with a gilded surface. See also *HC* 4§§213–214, with further details.

> Particularly stressed [in the narrative of the Gigantomachy as metal-worked into the bronze shield of Athena] is the presence of Zeus in the centre top of the heavenly arch: other gods converge toward him symmetrically from either side. [Pheidias] seems to announce in this way to the spectator that Zeus is not only in the centre of the battle but also at its culminating point. The same conception is found on the Panathenaic [F]rieze where the human procession, starting from the south-west corner, proceeds in two directions along the north and south sides of the temple to converge over the east end where the gods are assembled to witness the culmination of the ceremony.[64]

3§90. The comparison here with the point of convergence in the narrative of the Parthenon Frieze is most apt. It is at this point in that narrative, as I have noted all along, that we find its defining moment, which is, the presentation of the Peplos.

Linking the Robe of Athena to the Sculptures on the Exterior of the Parthenon

3§91. By now we have seen two links to the Peplos of Athena in the visual art of the Parthenon. In one case, the pictorial narrative that is sculpted into Block 5 on the east side of the Parthenon Frieze in the interior of the Parthenon refers to the form of the woven Peplos. In the other case, the pictorial narrative that is metalworked into the bronze interior of the Shield of Athena is a myth that matches the content that is pattern-woven into the Peplos of Athena, that is, the myth of the Gigantomachy.[65] And now we will see a third link to the Peplos, sculpted into the exterior of the Parthenon.

3§92. I quote from a relevant formulation that I presented in the book *Homer the Classic*, where I highlighted this third link in the overall context of all the sculptures adorning the exterior of the temple:

> On the surface of this exterior [of the Parthenon] are the grand relief sculptures of the pediments and the metopes, featuring a set of connected mythical and ritual themes. The east and the west pediment show respectively the birth of Athena and her victory over Poseidon in their struggle over the identity of Athens; the metopes show the battle of the gods and giants on the east side, the battle of the Athenians and

[64] Leipen 1971:48. On the evidence that comes from ancient representations that were modeled on the original work of Pheidias, see *HC* 1§131.

[65] *HC* 4§223.

> Amazons on the west, the battle of the Lapiths and Centaurs on the south, and the battle of the Achaeans and Trojans on the north. So once again we see a sculpted narrative that matches the woven narrative of the Peplos of Athena: it is the myth of the Gigantomachy, sculpted into the east metopes, featuring Athena herself battling in the forefront [...]. In this case, the Gigantomachy balances the Amazonomachy that is sculpted into the west metopes. Similarly, the Gigantomachy that is metalworked into the concave interior of the Shield of Athena balances the Amazonomachy that is metalworked into the convex exterior. So the contents of the east and the west metopes of the Parthenon's exterior correspond respectively to the contents of the concave interior and convex exterior of the Shield of Athena.[66]

Linking the Robe of Athena to the Pandora Frieze

3§93. There is a fourth link to the Peplos of Athena in the narratives of visual art adorning the Parthenon. It is the Pandora Frieze, a creation by Pheidias, which he metalworked into the base of the statue of Athena Parthénos.[67] In order to appreciate the significance of this fourth link, I propose that we take the perspective of a viewer standing before the entrance to the temple:

> Facing the east side of the temple and looking for highlights that catch the eye, starting from the top, we would first of all see the birth of Athena sculpted into the pediment on high; next, looking further below, we would see the battle of the gods and giants sculpted into the metopes; next, looking even further below and into the interior, we would see the presentation of the Peplos of Athena sculpted into the Parthenon Frieze that wraps around this interior above the columns of the porch.[68]

3§94. What do we see, then, after experiencing these three spectacular views, that is, after beholding (1) the birth of Athena as sculpted into the pediment above, (2) the Gigantomachy as sculpted into the metopes below, and (3) the prototypical Panathenaic Procession as sculpted further below into the Parthenon Frieze? Ascending the steps of the temple and entering its open

[66] *HC* 4§224. Also relevant to the Peplos of Athena, as I show elsewhere, is what we see sculpted into the north metopes of the Parthenon's exterior: it is the battle of the Achaeans and Trojans, the topical centerpiece of the Homeric *Iliad* and *Odyssey*. I analyze the narrative of the north metopes in *HC* 4§§246–251, 256.

[67] What follows is a recasting of what I argued in *HC* 4§§225–231.

[68] *HC*§225, following Berczelly 1992:54.

doors, we now behold the most spectacular sight of them all—the gigantic figure of Athena Parthénos standing on top of a commensurately gigantic base. And, at the same time, we also behold, metalworked into the surface of this base, the Pandora Frieze.

3§95. Here is why I just said *metalworked*, not *sculpted*. As we know from Pliny the Elder (*Natural History* 36.19), the relief work of the Pandora Frieze was executed not in marble but in bronze. In other words, the Pandora Frieze was 'chased', *caelātum* (verb *caelāre* 'chase'). The bronze metalwork must have featured a gilded surface, which is to be inferred from what Pausanias says about the corresponding relief work gracing the base of the statue of Zeus in Olympia (5.11.8).[69]

3§96. Let us continue to follow the perspective of a viewer who has just entered the interior of the temple. As we enter, we are looking straight ahead at the glittering figure of Pandora at the center of the Pandora Frieze, her radiance enhanced by her reflection in the pool at the front of the base; this view gives the viewer "a premonition of what, once he had accustomed himself to the semi-darkness in the cella, he would, on directing his gaze upwards, experience in the statue of the Athena Parthénos herself."[70] Even before the viewer "could have been alerted to the astonishing height and polychromatic splendour of the chryselephantine statue of Athena itself, he would have looked straight ahead and glanced at its base."[71]

3§97. In Extract 3-B, I quoted what Pausanias says (1.24.7), about the myth that is narrated in the metalwork that adorns the base of the statue of Athena Parthénos. This myth, as Pausanias says, centered on the genesis of Pandora. What Pausanias does not say, however, is that Pandora is the first Athenian woman in the Athenian version of the myth, and that she is represented as wearing the first *peplos* ever worn—by a woman. The narrative of this myth about Pandora, as metalworked into the frieze of the base of the statue of Athena Parthénos, can be reconstructed primarily on the basis of vase paintings that narrate this myth.[72] In terms of these narrations, Pandora is represented as wearing the first *peplos*, given to her by the goddess Athena herself:

> This robe, the first *peplos*, might have been understood in the widest sense of the word as the archetypal *peplos*, given by Athena to the primordial woman. For that reason its concept was not confined to the bare image of a beautiful garment, but involved women's ability

[69] *HC*§226, following Berczelly 1992:55.
[70] Berczelly 1992:55.
[71] Berczelly 1992:54–55.
[72] *HC* 4§227, following Berczelly 1992:61–67.

to weave *peploi* as well.[73] Thus the *peplos* of Pandora could have represented the mythical pattern or prototype for all the *peploi* in the world.[74]

3§98. This formulation is backed up by the narratives of two relevant vase paintings. Both paintings are dated to the second quarter of the fifth century BCE; so they predate the Pandora Frieze itself.[75]

3§98-A. The first of these paintings shows a frontal view of Pandora, who has just been created by Hephaistos with the help of Athena. She is wearing a *peplos* and is flanked by Athena, who is presenting her with a garland of flowers:[76]

Extract 3-Ga

Attic red-figure calyx krater: the Birth of Pandora. Attributed to the Niobid Painter, ca. 475–425 BCE. London, British Museum, GR 1856.12–13.1 (Vase E 467). Line drawing by Valerie Woelfel.

3§98-B. The second of these two paintings shows Pandora flanked by Athena and Hephaistos on either side. It is the moment when the two divinities have just finished creating this female prototype by way of their combined crafts:

[73] The author refers here to Hesiod *Works and Days* 63–64.

[74] Berczelly 1992:61.

[75] *HC* 4§228, following Berczelly 1992:61.

[76] On the association of Pandora with garlands of flowers, see also Hesiod *Theogony* 576–580 and *Works and Days* 74–75. See also Blech 1982:34 and Berczelly 1992:63.

Extract 3-Gb

Attic red-figure cup: the Creation of Pandora. Attributed to the Tarquinia Painter, ca. 475–425 B. C. London, British Museum, 1885.1-28.1. Line drawing by Valerie Woelfel.

3§98-C. I quote this description:

> We see here only three figures: Hephaistos in company with Athena, respectively on the left (spectator's right) and right side of Pandora. Hephaistos has completed the modelling of Pandora with a small hammer, which he still holds in his left hand. Lifting his right hand over her head he now has a closer look at the results, whereas Athena is engaged in fastening the *peplos* to Pandora's shoulders. It is not accidental that just these two deities should be flanking her. After all, the part Hephaistos, the creator of Pandora, takes in the myth, is no less significant than that of Athena. As an allusion to his rôle in the artificial birth of Pandora, a cave behind the figures indicates the smithy where Hephaistos and his helpers executed the work. Another reason for his presence in the scene might have been that Hephaistos and Athena *Erganē* very often appear together in Classical Attic art.[77]

[77] Berczelly 1992:62. In support of what he says about Hephaistos, he refers to Hesiod *Works and Days* 60–63; also *Theogony* 571 and following.

3§98-D. The naming here of Athena as *Erganē* is most noteworthy, since this name *Erganē* is an epithet of the goddess in her role as the divine force that presides over the *ergasiā* 'work' of women:

Extract 3-H

> *Erganē* is Athena, in that she oversees the work [*ergasiā*] of *women*. This is the way she is called by the Athenians, also by the people of Samos. The word indicates 'work' [*ergasiā*].
>
> Suda s.v. ἐργάνη[78]

3§98-E. This epithet of the goddess, *Erganē*, is relevant to the *Khalkeia*, an Athenian festival that inaugurated the weaving of the Peplos of Athena, and the name of this festival, derived from the word *khalkos* 'bronze', is in turn relevant to the epithet of the goddess:

Extract 3-I

> *Khalkeia* was the name of an ancient festival [*heortē*], once celebrated by the entire population [of Athens], but later only by the artisans. It was named this way because [the god] Hephaistos in the region of Athens [= Attica] was known for the working [*ergazesthai*] of bronze [*khalkos*]. It [= the festival] was celebrated on the last day of the month Pyanepsion. And it is on this day that the priestesses [*hiereiai*], together with the [selected girls known as the] *Arrhēphoroi*, set the warp [of the Peplos of Athena] in the loom.
>
> *Suda* s.v. Χαλκεῖα[79]

3§99. The day when this festival of the Khalkeia was celebrated, which was the last day of the month Pyanepsion, preceded by nine months the 28th day of the month Hekatombaion, which as we have seen was the birthday of the goddess Athena and the last day of the festival of the Panathenaia. That day, as we have seen, was the sacred occasion for the climactic presentation of the Peplos to the goddess. And the nine months that elapsed between the time when the weaving of the Peplos was started at the festival of the Khalkeia and the time when the fabric was presented to Athena at the festival of the

[78] Ἐργάνη: ἡ Ἀθηνᾶ, παρ' ὅσον ἔφορός ἐστι τῆς τῶν γυναικῶν ἐργασίας, ταύτῃ παρὰ Ἀθηναίοις καὶ Σαμίοις εἴρηται. σημαίνει δὲ καὶ τὴν ἐργασίαν.

[79] Χαλκεῖα: ἑορτὴ ἀρχαία καὶ δημώδης πάλαι, ὕστερον δὲ ὑπὸ μόνων ἤγετο τῶν τεχνιτῶν, ὅτι ὁ Ἥφαιστος ἐν τῇ Ἀττικῇ χαλκὸν εἰργάσατο. ἔστι δὲ ἕνῃ καὶ νέᾳ τοῦ Πυανεψιῶνος· ἐν ᾗ καὶ ἱέρειαι μετὰ τῶν ἀρρηφόρων τὸν πέπλον διάζονται.

Panathenaia matched symbolically the period of gestation leading up to the birth of the goddess.[80]

3§100. This festival of the Khalkeia celebrated the synergism of the divinities Athena and Hephaistos as models for the practice of crafts like weaving and metalworking. As the synergistic partner of Hephaistos, Athena performed her role as the *Erganē*, that is, as the divinity who presided over the *ergon* or work of weaving and even of craftsmanship in general.[81] It is relevant to note here that the traditional name for the female weavers of the Peplos at the annual Panathenaia was *Ergastīnai*:

Extract 3-J

> *Ergastīnai* are the women who weave the Peplos.
>
> Hesychius s.v. ἐργαστῖναι[82]

3§101. So, there was a link between the work of Athena, who practiced the craft of weaving her own Peplos, and the work of Hephaistos, who practiced the craft of metalwork in bronze. And, from what we have seen concerning the myth of Pandora, I can now also argue for a link between the work of the weavers who produced the Peplos of Athena and the work of the metalworkers who produced artifacts made of bronze in the sacred space of Athena. The fact that Athena presided over the craft of weaving the Peplos in conjunction with the craft of bronze metalwork is relevant to the fact that the relief work of the Pandora Frieze, which showed Pandora being dressed in a prototypical *peplos* given to her by Athena, was an artifact of metalwork in bronze. It is also relevant to the fact that the metalworker who sculpted the narrative about Pandora and her *peplos* was none other than Pheidias himself, who also metalworked the narrative of the Gigantomachy into the concave interior of the Shield of Athena—matching the narrative of the Gigantomachy woven into the Peplos of Athena.[83]

80 Scheid and Svenbro 1994:27n43.

81 Nagy *HC* 4§§192 and 229, following Parke 1977:92–93.

82 ἐργαστῖναι· αἱ τὸν πέπλον ὑφαίνουσαι. See Nagy *HC* 4§§192 and 229, with reference to the work of B. Nagy 1972. See also Aleshire and Lambert 2003, especially pp. 75–76 on the semantics of *ergazesthai* 'work', which can apply to work done on woolen fabric (just as it can apply to work done on bronze).

83 *HC* 4§230.

The Parthenon as a Perfect Masterpiece of Metonymy

3§102. Having considered, in reverse order, (1) the Pandora Frieze, (2) the interior surface of the bronze shield of Athena, (3) the relief sculptures showing the Gigantomachy on the east metopes, and (4) the presentation of the Peplos at Block 5 on the east side of the Parthenon Frieze, we have by now traced four links to the Peplos of Athena in the works of art adorning the Parthenon. Taken together, all four show that the Peplos was relevant to Athena Parthénos, the occupant of the Parthenon, not only to Athena Polias, who was the official recipient of the Peplos by virtue of being the occupant of the older temple of the goddess on top of the Acropolis. Moreover, these four links all show that the making of the Parthenon, as an artistic process, was modeled on the making of the Peplos of Athena.[84] So, if we think of these four links in terms of my definition of metonymy as an expression of meaning by way of connections, what we see in the art that went into the creation of the Parthenon is a system of connections, of mental associations, and this system matches the system of connections that we see when we contemplate the overall idea of the Peplos. So, just as the Peplos of Athena was a notionally perfect masterpiece of metonymy, so too was the Parthenon.

[84] *HC* 4§231.

Part Four

The Metonymy of a Perfect Festive Moment

4§01. In Part Three, we saw how the Parthenon Frieze tells the myth of a prototypical Panathenaic Procession. And we also saw how this myth, like the ritual of the recurrent Panathenaic Procession that it aetiologizes, follows the logic of a *metonymic sequence*. Here in Part Four, we will see in general that the culmination of such a sequence—the most decisive step in a series of consecutive steps—is a perfect festive moment. It is a moment of feeling delight in experiencing the beauty and the pleasure of attending a festival. In the ancient Greek passages that I am about to analyze, the relevant word for 'feeling delight' is *terpesthai*.

4§02. At first sight, there is a problem with the formulation I just offered. The English expression *feeling delight* seems at first too subjective for describing something that someone actually experiences at a festival: does the Greek word *terpesthai*, translated as 'feeling delight', really say anything objective about an ancient Greek festival?

4§03. In confronting this problem, I will concentrate on one particular aspect of festivals, which is, *the singing and the dancing* as described in Homeric poetry and beyond. In the course of reading these poetic descriptions, we will have ample opportunity to reconsider our first impressions about the idea of 'feeling delight' at a festival. What we will find is that the wording that expresses this idea is in fact not subjective but programmatic.

4§04. The word that I translate as 'feeling delight', *terpesthai*, is present in every one of the first eleven passages that I have selected to analyze here in Part Four: Extracts 4-A, 4-B, 4-C, 4-D, 4-E, 4-F, 4-G, 4-H, 4-I, 4-J, 4-K. The last of these eleven passages, Extract 4-K, will reveal the most decisive contextual evidence, and, by the time we reach this passage, we will have seen clearly the programmatic function of the word *terpesthai* 'feeling delight' in referring to festive moments of singing and dancing. At the end of each one of the eleven Extracts, I will add a special note drawing attention to the presence of this word *terpesthai*.

Introducing the Most Festive of All Moments in the *Iliad*

4§1. The setting for my first example of festive moments signaled by the word *terpesthai* 'feeling delight' is a passage describing a picture created by the divine artisan Hephaistos in the process of his metalworking the Shield of Achilles in *Iliad* XVIII. The picture is metalworked into the bronze surface of the shield. The text that describes this picture, which I will quote presently in Extract 4-A, is relevant to the ten texts that will follow it in Extracts 4-B, 4-C, 4-D, 4-E, 4-F, 4-G, 4-H, 4-I, 4-J, 4-K.

4§2. In this picture, we will see a festive moment of singing and dancing, and the key word describing the reaction of all those attending is *terpesthai* 'feeling delight' at line 604 of *Iliad* XVIII here. Before we can view the text and the context, however, I need to give some background about the Homeric Shield of Achilles as a work of art in its own right.

Pattern-Weaving as a Metaphor For Metalworking

4§3. In Part Three, we saw how the visual art of weaving the Peplos of Athena was a model for the various forms of visual art that adorned the Parthenon. Relevant here is one special detail, which is the fact that the sacred charter myth about a cosmic battle between the Giants and the Olympians was not only pattern-woven into the Peplos but also metalworked into the concave interior surface of the gigantic bronze shield that was positioned next to the commensurately gigantic gold-and-ivory statue of the goddess. As we will now see, this convergence of visual narration as pattern-woven into a fabric and as metalworked into bronze is re-enacted in the picture that I am about to analyze.

4§4. This picture, metalworked into the surface of the Shield of Achilles in *Iliad* XVIII, is a Homeric masterpiece of *ekphrasis*. I have in mind here the most basic sense of this technical term *ekphrasis*, which is, *an imitation of visual art by verbal art*. In this case, the verbal art of poetry performs a narration that was supposedly performed by the visual art of metalwork in bronze. And the poetry visualizes the performer of this narration as none other than the god of metalwork himself, the divine smith Hephaistos, whose primary medium of metalwork is bronze, as we know from the Homeric description of the god as a *khalkeus* 'bronzeworker' (*Iliad* XV 309).

4§5. The performance of metalwork by Hephaistos, as we will see, is expressed by way of a powerful metaphor: in the extract that I am about to quote from *Iliad* XVIII, the god's act of metalworking his narration into bronze is compared to an act of pattern-weaving that same narration into fabric, as if the divine metalworker were pattern-weaving a *peplos*. And the word here for *pattern-weave* is *poikillein*, which occurs in the very first line of my quoted extract:

Extract 4-A

> |$_{590}$ The renowned one [= Hephaistos], the one with the two strong arms, pattern-wove [*poikillein*][1] into it [= the Shield of Achilles] a place for singing-and-dancing [*khoros*].[2] |$_{591}$ It [= the *khoros*] was just like the one that, once upon a time in far-ruling Knossos, |$_{592}$ Daedalus made for Ariadne, the one with the beautiful tresses [*plokamoi*]. |$_{593}$ There were young men there,[3] and young women who are courted with gifts of cattle, |$_{594}$ and they all were dancing [*orkheîsthai*] with each other, holding hands at the wrist. |$_{595}$ The girls were wearing delicate dresses, while the boys were clothed in tunics [*khitōn* plural] |$_{596}$ well woven, gleaming exquisitely, with a touch of olive oil. |$_{597}$ The girls had beautiful garlands [*stephanai*], while the boys had knives |$_{598}$ made of gold, hanging from knife-belts made of silver. |$_{599}$ Half the time they moved fast in a circle, with expert steps, |$_{600}$ showing the greatest ease, as when a wheel, solidly built, is given a spin by the hands |$_{601}$ of a seated potter, who is testing it whether it will run well. |$_{602}$ The other half of the time they moved fast in straight lines, alongside each other. |$_{603}$ A huge crowd stood around the place of the song-and-dance [*khoros*] that rouses desire, |$_{604}$ and they were feeling delight [*terpesthai*];[4] in their midst sang-and-danced [*melpesthai*] a divine singer [*aoidos*], |$_{605}$ playing on the special lyre [*phorminx*];[5] two special dancers [*kubistētēre*] among them |$_{606}$ were swirling as he led [*ex-arkhein*][6] the singing-and-dancing [*molpē*] in their midst.
>
> *Iliad* XVIII 590–606[7]

1 The Homeric textual tradition shows a textual variation here: besides ποίκιλλε (*poikillein*) in the specific sense of 'pattern-weave' we find also the variant ποίησε (*poieîn*) in the general sense of 'make'.

2 As we will see, this word *khoros* can designate either the place where singing-and-dancing takes place or the group of singers-and-dancers who perform at that place.

3 The 'there' is both the place for song-and-dance and the place in the picture that is the Shield.

4 The form of the participle here, *terpomeno-* 'feeling delight', is plural (τερπόμενοι) in the majority of the medieval manuscripts, but singular (τερπόμενος) in a small minority. My translation is not affected by this textual variation. In the Greek text as I quote it in the corresponding note below, I show τερπόμενοι.

5 My translation here follows the Greek text as I quote it in the corresponding note below.

6 Again, my translation here follows the Greek text as I quote it in the corresponding note below.

7 |$_{590}$ Ἐν δὲ χορὸν ποίκιλλε περικλυτὸς ἀμφιγυήεις, |$_{591}$ τῷ ἴκελον οἷόν ποτ' ἐνὶ Κνωσῷ εὐρείῃ |$_{592}$ Δαίδαλος ἤσκησεν καλλιπλοκάμῳ Ἀριάδνῃ. |$_{593}$ ἔνθα μὲν ἠΐθεοι καὶ παρθένοι ἀλφεσίβοιαι |$_{594}$ ὀρχεῦντ' ἀλλήλων ἐπὶ καρπῷ χεῖρας ἔχοντες. |$_{595}$ τῶν δ' αἳ μὲν λεπτὰς ὀθόνας ἔχον, οἳ δὲ

Special note: As in the other ten passages in the sequence of Extracts 4-A through 4-K, I highlight here the context of *terpesthai* 'feeling delight' at line 604.

4§6. In contemplating this picture, the mind's eye sees the metalwork executed by the god Hephaistos, that ultimate bronzeworker: as I have already noted, that is what Hephaistos is actually called by Homeric poetry, a *khalkeus* 'bronzeworker' (*Iliad* XV 309). Metaphorically, however, the actual epic narration of the Shield in the *Iliad* is figured not only as metalwork, specifically as bronzework, but also as pattern-weaving: we have just seen the decisive word, *poikillein*, in the first line of the extract I just quoted (XVIII 590).

Back To Pattern-Weaving as a Metaphor For Homeric Poetry

4§7. The craft of pattern-weaving is especially privileged as a metaphor for the craft of metalworking, since it is also a metaphor for the craft of making Homeric poetry, as we saw in Part Two when we considered the Iliadic passages picturing the web that was pattern-woven by Andromache, quoted in Extract 2-O, and the web that was pattern-woven by Helen, quoted in Extract 2-P. Virgil understood this privileging of the metaphor of pattern-weaving: in the *Aeneid*, the metalwork of the divine smith Vulcan in producing the Shield of Aeneas is described there as an act of weaving a 'web', a *textus* (*Aeneid* 8.625).[8]

4§8. So, the *ekphrasis* of the Shield of Achilles in *Iliad* XVIII is one step removed from a metaphor for Homeric poetry, since the metaphor that compares the metalworking of this Shield to the pattern-weaving of a web can be seen as an ingenious substitution for the metaphor that compares the making of Homeric poetry itself to this same privileged process of pattern-weaving.

χιτῶνας |$_{596}$ εἵατ' ἐϋννήτους, ἦκα στίλβοντας ἐλαίῳ· |$_{597}$ καί ῥ' αἳ μὲν καλὰς στεφάνας ἔχον, οἳ δὲ μαχαίρας |$_{598}$ εἶχον χρυσείας ἐξ ἀργυρέων τελαμώνων. |$_{599}$ οἳ δ' ὁτὲ μὲν θρέξασκον ἐπισταμένοισι πόδεσσι |$_{600}$ ῥεῖα μάλ', ὡς ὅτε τις τροχὸν ἄρμενον ἐν παλάμῃσιν |$_{601}$ ἑζόμενος κεραμεὺς πειρήσεται, αἴ κε θέῃσιν· |$_{602}$ ἄλλοτε δ' αὖ θρέξασκον ἐπὶ στίχας ἀλλήλοισι. |$_{603}$ πολλὸς δ' ἱμερόεντα χορὸν περιίσταθ' ὅμιλος |$_{604}$ τερπόμενοι· μετὰ δέ σφιν ἐμέλπετο θεῖος ἀοιδὸς |$_{605}$ φορμίζων· δοιὼ δὲ κυβιστητῆρε κατ' αὐτοὺς |$_{606}$ μολπῆς ἐξάρχοντος ἐδίνευον κατὰ μέσσους. The Greek text that I quote in lines 605–606 here follows the reading given in the edition of the *Iliad* by Wolf 1804. In the analysis that follows, I will defend the validity of this reading. I also note here, in passing, the textual variation between τερπόμενοι and τερπόμενος at line 604 in the medieval manuscript tradition. We find the plural form τερπόμενοι in a majority of the manuscripts, while the singular τερπόμενος is attested in a small minority. My translation of line 604, as I indicate in my corresponding note on this line, is not affected by this textual variation. In the text of Athenaeus (5.181b and 5.181d) where he quotes this same line 604 of *Iliad* XVIII and the corresponding line 17 of *Odyssey* iv, which I will quote in Extract 4-D, we read τερπόμενος in the case of the *Odyssey* and τερπόμενοι in the case of the *Iliad*.

8 *HPC* II§413 p. 291.

Pattern-Weaving Homer Himself into his Own Web

4§9. Having just considered again the centrality of pattern-weaving as a metaphor for the verbal art of Homeric poetry, this time in the context of lines 590–606 in *Iliad* XVIII, quoted in Extract 4-A, I now take a closer look at lines 603–606 in that same extract. We find in these four lines something we see nowhere else in texts of the *Iliad* as they have survived into our time. Right in the center of the festive scene that is pattern-woven into the metaphorical web of pictures created by Homeric poetry is a singer who is none other than Homer himself.

4§10. Perhaps this Homer is not the kind of Homer we may have expected to find, but here he is, for all to see. That is what I will now argue.

Homer as a Lead Singer

4§11. In arguing that the singer we see in lines 603–606 of *Iliad* XVIII is meant to be Homer himself, I start by focusing on the fact that this singer is shown here in the act of taking the lead in the performance of a *khoros*. This word *khoros* means 'chorus' in the sense of *a singing-and-dancing group*.[9] I quickly add here in passing that I have started to use hyphens in saying *singing-and-dancing*, but I will postpone till a later point my rationale for using such a format.

4§12. To reword my argument in terms of this meaning of *khoros* 'chorus' as *a singing-and-dancing group*, I am saying that Homer in the present context is imagined as a lead singer who participates in the singing-and-dancing of such a choral group. In making this argument, I will highlight five words that we find in lines 603–606 of *Iliad* XVIII. I start by quoting again these four lines:

Extract 4-B (four lines re-quoted from Extract 4-A)

> $|_{603}$ A huge crowd stood around the place of the song-and-dance [*khoros*] that rouses desire, $|_{604}$ and they were feeling delight [*terpesthai*]; in their midst sang-and-danced [*melpesthai*] a divine singer [*aoidos*], $|_{605}$ playing on the special lyre [*phorminx*];[10] two special dancers [*kubistētēre*] among them $|_{606}$ were swirling as he led [*ex-arkhein*][11] the singing-and-dancing [*molpē*] in their midst.
>
> *Iliad* XVIII 603–606[12]

9 For me the ideal introduction to the subject of ancient Greek choruses is Calame 2001.

10 My translation here follows the Greek text as I quote it in the corresponding note below.

11 Again, my translation here follows the Greek text as I quote it in the corresponding note below.

12 $|_{603}$ πολλὸς δ' ἱμερόεντα χορὸν περιίσταθ' ὅμιλος $|_{604}$ τερπόμενοι· μετὰ δέ σφιν ἐμέλπετο θεῖος ἀοιδὸς $|_{605}$ φορμίζων· δοιὼ δὲ κυβιστητῆρε κατ' αὐτοὺς $|_{606}$ μολπῆς ἐξάρχοντος ἐδίνευον κατὰ μέσσους.

Special note: As in the other ten passages in the sequence of Extracts 4-A through 4-K, I highlight here the context of *terpesthai* 'feeling delight' at line 604.

4§13. I have already indicated, in the special note immediately above, the first of the five words that especially concern me in Extract 4-B here, which is *terpesthai* 'feeling delight' at line 604. But I am not yet ready to explain my reasons for highlighting this word.

4§14. So, without any further explanation for now, I proceed to the second of the five words that I highlight here, which is the noun *khoros* 'chorus' at line 603. In general, as I have already observed with reference to an earlier occurrence of *khoros*, at line 590 as quoted in Extract 4-A, this word can refer not only to a choral group of singers-and-dancers but also to the place where the singing-and-dancing happens, and the relationship of the place to the group inside that place is a fine example of *synecdoche*: the place for the grouping is seen as the grouping itself. And, to return to my translation of line 603, the word *khoros* in this context can refer not only to a singing-and-dancing group but also to the place where the group is performing.

4§15. The third and the fourth words that I highlight here in lines 603–606 of *Iliad* XVIII are the verb *melpesthai* at line 604 and the noun *molpē* at line 606: both of these words, as we know from other contexts, refer to the combined activities of singing and dancing in a *khoros* or choral group.[13] Because these words *melpesthai* and *molpē* combine the idea of singing with the idea of dancing, I will consistently translate them in a hyphenated format, 'singing-and-dancing'. In fact, I have been using this format from the start in defining the word *khoros* as a 'singing-and-dancing group', in order to highlight the fact that this Greek word *khoros*, unlike the borrowed English word *chorus*, includes dance.

4§16. The fifth and last word that I highlight in this passage is the verb *ex-arkhein* at line 606, which signals an individuated act of performance that interacts with the collective performance of a *khoros* as a singing-and-dancing group.[14]

4§17. I now offer an overall interpretation of *Iliad* XVIII 603–606, as just quoted in Extract 4-B, in which these five words occur. I focus on the picturing of an individuated singer who is singing while playing on a *phorminx*, which is a special kind of lyre. He is flanked by two individuated dancers, *kubistētēre*. The three of them are surrounded by a choral group of radiant young men and women who are not only dancing but also evidently singing, as we see from the contexts of the words *khoros* at line 603 and *melpesthai*/*molpē* at lines 604/606.

[13] *PH* 12§29 p. 350 and p. 351n64. Also *HC* 2§75.

[14] *HC* 2§74. See also *HC* 2§§65–82, with reference to the formulation of Aristotle *Poetics* 1449a10–11, which is relevant to a wide variety of poetic contexts involving the verb *ex-arkhein* (also *arkhein*) in the sense of 'lead a performance of singers-dancers'.

The lead singer himself is not only singing but also dancing—*or at least he is participating in the overall choral dancing*, as we see again from the contexts of the words *melpesthai/molpē* at lines 604 /606. So, this lead singer too is part of the overall *khoros*. And all of them—the lead singer together with the choral group—are performing to the delight of a huge crowd. Here I come back to the programmatic word *terpesthai* 'feeling delight' at line 604.

4§18. I said a while ago that Homer, as pattern-woven into the metaphorical web created by Homeric poetry, is here for all to see. But now I must add a major qualification. The fact is, Homer is "here" only in one version of the Homeric textual tradition. We will now consider an alternative version—and this version is the one that actually survives in the medieval manuscripts—*where we see no Homer at all*. I now show the text of this alternative version:

Extract 4-C (three lines different in meaning from the four lines quoted in Extract 4-B)

> |$_{603}$ A huge crowd stood around the place of the song-and-dance [*khoros*] that rouses desire, |$_{604}$ and they were feeling delight [*terpesthai*]; in their midst *sang-and-danced* [*melpesthai*] a divine singer [*aoidos*], |$_{605}$ playing on the special lyre [*phorminx*];[15] two special dancers [*kubistētēre*] among them |$_{606}$ were swirling as they led [*ex-arkhein*][16] the singing-and-dancing [*molpē*] in their midst.
>
> *Iliad* XVIII 603–606[17]

Special note: as in the other ten passages in the sequence of Extracts 4-A through 4-K, I highlight here the context of *terpesthai* 'feeling delight' at line 604.

4§19. A part of the wording here—the part that I indicate with a double strikethrough—is not attested in the medieval manuscript tradition: "|$_{604}$ and they were feeling delight [*terpesthai*]; in their midst *sang-and-danced* [*melpesthai*] a divine singer [*aoidos*], |$_{605}$ playing on the special lyre [*phorminx*]; two special dancers [*kubistētēre*] among them |$_{606}$ ..."[18] This missing part in *Iliad* XVIII 603–606

[15] The deletion here is in line with the Greek text as I quote it in the corresponding note below, where we see an omission of the wording μετὰ δέ σφιν ἐμέλπετο θεῖος ἀοιδὸς |$_{605}$ φορμίζων.

[16] My translation here follows the Greek text as I quote it in the corresponding note below, where we read ἐξάρχοντες and not ἐξάρχοντος.

[17] |$_{603}$ πολλὸς δ' ἱμερόεντα χορὸν περιίσταθ' ὅμιλος |$_{604}$ τερπόμενοι· μετὰ δέ σφιν ἐμέλπετο θεῖος ἀοιδὸς |$_{605}$ φορμίζων· δοιὼ δὲ κυβιστητῆρε κατ' αὐτοὺς |$_{606}$ μολπῆς ἐξάρχοντες ἐδίνευον κατὰ μέσσους. The Greek text that I quote here in lines 604 and 606 follows the reading given in the medieval manuscript tradition of the *Iliad*, omitting the words μετὰ δέ σφιν ἐμέλπετο θεῖος ἀοιδὸς |$_{605}$ φορμίζων· as printed in the edition of Wolf 1804.

[18] |$_{604}$ τερπόμενοι· μετὰ δέ σφιν ἐμέλπετο θεῖος ἀοιδὸς |$_{605}$ φορμίζων· δοιὼ δὲ κυβιστητῆρε κατ' αὐτοὺς |$_{606}$ ...

was restored by Friedrich August Wolf in his 1804 edition of the *Iliad*, and the relevant line-numbering 604–605 in current editions of the *Iliad* reflects that restoration, going back to the edition of Wolf.[19] The restoration, as I call it, is based on what we read in a source that dates back to the late second century CE, Athenaeus (his relevant text can be found at 5.180c–e, 181a–f).[20] From this source, we learn about the treatment of *Iliad* XVIII 603–606 in the Homeric text edited by Aristarchus, whose editorial work can be dated to the middle of the second century BCE. As we learn from Athenaeus (5.181c), Aristarchus rejected as un-Homeric the part of the wording that I have translated this way: "$|_{604}$ ... in their midst sang-and-danced [*melpesthai*] a divine singer [*aoidos*], $|_{605}$ playing on the special lyre [*phorminx*] ... $|_{606}$ ..."[21] But, as we also learn from Athenaeus (again 5.181c), Aristarchus did not reject the same wording in another Homeric context, at *Odyssey* iv 17–18, where we read once again: "$|_{17}$ ... in their midst sang-and-danced [*melpesthai*] a divine singer [*aoidos*], $|_{18}$ playing on the special lyre [*phorminx*] ... $|_{19}$ ..."[22] And, in fact, this wording is preserved for *Odyssey* iv 17–18 in the medieval manuscript tradition.

4§20. I quote here the full context of the passage I just cited from the *Odyssey*:

Extract 4-D

> $|_{15}$ So they feasted throughout the big palace with its high ceilings, $|_{16}$ both the neighbors and the kinsmen of glorious Menelaos, $|_{17}$ and they were feeling delight [*terpesthai*]; in their midst sang-and-danced [*melpesthai*] a divine singer [*aoidos*], $|_{18}$ playing on the special lyre [*phorminx*]; two special dancers [*kubistētēre*] among them $|_{19}$ were swirling as he led [*ex-arkhein*][23] the singing-and-dancing [*molpē*] in their midst.
>
> *Odyssey* iv 15–19[24]

Special note: As in the other ten passages in the sequence of Extracts 4-A through 4-K, I highlight here the context of *terpesthai* 'feeling delight' at line 17.

19 Wolf in his *Prolegomena ad Homerum* (1795 §49n49) already comments on his restoration. Revermann 1998 tracks the vast array of published opinions on *Iliad* XVIII 603–606 since Wolf's *Prolegomena*.

20 The relevant testimony of this ancient source is dismissed by Revermann 1998. I strongly disagree with this move.

21 $|_{604}$ ... μετὰ δέ σφιν ἐμέλπετο θεῖος ἀοιδὸς $|_{605}$ φορμίζων· ... $|_{606}$ ...

22 $|_{17}$ ... μετὰ δέ σφιν ἐμέλπετο θεῖος ἀοιδὸς $|_{18}$ φορμίζων· ... $|_{19}$ ...

23 My translation here follows the Greek text as I quote it in the corresponding note below.

24 $|_{15}$ ὣς οἱ μὲν δαίνυντο καθ' ὑψερεφὲς μέγα δῶμα $|_{16}$ γείτονες ἠδὲ ἔται Μενελάου κυδαλίμοιο, $|_{17}$ τερπόμενοι· μετὰ δέ σφιν ἐμέλπετο θεῖος ἀοιδὸς $|_{18}$ φορμίζων· δοιὼ δὲ κυβιστητῆρε κατ' αὐτοὺς $|_{19}$ μολπῆς ἐξάρχοντος ἐδίνευον κατὰ μέσσους.

4§21. I just quoted the reading 'as he led' (*ex-arkhontos*), indicated by Athenaeus (5.180d, 5.181d) both for this line, at *Odyssey* iv 19, and for the line at *Iliad* XVIII 606.[25] With regard to this reading, Athenaeus (5.180d) also indicates that the editor Aristarchus and his followers had accepted an alternative reading 'as they led' (*ex-arkhontes*) at *Odyssey* iv 19—as also in *Iliad* XVIII 606.[26] In fact, it is this alternative reading (*ex-arkhontes*) that we find preserved in the medieval manuscripts of both the *Iliad* and the *Odyssey*. Still, as the wording of Athenaeus indicates further, his own preferred reading 'as he led' (*ex-arkhontos*) existed in ancient times as a textual variant that had been noted by Aristarchus—even though that editor preferred the alternative textual variant 'as they led' (*ex-arkhontes*).

4§22. I focus here on the methodology of Aristarchus in making these judgments. Here was a scholar whom the ancient world generally acclaimed as the greatest of all experts in the editing of the Homeric texts. His working procedure was to track variations in the Homeric textual tradition by collating manuscripts that were available to him—and then to publish in his *hupomnēmata* or 'commentaries' his scholarly judgments in choosing which textual variants were authentically Homeric and which ones were supposedly not.[27] In the case of line 606 in *Iliad* XVIII, I argue, we are dealing with two textual variants that were known to Aristarchus, 'as he led' (*ex-arkhontos*) and 'as they led' (*ex-arkhontes*); in his commentaries, he evidently expressed his judgment that the second of these variants was authentically Homeric while the first was supposedly un-Homeric.[28]

4§23. Then, about 350 years later, Athenaeus seized an opportunity to show off his own learning by criticizing this particular judgment of Aristarchus about the two textual variants, arguing that the authentically Homeric version is really the first one, 'as he led' (*ex-arkhontos*) and not the second one, 'as they led' (*ex-arkhontes*).

4§24. In the larger context of the passage where line 606 occurs, that is, in lines 603–606 of *Iliad* XVIII, Aristarchus had evidently found a related textual variation, in the form of a longer four-line version as quoted in Extract 4-B and a shorter three-line version as quoted in Extract 4-C. In the case of these lines 603–606 of *Iliad* XVIII, Aristarchus judged the shorter three-line textual variant of this passage to be the authentically Homeric one. And the three-line variant requires the reading 'as they led' (*ex-arkhontes*), since there exists in this version no singular referent to which the alternative reading 'as he led' (*ex-arkhontos*)

25 $|_{19}$ ... ἐξάρχοντος and $|_{606}$ ... ἐξάρχοντος.

26 $|_{19}$ ... ἐξάρχοντες and $|_{606}$ ... ἐξάρχοντες.

27 More in *HTL* 48–54, 63–64, 70–71 on the editorial methodology of Aristarchus in analyzing textual variants that he collected on the basis of collating Homeric texts.

28 *HC* 2§74.

could refer. Only in the case of the four-line variant could there be room for allowing either the reading 'as they led' (*ex-arkhontes*), with the plural referent, or the reading 'as he led' (*ex-arkhontos*), with the singular referent. In this case, it all depends on whether the leading of the chorus is ascribed respectively to the one singer or to the two dancers.

4§25. And, here again, Aristarchus is criticized for his judgment by Athenaeus, who argues on the basis of comparable contexts that only a singer can lead off a choral performance, not dancers. In terms of this criticism, only the longer four-line version could be authentic, and, even in this case, such a longer version would require the reading 'as he led' (*ex-arkhontos*), which refers to the singer, since the reading 'as they led' (*ex-arkhontes*) would be simply wrong.

4§26. In terms of my argument, however, the authenticity of the longer version does not rule out the possibility that the shorter version is also authentic. As we will see, both versions can be authenticated. And what really matters, I argue, is that Aristarchus in the course of his collating Homeric manuscripts could verify here the existence of both a longer and a shorter textual variant, and that he makes note of the variation itself in his commentaries.[29] What Athenaeus is criticizing here is simply the judgment of Aristarchus in preferring one textual variant instead of another. But the fact is, if Aristarchus had not mentioned two variants in this case, Athenaeus would have had nothing to criticize.

4§27. More important for now, both of the textual variants at line 606 of *Iliad* XVIII, 'as he led' (*ex-arkhontos*) and 'as they led' (*ex-arkhontes*), can be shown to be formulaic variants as well.[30] To say it more forcefully, the existence of these forms as textual variants was determined by their pre-existence as formulaic variants.

4§28. Here is what I mean. The form and the meaning of both variants can be explained in terms of variations that existed in the formulaic system of the Homeric language, which stemmed from an oral poetic tradition and thus did not depend on the technology of writing for either the composition or the performance of Homeric poetry. Just as any language is a system, so also the special language of Homeric poetry was a system, albeit a specialized one, and therefore this special language has to be analyzed as a system in its own right. The basic formal components of this system are known as *formulas*, and that is why I describe Homeric poetry in terms of a *formulaic system*. In using these terms *formulas* and *formulaic system*, I follow the lead of Milman Parry and

[29] I agree with Revermann 1998:36 when he says in passing that the editorial work of Aristarchus included the collating of Homeric manuscripts.

[30] Once again, *HC* 2§74; *HPC* II§435 pp. 300–301n88.

Albert Lord, who perfected a methodology for analyzing the textual tradition of Homeric poetry in terms of the formulaic system underlying the textualization of this poetry.[31]

4§29. So, applying the approach of Parry and Lord, I am arguing that the variants 'as he led' (*ex-arkhontos*) and 'as they led' (*ex-arkhontes*), attested in *Odyssey* iv 19 and in *Iliad* XVIII 606, are independent of the Homeric textual tradition and depend instead on pre-existing variations that derive from the formulaic system of Homeric poetry.[32]

4§30. These two variants, I will now go on to argue, stem from two different narrative scenarios corresponding to the longer and the shorter versions of the wording transmitted for lines 603–606 of *Iliad* XVIII. According to the shorter version as signaled by 'as they led' (*ex-arkhontes*) at line 606, which is the reading I quote in Extract 4-C, it is the two individuated dancers whose performance leads into the choral singing-and-dancing. According to the longer version as signaled by 'as he led' (*ex-arkhontos*), which is the reading I quote in Extract 4-B, the individuated singer combines his performance with the corresponding performance of two individuated dancers who flank him as he leads into the choral singing-and-dancing.

4§31. These two scenarios both resemble, in different ways, what happens in *Odyssey* viii when Demodokos the blind singer performs the second of his three songs:

Extract 4-E

> $|_{250}$ [Alkinoos is speaking.] "Let's get started. I want the best of the Phaeacian acrobatic dancers [*bētarmones*] $|_{251}$ to perform their sportive dance [*paizein*],[33] so that the stranger, our guest, will be able to tell his near-and-dear ones, $|_{252}$ when he gets home, how much better we (Phaeacians) are than anyone else $|_{253}$ in sailing and in footwork, in dance [*orkhēstus*] and song [*aoidē*]. $|_{254}$ One of you go and get for Demodokos the clear-sounding special lyre [*phorminx*], $|_{255}$ bringing it to him. It is in the palace somewhere." $|_{256}$ Thus spoke Alkinoos, the one who looks like the gods, and the herald [*kērux*] got up, $|_{257}$ ready

[31] I offer an overview of this methodology in *HQ* 13–27, focusing on the primary publications of Parry [1971] and Lord 1960.

[32] See *HC* 2§74, where I criticize the approach of Revermann 1998 in dealing with variants that he finds in Homeric references to singing and dancing and lyre-playing. In his study of these references, with a focus on *Iliad* XVIII 603–606, he persistently misreads the relevant formulaic variants as if they were exclusively textual variants, ignoring the methodology of Parry and Lord.

[33] On *paizein* as 'perform a sportive dance', see especially *Odyssey* xxiii 147. See also the Hesiodic *Shield* 277. For more on this word, see Bierl 2009:67–75.

> to bring the well carved *phorminx* from the palace of the king. $|_{258}$ And the organizers [*aisumnētai*], the nine selectmen, all got up $|_{259}$ —they belonged to the district [*dēmos*]—and they started arranging everything according to the rules of the competition [*agōn*]: $|_{260}$ they made smooth the place of the singing-and-dancing [*khoros*], and they made a wide space of competition [*agōn*]. $|_{261}$ The herald [*kērux*] came near, bringing the clear-sounding *phorminx* $|_{262}$ for Demodokos. He moved to the center [*es meson*] of the space. At his right and at his left were boys [*kouroi*] $|_{263}$ in the first stage of adolescence [*prōthēboi*], standing there, well versed in dancing [*orkhēthmos*]. $|_{264}$ They pounded out with their feet a dance [*khoros*], a thing of wonder, and Odysseus $|_{265}$ was observing the sparkling footwork. He was amazed in his heart [*thūmos*]. $|_{266}$ And he [= Demodokos], playing on the *phorminx* [*phormizein*], started [*anaballesthai*] singing beautifully $|_{267}$ about [*amphi*] the bonding [*philotēs*] of Ares and of Aphrodite, the one with the beautiful garlands [*stephanoi*], $|_{268}$ about how they, at the very beginning,[34] mated with each other in the palace of Hephaistos, $|_{269}$ in secret. [The story that has just started at line 266 now continues, ending at line 366.] $|_{367}$ These things, then, the singer [*aoidos*] was singing [*aeidein*], that very famous singer. As for Odysseus, $|_{368}$ he felt delight [*terpesthai*] in his heart as he was listening—and so too did all the others feel, $|_{369}$ the Phaeacians, those men with their long oars, men famed for their ships.
>
> *Odyssey* viii 250–269, 367–369[35]

Special note: As in the other ten passages in the sequence of Extracts 4-A through 4-K, I highlight here the context of *terpesthai* 'feeling delight' at line 368.

[34] The syntax of the indirect question here, appropriate to the introduction of the main subject of the performance, includes the concept of *ta prōta* 'in the beginning'—which has cosmogonic implications.

[35] $|_{250}$ "ἀλλ' ἄγε, Φαιήκων βητάρμονες ὅσσοι ἄριστοι, $|_{251}$ παίσατε, ὥς χ' ὁ ξεῖνος ἐνίσπῃ οἷσι φίλοισιν, $|_{252}$ οἴκαδε νοστήσας, ὅσσον περιγινόμεθ' ἄλλων $|_{253}$ ναυτιλίῃ καὶ ποσσὶ καὶ ὀρχηστυῖ καὶ ἀοιδῇ. $|_{254}$ Δημοδόκῳ δέ τις αἶψα κιὼν φόρμιγγα λίγειαν $|_{255}$ οἰσέτω, ἥ που κεῖται ἐν ἡμετέροισι δόμοισιν." $|_{256}$ ὣς ἔφατ' Ἀλκίνοος θεοείκελος, ὦρτο δὲ κῆρυξ $|_{257}$ οἴσων φόρμιγγα γλαφυρὴν δόμου ἐκ βασιλῆος. $|_{258}$ αἰσυμνῆται δὲ κριτοὶ ἐννέα πάντες ἀνέσταν, $|_{259}$ δήμιοι, οἳ κατ' ἀγῶνα ἐῢ πρήσσεσκον ἕκαστα, $|_{260}$ λείηναν δὲ χορόν, καλὸν δ' εὔρυναν ἀγῶνα. $|_{261}$ κῆρυξ δ' ἐγγύθεν ἦλθε φέρων φόρμιγγα λίγειαν $|_{262}$ Δημοδόκῳ· ὁ δ' ἔπειτα κί' ἐς μέσον· ἀμφὶ δὲ κοῦροι $|_{263}$ πρωθῆβαι ἵσταντο, δαήμονες ὀρχηθμοῖο, $|_{264}$ πέπληγον δὲ χορὸν θεῖον ποσίν. αὐτὰρ Ὀδυσσεὺς $|_{265}$ μαρμαρυγὰς θηεῖτο ποδῶν, θαύμαζε δὲ θυμῷ. $|_{266}$ αὐτὰρ ὁ φορμίζων ἀνεβάλλετο καλὸν ἀείδειν $|_{267}$ ἀμφ' Ἄρεος φιλότητος ἐϋστεφάνου τ' Ἀφροδίτης, $|_{268}$ ὡς τὰ πρῶτ' ἐμίγησαν ἐν Ἡφαίστοιο δόμοισι $|_{269}$ λάθρῃ. [The story that has just started at line 266 now continues, ending at line 366.] $|_{367}$ ταῦτ' ἄρ' ἀοιδὸς ἄειδε περικλυτός· αὐτὰρ Ὀδυσσεὺς $|_{368}$ τέρπετ' ἐνὶ φρεσὶν ᾗσιν ἀκούων ἠδὲ καὶ ἄλλοι $|_{369}$ Φαίηκες δολιχήρετμοι, ναυσικλυτοὶ ἄνδρες. At line 267, there is a variant reading attested: φιλότητα in the accusative, instead of φιλότητος in the genitive.

4§32. I paraphrase what we have just seen narrated here, in the larger context of *Odyssey* viii 248–380.[36] To start, a special lyre called the *phorminx* is brought to Demodokos (lines 254, 257), and then he proceeds *es meson* 'to the center' (262) of the space where the performance is to take place; that space is a *khoros* 'chorus' (260)—and we have already seen that this word can refer both to a singing-and-dancing group and to the place where the group performs. This space has been smoothed over (260), and it is enveloped by a wider overall space that is marked out for accommodating a vast assembly of people attending what is described here as a competitive event. The one word that is used in this context to express two meanings, both 'assembly of people' and 'competitive event', is *agōn* (259 and 260). Participating in this competitive event of choral performance are the young men of the Phaeacians, who are described as specially skilled performers at such events (248–253); among the words that we see in this description are *khoroi* 'choruses' (248), *orkhēstus* 'dancing' (253), and *aoidē* 'singing' (253). Also participating in this competitive event is the singer in the center, Demodokos himself. When this singer makes his way *es meson* 'to the center' (again, 262) of the space set aside for the performance, he is surrounded by *kouroi* 'boys' (262) whose nimble feet are already pounding out the rhythm of the song on the surface of the space set aside for singing-and-dancing. And the word for this space here again is *khoros* (264). Meanwhile the singer starts 'singing', *aeidein* (266), while accompanying himself on the special lyre called the *phorminx* (266). His song, about the love affair of Ares and Aphrodite, is now retold, and the retelling takes one hundred lines exactly within the framing narrative of the *Odyssey*: he starts at 266 and ends at 366. So, what is the reaction of the disguised Odysseus, who is the primary character attending this performance of Demodokos? The answer is, as we see in the text as I quoted it here in Extract 4-E, Odysseus *terpeto* 'felt delight' (368), and the same delighted reaction was experienced, it is said, by everyone else attending the performance (368–369). Then the virtuoso song of this individuated singer Demodokos leads into a virtuoso performance by two individuated dancers (370–379). Responding to these dancers in choral performance are the rest of the *kouroi* 'boys' (379–380).

4§33. So, in the formulaic wording that I have just paraphrased from *Odyssey* viii, we find a wealth of free-standing comparative evidence that I can cite in support of authenticating both the longer and the shorter versions of lines 603–606 in *Iliad* XVIII, as quoted respectively in Extract 4-B and Extract 4-C. These two different versions, I argue, would have suited two different eras in the evolution of Homeric poetry as a formulaic system. In an earlier era, Homer would have been appreciated as a lead singer who could interact with choral

[36] In *HPC* I§§206–209 pp. 86–88, I offer a fuller commentary on *Odyssey* viii 248–249 and 250–269.

singing-and-dancing; in a later era, by contrast, he would be a solo singer, and so he could no longer fit into a festive scene of choral performance.

4§34. For the moment, I highlight one detail that stands out in the longer and older version of lines 603–606 in *Iliad* XVIII as quoted in Extract 4-B: there is an individuated lead singer here, flanked by two individuated dancers, and this picture matches closely what we see in *Odyssey* viii 370–379, which likewise shows an individuated lead singer flanked by two individuated dancers. Conversely, the focus on the two individuated dancers instead of the one individuated singer in this part of the description in *Odyssey* viii 370–379 is comparable to what we see in the shorter and newer version of lines 603–606 in *Iliad* XVIII, quoted in Extract 4-C, where the figure of the lead singer is occluded—and thus excluded from any possibility of interacting with the choral performance that is being described.

4§35. Pursuing further my argument that the *Iliad*, like the *Odyssey*, shows a lead singer whose performance interacts with choral singing-and-dancing, I now come to a new piece of evidence. We see it in *Odyssey* xiii, where the singer Demodokos performs one last song before Odysseus leaves the land of the Phaeacians. The occasion is most festive, marking the conclusion of the overall festivities that had started in *Odyssey* viii—and had continued ever since then. Bringing these festivities to a spectacular close, Alkinoos the king of the Phaeacians slaughters a sacrificial ox to the god Zeus, and this animal sacrifice is the cue for Demodokos to emerge once again as the lead singer in the midst of a festive crowd:

Extract 4-F

> $|_{24}$ On their [= the Phaeacians'] behalf Alkinoos, the one with the holy power, sacrificed an ox $|_{25}$ to Zeus, the one who brings dark clouds, the son of Kronos, and he rules over all. $|_{26}$ Then, after burning the thigh-pieces, they feasted, feasting most gloriously, $|_{27}$ and they were feeling delight [*terpesthai*]; in their midst sang-and-danced [*melpesthai*] the divine singer [*aoidos*], $|_{28}$ Demodokos, honored by the people.
>
> *Odyssey* xiii 24–28[37]

Special note: As in the other ten passages in the sequence of Extracts 4-A through 4-K, I highlight here the context of *terpesthai* 'feeling delight' at line 27.

[37] $|_{24}$ τοῖσι δὲ βοῦν ἱέρευσ' ἱερὸν μένος Ἀλκινόοιο $|_{25}$ Ζηνὶ κελαινεφέϊ Κρονίδῃ, ὃς πᾶσιν ἀνάσσει. $|_{26}$ μῆρα δὲ κήαντες δαίνυντ' ἐρικυδέα δαῖτα $|_{27}$ τερπόμενοι· μετὰ δέ σφιν ἐμέλπετο θεῖος ἀοιδός $|_{28}$ Δημόδοκος, λαοῖσι τετιμένος.

4§36. We see here in line 27 of *Odyssey* xiii exactly the same wording that we saw in line 17 of *Odyssey* iv, quoted in Extract 4-D. More important, we see the same wording also in line 604 of *Iliad* XVIII, quoted in Extract 4-B and already in Extract 4-A, that is, in the line that shows a part of the longer version of *Iliad* XVIII 603–606 as restored by Wolf. In each one of these three lines that I just listed, *Odyssey* xiii 27 and iv 17 and *Iliad* XVIII 604, a solo singer is shown, but the individuated soloist is leading into a choral song combined with dance, as signaled by the word *melpesthai* in all three contexts. This word, as we have seen, combines the idea of singing with the idea of dancing—that is, choral dancing. That is why I have translated *melpesthai* all along in a hyphenated format, 'singing-and-dancing'.

4§37. The passage I have just quoted in Extract 4-F from *Odyssey* xiii 24–28 is a most decisive piece of comparative evidence validating the authenticity of the corresponding passage in the longer version of *Iliad* XVIII 603–606, quoted earlier in Extract 4-B and even earlier in Extract 4-A. Both of these two passages show an individuated lead singer in the midst of a festive crowd surrounding a choral performance that brings delight to all. Both in *Odyssey* xiii 27 and in *Iliad* XVIII 604, the decisive word that shows the interaction of the individuated lead singer with choral performance is *melpesthai* 'sing-and-dance'.[38] But the passage in *Odyssey* xiii 24–28 occludes any direct mention of dancers, thus differing from the corresponding passage in the longer version of *Iliad* XVIII 603–606, which highlights two individuated dancers as well as a chorus. Conversely, the passage in the shorter version of *Iliad* XVIII 603–606, quoted earlier in Extract 4-C, occludes any direct mention of a singer, thus differing from the corresponding passage in *Odyssey* xiii 24–28, quoted just now in Extract 4-F, which highlights Demodokos as an individuated lead singer.

4§38. The decisive evidence of this passage in *Odyssey* xiii 24–28 is missing from the reportage of Athenaeus (5.181c) about the editorial decisions of Aristarchus concerning *Odyssey* iv 15–19 and *Iliad* XVIII 603–606. And it is missing also from the argumentations of those who build theories about various kinds of textual interpolation; according to one such theory, for example, the longer version of *Iliad* XVIII 604–605 results from some kind of "rhapsodic intervention," which supposedly happened at some undetermined stage in the history

[38] The verb *melpesthai* 'sing-and-dance' at line 604 of *Iliad* XVIII is picked up by the corresponding noun *molpē* 'singing-and-dancing' at line 606. This noun here at line 606 continues to convey the idea of singing as started by the lead singer at line 604. The singing at line 606 is now choral, combined with the choral dancing that is being highlighted in the description. Despite this highlighting of choral dance, however, the aspect of choral song in the meaning of *molpē* as 'singing-and-dancing' is maintained. Revermann 1998:29 recognizes that *molpē* at line 606 refers to choral singing as well as dancing. In this context, he describes *molpē* as "this blunt and colourless noun." I can agree only with the first part of this description.

the Homeric textual tradition.[39] The problem with this kind of theorizing is that it fails to account for the formulaic nature of such an "intervention."[40] As we have seen by now, the evidence of the wording in *Iliad* XVIII 604–605 indicates that both the shorter and the longer versions result from formulaic variation.[41]

Homer as the Lead Singer of the *Homeric Hymn to Apollo*

4§39. So far, I have highlighted three Homeric passages, two of them in the *Odyssey* and one in the *Iliad*, where we see a lead singer interacting with the performance of a choral group. Now we turn to the *Homeric Hymn* [3] *to Apollo*, where we are about to see once again a lead singer in the act of interacting with a choral performance. And, in this case, we have evidence from the historical period that the lead singer was actually recognized as Homer himself, as we learn from the explicit testimony of the historian Thucydides:

Extract 4-G

> $|_{3.104.2}$ ... After the ritual purification [of the sacred island of Delos], the Athenians at that point for the first time turned the festival known as the Delia into a quadrennial [instead of an annual] festival. $|_{3.104.3}$ Even in the remote past, there had been at Delos a great [annual] coming together of Ionians and neighboring islanders [*nēsiōtai*], and they were celebrating [ἐθεώρουν 'were making *theōriā*'] along with their wives and children, just as the Ionians in our own times come together [= at Ephesus] for [the festival of] the Ephesia. A competition [*agōn*] was held there [= in Delos], both in athletics and in *mousikē* (*tekhnē*),[42] and the cities brought choruses [*khoroi*]. $|_{3.104.4}$ Homer makes it most clear that such was the case in the following verses [*epos* plural], which come from a *prooimion*[43] of Apollo:

39 Revermann 1998:37.

40 This criticism meshes with what I said in my earlier note about the ignoring of formulaic variants.

41 There is an abbreviated version of this argument in *HC* 2§74.

42 Comparable to the *agōn* 'competition' mentioned here by Thucydides (3.104.3) is the *agōn* 'competition' in *mousikē* 'craft of the Muses' at the festival of the Panathenaia, where the word *mousikē* includes the *tekhnē* 'craft' of *rhapsōdoi* 'rhapsodes'. As my argumentation proceeds, I will have more to say about this Athenian *agōn*.

43 I leave this word *prooimion* untranslated for now. It can be used with reference to the beginning of a *humnos* or 'hymn', as in the case of the *Homeric Hymns*. At a later point, I will analyze the technical meaning of this word and its etymology.

[[beginning of quotation by Thucydides]] |$_{146}$ But when, O Phoebus [Apollo], in Delos more than anywhere else you feel delight [*terpesthai*] in your heart [*thūmos*], |$_{147}$ there the Ionians, with tunics [*khitōn* plural] trailing, gather |$_{148}$ with their children and their wives, along the causeway [*aguia*],[44] |$_{149}$ and there with boxing [*pugmakhiē*] and dancing [*orkhēstus*] and song [*aoidē*] |$_{150}$ they have you in mind and make you feel delight [*terpein*], whenever they set up a competition [*agōn*]. [[end of quotation by Thucydides, who now resumes his own comments]]

|$_{3.104.5}$ That there was also a competition [*agōn*] in *mousikē* (*tekhnē*),[45] in which the Ionians went to engage-in-competition [*agōnizesthai*], again is made clear by him [= Homer] in the following verses, taken from the same *prooimion*.[46] After making the subject of his hymn [*humnos*] the Delian chorus [*khoros*] of women, he was drawing toward the completion [*telos*] of his song of praise, drawing toward these verses [*epos* plural], in which he also makes mention of himself—

[[beginning of further quotation by Thucydides]] |$_{165}$ But come now, may Apollo be gracious, along with Artemis; |$_{166}$ and you all also, hail [*khairete*] and take pleasure, all of you [Maidens of Delos]. Keep me, even in the future, |$_{167}$ in your mind, whenever someone, out of the whole mass of earthbound humanity, |$_{168}$ comes here [to Delos], after arduous wandering, someone else, and asks this question: |$_{169}$ "O Maidens, who is for you the most pleasurable of singers |$_{170}$ that wanders here? In whom do you take the most delight [*terpesthai*]?" |$_{171}$ Then you, all of you [Maidens of Delos], must very properly respond [*hupokrinasthai*], without naming names [*aphēmōs*]:[47] |$_{172}$ "It is a blind man, and he dwells in Chios, a rugged land." [[end of quotation by Thucydides, who now resumes his own comments]]

44 On this *aguia* as the *via sacra* of Delos, see Aloni 1989:117–118.

45 The word *agōn* 'competition' as used here by Thucydides (3.104.5) needs to be correlated with his use of the same word earlier on in the passage that I am quoting here (3.104.3).

46 See my earlier note on this word.

47 In *HC* 2§27n25, I make an argument for interpreting this word *aphēmōs* (ἀφήμως) to mean 'without naming names'. The adjective ἄφημος was understood to be a synonym of ἀπευθής (as we see in the scholia to Aratus 1.270.2 ed. J. Martin 1974). This word ἀπευθής is used in the sense 'without information', as in *Odyssey* iii 88 and 184. When the Delian Maidens are asked to respond to the question "Who is the singer?", they respond without naming names, that is, without giving information about the singer's name. See also De Martino 1982:92–94. For a similar explanation, see also Burkert 1979:61.

> $|_{3.104.6}$ So much for the evidence given by Homer concerning the fact that there was even in the remote past a great coming together and festival [*heortē*] at Delos; later on, the islanders [*nēsiōtai*] and the Athenians continued to send choruses [*khoroi*], along with sacrificial offerings, but various misfortunes evidently caused the discontinuation of the things concerning the competitions [*agōnes*] and most other things—that is, up to the time in question [= the time of the ritual purification] when the Athenians set up the [quadrennial] competition [*agōn*], including chariot races [*hippodromiai*], which had not taken place before then.
>
> Thucydides 3.104.3–6[48]

Special note: As in the other ten passages in the sequence of Extracts 4-A through 4-K, I highlight here the contexts of *terpesthai* 'feeling delight' at lines 146 and 170 of the *Homeric Hymn* as quoted here.

4§40. The two sequences of verses here, as quoted by Thucydides and as attributed by him to Homer himself as the speaker of these verses, correspond to the following sequences of verses transmitted by the medieval manuscript traditions of the *Homeric Hymn* [3] *to Apollo*:

Extract 4-H

> $|_{146}$ But you, O Phoebus [Apollo], in Delos more than anywhere else feel delight [*terpesthai*] in your heart [*ētor*], $|_{147}$ where the Ionians, with tunics [*khitōn* plural] trailing, gather $|_{148}$ with their children and their

48 $|_{3.104.2}$ ... καὶ τὴν πεντετηρίδα τότε πρῶτον μετὰ τὴν κάθαρσιν ἐποίησαν οἱ Ἀθηναῖοι τὰ Δήλια. $|_{3.104.3}$ ἦν δέ ποτε καὶ τὸ πάλαι μεγάλη ξύνοδος ἐς τὴν Δῆλον τῶν Ἰώνων τε καὶ περικτιόνων νησιωτῶν· ξύν τε γὰρ γυναιξὶ καὶ παισὶν ἐθεώρουν, ὥσπερ νῦν ἐς τὰ Ἐφέσια Ἴωνες, καὶ ἀγὼν ἐποιεῖτο αὐτόθι καὶ γυμνικὸς καὶ μουσικός, χορούς τε ἀνῆγον αἱ πόλεις. $|_{3.104.4}$ δηλοῖ δὲ μάλιστα Ὅμηρος ὅτι τοιαῦτα ἦν ἐν τοῖς ἔπεσι τοῖσδε, ἅ ἐστιν ἐκ προοιμίου Ἀπόλλωνος· [[beginning of quotation by Thucydides]] $|_{146}$ ἀλλ' ὅτε Δήλῳ, Φοῖβε, μάλιστά γε θυμὸν ἐτέρφθης, $|_{147}$ ἔνθα τοι ἑλκεχίτωνες Ἰάονες ἠγερέθονται $|_{148}$ σὺν σφοῖσιν τεκέεσσι γυναιξί τε σὴν ἐς ἀγυιάν· $|_{149}$ ἔνθα σε πυγμαχίῃ τε καὶ ὀρχηστυῖ καὶ ἀοιδῇ $|_{150}$ μνησάμενοι τέρπουσιν, ὅταν καθέσωσιν ἀγῶνα. [[end of quotation by Thucydides]] $|_{3.104.5}$ ὅτι δὲ καὶ μουσικῆς ἀγὼν ἦν καὶ ἀγωνιούμενοι ἐφοίτων ἐν τοῖσδε αὖ δηλοῖ, ἅ ἐστιν ἐκ τοῦ αὐτοῦ προοιμίου· τὸν γὰρ Δηλιακὸν χορὸν τῶν γυναικῶν ὑμνήσας ἐτελεύτα τοῦ ἐπαίνου ἐς τάδε τὰ ἔπη, ἐν οἷς καὶ ἑαυτοῦ ἐπεμνήσθη· [[beginning of further quotation by Thucydides]] $|_{165}$ ἀλλ' ἄγεθ', ἱλήκοι μὲν Ἀπόλλων Ἀρτέμιδι ξύν, $|_{166}$ χαίρετε δ' ὑμεῖς πᾶσαι. ἐμεῖο δὲ καὶ μετόπισθε $|_{167}$ μνήσασθ', ὁππότε κέν τις ἐπιχθονίων ἀνθρώπων $|_{168}$ ἐνθάδ' ἀνείρηται ταλαπείριος ἄλλος ἐπελθών· $|_{169}$ ὦ κοῦραι, τίς δ' ὔμμιν ἀνὴρ ἥδιστος ἀοιδῶν $|_{170}$ ἐνθάδε πωλεῖται, καὶ τέῳ τέρπεσθε μάλιστα; $|_{171}$ ὑμεῖς δ' εὖ μάλα πᾶσαι ὑποκρίνασθαι ἀφήμως· $|_{172}$ τυφλὸς ἀνήρ, οἰκεῖ δὲ Χίῳ ἔνι παιπαλοέσσῃ." [[end of quotation by Thucydides]] $|_{3.104.6}$ τοσαῦτα μὲν Ὅμηρος ἐτεκμηρίωσεν ὅτι ἦν καὶ τὸ πάλαι μεγάλη ξύνοδος καὶ ἑορτὴ ἐν τῇ Δήλῳ· ὕστερον δὲ τοὺς μὲν χοροὺς οἱ νησιῶται καὶ οἱ Ἀθηναῖοι μεθ' ἱερῶν ἔπεμπον, τὰ δὲ περὶ τοὺς ἀγῶνας καὶ τὰ πλεῖστα κατελύθη ὑπὸ ξυμφορῶν, ὡς εἰκός, πρὶν δὴ οἱ Ἀθηναῖοι τότε τὸν ἀγῶνα ἐποίησαν καὶ ἱπποδρομίας, ὃ πρότερον οὐκ ἦν.

circumspect wives. $|_{149}$ And they with boxing and dancing [*orkhēthmos*] and song [*aoidē*] $|_{150}$ have you in mind and make you feel delight [*terpein*], whenever they set up a competition [*agōn*].

Homeric Hymn [3] *to Apollo* 146–150[49]

Special note: As in the other ten passages in the sequence of Extracts 4-A through 4-K, I highlight here the context of *terpesthai* 'feeling delight' at line 146.

Extract 4-I

$|_{165}$ But come now, may Apollo be gracious, along with Artemis; $|_{166}$ and you all also, hail [*khairete*] and take pleasure, all of you [Maidens of Delos]. Keep me, even in the future, $|_{167}$ in your mind, whenever someone, out of the whole mass of earthbound humanity, $|_{168}$ arrives here [to Delos], after arduous wandering, as a guest entitled to the rules of hosting, and asks this question: $|_{169}$ "O Maidens, who is for you the most pleasurable of singers $|_{170}$ that wanders here? In whom do you take the most delight [*terpesthai*]?" $|_{171}$ Then you, all of you [Maidens of Delos], must very properly respond [*hupokrinasthai*] about me [*aph' hēmeōn*]: $|_{172}$ "It is a blind man, and he dwells in Chios, a rugged land."

Homeric Hymn [3] *to Apollo* 165–172[50]

Special note: As in the other ten passages in the sequence of Extracts 4-A through 4-K, I highlight here the context of *terpesthai* 'feeling delight' at line 170.

4§41. At line 171 of this version as we find it in the medieval manuscript tradition, I show the variant reading *aph' hēmeōn* (ἀφ' ἡμέων). There are other corresponding variant readings also attested in the manuscripts, but I single out this one because it is comparable in its formulaic function to the variant reading *aphēmōs* (ἀφήμως) that we have already seen in the version quoted by Thucydides. I translate the variant reading *aph' hēmeōn* (ἀφ' ἡμέων) as 'about me', to be contrasted with the variant reading *aphēmōs* (ἀφήμως), which I translated as meaning 'without naming names'. As I will argue, both *aph' hēmeōn* and *aphēmōs* are authentic formulaic variants, and both of them are relevant to the

49 $|_{146}$ ἀλλὰ σὺ Δήλῳ, Φοῖβε, μάλιστ' ἐπιτέρπεαι ἦτορ, $|_{147}$ ἔνθα τοι ἑλκεχίτωνες Ἰάονες ἠγερέθονται $|_{148}$ αὐτοῖς σὺν παίδεσσι καὶ αἰδοίῃς ἀλόχοισιν. $|_{149}$ οἱ δέ σε πυγμαχίῃ τε καὶ ὀρχηθμῷ καὶ ἀοιδῇ $|_{150}$ μνησάμενοι τέρπουσιν, ὅταν στήσωνται ἀγῶνα.

50 $|_{165}$ ἀλλ' ἄγεθ', ἱλήκοι μὲν Ἀπόλλων Ἀρτέμιδι ξύν, $|_{166}$ χαίρετε δ' ὑμεῖς πᾶσαι· ἐμεῖο δὲ καὶ μετόπισθε $|_{167}$ μνήσασθ', ὁππότε κέν τις ἐπιχθονίων ἀνθρώπων $|_{168}$ ἐνθάδ' ἀνείρηται ξεῖνος ταλαπείριος ἐλθών· $|_{169}$ ὦ κοῦραι, τίς δ' ὔμμιν ἀνὴρ ἥδιστος ἀοιδῶν $|_{170}$ ἐνθάδε πωλεῖται, καὶ τέῳ τέρπεσθε μάλιστα; $|_{171}$ ὑμεῖς δ' εὖ μάλα πᾶσαι ὑποκρίνασθαι ἀφ' ἡμέων· $|_{172}$ τυφλὸς ἀνήρ, οἰκεῖ δὲ Χίῳ ἔνι παιπαλοέσσῃ.

role of Homer as lead singer. In both versions, as we will see, the context is opaque and riddling.

The Riddling of Homer in the *Homeric Hymn to Apollo*

4§42. In the case of the variant *aph' hēmeōn* at line 171 of the *Homeric Hymn to Apollo* in a version that survives in the medieval manuscript tradition, as we read it in Extract 4-I, my translation 'about me' is a cover for the deeper meaning of this expression, which is 'by me'. As I will argue, the Maidens of Delos are being prompted 'by me' to respond dialogically to a question 'about me'.[51] And the reference to 'me' here, as we will see, is a riddling way of referring to Homer himself. The wording of Homer is coming 'from me' and is thus worded 'by me' to become the wording 'about me'.

4§43. Similarly in the case of the variant *aphēmōs* in the version of line 171 quoted by Thucydides, as we read in in Extract 4-G, the meaning 'without naming names' signals the fact that the Maidens are being prompted to identify Homer in a riddling way, without naming him directly.[52]

4§44. And who are these Maidens of Delos, so prominently featured here in the *Homeric Hymn to Apollo*? As I argue in the book *Homer the Classic*, the *Hymn* pictures the Maidens as the local Muses of Delos who sing-and-dance as a prototypical chorus, which is parallel to the picturing of Homer as a prototypical lead singer.[53]

4§45. In this context of choral performance, I highlight the fact that the Delian Maidens in the *Homeric Hymn to Apollo* are described as masters of mimesis or 're-enactment' (verb *mīmeîsthai* at verse 163).[54] This reference is saying something that is fundamentally true about choral performance in general, which as we know from the surviving textual evidence is highly mimetic. A shining example is the extant body of choral "lyric" songs composed by Pindar in the fifth century BCE.[55]

4§46. At a later point in my argumentation, I will elaborate on the mimetic power of Pindar's songs. For now, however, I extend the analysis from the

[51] There is an earlier version of my argument in *HPC* I§26 p. 17n27.

[52] Again, there is an earlier version of my argument in *HPC* I§26 p. 17n25.

[53] *HC* 2§§27–40.

[54] Commentary in *HC* 2§27n22.

[55] In the case of Pindar's victory odes, for example, the speaking "I" can make a mimesis of everyone and anyone who may be relevant to the act of praising the victor: the laudator, the laudandus, the *kōmos*, an optional *khoros* embedded within the *kōmos*, the ancestor, the athlete, the hero, and so on. Pindar's odes also make mimesis of a wide variety of poetic functions, including what Bundy 1972 describes as a "hymnal" function (pp. 55–57). As Bundy shows, Pindar's odes can even make mimesis of "the actual process of thought in arriving at its goal" (p. 59n59; see also pp. 61–62).

medium of choral performance to another medium. What I just said about choral performance applies to the medium of rhapsodic performance as well: this medium too is highly mimetic. A most striking example is the interaction of Homer with the Delian Maidens in the *Homeric Hymn to Apollo*. In this hymn, as we will now see, the rhapsodic medium is making a mimesis of the choral medium.

4§47. When I say *rhapsodic* here, I am referring to a non-choral medium of performance, which is a medium that is not *sung-and-danced* and not even *sung*—but *recited*. As I already noted in Part One, this medium of recitative performance was practiced by professional performers known as *rhapsōidoi* 'rhapsodes', who both competed and collaborated with each other in the performance of epic at Panhellenic festivals like the Panathenaia in Athens. I have studied this rhapsodic medium extensively in other projects, especially in the 2002 book *Plato's Rhapsody and Homer's Music*, and I present here only a brief summary of what is relevant to my ongoing argument.[56]

4§48. Presiding over the rhapsodic competitions at the festival of the Panathenaia, as we know from a fleeting reference in Plato's *Ion* (*Ion* 530d), were the *Homēridai*, who were a corporation of epic performers stemming from the island of Chios and claiming to be descended from Homer himself.[57] These *Homēridai*, masters of rhapsodic performance, also performed hymns. Unlike other hymns, which were conventionally performed in a choral mode, the hymns of the *Homēridai* were composed as well as performed only in a rhapsodic mode, as characterized by a single meter known as the dactylic hexameter. And it is these hymns that have survived down to our time in a collection of hexametric hymns that we now call the *Homeric Hymns*. As for the choral mode of composing and performing hymns, it too has survived—in the form of choral "lyric" singing, characterized by a vast multiplicity of meters. I have already highlighted the example of choral "lyric" songs composed by Pindar in the fifth century BCE. As we will now see, the Homer of the *Homeric Hymn to Apollo* performs a mimesis of such a non-rhapsodic choral mode of singing when he interacts with the chorus of the Delian Maidens—though this interaction is composed in the rhapsodic medium of the dactylic hexameter.

4§49. In the *Homeric Hymn to Apollo*, Homer re-enacts the Maidens by quoting what they say, which is said not in their own choral medium but in the rhapsodic medium of the *Hymn*.[58] So the medium of rhapsodic performance shows that it can make a mimesis of the medium of choral performance as exemplified by the Delian Maidens, who are described as the absolute masters of choral

56 In *PR* 9–35, I offer a more extensive summary.

57 More on the *Homēridai* in *HPC* I§§52–54, 138–167 pp. 28, 57–69.

58 *HC* 2§40.

mimesis. This way, Homer demonstrates that he is the absolute master of rhapsodic mimesis.[59]

4§50. The argument can be taken further: the figure of Homer in the *Homeric Hymn to Apollo* is acting as a lead singer when he prompts the Delian Maidens to perform a response, in choral song-and-dance, to a question. As we will see, the question will be a perennial one, just as the response of the Maidens will be perennial.

4§51. To understand this question that is addressed to the Delian Maidens, we need to consider the entire context of the dialogue that takes place between them and Homer. The complete wording of this dialogue is not quoted by Thucydides, and we find it attested only in the medieval manuscript tradition of the *Homeric Hymn to Apollo*. I now quote here the complete wording as preserved in that textual tradition:

Extract 4-J (including lines 165–172 as quoted already in Extract 4-I)

> $|_{165}$ But come now, may Apollo be gracious, along with Artemis; $|_{166}$ and you all also, hail [*khairete*] and take pleasure, all of you [Maidens of Delos]. Keep me, even in the future, $|_{167}$ in your mind, whenever someone, out of the whole mass of earthbound humanity, $|_{168}$ arrives here [to Delos], after arduous wandering, as a guest entitled to the rules of hosting, and asks this question: $|_{169}$ "O Maidens, who is for you the most pleasurable of singers $|_{170}$ that wanders here? In whom do you take the most delight [*terpesthai*]?" $|_{171}$ Then you, all of you [Maidens of Delos], must very properly respond [*hupokrinasthai*] about me [*aph' hēmeōn*]: $|_{172}$ "It is a blind man, and he dwells in Chios, a rugged land. $|_{173}$ and all his songs will in the future prevail as the very best." $|_{174}$ And I[60] in turn will carry your fame [*kleos*] as far over the earth $|_{175}$ as I wander, throughout the cities of men, with their fair populations. $|_{176}$ And they will all believe—I now see—[61] since it is genuine [*etētumon*]. $|_{177}$ As for me, I will not leave off [*lēgein*] making far-shooting Apollo $|_{178}$ [the subject of] my hymn [*humnos*]—the one with the silver quiver, who was borne by Leto of the fair tresses.
>
> *Homeric Hymn* [3] *to Apollo* 165–178[62]

59 Nagy 2011d:305–306.

60 Literally, 'we'.

61 The particle δή here has an "evidentiary" force, indicating that the speaker has just *seen* something, in other words, that the speaker has achieved an insight just a moment ago ("Aha, now I see that ..."). See Bakker 1997:74–80 and 2005:146.

62 $|_{165}$ ἀλλ' ἄγεθ', ἱλήκοι μὲν Ἀπόλλων Ἀρτέμιδι ξύν, $|_{166}$ χαίρετε δ' ὑμεῖς πᾶσαι· ἐμεῖο δὲ καὶ μετόπισθε $|_{167}$ μνήσασθ', ὁππότε κέν τις ἐπιχθονίων ἀνθρώπων $|_{168}$ ἐνθάδ' ἀνείρηται ξεῖνος ταλαπείριος

Special note: As in the other ten passages in the sequence of Extracts 4-A through 4-K, I highlight here the context of *terpesthai* 'feeling delight' at line 170.

4§52. Our first impression is that the question addressed here to the Delian Maidens, as quoted directly at lines 169–170, is simple and straightforward: "'|$_{169}$ O Maidens, who is for you the most pleasurable of singers |$_{170}$ that wanders here? In whom do you take the most delight [*terpesthai*]?'"[63] And the response of the Maidens at line 172, as also quoted directly, seems likewise simple and straightforward: "'|$_{172}$ It is a blind man, and he dwells in Chios, a rugged land.'"[64]

4§53. What complicates both the question and the answer, however, is that the person who originally asks the question seems at first to be distinct from Homer. Homer seems at first to be simply quoting the question. The original questioner is described at line 168 as some nameless wanderer who will come to visit Delos in the future. Let us consider again lines 167–168 in the medieval manuscript tradition, where the nameless wanderer who addresses the question to the Delian Maidens is described in this way: "'|$_{167}$ ... whenever someone, out of the whole mass of earthbound humanity, |$_{168}$ arrives here [to Delos], after arduous wandering, as a guest entitled to the rules of hosting, and asks this question ...'"[65] So, it is as if someone other than Homer were asking the question quoted by Homer.

4§54. This complication is what turns both the question and the answer into a riddle, since the nameless questioner is kept distinct here from Homer, even though the description of this nameless person as a wanderer who claims the right to be treated as a guest makes him look as if he were Homer himself. After all, Homer too is a wanderer, just as the nameless questioner is a wanderer. And Homer is a wandering singer who claims the right to be treated as a guest at whatever place he visits, as we see later on at lines 174–175, where he describes in his own words the fame that he will create for the Delian Maidens: "|$_{174}$ And I in turn will carry your fame [*kleos*] as far over the earth |$_{175}$ as I wander, throughout the cities of men, with their fair populations."[66]

ἐλθών· |$_{169}$ ὦ κοῦραι, τίς δ' ὔμμιν ἀνὴρ ἥδιστος ἀοιδῶν |$_{170}$ ἐνθάδε πωλεῖται, καὶ τέῳ τέρπεσθε μάλιστα; |$_{171}$ ὑμεῖς δ' εὖ μάλα πᾶσαι ὑποκρίνασθαι ἀφ' ἡμέων· |$_{172}$ τυφλὸς ἀνήρ, οἰκεῖ δὲ Χίῳ ἔνι παιπαλοέσσῃ. |$_{173}$ τοῦ πᾶσαι μετόπισθεν ἀριστεύουσιν ἀοιδαί. |$_{174}$ ἡμεῖς δ' ὑμέτερον κλέος οἴσομεν ὅσσον ἐπ' αἶαν |$_{175}$ ἀνθρώπων στρεφόμεσθα πόλεις εὖ ναιεταώσας· |$_{176}$ οἱ δ' ἐπὶ δὴ πείσονται, ἐπεὶ καὶ ἐτήτυμόν ἐστιν. |$_{177}$ αὐτὰρ ἐγὼν οὐ λήξω ἑκηβόλον Ἀπόλλωνα |$_{178}$ ὑμνέων ἀργυρότοξον ὃν ἠΰκομος τέκε Λητώ.

63 |$_{169}$ ὦ κοῦραι, τίς δ' ὔμμιν ἀνὴρ ἥδιστος ἀοιδῶν |$_{170}$ ἐνθάδε πωλεῖται, καὶ τέῳ τέρπεσθε μάλιστα;

64 |$_{172}$ τυφλὸς ἀνήρ, οἰκεῖ δὲ Χίῳ ἔνι παιπαλοέσσῃ.

65 |$_{167}$ ... ὁππότε κέν τις ἐπιχθονίων ἀνθρώπων |$_{168}$ ἐνθάδ' ἀνείρηται ξεῖνος ταλαπείριος ἐλθών·

66 |$_{174}$ ἡμεῖς δ' ὑμέτερον κλέος οἴσομεν ὅσσον ἐπ' αἶαν |$_{175}$ ἀνθρώπων στρεφόμεσθα πόλεις εὖ ναιεταώσας.

4§55. Homer will create fame for the Delian Maidens as an act of reciprocation for the fame that the Maidens will create for Homer when they respond to the question in the words quoted by Homer himself. The difference is, the Maidens create fame for Homer in their role as singers-dancers who are *stationary*, while Homer creates fame for the Maidens in his role as a lead singer who is *mobile*, a wanderer. And Homer is the best of all wandering singers, as predicted by the wording of the question directly quoted at lines 169–170, where we read: "'$|_{169}$ O Maidens, who is for you the most pleasurable of singers $|_{170}$ that wanders here?...'"[67] This question already presupposes that Homer is that wandering singer. So, now the meaning loops back again to lines 167–168, where the person who addresses the question to the Delian Maidens is described in this way: "'$|_{167}$ ... whenever someone, out of the whole mass of earthbound humanity, $|_{168}$ arrives here [to Delos], after arduous wandering, as a guest entitled to the rules of hosting, and asks this question ...'"[68] By now we see that this nameless wanderer, even though he seemed at first to be distinct from Homer, must be identical with Homer. And he is pictured as returning to Delos year after year to ask a question that requires the same answer year after year, and that answer is "Homer."

4§56. Similarly, as I have argued in the book *Homer the Classic*, even the alternative wording of line 168 of the *Hymn* as quoted by Thucydides about the "other someone" who comes to Delos leaves open the option of imagining that the "other someone" who asks the riddling question could still be the same singer returning again and again to Delos, and this singer could still be Homer, not a substitute for Homer.[69] The "other someone" is an "other" only so long as the identification is not yet made, since this "other" is nameless. But Homer does have a name, which is ostentatiously not spoken. If that name were in fact spoken, however, then the identification of the "other" as Homer himself could become clear. But Homer is here being identified without being named. That, I argue, is the force of the riddling expression *aphēmōs* at verse 171 of the *Homeric Hymn to Apollo* as quoted by Thucydides: as I already noted, this expression means 'without naming names'. So, the Maidens are being prompted by Homer to identify Homer in a riddling way, without naming him directly.[70]

4§57. What makes the riddle work is that Homer remains unnamed, just as the wanderer who is quoted as asking the question is not named. But the response of the Maidens, about that blind singer who dwells in Chios, gives away the answer: this wandering singer must be Homer, who is known to be blind and

67 $|_{169}$ ὦ κοῦραι, τίς δ' ὔμμιν ἀνὴρ ἥδιστος ἀοιδῶν $|_{170}$ ἐνθάδε πωλεῖται, καὶ τέῳ τέρπεσθε μάλιστα;

68 $|_{167}$ ... ὁππότε κέν τις ἐπιχθονίων ἀνθρώπων $|_{168}$ ἐνθάδ' ἀνείρηται ξεῖνος ταλαπείριος ἐλθών.

69 *HC* 2§39. On the formulaic integrity of both versions of lines 166–168 of the *Homeric Hymn to Apollo*, see Aloni 1989:111–112.

70 *HPC* I§26 p. 17n25.

who claims Chios as his residence. As we know from the *Life of Homer* traditions, which preserve evidence that is independent of the *Homeric Hymn to Apollo*, the blind singer who once resided in Chios can in fact be identified as Homer. I refer here to a detailed study of this evidence in the book *Homer the Preclassic*, where I focus on the evidence we can find in the *Herodotean Life of Homer*.[71]

4§58. So, the response of the Maidens as quoted at lines 172–173 of the *Homeric Hymn to Apollo* can be seen as a mimesis of Homer by Homer about Homer; and, to complicate matters further, this mimesis is performed for Homer by the Maidens of Delos, whose existence in the song is a mimesis by Homer because it is Homer who quotes what they say.[72] In a sense, then, the whole performance originates from this lead singer. And that, I argue, is the force of the complex expression *aph' hēmeōn* at verse 171 of the *Hymn*: the Maidens are prompted 'by me' to respond dialogically to a question 'about me', and the prompt originates 'from me'.[73]

Homer's Eternal Return to Delos in the *Homeric Hymn to Apollo*

4§59. The riddling dialogic response of the Delian Maidens to Homer is made perennial by their recurrent choral performance in response to the recurrent visit of Homer to Delos in his role as their lead singer. According to the *Homeric Hymn to Apollo*, the performance of Homer in choral interaction with the Maidens of Delos will become a perennial event. In terms of the myth that we see encapsulated in the *Hymn*, there will be an eternal return of Homer to Delos.

4§60. To back up this formulation, I will show that the *Homeric Hymn to Apollo* foretells in a riddling way a seasonally recurring re-enactment of the prototypical visit of Homer to Delos. The visit will be re-enacted year after year, in a loop that loops back eternally, so that Homer may forever interact with succeeding generations of young women who will re-enact in song-and-dance the prototypical Maidens of Delos in the act of chorally responding to Homer about Homer for Homer.

4§61. As we will now see, the occasion for Homer's eternal return to Delos was the annual festival of the Delia, and the word that signals this festival in the *Homeric Hymn to Apollo* is *agōn*, which as I already noted means 'competition'.

[71] *HPC* I§126 pp. 51–52.

[72] *HPC* I§26 p. 17n27.

[73] Again, *HPC* I§26 p. 17n27. There I note the relevance of the formulation of Bakker 2002:21 about the preverb *apo*: "In the case of verbs denoting speech, the addition of *apo-* turns the sensibility to context into an immediately dialogic sense: *apo-logeomai* 'speak in return', 'defend oneself against', *apo-krinomai* 'reason in return', 'answer'."

Homer as the Lead Singer at an Agonistic Choral Event

4§62. In *Odyssey* viii 250–269, quoted in Extract 4-E, we have seen the figure of Demodokos performing as a lead singer who interacts with a chorus that is singing-and-dancing at a competitive choral event, and the word for this event at lines 259 and 260 is *agōn*, meaning 'competition'. Here again is the wording: "$|_{259}$ ... they started arranging everything according to the rules of the competition [*agōn*]: $|_{260}$ they made smooth the place of the singing-and-dancing [*khoros*], and they made a wide space of competition [*agōn*]."[74] So too in the *Homeric Hymn to Apollo* we see the figure of Homer himself performing as a lead singer in his own right, and he too is interacting with a chorus that is singing-and-dancing at a competitive choral event called an *agōn*. That is what I will show here, arguing that the figure of Homer qualifies as a lead singer in the context of such an *agōn*. Or, to put it in terms of a modern word derived from *agōn*, Homer is a lead singer at the agonistic choral event of the Delia.

4§63. If we look back at the lengthy passage I quoted from Thucydides (3.104.3–6) in Extract 4-G, we can see that the historian uses this word *agōn* with reference to both choral and athletic competitions at the festival of the Delia (3.104.3 [choral], 3.104.5 [choral and athletic], 3.104.6 [choral and athletic]). As we can see further in Extract 4-G, Thucydides also quotes from the *Homeric Hymn to Apollo* a passage that features the same word *agōn* with reference to both choral and athletic competitions at the festival of the Delia: in one of the lines (149) quoted from the *Hymn*, the words *orkhēstus* 'dancing' and *aoidē* 'singing' indicate the choral competition, while the word *pugmakhiē* 'boxing' indicates one example of the various athletic competitions. The same three words, with one slight formal variation (*orkhēthmos* instead of *orkhēstus* for 'dancing'), are also attested in the corresponding line (149) of the version found in the medieval manuscripts of the *Hymn to Apollo* and quoted in Extract Q. From here on, whenever I refer to competitive choral events, I will substitute the term *agonistic* for *competitive* in order to evoke the meaning of *agōn* as this word is used in the contexts we have just considered.

4§64. In the case of *Odyssey* viii, the agonistic choral event is ostentatiously *festive*, as we have already seen from my overall paraphrase of the relevant narrative, but it cannot be tied to any specific *festival*. In the case of the *Homeric Hymn to Apollo*, by contrast, the corresponding agonistic choral event is pictured as taking place on a very specific occasion, at the festival of the Delia in Delos. And the choral aspect of this agonistic event that took place at the seasonally

[74] $|_{259}$ ... οἳ κατ' ἀγῶνα ἐῢ πρήσσεσκον ἕκαστα, $|_{260}$ λείηναν δὲ χορόν, καλὸν δ' εὔρυναν ἀγῶνα.

recurrent festival of the Delia is highlighted by Thucydides: he uses the word *khoros* 'chorus' in referring to female singers-and-dancers who performed at this festival (3.104.3, 3.104.5, 3.104.6). It is clear that Thucydides, in analyzing the *Homeric Hymn to Apollo*, imagined that Homer himself had once interacted with a prototypical *khoros* of these female singers-and-dancers (3.104.5), and it is also clear that he connected this prototypical *khoros* with the historical attestations of agonistic choral events that were taking place at the annual festival of the Delia (3.104.3, 3.104.6). This connection made by Thucydides is justified, since the *Homeric Hymn* in its own wording connects the Maidens of Delos with an agonistic choral event that is celebrated at the festival of the Delia in Delos. Highlighted in the *Hymn*, as I already noted, are the words *orkhēstus/orkhēthmos* 'dancing' and *aoidē* 'singing' (line 149). And here I return to a comparable highlighting in *Odyssey* viii, with reference to the skills of the Phaeacian youths in choral as well as athletic competitions (248–253): among the words that we see in this context are *khoroi* 'choruses' (248), *orkhēstus* 'dancing' (253), and *aoidē* 'singing' (253). And we have also seen the word *khoros* in the specific context of referring to the place of the singing-and-dancing (260).

4§65. In *Odyssey* viii, the reaction of all those who attend such an agonistic choral event is *delight*, as expressed by the verb *terpesthai*, meaning 'feeling delight', and such a reaction is best exemplified by the disguised Odysseus as the primary character attending the performance of Demodokos in concert with the choral singers-dancers: it is said that Odysseus, in reacting to this performance, *terpeto* 'felt delight' (368), and the same delighted reaction was experienced, it is also said, by everyone else attending the performance (368–369). Again in *Odyssey* xiii, where Demodokos is performing as a lead singer for the last time, the entire community is described as *terpomenoi* 'feeling delight' (27), as we saw in the passage I quoted in Extract 4-F.

4§66. And there is a comparable reaction in the *Homeric Hymn to Apollo*: at lines 146–150, which I have already quoted in Extract 4-G, the Ionian Greeks who celebrate the festival of the Delia, which is called an *agōn* here (150), are delighting Apollo himself: as Homer says to the god, these celebrants 'give you delight', *terpousin* (again, 150), precisely because they are celebrating the festival by way of both choral and athletic competitions (149). As the principal god who presides over the festival of the Delia, Apollo is told by Homer that 'you feel delight', *epi-terpeo*, at each recurring occasion when the festival is celebrated. Here again is the wording of the relevant lines 146–150 in the *Hymn*, which I quoted already in Extract 4-G: "$|_{146}$ But when, O Phoebus [Apollo], in Delos more than anywhere else you feel delight [*terpesthai*] in your heart [*thūmos*], $|_{147}$ there the Ionians, with tunics [*khitōn* plural] trailing, gather $|_{148}$ with their children and their wives, along the causeway [*aguia*], $|_{149}$ and there with boxing [*pugmakhiē*] and dancing [*orkhēstus*] and song [*aoidē*] $|_{150}$ they have you in mind and make you feel delight [*terpein*], whenever they set up a competition [*agōn*]."[75] The same wording, with minor variations, is attested in the corresponding text of the medieval manuscripts, and I have already quoted that text in Extract 4-H.

4§67. So the god Apollo, as a god, is the perfect model for everyone who attends the festival of the Delia: he reacts to the beauty and the pleasure of the *Hymn to Apollo* by feeling utter delight. We can see in this reaction another example of the theological principle of *do as I do*.[76] And the god's reaction is re-enacted by the Delian Maidens when they identify Homer, without naming him, as the one who surpasses all other singers in making them too feel delight, just as Homer makes everyone feel delight. Already the question asked by the nameless singer makes it clear that the ultimate purpose of Homer is to give that feeling of delight to all: "'$|_{169}$ O Maidens, who is for you the most pleasurable of singers $|_{170}$ that wanders here? In whom do you take the most delight [*terpesthai*]?'"[77] That singer, as the response of the Delian Maidens indicates in its own riddling way, must be identified as Homer.

Homer and Demodokos as Masters of Hymnic Singing

4§68. We have just seen, then, how the *Homeric Hymn to Apollo* idealizes the sheer delight that must surely be felt by all when they hear Homer himself singing at the agonistic choral event of Apollo's festival, the Delia. In the *Hymn*, a clear signal of this idealization is the programmatic use of the word *terpesthai* 'feeling delight' (146, 150, 170) in describing the reaction to Homer's song. Also in *Odyssey* viii, we have seen the same programmatic use of this word *terpesthai* 'feeling delight' in describing the reaction of all those who hear the song of Demodokos about Ares and Aphrodite (368–369). And the key word for referring to the form of singing that we see being performed in both these cases is *humnos*, which I have translated so far simply as 'hymn'. As the argumentation advances, we will see that both Homer and Demodokos are masters of such hymnic singing.

4§69. Essential for my argument is an extraordinary single line, *Odyssey* viii 429, referring to the singing of a *humnos* by Demodokos. Nowhere else in the *Odyssey*—or in the *Iliad*, for that matter—is this word *humnos* attested. For the moment, I translate the line without translating the word *humnos* itself:

[75] $|_{146}$ ἀλλ' ὅτε Δήλῳ, Φοῖβε, μάλιστά γε θυμὸν ἐτέρφθης, $|_{147}$ ἔνθα τοι ἑλκεχίτωνες Ἰάονες ἠγερέθονται $|_{148}$ σὺν σφοῖσιν τεκέεσσι γυναιξί τε σὴν ἐς ἀγυιάν· $|_{149}$ ἔνθα σε πυγμαχίῃ τε καὶ ὀρχηστυῖ καὶ ἀοιδῇ $|_{150}$ μνησάμενοι τέρπουσιν, ὅταν καθέσωσιν ἀγῶνα.

[76] For a general examination of this theological principle, I cite again Patton 2009.

[77] $|_{169}$ ὦ κοῦραι, τίς δ' ὔμμιν ἀνὴρ ἥδιστος ἀοιδῶν $|_{170}$ ἐνθάδε πωλεῖται, καὶ τέῳ τέρπεσθε μάλιστα;

Extract 4-K

> ... so that he [= Odysseus] may feel delight [*terpesthai*] at the feast [*dais*] and in listening to the *humnos* of the song.
>
> *Odyssey* viii 429[78]

Special note: As in the other ten passages in the sequence that comes to an end with this passage, Extract 4-K, I highlight here the context of *terpesthai* 'feeling delight'.

An Idealization of the Delight Experienced at a Festival

4§70. The context of line 429 in *Odyssey* viii is this: at lines 424–428, Alkinoos is speaking of his plans for the further hosting of his guest Odysseus, who has not yet identified himself. As a gracious host, Alkinoos says that he wants to arrange for his guest to be bathed in a lustral basin and then to be clothed in luxurious new garments before they all sit down to dine together, at which occasion Odysseus will receive going-away presents. The syntax of the expression 'so that he may feel delight [*terpesthai*]' at line 429 carries two levels of meaning here, since the host's wish is both general and specific. Generally, the guest should be gratified by the good hosting. But there is also the specific gratification of dining well while hearing the performance of song. The idea of dining at line 429, as expressed by the word *dais*, meaning 'feast', is closely combined here with the idea of hearing the performance of 'song', as expressed by the word *aoidē* together with *humnos*, and this combination is viewed as the best of all gratifications. In this same line 429, such sheer gratification is signaled by the programmatic word *terpesthai*, 'feeling delight'. As I will now argue, what we see here is an idealization of the experience of 'feeling delight' in the context of a *dais* 'feast', which in turn is an idealization of a festival.

4§71. As Odysseus himself says later on in *Odyssey* ix, when he finally identifies himself, there is in fact no greater gratification in the whole world that the combination of good feasting and good singing, and the model for the general reference to singing here is the singer Demodokos:

Extract 4-L

> |$_{3}$ This is indeed a beautiful thing, to listen to a singer [*aoidos*] |$_{4}$ such as this one [= Demodokos], the kind of singer that he is, comparable to the gods with the sound of his voice [*audē*], |$_{5}$ for I declare, there is no

[78] δαιτί τε τέρπηται καὶ ἀοιδῆς ὕμνον ἀκούων.

> outcome [*telos*] that has more pleasurable beauty [*kharis*] |$_{6}$ than the moment when the spirit of festivity [*euphrosunē*][79] prevails throughout the whole community [*dēmos*] |$_{7}$ and the people at the feast [*daitumones*], throughout the halls, are listening to the singer [*aoidos*] |$_{8}$ as they sit there—you can see one after the other—and they are seated at tables that are filled |$_{9}$ with grain and meat, while wine from the mixing bowl is drawn |$_{10}$ by the one who pours the wine and takes it around, pouring it into their cups. |$_{11}$ This kind of thing, as I see it in my way of thinking, is the most beautiful thing in the whole world.
>
> *Odyssey* ix 3–12[80]

4§72. The feast that is going on here is a continuation of the feast that is already signaled by the word *dais* at line 429 of *Odyssey* viii, quoted in Extract 4-K, which basically means 'feast'. In that context, *dais* refers short-range to an occasion of communal dining (*dorpon* 'dinner': 395), which will take place after sunset (417). The intended guest of honor at this feast will be Odysseus. This occasion of communal dining leads into the third song of Demodokos (484–485). But this same word *dais* at line 429 of *Odyssey* viii is also making a long-range reference: it refers metonymically to a stylized festival that has been ongoing ever since an earlier occasion of communal dining (71–72), which actually led into the first song of Demodokos (73–83). And let me go even further back in time. Leading up to the communal dining, there had been an animal sacrifice (as expressed by the word *hiereuein* 'sacrificially slaughter': 59). Then, the meat of the sacrificed animals (twelve sheep, eight pigs, and two oxen: 59–60) had been prepared to be cooked at the feast (61). And I stress that the word at line 61 for 'feast' is once again *dais*.

4§73. The noun *dais* 'feast' is derived from the verb *daiesthai* in the sense of 'distribute', which is used in contexts of animal sacrifice in referring to the 'distribution' of cooked meat among the members of a community (as in *Odyssey* xv 140 and xvii 332). Then, by way of synecdoche, the specific idea of *distribution* extends metonymically to the general idea of *feasting* and further to the even more general idea of a *festival*. Following the logic of this sequence of meanings, we see that the animal sacrifice in *Odyssey* viii (59) had led to the cooking and

[79] On the programmatic implications of *euphrosunē* 'mirth' as the atmosphere, as it were, of the poetic occasion, see *BA* 5§39 p. 91, 12§15 p. 235, and *PH* 6§92 = p. 198, following Bundy 1986:2.

[80] |$_{3}$ ἦ τοι μὲν τόδε καλὸν ἀκουέμεν ἐστὶν ἀοιδοῦ |$_{4}$ τοιοῦδ', οἷος ὅδ' ἐστί, θεοῖσ' ἐναλίγκιος αὐδήν. |$_{5}$ οὐ γὰρ ἐγώ γέ τί φημι τέλος χαριέστερον εἶναι |$_{6}$ ἢ ὅτ' ἐϋφροσύνη μὲν ἔχῃ κάτα δῆμον ἅπαντα, |$_{7}$ δαιτυμόνες δ' ἀνὰ δώματ' ἀκουάζωνται ἀοιδοῦ |$_{8}$ ἥμενοι ἑξείης, παρὰ δὲ πλήθωσι τράπεζαι |$_{9}$ σίτου καὶ κρειῶν, μέθυ δ' ἐκ κρητῆρος ἀφύσσων |$_{10}$οἰνοχόος φορέῃσι καὶ ἐγχείῃ δεπάεσσι· |$_{11}$ τοῦτό τί μοι κάλλιστον ἐνὶ φρεσὶν εἴδεται εἶναι.

the distribution of the meat (61), which had led to the communal dining (71–72), which had led to the first song of Demodokos (73–83), and so on. In terms of this logic, the metonymic use of the word *dais* 'feast' marks a whole complex of events that are typical of festivals: animal sacrifice, communal feasting, singing as well as dancing at the feast.[81]

4§74. Besides these events in *Odyssey* viii, we find another set of events that are likewise typical of festivals. Right after the first song of Demodokos has come to an end (83), the king of the Phaeacians announces that there will now be a pause in the eating and the drinking, to which he refers generally as a *dais* 'feast' (98 and 99), and the pause extends to the singing that has so far accompanied the *dais* (99). The time has come for athletic contests, that is, *aethloi/aethla* (100), to be held outside the palace, in the public gathering space of the Phaeacians (100–101, 109). The king refers to boxing, wrestling, jumping, and footracing (103). The first athletic event turns out to be the footrace (120–125), followed by wrestling (126–127), jumping (128), discus throwing (129), and boxing (130). The general term that refers to the occasion of all these events is *agōn*, meaning 'competition' or 'place of competition' (200, 238).

4§75. There is a striking parallel to be found in a passage we have already examined in the *Homeric Hymn to Apollo* (146–155), describing a festival of all Ionians gathered on the island of Delos. In this case as well, the occasion of that Delian festival is described as an *agōn* 'competition' (149). The competitive events at that festival include athletics—boxing is the example that is highlighted—as well as dancing and singing (149). Similarly in *Odyssey* viii, the competition includes singing as well as athletics, as we see from the fact that the three songs performed by Demodokos become a foil for the later performance of Odysseus starting in *Odyssey* ix. And the occasion for the singing of Demodokos in *Odyssey* viii, as we have already seen, is the ongoing *dais* 'feast' (429), which is a stylized festival—and which continues to be the occasion for the competitive performance of Odysseus in *Odyssey* ix.[82]

4§76. For the moment I concentrate not on the singing but on the athletics. As in the case of singing, athletics too can be seen as a source of 'feeling delight', *terpesthai*, to be experienced at a festival. I cite yet again the relevant lines 146–150 in the *Homeric Hymn to Apollo*, as quoted in Extract 4-G, concerning the festival of the Delia: "$|_{146}$ But when, O Phoebus [Apollo], in Delos more than anywhere else you feel delight [*terpesthai*] in your heart [*thūmos*], $|_{147}$ there the Ionians, with tunics [*khitōn* plural] trailing, gather $|_{148}$ with their children and their wives, along the causeway [*aguia*], $|_{149}$ and there with boxing [*pugmakhiē*]

[81] *HPC* I§192 p. 81.
[82] *HPC* I§§190–191 pp. 80–81.

and dancing [*orkhēstus*] and song [*aoidē*] $|_{150}$ they have you in mind and make you feel delight [*terpein*], whenever they set up a competition [*agōn*]."[83]

The Relevant Etymology of a Hittite Word

4§77. The idea of 'feeling delight' on a festive occasion, as expressed by the Greek verb *terpesthai*, is built into a related form that we find attested in the Hittite language. It is the noun *tarpa-*, attested in a Hittite text dating from the second millennium BCE. This particular text (*Keilschrifttexte aus Boghazköi* XXIII 55 I, 2–27), analyzed by Jaan Puhvel, is describing a festive occasion. There is to be an animal sacrifice (four rams and an unspecified number of bulls), and there are athletic events, which include boxing and wrestling. As Puhvel notes, "a military gathering in the iconic presence of the solar deity seems to be the occasion."[84] And the word that refers to this occasion is *tarpa-*. This word, Puhvel suggests, "would then be the 'pleasure part' of the event, the distribution, celebration, and enjoyment of winnings, perhaps even etymologically cognate with the Greek *terp*[*esthai*], 'to delight', which crops up so often in the Homeric vocabulary of sports."[85]

4§78. In making this argument, Puhvel cites a number of Homeric lines that feature this word *terpesthai*, and among them is line 131 of *Odyssey* viii, where the Phaeacians are said to be 'feeling delight' in response to the spectacular *aethloi*/*aethla* or 'contests' that are then taking place. These contests are athletic competitions, which as we have just seen are imagined as part of the ongoing festivities that are narrated in *Odyssey* viii. At line 131, the word *terpesthai* 'feeling delight' focuses on athletics as one particular aspect of the festivities, whereas later on at line 429, as quoted in Extract 4-K, the same word focuses on another aspect, which is the singing of Demodokos. In both lines, the overall context is a stylized festival.

The Festive Context of Hymnic Singing

4§79. I now turn to the *humnos* that Demodokos is singing at line 429 of *Odyssey* viii. As we have just seen in the same line, the overall context for this singing is a stylized festival, signaled by the word *dais* 'feast'. This festive context, as we will now see, is the key to understanding what the word *humnos* means here.

83 $|_{146}$ ἀλλ' ὅτε Δήλῳ, Φοῖβε, μάλιστά γε θυμὸν ἐτέρφθης, $|_{147}$ ἔνθα τοι ἑλκεχίτωνες Ἰάονες ἠγερέθονται $|_{148}$ σὺν σφοῖσιν τεκέεσσι γυναιξί τε σὴν ἐς ἀγυιάν· $|_{149}$ ἔνθα σε πυγμαχίῃ τε καὶ ὀρχηστυῖ καὶ ἀοιδῇ $|_{150}$ μνησάμενοι τέρπουσιν, ὅταν καθέσωσιν ἀγῶνα.

84 Puhvel 1988:29.

85 Again, Puhvel 1988:29.

4§80. As I showed in the book *Homer the Classic*, this word *humnos* fits all the forms of singing performed by Demodokos at the ongoing festival narrated in *Odyssey* viii, including the song that he finishes performing at line 367, which is a story about Ares and Aphrodite.[86] As I also showed in that book, the morphology of this particular song is cognate with the morphology of the so-called *Homeric Hymns*, including the *Homeric Hymn to Apollo*.[87] And, as we will see, many of the *Homeric Hymns* actually refer to themselves in terms of *humnos*. This is not to say, however, that the translation of *humnos* as 'hymn' is sufficient for helping us understand the combination of this noun with the genitive of the noun *aoidē* at line 429 of *Odyssey* viii, where Alkinoos expresses the wish that Odysseus 'may feel delight [*terpesthai*] at the feast [*dais*] and in listening to the *humnos* of the song [*aoidē*]'. We are still left with the problem of translating *humnos* in the actual context of a '*humnos* of the song [*aoidē*]'. Here is where I shift from the figure of Demodokos as a master of hymnic singing to the figure of Homer as represented in the *Homeric Hymns*, especially in the *Homeric Hymn to Apollo*. Homer too, as we will now see, is a master of hymnic singing.

A Metonymy of Hymning

4§81. The English words *hymn/hymnic/hymning* derive from the programmatic use of the Greek word *humnos* in poetry as exemplified by the *Homeric Hymns*. Each one of these *Hymns* is addressed to a god or goddess who notionally presides over the performance of the hymn, and this link to divinity is in fact the key to the meaning of *humnos*. As we will see from attestations of this word in the *Hymns*, a *humnos* is seen as a perfect beginning of a perfect song. And the beginning is perfect if the divinity to whom the song is addressed favors the performance of the beginning. But the *humnos* is not just a perfect beginning. It is also the signal of a perfect transition to the rest of the performance. By metonymy, the *humnos* includes the rest of the performance, proceeding sequentially all the way to the conclusion of the whole performance. If the performance is sequential, consequential, you know it was started by a *humnos* and you know it is really a *humnos*.[88]

The Hymnic Subject

4§82. To analyze further the programmatic use of the word *humnos* in the *Homeric Hymns*, I find it useful to introduce a relevant term, the *hymnic subject*. In the *Homeric Hymns*, the invoked divinity who presides over a given festival is the

86 *HC* 2§321.

87 Again, *HC* 2§321.

88 *HC* 2§98

hymnic subject of the hymn. In the language of the *Hymns*, however, the divinity who figures as the *subject* of any hymn is normally the grammatical *object* of the verb of singing the hymn (as at the beginnings of *Homeric Hymns* 2, 4, 6, 9, 10, 11, 12, 13, 14, 15, 16, 17, 18, 20, 21, 23. 26, 27, 28, 30, 31, 32). In the logic of the *Hymns*, the hymnic subject is the divinity that presides over the occasion of performance and becomes continuous with the occasion and thus becomes the occasion.[89]

A Theology of Perfection in the *Homeric Hymn to Apollo*

4§83. The occasion of a *humnos* is notionally perfect because the divinity who is the occasion is perfect. The theological notion of such perfection is expressed by way of the word *eu-humnos* (εὔυμνος) 'good for hymning', as in the sublime aporetic question that is asked twice in the *Homeric Hymn* [3] *to Apollo* (verses 19 and 207):[90]

Extract 4-M

> For how shall I hymn you, you who are so absolutely [*pantōs*] good for hymning [*eu-humnos*]?
>
> *Homeric Hymn* [3] *to Apollo* 19 and 207[91]

4§84. The theological rationale of this aporetic question can be formulated this way:

> Faced with the absoluteness of the god, the performer experiences a rhetorical hesitation: how can I make the subject of my *humnos* something that is perfect, absolute? The absoluteness of this hymnic subject is signaled by the programmatic adverb *pantōs* 'absolutely', which modifies not only the adjective *eu-humnos* 'good for hymning' but also the entire phrasing about the absoluteness of the subject. The absoluteness of the god Apollo is continuous with the absoluteness of the *humnos* that makes Apollo its subject. This *Homeric Hymn* is saying about itself that it is the perfect and absolute *humnos*. As such, it is not only the beginning of a composition but also the totality of the composition, authorizing everything that follows it, because it was begun so

89 *HC* 2§83.

90 On the term *aporetic question*, see Bundy 1972:47. On "apologetic" and "aporetic" rhetorical strategies, see Bundy p. 59n59; also pp. 60–61 and 65.

91 πῶς γάρ σ' ὑμνήσω πάντως εὔυμνον ἐόντα. At verse 19 of the *Homeric Hymn to Apollo*, the manuscript reading is γάρ, while at 207, it is τ' ἄρ.

perfectly. And the source of the perfection is the god as the subject of the *humnos*.[92]

4§85. The naming of the divinity as the subject of the *humnos*, together with the initial describing of the divinity, is the notionally perfect beginning of the *humnos*, and this beginning is the *prooimion*. We have already seen in Extract 4-G that Thucydides refers to the *Homeric Hymn to Apollo* explicitly as a *prooimion* (3.104.4, 5).

4§86. Whereas the word *prooimion* is a term referring only to the start of the continuum that is activated by a hymn, the word *humnos* retains the full extent of the poetic agenda, referring both to the start of the continuum and to the continuum itself. This connecting of the start to the continuity, as expressed by the word *humnos*, is a sublime act of metonymy. And the *Homeric Hymn to Apollo* is a perfect example: it refers to itself in terms of a *humnos* (verses 158, 161, 178), while Thucydides, as I just noted again, refers to it in a more restrictive way as a *prooimion* (3.104.4, 5).[93]

The Etymologies of *Prooimion* and *Humnos*

4§87. This parallelism of the words *prooimion* and *humnos* in referring to the start of a continuum, which I have just described as a sublime act of metonymy, can be explained in terms of a parallelism that we find in their etymologies.

4§88. I will start with *prooimion*. The conventional meaning of this Greek word is conveyed by the Latin borrowing *prooemium*, which refers to the beginning of any work of verbal art. The original Greek form *pro-oimion* is a compound noun, and its etymology derives from a metaphorical reference to *pattern-weaving*: the word means literally the 'initial threading' of a song, parallel to the etymology of Latin *ex-ordium*, which is a synonym of *pro-oemium* in poetic and rhetorical contexts and which can likewise be traced back to the basic idea of an 'initial threading'. To say it more technically in Greek, using the terminology of fabric work, the 'initial threading' is the *exastis* or 'selvedge'.[94]

4§89. As for the etymology of the simplex noun *humnos*, I argue that it too derives from a metaphorical reference to pattern-weaving. According to one explanation, *humnos* is derived from the root of the verb *huphainein* 'weave'; according to another, the root of *humnos* is cognate with the root of *humēn*

[92] *HC* 2§24. On the syntax of *pantōs* 'absolutely' as an overall modifier of absolute phraseology, see for example Solon F 4.16 ed. West and the commentary in Nagy 1985:59–60, *PH* 9§7 p. 256n38.

[93] *HC* 2§89. See also Petrović 2013.

[94] *HC* 2§92. See also *PP* 63n20 and *PR* 72, 81,with reference to Latin *exordium* as a semantic equivalent of Greek *prooimion*.

'membrane'.[95] Either way, the basic idea conveyed by this noun is 'web'. In terms of my overall argument, then, a *humnos* is metaphorically the product of *weaving* in general and of *pattern-weaving* in particular.

Starting Again with Homer and Demodokos as Masters of Hymnic Singing

4§90. These parallel etymologies of words referring to the hymning of Apollo are relevant to the figuring of both Homer and Demodokos as masters of hymnic singing. If in fact such hymnic singing is to be understood in terms of a metaphor for pattern-weaving, then what we see at work here once again is the metaphorization of Homeric poetry as a masterpiece of such pattern-weaving. We have already seen such a metaphorization when we considered the passages in the *Iliad* describing the web pattern-woven by Andromache, as quoted in Extract 2-O, and the web pattern-woven by Helen, as quoted in Extract 2-P. In those cases, we also saw that such masterpieces of pattern-weaving are likewise masterpieces of metonymy. And now I will develop a parallel argument about the *humnos* that refers to the ongoing performance of Demodokos in *Odyssey* viii 429 and about the *humnos* that refers to the ongoing performance of Homer in the *Homeric Hymn to Apollo* 178.

The Hymnic Metabasis and the Hymnic Consequent

4§91. Here I introduce two relevant terms, the *hymnic consequent* and the *hymnic metabasis*. The first, *hymnic consequent*, refers to a performance that follows the performance of a *humnos*. The second term, *hymnic metabasis*, refers to the transition that actually makes it possible for the hymnic consequent to follow the *humnos*.[96]

4§92. Here are three most telling examples of hymnic metabasis in the *Homeric Hymns*:

Extract 4-Na

> $|_{292}$ Hail and take pleasure [*khaire*], goddess, queen of well-founded Cyprus. $|_{293}$ But, having started off from you, I will move ahead and shift forward [*metabainein*] to the rest of the *humnos*.
>
> *Homeric Hymn* [5] *to Aphrodite* 292–293[97]

[95] *HC* 2§91, with bibliography on alternative etymological solutions. On a possible Avestan parallel, see Skjærvø 2005:274.

[96] *HC* 2§§97, 109, 113–114, 116.

[97] $|_{292}$ χαῖρε θεὰ Κύπροιο ἐϋκτιμένης μεδέουσα· $|_{293}$ σεῦ δ' ἐγὼ ἀρξάμενος μεταβήσομαι ἄλλον ἐς ὕμνον.

Extract 4-Nb

> $|_7$ So, with all this said, I say to you [= Artemis] now: hail and take pleasure [*khaire*], and along with you may all the other goddesses [take pleasure] from my song. $|_8$ As for me, I sing you first of all and from you do I start off [*arkhesthai*] to sing. $|_9$ And, having started off from you, I will move ahead and shift forward [*metabainein*] to the rest of the *humnos*.[98]
>
> *Homeric Hymn* [9] *to Artemis* 7–9[99]

Extract 4-Nc

> $|_{10}$ So, with all this said, I say to you [= Hermes] now: hail and take pleasure, son of Zeus and Maia. $|_{11}$ And, having started off from you, I will move ahead and shift forward [*metabainein*] to the rest of the *humnos*. $|_{12}$ Hail and take pleasure [*khaire*], Hermes, giver of pleasurable beauty [*kharis*], you who are conductor [of *psūkhai*] and giver of good things.
>
> *Homeric Hymn* [18] *to Hermes* 10–12[100]

4§93. The transition in each one of these passages, as marked by *metabainein* 'move ahead and shift forward', is predicated on the idea of a perfect beginning. The idea is, "I begin, starting from the god." This process of transition, to which I refer by way of the prosaic noun *metabasis*, which is derived from the poetic verb *metabainein* as we see it used in these three passages, is activated by the hymnic salutation *khaire/khairete*, which I interpret as 'hail and take pleasure'. Implicit in these imperative forms of the verb *khairein* is the meaning of the related noun *kharis*, which conveys the idea of a 'favor' achieved by *reciprocating the pleasure of beauty*. Making this idea explicit, I have formulated a paraphrase of *khaire/khairete* in the context of all its occurrences in the *Homeric Hymns*:

> Now, at this precise moment, with all this said, I greet you, god (or gods) presiding over the festive occasion, calling on you to show favor [*kharis*] in return for the beauty and the pleasure of this, my performance.[101]

98 Note the wording in the beginning of this hymn, in verse 1: Ἄρτεμιν ὕμνει Μοῦσα "make Artemis, O Muse, the subject of my *humnos*."

99 $|_7$ καὶ σὺ μὲν οὕτω χαῖρε θεαί θ' ἅμα πᾶσαι ἀοιδῇ· $|_8$ αὐτὰρ ἐγώ σε πρῶτα καὶ ἐκ σέθεν ἄρχομ' ἀείδειν, $|_9$ σεῦ δ' ἐγὼ ἀρξάμενος μεταβήσομαι ἄλλον ἐς ὕμνον.

100 $|_{10}$ καὶ σὺ μὲν οὕτω χαῖρε Διὸς καὶ Μαιάδος υἱέ· $|_{11}$ σεῦ δ' ἐγὼ ἀρξάμενος μεταβήσομαι ἄλλον ἐς ὕμνον. $|_{12}$ χαῖρ' Ἑρμῆ χαριδῶτα διάκτορε, δῶτορ ἐάων.

101 *HC* 2§99. See also Bundy 1972:44, 49. For more on the rhetoric of seeking the pleasure of the gods, see his p. 62n65.

4§94. What drives the performative gesture of *khaire/khairete* is the fundamental idea that the reciprocal favor of *kharis* is the same beautiful thing as the pleasure that it gives. And to give such pleasure, I argue, is seen as an essential requirement for achieving a successful reception.[102]

4§95. After the signal *khaire/khairete* in the *Homeric Hymns*, the actual process of metabasis can be activated. This process is made explicit in the expression we have just seen in the three passages that I quoted, 'I will move ahead and shift forward [*metabainein*] to the rest of the *humnos*' (*Homeric Hymns* 5.292–293, 9.7–9, 18.10–12).[103] The word *humnos* in the wording ἄλλον ἐς ὕμνον in the *Homeric Hymns* marks the whole performance, so that ἄλλον ἐς ὕμνον means not 'extending into another performance' but 'extending into the rest of the performance'.[104]

4§96. Here I summarize my earlier findings about these transitions, which I continue to describe in terms of *metabasis*:

> Metabasis is a device that signals a shift from the subject of the god with whom the song started—what I have been calling the hymnic subject—and then proceeds to a different subject—in what must remain notionally the same song. Ideally, the shift from subject to different subject will be smooth. Ideally, the different subject will be consequential, so that the consequent of what was started in the *humnos* may remain part of the *humnos*. This way, the transition will lead seamlessly to what is being called 'the rest of the song'. In other words, the concept of *humnos* is the concept of maintaining the song as the notionally same song by way of successfully executing a metabasis from the initial subject to the next subject. The initial subject of the god and the next subject are linked as one song by the *humnos* in general and by

[102] With reference to the use of *kharis* in the *Homeric Hymn* [24] *to Hestia* [5], Bundy 1972:83 speaks of a "concern for the pleasure of a critical audience as well as for that of the god."

[103] μεταβήσομαι ἄλλον ἐς ὕμνον.

[104] *PH* 12§33 pp. 353–354, following Koller 1956:174–182; see also Bakker 2005:144, disagreeing with Clay 1997:493. Further discussion in Petrović 2012. So also the expression ἄλλης ... ἀοιδῆς in other *Homeric Hymns* means not 'another song' but 'the rest of the song', as in the case of *Homeric Hymn* [2] *to Demeter* 494–495. Other examples of this type include *Homeric Hymn* [3] *to Apollo* 545–546, *Homeric Hymn* [4] *to Hermes* 579–580, *Homeric Hymn* [6] *to Aphrodite* 19–21, *Homeric Hymn* [10] *to Aphrodite* 4–6, *Homeric Hymn* [19] *to Pan* 48–49, *Homeric Hymn* [25] *to the Muses and Apollo* 6–7, *Homeric Hymn* [27] *to Artemis* 21–22, *Homeric Hymn* [28] *to Athena* 17–18, *Homeric Hymn* [29] *to Hestia* 13–14, *Homeric Hymn* [30] *to Gaia* 17–19, *Homeric Hymn* [33] 18–19 *to the Dioskouroi*. Further analysis in Nagy 2011d:328–329, where I note that these and other such examples of the expression ἄλλης ... ἀοιδῆς have been described in terms of a "break-off formula" by Bundy 1972:52–53, even though he recognizes the "transitional" function of this formula (pp. 52). I find the term "break-off" misleading because it blunts the idea of "transitional" (for more on Bundy's use of the term "transitional," see his p. 87).

the device of hymnic metabasis in particular. What comes before the metabasis is the *prooimion*, the beginning of the *humnos*. What comes after the metabasis is no longer the *prooimion*—but it can still be considered the *humnos*.[105]

4§97. In this formulation centering on the *hymnic metabasis*, I have already anticipated the concept of the *hymnic consequent*. Following up, I now propose to show examples of the kind of performance that "comes after" the hymnic metabasis. In the book *Homer the Preclassic*, I have worked up a set of relevant arguments that take up more than twenty-five paragraphs of space, and there is no time for me here to recapture all that argumentation. Instead, I have to content myself here with a brief summary, which I divide into five comments that all relate to the concept of a hymnic consequent.[106]

4§98. Each one of the five comments will refer to the ongoing performance of the blind singer Demodokos in *Odyssey* viii. The word for this performance, as we have already seen at line 429 as quoted in Extract 4-K, is *humnos*. And the context for this ongoing *humnos*, as we have also already seen, is described in the same line 429 as a *dais* 'feast', indicating a stylized festival. This ongoing *humnos* is envisaged as an alternative to—and a rival of—the future performance of Odysseus when he gets to tell his own story in *Odyssey* ix x xi xii. And what makes the performing of Demodokos so different from the future performing of Odysseus? As I show in *Homer the Preclassic*, Demodokos is represented as performing forms of song that resemble (a) the epic form of the so-called epic Cycle, in the case of his first and third songs, which are about the Trojan War, and (b) the hymnic form of the *Homeric Hymns*, in the case of his second song, which is about the love affair of Ares and Aphrodite.[107] By contrast, Odysseus is represented as performing a form of song that resembles the epic form of the Homeric *Odyssey* itself.

4§99. With this background in place, I am now ready to make my five comments relating to the concept of a *hymnic consequent*.

4§99-1. Each one of the three songs of Demodokos in *Odyssey* viii starts with a new hymnic *prooimion*, and each one of these three new *prooimia* is followed by a new hymnic consequent.[108]

4§99-2. In the case of the first and the third songs, the hymnic consequent is epic poetry about the Trojan War (73–83 and 486–520 respectively). In the case of the second song, the hymnic consequent is a choral song-and-dance

[105] *HC* 2§109.

[106] There is a longer summary, featuring ten comments, in Nagy 2011d:330–332.

[107] *HPC* I§§188–23 pp. 203–214.

[108] *HPC* I§§242 p. 222.

that narrates the love affair of Ares and Aphrodite (370–380; supplemented by 262–265); in the overall narration, the performance of choral song-and-dance is preceded by an embedded narration of this love affair, performed by Demodokos and quoted by the epic medium of the Homeric *Odyssey* (266–366).[109]

4§99-3. Just as the *Homeric Hymns* have hymnic *prooimia* and allow for metabasis to follow, so also the third song of Demodokos has a hymnic *prooimion* followed by a metabasis, which is performed by Demodokos after the disguised guest Odysseus challenges the singer to *metabainein* 'move ahead and shift forward' to the story of the Wooden Horse in the epic narration of the Trojan War (492 μετάβηθι).[110]

4§99-4. The god invoked in each one of the three hymnic *prooimia* performed by Demodokos in *Odyssey* viii turns out to be one and the same god, but the identity of this god is revealed only in *Odyssey* xiii, after both Demodokos and Odysseus have finished their rival performances. We are about to see in my next and last comment, the fifth, that this god is Zeus himself. But before we turn to the subject of Zeus, I must emphasize here in this fourth comment that the performance of Odysseus in *Odyssey* ix x xi xii, just like the performance of Demodokos in *Odyssey* viii, takes place in the context of one single ongoing festival, which as I am arguing is stylized as a *dais* 'feast' in *Odyssey* viii (429; also already at 61).[111]

4§99-5. The word *agōn* 'competition' in *Odyssey* viii (259, 260, 380) points to the festivities that have been ongoing at this festival ever since it started with an animal sacrifice (59–61), which inaugurates the *dais* 'feast' (61). Here I recall the *Homeric Hymn* [3] *to Apollo*, where we have seen this same word *agōn* 'competition' used with reference to the recurrent festival of Apollo on the island of Delos (150). The feasting and the competition that start in *Odyssey* viii continue all the way through the narrative performed by Odysseus in *Odyssey* ix x xi xii, lasting all night. Then, after dawn finally arrives in *Odyssey* xiii (23), there is another animal sacrifice (24), and this time the divine recipient of the sacrifice is mentioned by name: he is Zeus himself (25). This god, I argue, is the transcendent *hymnic subject* of the *Homēridai*, who as I noted already were a corporation of epic performers claiming to be descended from Homer of Chios.[112] So we see here a signature, as it were, of the Homeric tradition as represented by the *Homēridai* of Chios. The Homeric way of narrating epic, as exemplified by the performance of Odysseus in *Odyssey* ix x xi xii, is recognized by way of a concluding sacrifice to Zeus, who is the primary hymnic subject of the *Homēridai*.

[109] *HPC* I§§207–208 pp. 207–208.
[110] *HPC* I§§225–226 pp. 214–216.
[111] Again, *HPC* I§298 p. 240.
[112] Again, *HPC* I§298 p. 240.

4§100. On the basis of the analysis I have offered in these five comments, I can offer an overall formulation about the device of metabasis as we find it activated at line 492 of *Odyssey* viii (μετάβηθι): in the ongoing performance of Demodokos, viewed as a *humnos* at line 429 (ὕμνον ἀοιδῆς), the hymnic consequence of the hymnic metabasis is epic itself.

4§101. But the ongoing performance of Demodokos in Odyssey viii, as signaled by the word *humnos* at line 429, is more complicated. A distinctive feature of the outer narrative in *Odyssey* viii is that it separates the three songs of Demodokos from each other: each one of his three songs is represented as having its own separate starting point. And yet, these three separate inner narratives show signs of a narrative continuum connecting the three songs. The connectedness of this continuum will be made evident through the privileged perspective of Odysseus as he listens to the three stories of the inner narrative. The hero will make the mental connections that need to be made by the outer narrative, and his own performance of epic in *Odyssey* ix x xi xii shows that these connections were successfully made. That is what I argue in the book *Homer the Classic*.[113] In terms of this argument, the process of making the *humnos* in *Odyssey* viii, as signaled at line 429, is the process of making such mental connections. By indicating connections that achieve a narrative continuum in the Homeric *Odyssey*, the word *humnos* is self-referential: in referring to the ongoing *humnos*, Homeric poetry is referring to itself.

4§102. The *Homeric Hymn to Apollo*, featuring the ongoing performance of the singer who is figured as Homer, is likewise quite complicated. This figure addresses the Delian Maidens with the hymnic salutation *khairete* 'hail and take pleasure' at line 166—just as the figure of Hesiod addresses the Olympian Muses with the same hymnic salutation *khairete* at line 104 of the *Theogony*. The parallelism indicates that Homer in the *Homeric Hymn to Apollo* is in effect hymning not only the divine Apollo but also the Delian Maidens, who can be seen as the local Muses of Delos and who are therefore divine in their own right.[114]

4§103. In fact, the role of the Delian Maidens as divine hymnic counterparts of the god Apollo is what directly authorizes the role of Homer as master of the *humnos*. These Maidens are figured not only as attendants of Apollo (157) but also as the prototypical singers of a *humnos* or 'hymn' (161: ὕμνον), which is a song that makes Apollo the subject of that song (158: ὑμνήσωσιν). That song, of course, is the prototype of the *Homeric Hymn to Apollo* as sung by Homer himself, who declares that he in his own right is making Apollo the subject of the *humnos* that he himself sings (178).

[113] *HC* 2§278.
[114] *HC* 2§34.

4§104. But Homer is also making the Delian Maidens the subject of this same *humnos*, since he addresses them in the *Homeric Hymn to Apollo* as if they were a sacred chorus led by the god Apollo himself as their lead singer. The Delian Maidens must be delighted by Homer's song just as Apollo is delighted.

4§105. So, what really complicates things here is the fact that the hymnic salutation *khairete* 'hail and take pleasure' that signals a hymnic metabasis at line 166 in the *Homeric Hymn to Apollo* is addressed not to Apollo but to the Delian Maidens. The *Homeric Hymn to Apollo* is not yet directing its hymnic salutation at Apollo, who is still to be hymned as the god of Delphi after he is hymned as the god of Delos. And what follows the hymnic salutation to the Delian Maidens at line 166 of the *Hymn* is not a metabasis or transition to a new subject in the rest of the performance, as in other *Homeric Hymns*. Instead, the primary subject remains Apollo, and the performance itself continues in a hymnic mode, with a transition from hymning Apollo as worshipped at Delos to Apollo as worshipped at Delphi. In the meantime, however, there is another kind of transition going on. Homer himself will be transitioning out of Delos and taking his performance on the road, as it were, throughout the cities of the Greek world. He will be a wandering singer of epic while the Delian Maidens, as stationary singers-dancers of the *Hymn to Apollo*, will stay in Delos, awaiting the return of Homer on the occasion of the upcoming year's festival of the Delia.

4§106. Homer's hymnic salutation of the Maidens at line 166, *khairete* 'hail and take pleasure', is a wish that is fulfilled every year, and the Maidens affirm this annual wish-fulfillment when they respond to the question "'|$_{169}$ O Maidens, who is for you the most pleasurable of singers |$_{170}$ that wanders here? In whom do you take the most delight [*terpesthai*]?'"[115] Each and every year at the Delia, the answer will be the same: this most pleasurable of all singers will be Homer himself, and Homer's hymnic salutation to the Maidens, wishing that they take pleasure in his singing, will be his eternal wish-fulfillment.

4§107. Thucydides himself shows that he understands the significance of Homer's hymnic salutation of the Delian Maidens in the context of his paraphrasing what Homer tells the Maidens at lines 165–172 of the *Hymn*: in the words of the historian (3.104.5), as quoted in Extract 4-G, Homer in his *prooimion* praises these prototypical singers of the *humnos* as the subject of his own *humnos*, just as he praises the god Apollo himself. The noun used here by Thucydides (3.104.5) with reference to the *humnos* performed by Homer is not *humnos* but *prooimion*, but the corresponding verb that he uses in this same context to express the idea of Homer's performance is *humneîn* (ὑμνήσας). This verb here takes as its grammatical object the noun referring to the female singers-dancers

[115] |$_{169}$ ὦ κοῦραι, τίς δ' ὔμμιν ἀνὴρ ἥδιστος ἀοιδῶν |$_{170}$ ἐνθάδε πωλεῖται, καὶ τέῳ τέρπεσθε μάλιστα;

who represent the Delian Maidens themselves. So, in the reading of Thucydides, Homer in his *prooimion* is 'hymning' the Delian Maidens, not only the god Apollo.

4§108. It is not a contradiction, however, to maintain that the Delian Maidens are simultaneously envisioned as members of a local *khoros* 'chorus' of girls or women.[116] In terms of my argument, the role of divinity can be appropriated by members of a chorus during choral performance. That is to say, the Delian Maidens as a choral ensemble can re-enact the local Delian Muses.[117]

4§109. By now we have seen a wide variety of complications and subtleties involved in the making of metabasis, which I define overall as a transition from a notionally perfect beginning into a continuum that will ultimately come to a perfect close. Viewing the poetics of transition from this standpoint, I bring this section to a close by citing a relevant formulation by Elroy Bundy: "Beginnings, middles, and ends: the meaning of literature resides in its transitions."[118]

The Festive *Humnos* in the Homeric *Odyssey*

4§110. Having analyzed the meaning of the word *humnos* as we see it at work in the *Homeric Hymns*, I now look back at the unique attestation of this same word at verse 429 of *Odyssey* viii, quoted in Extract 4-K. By now we can see that *humnos* here signals an ongoing performance by the singer Demodokos, and the occasion is a correspondingly ongoing festival, as signaled by the word *dais* 'feast' at the same line 429.[119] Part of the ongoing *humnos* is the second performance of Demodokos in *Odyssey* viii, where he sings the story of the love affair of Ares and Aphrodite, and I already referred to the occasion of this performance as a

[116] *HC* 2§34. See also Peponi 2009:54–55, 66n71 and Calame 2001:30, 104, 110. Thucydides 3.104.5 refers to this chorus as *gunaikes* 'women', but I think that this description does not exclude young women.

[117] See my note for *Homeric Hymn to Apollo* verse 163 at 2§27. The designation of the Delian Maidens as *therapnai* 'attendants' of the god Apollo in the *Homeric Hymn to Apollo* (157) is comparable to the designation of the generic *aoidos* 'singer' as *therapōn* 'attendant' of the Muses (Μουσάων θεράπων), as in the Hesiodic *Theogony* (100). Since the feminine form *therapnē* is related to the masculine *therapōn*, I suggest that the Delian Maidens as choral performers are surrogates of Apollo and, by extension, of his choral ensemble of Muses, just as the generic *aoidos* 'singer' in the *Theogony* is a surrogate of the Muses, and by extension, of their choral leader Apollo. On Apollo as a metonym for Apollo and the Muses in choral contexts, see *PH* 12§29 pp. 350–351 and §58 p. 370. On *therapōn* 'attendant' in the earlier sense of 'ritual substitute', I refer again to *BA* 18§1–9 pp. 301–307, with special reference to the use of the epithet Μουσάων θεράπων '*therapōn* of the Muses' in the Life of Archilochus and Life of Aesop traditions. On the Hesiodic model of Μουσάων θεράπων '*therapōn* of the Muses' (*Theogony* 100), I refer again to *GM* 47–51. With reference to the word *therapnai* 'attendants', consider also the Laconian place-name *Therapna* (*Serapna*), which I interpret as a metonym like *Mukēnē*, *Thēbē*, and so on (on these place names, see *HTL* 163).

[118] Bundy 1972:59n58.

[119] *HPC* I§223 p. 94.

festival. I noted, though, that this occasion cannot be tied to any specific festival as in the case of the *Homeric Hymn to Apollo*, where that particular occasion is clearly the festival of the Delia. Still, the performance of Demodokos happens at a festival, even if that festival is only a virtual one. And, as I say, it is an ongoing festival.

Returning to that Most Festive of All Moments in the *Iliad*

4§111. From our reading of the narrative in *Odyssey* viii about the ongoing performance of Demodokos at a festival that is stylized as a correspondingly ongoing feast, we can see at least in broad outlines the figuring of an earlier kind of Homer as he existed in an earlier phase of his evolution. In this earlier phase, Homer is pictured as a master of hymnic singing, which would be an older kind of performance. In a later phase, he becomes a master of epic recitation, which would be a newer kind of performance. I have already described the occasion of hymnic singing as an *agonistic choral event*. As for the occasion of epic recitation, it is likewise an agonistic event, but the competition is in this case no longer *choral* but *rhapsodic*. In speaking here of an *agonistic rhapsodic event*, I have in mind once again the recitative and non-choral medium of performance practiced by professionals called *rhapsōidoi* 'rhapsodes'.

4§112. This formulation, as we will now see, is relevant to what I described earlier as that most festive of all moments in the *Iliad*. It is the moment at lines 603–606 of *Iliad* XVIII where we either see or do not see Homer himself performing at a festival. In the longer version of this Iliadic passage, as quoted in Extract 4-B, we do see Homer performing, but in the shorter version, as quoted in Extract 4-C, he has been removed from view.

4§113. This dichotomy reflects a differentiation between rhapsodic and choral performance, and I review here the relevant parts of what I said earlier about this differentiation:

- Rhapsodes both competed and collaborated with each other in the performance of epic at Panhellenic festivals like the Panathenaia in Athens.
- Presiding over the agonistic rhapsodic events at that particular festival were the *Homēridai*, epic performers claiming to be descended from Homer of Chios.
- These *Homēridai*, masters of epic performance, also performed hymns, but these hymns were composed as well as performed only in a rhapsodic mode, as characterized by a single meter known as the dactylic

hexameter. And it is these hymns that have survived down to our time as the *Homeric Hymns*.

- As for the choral mode of composing and performing hymns, it too has survived—in the form of choral "lyric" song, characterized by a vast multiplicity of meters.[120]

4§114. That said, I confront here a simple historical fact: the rhapsodic recitation of the Homeric *Iliad* and *Odyssey* in historical times is not a choral mode for performance. Similarly, the figure of Odysseus does not engage in a choral mode of performance when he recites his own epic narrative in *Odyssey* ix x xi xii. By contrast, Demodokos still needs the old choral mode when he interacts with a stylized chorus of Phaeacians in performing the story of the love affair between Ares and Aphrodite. And even the Homer of the *Homeric Hymn to Apollo* is at least performing a mimesis of the old choral mode when he interacts with the chorus of the Delian Maidens—though this interaction is performed in the rhapsodic medium of the dactylic hexameter.

4§115. A comparable formulation applies in the case of the variation we see between the longer version of *Iliad* XVIII 603–606 as quoted in Extract 4-B and the shorter version as quoted in Extract 4-C. In the longer version, we find Homer himself engaging in the earlier choral mode of performance, while the shorter version has no room for him any more, because he has already become a rhapsodic specialist. So, in the shorter version, Homer is elided from the choral scene. We can no longer see him there.

4§116. By contrast, it is the chorus that we can no longer see in *Odyssey* xiii 24–28 as quoted in Extract 4-F, where Demodokos is shown performing for the last time. Here the choral mode of his performance is shaded over while the rhapsodic mode is highlighted. There is no direct mention of a participating chorus here. Such an elision of the chorus in *Odyssey* xiii reflects a transition in the narrative—from the generally choral mode of performance by Demodokos in *Odyssey* viii to the specifically rhapsodic mode of Odysseus as a precursor of a newer non-choral Homer in *Odyssey* ix x xi xii. And the naming of Zeus as the recipient of the sacrifice that concludes the feast in *Odyssey* xiii 24–28, as quoted in Extract 4-F, can be seen here as a signature of the *Homēridai* as the rhapsodic heirs of Homer, since the form of their hymns—specifically, of their *prooimia*—allowed for Zeus to become the ultimate hymnic subject of any Homeric performance—even if that performance took place at a festival celebrating some other god. No matter which god was the immediate hymnic subject of a Homeric *prooimion*, the ultimate hymnic subject for the *Homēridai* was normally Zeus.[121]

[120] Especially relevant is what Bundy 1972:55–57 says about the "hymnal" function.

[121] *HC* 2§72, *HPC* I§§199–201 pp. 84–85; I§§248–259 pp. 105–109.

4§117. This Homeric signature of the *Homēridai* in starting any Homeric *prooimion* with Zeus is most tellingly echoed in the words of Pindar. These words, which I now quote, start off a song that we know as *Nemean* 2:

Extract 4-O

> [Starting] from the point where [*hothen*] the *Homēridai*, singers, most of the time [*ta polla*] begin [*arkhesthai*] their stitched-together [*rhapta*] words, from the *prooimion* of Zeus ...
>
> Pindar *Nemean* 2.1–3[122]

4§118. To say that Zeus is the song's point of departure in Pindar's *Nemean* 2 is the equivalent of saying that this point of departure is the *prooimion* of Zeus, in that the *prooimion* starts with the god and is a continuation from the god. Further, the continuity that is started by the *prooimion* becomes the continuum that is the *humnos*.[123]

4§119. With this formulation in place, I can now return to my earlier argument about a basic divergence between the meanings of *prooimion* and *humnos*: whereas the word *prooimion* refers only to the start of the continuum, the word *humnos* refers to both the start of the continuum and the continuum itself. To put it another way, the naming of the god is a metonymy—of and by itself—from the standpoint of the *prooimion* that starts off with the naming of the god, and the whole process of starting and then continuing is the essence of *humnos*. Then, in the logic of the *humnos*, there is even further metonymy: the god who presides over the occasion of performance becomes continuous with the occasion and thus becomes the occasion.[124]

4§120. At the very end of Pindar's *Nemean* 2, the wording of the song most tellingly loops back to the very beginning:

Extract 4-P

> Him [= Zeus, presiding over the festival of the Némea] you O citizens of the city must celebrate [*kōmazein*] for the sake of Timodemos, at the moment of his homecoming marked by genuine fame [*kleos*], and, in sweet-sounding song, you must lead off [*ex-arkhein*] with your voice.
>
> Pindar *Nemean* 2.23–25[125]

122 |$_1$ Ὅθεν περ καὶ Ὁμηρίδαι |$_2$ ῥαπτῶν ἐπέων τὰ πόλλ' ἀοιδοί |$_3$ ἄρχονται, Διὸς ἐκ προοιμίου.
123 *PH* 12§§33–43 pp. 353–360.
124 *HC* 2§83.
125 τόν, ὦ πολῖ|ται, κωμάξατε Τιμοδήμῳ σὺν εὐκλέϊ νόστῳ·| ἁδυμελεῖ δ' ἐξάρχετε φωνᾷ.

4§121. Here at the end of the song, the chorus of performers is imagined as an assembly of the citizens of the city who are called upon to 'begin' or 'lead off', *ex-arkhein*, as if they had become transformed into a lead singer whose song will lead into the collective choral singing-and-dancing. So the chorus here is pictured as making a mimesis of its own lead singer—who could be imagined as Homer himself, the notional ancestor of the *Homēridai*.

4§122. In terms of my argument, we have already seen such a lead singer. He was pictured at lines 603–606 of *Iliad* XVIII, as quoted in Extracts 4-A and 4-B. The word *ex-arkhein* 'lead off' at line 606 there, as we saw, signals an individuated performer who interacts with the collective performance of a singing-and-dancing chorus.[126] So also in the mimetic world of Pindar's *Nemean* 2, the same word *ex-arkhein* 'lead off' at the last line of this song signals a new beginning for the singing-and-dancing of the chorus—a beginning that is 'led off' by an imagined Homer who gives 'voice' to the words of song.[127]

4§123. This imagined Homer matches not only the anonymous singer of *Iliad* XVIII 606 but also another ostentatiously anonymous singer. I have in mind here the Homer who refers to himself without naming himself in the *Homeric Hymn to Apollo*. That other Homer seems at first to be simply a solo singer, but he is not. Rather, that Homer is a solo singer only in the making. The self-portrait of that Homer in the *Homeric Hymn to Apollo* pictures a singer in the act of taking the lead in the performance of a singing-and-dancing chorus.[128] That Homer in the *Homeric Hymn to Apollo* is making a mimesis of himself as the lead singer of a chorus, and the model for his emergence as an individual performer is the god Apollo himself.[129]

Homer as a Metonym

4§124. In the light of all the internal and comparative evidence I have surveyed up to now, I am ready to conclude that not only Demodokos in *Odyssey* viii and xiii but also the anonymous singer in the longer version of lines 603–606 in *Iliad* XVIII are representations of Homer himself as a lead singer. Essential for this conclusion is the idea that a lead singer is connected to a choral group of singers-and-dancers as he leads into the choral singing-and-dancing. Such a connection is metonymic, in the sense that the singer's meaning is achieved by

126 See again *HC* 2§74; also *HC* 2§§65–82, with reference to the formulation of Aristotle *Poetics* 1449a10–11 involving the verb *ex-arkhein* (also *arkhein*) in the sense of 'lead a performance of singers-dancers'.

127 *HC* 2§73.

128 *HC* 2§75.

129 Again, *HC* 2§75.

way of his connecting with the performers in the chorus, who in turn connect with the crowd that surrounds these performers. This way, to the extent that this metonymic lead singer is Homer, Homer himself can be seen as a metonym.

Homeric Poetry as a Perfect Masterpiece of Metonymy

4§125. In Part Two, I had argued that the Peplos of Athena could be viewed as a perfect masterpiece of metonymy. Here in Part Four, I am ready to make a comparable argument about Homeric poetry. What justifies the description *perfect* in this case is the idealized representation of Homer himself by Homeric poetry.

4§126. Here I build on the idea of Homer as a metonym. If, as I said a minute ago, Homer himself is potentially connected to everyone because he had once been idealized as everyone's lead singer, then it follows that all Homeric poetry could be viewed as a system of connections that leads back to Homer as an absolute model for actually making these connections.

4§127. And the metaphor for the making of connections by Homer is the craft of pattern-weaving. This craft, as I argued in Part Two, was actually driven by a metonymic way of thinking, and we saw already at the very start of Part Four here that Homer himself is metaphorically pattern-woven into a web that is pictured as the work of the divine artisan, Hephaistos himself. So, the pattern-weaving of Homeric poetry would surely have produced a work of art that was thought to be absolutely perfect—a perfect masterpiece of metonymy.

Viewing Homeric Poetry through the Lens of Synecdoche

4§128. I have reached a point here, in the course of collecting masterpieces of metonymy, where the sheer size of a given masterpiece simply overwhelms the framework of my argumentation. Even if I am right in arguing that all of Homeric poetry can be viewed as a perfect masterpiece of metonymy, how can I possibly show, in my collection of extracts, the entirety of this poetry? Obviously, I am faced with an impossibility. What I have done instead is to view the wording of one single line, *Odyssey* viii 429, quoted in Extract 4-K, as a placeholder for all the thousands of lines of Homeric poetry. In viewing this one line, I first argued that the word *humnos* as we find it here refers metaphorically to the singing of Demodokos *as if this singing were the same thing as the weaving of a web.* Anyone who hears this singing is "hearing the web [*humnos*] of song [*aoidē*]."

Then I argued that there is also an all-pervasive metonymic reference at work here. The unique occurrence here in *Odyssey* viii 429 of the word *humnos*, found nowhere else in the *Odyssey* and the *Iliad* taken together, signals a metonymic reference to a part of Homeric poetry *as if this part were the same thing as the whole*, that is, as if one word in Homeric poetry could represent *the entire continuum* of this poetry. Such a metonymic reference is of course a shining example of synecdoche as I had defined it back in Part One.

4§129. And there is also a second example of synecdoche at work here, since the word *dais* in this same line 429 of *Odyssey* viii refers metonymically to a 'feast', that is, to a scene of dining, as if this feast could represent *the entire continuum* of the stylized festival that we see described throughout the length of *Odyssey* viii. In other words, this word *dais* makes it possible to view, through the lens of synecdoche, an idealized occasion for hearing "the web of song" that represents Homeric poetry. And the best person to hear this song is the main hero of the epic that represents him here, Odysseus himself:

Extract 4-Q (repeating Extract 4-K)

> ... so that he [= Odysseus] may feel delight [*terpesthai*] at the feast [*dais*] and in listening to the *humnos* of the song.
>
> *Odyssey* viii 429[130]

4§130. So, we have just seen Odysseus as a model for hearing Homeric poetry performed in the older ways exemplified by Demodokos. Later on, in *Odyssey* ix x xi xii, Odysseus becomes a model for performing this poetry in the newer ways of rhapsodic recitation. And, still later, he becomes a model for performing song in general—not in a rhapsodic way but in an old-fashioned choral way. In the passage we are about to read, we see his words re-enacting the way a lead singer could lead into the singing-and-dancing of a chorus at a festive occasion. After Odysseus arrives in Ithaca, he is hosted at a humble feast arranged for him by the swineherd Eumaios, and, at this festive occasion, the hero expresses his feelings of exuberance by saying, in a singing mode, that he feels the urge to sing-and-dance:

Extract 4-R

> $|_{462}$ Listen to me now, Eumaios and all you other companions! $|_{463}$ Speaking proudly, I will tell you a wording [*epos*]. The wine, which sets me loose, is telling me to do so. $|_{465}$ Wine impels even the thinking

[130] δαιτί τε τέρπηται καὶ ἀοιδῆς ὕμνον ἀκούων.

> man to sing [*aeidein*] and to laugh softly. And it urges him on to dance [*orkheîsthai*]. $|_{466}$ It even prompts a wording [*epos*] that may be better left unsaid. $|_{467}$ But now that I have shouted out loud [*an-e-kragon*], I will not suppress it.
>
> *Odyssey* xiv 462–467[131]

4§131. In the poetics of choral lyric song as exemplified by Pindar, we see what I think is an independent attestation of the same convention. Here the voice of the singers-dancers, speaking in an individuated mode, has this to say about the festivities that compensate for the previous toil or *ponos* 'pain' experienced by the victorious athlete in his successful struggle to achieve victory:

Extract 4-S

> If it [= the struggle for victory] was a pain [*ponos*], the feeling of delight [*tò terpnon*] that comes after it is greater. Let me do it. I'm doing it for the sake of bringing pleasure-and-beauty-as-compensation [*kharis*] for the victor. And if, in doing it, I soared too far upward and shouted out loud [*an-e-kragon*], I am not unversed in bringing it back down.
>
> Pindar *Nemean* 7.74–76[132]

4§132. Up to now, we have been reading passages where the verb *terpesthai* 'feel delight' signals programmatically the singing-and-dancing that takes place at a festival. But now we have found in a song of Pindar the absolutizing of such delight. Instead of the verb, what we see here is a neuter adjective *terpnon* 'delightful', absolutized as an abstract substantive noun *tò terpnon* meaning something like 'that delightful thing'. That thing could be the ultimate delight, and everyone attending a festive event could experience it—yes, everyone.

Viewing the Festival of Athena through the Lens of Synecdoche

4§133. In *Odyssey* viii 429, we saw that the word *dais* 'feast' refers metonymically to an ongoing festival, viewed as an idealized occasion for hearing Homeric poetry. The *metonymy* here could be described more specifically as *synecdoche*,

131 $|_{462}$ κέκλυθι νῦν, Εὔμαιε καὶ ἄλλοι πάντες ἑταῖροι, $|_{463}$ εὐξάμενός τι ἔπος ἐρέω· οἶνος γὰρ ἀνώγει, $|_{464}$ ἠλεός, ὅς τ' ἐφέηκε πολύφρονά περ μάλ' ἀεῖσαι $|_{465}$ καί θ' ἁπαλὸν γελάσαι καί τ' ὀρχήσασθαι ἀνῆκε, $|_{466}$ καί τι ἔπος προέηκεν, ὅ πέρ τ' ἄρρητον ἄμεινον. $|_{467}$ ἀλλ' ἐπεὶ οὖν τὸ πρῶτον ἀνέκραγον, οὐκ ἐπικεύσω.

132 $|_{7.74}$ εἰ πόνος ἦν, τὸ τερπνὸν πλέον πεδέρχεται. $|_{7.75}$ ἔα με· νικῶντί γε χάριν, εἴ τι πέραν ἀερθείς $|_{7.76}$ ἀνέκραγον, οὐ τραχύς εἰμι καταθέμεν. Commentary in *BA* 12§15 p. 236; also Nagy 1994:24.

since the feast here is part of the ongoing festival that is being imagined. Now we will see a comparable synecdoche involving another word, *thusiā*, which is conventionally translated as 'festival'. This word too can refer to an occasion for hearing Homeric poetry, but in this case the occasion is not idealized but real. In other words, we will see that this word *thusiā* is used with reference to a historical occasion for hearing the performance of Homeric poetry, and that this occasion is the seasonally recurring festival of the goddess Athena in Athens, the Panathenaia.

4§134. Essential here is the context of the word *thusiā* in the *Timaeus* of Plato (26e), where this word refers to the entire complex of events taking place at the festival of the Panathenaia in Athens. One of the greatest of these Panathenaic events—although Plato's text does not explicitly refer to it or to any other event that took place at that festival—was the relay performance of the Homeric *Iliad* and *Odyssey* by *rhapsōidoi* 'rhapsodes' who competed with each other for prizes.[133] The word for such rhapsodic competition is *agōn*, as attested for example in Plato's *Ion* (530a). This word *agōn*, as we have already seen, can mean literally 'competition'. Relevant is the wording of Thucydides 3.104.3–6, quoted in Extract 4-G, about the competitive events held at the festival of the Delia on the sacred island of Delos. In that context, we saw that the historian uses this same word *agōn* 'competition' with reference to events not only in athletics but also in *mousikē*, the 'craft of the Muses' (Thucydides 3.104.3 and 3.104.5, as analyzed in 4§63). So also in the case of competitive events held at the festival of the Panathenaia, as we can see from the wording of the Aristotelian *Constitution of the Athenians* (60.1), the same word *agōn* 'competition' applies to Panathenaic contests not only in athletics but also in *mousikē*, and the events in *mousikē* include the competitions of rhapsodes performing Homeric poetry.[134] In short, then, it is a historical fact that the Panathenaia, as a premier *thusiā* or 'festival' celebrated in honor of the goddess Athena in Athens, was a prime venue for hearing the performance of Homeric poetry.

4§135. The general meaning of *thusiā* as a *festival* needs to be reconsidered, however, in the context of this word's etymology, which as we will see points to the specific meaning of *slaughtering sacrificial animals*. In terms of this specific meaning for *thusiā*, a problem arises: how are we to square the idea of a *sacrificial slaughter* with the idea of hearing Homeric poetry performed at a festival like the Panathenaia? As I will now argue, there is a long-term solution to this problem if we consider, besides the event of the rhapsodic competitions, two other events that took place at this seasonally recurring festival in Athens.

133 *PR* 53, 83.

134 Further references in *HPC* I§26 p. 15n20.

4§136. In Part Three, we already examined in some detail these two other events. The first of these was the Panathenaic Procession, while the second was the presentation of the Peplos of Athena. Actually, the Panathenaic Procession could better be described as a multiple event—a metonymic sequence that led up to the climactic event of presenting the Peplos. And we have also considered in some detail a most spectacular visualization of this whole sequence, pictured in the relief sculptures of the Parthenon Frieze. But the fact is, the presentation of the Peplos was not the only climactic event of the Panathenaic Procession. Here we come to *another big thing that happened at the Panathenaia*—a happening that we have not yet considered. This happening was another essential part of the Panathenaic Procession—and of the whole festival of the Panathenaia. I have in mind here the *hekatombē* or 'hecatomb', which was a spectacular sacrificial slaughter of one hundred cattle that took place at the conclusion of the Panathenaic Procession. There is a striking attestation of this word *hekatombē* in an inscription concerning the quadrennial Panathenaia of 410/9 BCE (*IG* I[3] 375 lines 5 ... 7: παναθεναια τα μεγαλα ... ες τεν εκατομβεν).

4§137. If we keep in mind these spectacular animal sacrifices at the Panathenaia, we can learn to appreciate more fully the basic meaning of *thusiā* as 'sacrifice'. I emphasize again that the sacrifice of one hundred cattle at the Panathenaia was a decisively climactic moment in the metonymic sequence of the Panathenaic Procession, just as the presentation of the Peplos was a comparably climactic moment in the same procession. And I emphasize also that this spectacular animal sacrifice at the Panathenaia, as a climactic moment in the ritual sequence of the Panathenaic Procession, seems to be correlated with a climactic moment we saw in the mythological sequence of the Parthenon Frieze. Once again I have in mind here the primal scene that we see sculpted into Block 5 on the east side of the Parthenon Frieze, showing not only a presentation of the Peplos but also, if the argument holds, an act of preparation for a human sacrifice. In other words, the animal sacrifice in the ritual of the hecatomb seems to be correlated with the human sacrifice that is narrated in the myth about the mortal girl known simply as the Parthénos.

Viewing a Festival of Hera through the Lens of Synecdoche

4§138. Having just highlighted (1) the presentation of the Peplos and (2) the sacrifice of one hundred cattle as two climactic ritual events at the festival of the Panathenaia in Athens, I will now compare a similar pair of ritual events that took place at a festival in the ancient city of Argos. This Argive festival, sacred to the goddess Hera, was called the Heraia.

4§138.1a. I start with the first of the two ritual events I have in mind. This event, taking place at the festival of Hera in Argos, would have been the presentation of a robe to the goddess. The local Argive word for this robe was *patos* (Hesychius s.v.).[135] This *patos* 'robe', pattern-woven for Hera, was evidently presented to her on the seasonally recurring occasion of her own festival, the Heraia. There is a reference made to this robe in Callimachus (*Aetia* F 66.3), where the speaker is addressing a water-nymph who presides over one of the sacred springs of Argos:

Extract 4-T1

> For those women whose sacred concern it is to weave [*huphainein*] the holy robe [*patos*] of Hera, it is not sanctioned to be stationed at the weaving-bars [*kanones*] of their looms before having your [= the nymph's] water poured over their heads as they sit at the sacred rock.
>
> Callimachus *Aetia* F 66.2–5[136]

4§138.1b. I juxtapose what we have just seen concerning the robe of Hera with a text I have already quoted before, concerning the robe of Athena that is presented to the goddess at the conclusion of the *pompē* 'procession' that is held in her honor:

Extract 4-T2 (repeating Extract 2-S)

> For Athena the city-goddess [Polias] there was a robe [*peplos*] made. It was completely pattern-woven [*pan-poikilos*]. And it was ritually carried and presented to her in the procession [*pompē*] of the Panathenaia.
>
> Scholia for Aristophanes *Birds* 827[137]

4§138.2. Having reconstructed the first of two ritual events that took place at the festival of Hera in Argos, namely, the presentation of a robe to the goddess, I now turn to the second event, which was a hecatomb offered to Hera. This second event is related to the first. As we will see from a relevant text that I am about to quote from the scholia for Pindar's *Olympian* 7 (152), the *pompē* 'procession' that was held in honor of Hera at her festival in Argos culminated in a hecatomb, that is, in a ritual slaughter of one hundred cattle. In the case of the Athenian counterpart to this Argive procession, namely, the Panathenaic Procession, we already know that this ritual event likewise culminated in a hecatomb—*and that*

135 πάτος· ... ἔνδυμα τῆς Ἥρας.

136 $|_{66.2}$ ... οὐδὲ μὲν Ἥρης $|_{66.3}$ ἁγνὸν ὑ⌊φ⌋αινέμενα⌊ι⌋ τῇσι μέμη⌊λε⌋ πάτος $|_{66.4}$ στῆναι [πὰ]ρ κανόνεσσι πάρος θέμις ἢ τεὸν ὕδω[ρ] $|_{66.5}$ κὰκ κεφ[α]λῆς ἱρὸν πέτρον ἐφεζομένας χεύασθαι.

137 Τῇ Ἀθηνᾷ πολιάδι οὔσῃ πέπλος ἐγίνετο παμποίκιλος, ὃν ἀνέφερον ἐν τῇ πομπῇ τῶν Παναθηναίων.

this climactic moment of the hecatomb was synchronized with the presentation of the robe of the goddess. And now, in a text that refers to a comparable climactic moment of a hecatomb that takes place at the festival of Hera in Argos, we will be encountering the same word *pompē* 'procession' that we saw just a moment ago in the text I quoted about the festival of Athena in Athens. In the text that I am about to quote, the word *pompē* is used with reference to a procession that leads up to the ritual slaughtering of one hundred cattle at the festival of Hera. Further, as we will also be seeing in this text that I am about to quote, the word that actually refers to the slaughtering of the hundred cattle at the festival of Hera in Argos is the verb *thuein*, meaning literally 'sacrifice'. I highlight this detail in advance because it is relevant to the meaning of the noun *thusiā* as 'festival'. We already know, from the wording we have read in the *Timaeus* of Plato (26e), that this noun *thusiā* can be used as a general term for referring to the festival of Athena in Athens. And we also already know that this same noun *thusiā*, meaning 'festival', is actually derived from the verb *thuein*, meaning 'sacrifice'. So, the use of this word *thuein* 'sacrifice' in the text that I am about to quote is essential for my overall argumentation. That said, I now finally quote the relevant text, divided into four parts (Ua, Ub, Uc, Ud), describing the festival of the goddess Hera in Argos:

Extract 4-Ua

> "... and the *bronze* [khalkos] in Argos" [quotation from Pindar]: [It is the festival called] the *Heraia*. It is also called the *Hekatombaia* [derived from *hekatombē* = a sacrifice of one hundred cattle]. It is called that because of the number of cattle that are *sacrificed* [thuein]. What is received as prizes there [= at that festival] is *bronze* [khalkos] *not as raw material that has no work done on it* [a-ergon] but in the [worked] form of tripods and cauldrons and *shields* [aspis plural] and mixing bowls.
>
> Scholia for Pindar *Olympian* 7.152a 1 A[138]

Extract 4-Ub

> "... recognized him" [quotation from Pindar]: He [= the victor of the competition] was recognized by way of the *bronze* [khalkos] that is given as a prize [*athlon*] to the winner [of the competition] in Argos.
>
> Scholia for Pindar *Olympian* 7.152 b 1 ABDEQ[139]

[138] "ὅ τ' ἐν Ἄργει χαλκός": τὰ Ἥραια, ⟨ἃ⟩ καὶ Ἑκατόμβαια λέγεται διὰ τὸ πλῆθος τῶν θυομένων βοῶν. λαμβάνουσι δὲ ἐντεῦθεν οὐκ ἀργὸν χαλκὸν, ἀλλὰ τρίποδας καὶ λέβητας καὶ ἀσπίδας καὶ κρατῆρας.

[139] "ἔγνω νιν": ἐγνώρισε δὲ αὐτὸν καὶ ὁ ἐν τῷ Ἄργει διδόμενος χαλκὸς ἆθλον τῷ νικήσαντι.

Extract 4-Uc

> The festival of the *Heraia* or *Hekatombaia* at Argos *is ritually enacted* [*teleîsthai*] with the *sacrifice* [*thuein*] of one hundred cattle to the goddess. And the prize [*athlon*] to be won in the contest is a *bronze shield* [*aspis khalkē*]. According to other sources, the prizes are *garlands* [*stephanoi*] made *of myrtle*.
>
> Scholia for Pindar *Olympian* 7.152c 1 ABCEQ[140]

Extract 4-Ud

> According to an alternative source ... In Argos, at the *festival-of-competition* [*agōn*] called the Hekatombaia, *bronze* [*khalkos*] is awarded as the prize [*athlon*] (in the competition). That is because Arkhinos, when he became king of the Argives, was the first to establish a *festival-of-competition* [*agōn*] and, having been put in charge of the preparation of weapons, he proceeded from there to the establishment of the awarding of these weapons as prizes. This *festival-of-competition* [*agōn*] is called Hekatombaia because one hundred cattle are led forth in a grand *procession* [*pompē*], and their meat is divided by customary law among all the citizens of the city.
>
> Scholia for Pindar *Olympian* 7.152d 1 BCEQ[141]

Where It All Comes Together

4§139. I remember once saying about this four-part text, as I have just quoted it, that it brings together for me the pieces of a big picture. I said it spontaneously, just when I was nearing the end of the fourth of the four "live" Martin Classical Lectures in the spring of 2003 at Oberlin. Back then, I was arguing that this four-part prosaic description of a seasonally recurring festival of Hera as celebrated in the city of Argos contains a sufficient number of elements to make it possible for me to reconstruct a unified poetic description of such an event. And, to use again the words that I used then, I was thinking of such a reconstruction as some kind of big picture.

[140] τελεῖται δὲ κατὰ τὸ Ἄργος τὰ Ἥραια ἢ τὰ Ἑκατόμβαια διὰ τὸ ἑκατὸν βοῦς θύεσθαι τῇ θεῷ. τὸ δὲ ἆθλον, ἀσπὶς χαλκῆ· οἱ δὲ στέφανοι ἐκ μυρσίνης.

[141] ἄλλως· ἐν Ἄργει, ἐν τῷ Ἑκατομβαίων ἀγῶνι, χαλκὸς τὸ ἆθλον δίδοται, ὅτι Ἀρχῖνος Ἀργείων γενόμενος βασιλεύς, ὃς καὶ ἀγῶνα πρῶτος συνεστήσατο, ταχθεὶς ἐπὶ τῆς τῶν ὅπλων κατασκευῆς, ἀπὸ τούτων καὶ τὴν τῶν ὅπλων δόσιν ἐποιήσατο. Ἑκατόμβαια δὲ BC(D)EQ ὁ ἀγὼν λέγεται ὅτι πομπῆς μεγάλης προηγοῦνται ἑκατὸν βόες, οὓς νόμος κρεανομεῖσθαι πᾶσι τοῖς πολίταις.

4§140. Even earlier than that particular occasion at Oberlin, I had quoted the same four-part text just when I was nearing the end of the sixth of my six "live" Sather Classical Lectures in the spring of 2002 at Berkeley. Back then, I was arguing that this same four-part prosaic description of the festival of Hera in the city of Argos contains elements that we see on display in that ultimate big picture created by Homeric poetry, which is the Shield of Achilles. Much later on, in the online (2009) and the printed (2010) versions of the book *Homer the Preclassic*, I published the specifics of that argument about the Shield. Some of those specifics overlapped with what I had argued more generally in the fourth lecture of the Martin Classical Lectures about the festival of Hera in Argos. Here in the published version of the fourth lecture, I intend to synthesize this general argument centering on the festival of Hera with the specific argument, as already published in *Homer the Preclassic*, centering on the Shield of Achilles as we see it pictured in the context of the festival of Hera. In what follows, then, I offer such a synthesis.

The General Argument Centering on the Festival of Hera in Argos

4§141. Here I repeat the general argument: the elements we see at work in the four-part text as quoted in Extract 4-U (Ua, Ub, Uc, Ud) can be reconstructed as essential parts of a big picture that visualizes the festival of Hera at Argos, the Heraia. Each part is pointing metonymically toward the entirety of the festival. In other words, we see synecdoche at work here.

4§142. What follows is an inventory showing three events taking place at the festival, all three of which are mentioned in the text of Extract 4-U (Ua, Ub, Uc, Ud).

Event One: The Hecatomb

4§142. At the festival of Hera at Argos, there was a hecatomb, that is, a sacrifice of one hundred cattle (Ua, Uc, Ud), and the act of sacrifice is expressed by way of the verb *thuein* 'sacrifice' (Uc). The ritual of this mass sacrifice was a culminating event of the festival, and the corresponding ritual that led up to this event was a grand procession that was held in honor of the goddess. The word for this ritual lead-up is *pompē* 'procession' (Ud). I find it most significant that this procession is the actual setting for a celebrated story told by Herodotus (1.31.1–5) about a priestess of Hera and her two boys, Kleobis and Biton. The mother and the two sons are, all three of them, major characters in what turns out to be an aetiological myth about the ritual practice of sacrificially slaughtering one hundred cattle in the precinct of the goddess Hera at the climax of the festival celebrated in her honor at Argos. Also involved as major "characters" in the story are two sacrificial oxen. The two boys, who are described as *āthlophoroi* 'prize-winning athletes', willingly took the place of the two sacrificial oxen, chosen to pull the wagon carrying the priestess across the plain of Argos—over a distance of 45 stadium-lengths—along a sacred way leading up to the precinct of Hera (1.31.2). The oxen had been late in arriving at the starting-point of the procession (again, 1.31.2), *and this lateness, in terms of the story, is the aetiological explanation for their replacement by the two athletes.* If these two oxen had not been late, they would have been slaughtered along with the other ninety-eight oxen that had been chosen for the mass sacrifice of one hundred cattle at the finishing-point of the procession, inside the precinct of Hera. At the feast that followed the sacrifice inside the precinct, the two boys died a mystical death after having pulled the wagon of the priestess all the way to this finishing-point of the procession (1.31.5).[142] Thus, by way of this death that they shared with each other, the boys became sacrificial substitutes for the two premier victims of the animal sacrifice.[143]

Event Two: The Presentation of a Bronze Shield

4§143. A pre-eminent prize to be awarded in the athletic competitions at this festival of Hera was a bronze *aspis* 'shield' (Ua, Ub, Uc, Ud).[144] As we will see, the ritual of awarding the shield—like the ritual of slaughtering one hundred cattle—was another culminating event of the festival, and the corresponding ritual that led up to this event was, once again, the grand procession in honor of Hera. To repeat, the word for this ritual lead-up is *pompē* 'procession' (Ud). I add a related fact: the athletic competitions themselves were metonymically called the *Aspis* or 'Shield', as we see from a variety of inscriptions.[145] By way of synecdoche, then, the competition itself was the Shield. And there is even further synecdoche here. As we see from the wording that describes the athletic competition (Ub), the metallic substance of the bronze that goes into the making of the shield is seen as an extension of the very idea of victory in the competition, since this bronze is to be 'energized' (we can see that meaning at work in the Greek word *en-ergeia*). In other words, the bronze has work (*ergon*) done on it in

142 Commentary in *H24H* 13§§11–21.

143 For documentation on the ritual practice of choosing two premier animal victims out of a mass of animals destined for slaughter at a sacrifice, see *PR* 51–52.

144 See also Hesychius s.v. *agōn khalkeios*.

145 *HPC* II§417 p. 293. There are several attestations of the expression τὴν ἐξ Ἄργους ἀσπίδα 'shield [*aspis*] of Argos', as in *IG* IV 591.6–7.

the form of the shields—and tripods and cauldrons and mixing bowls—that are awarded as prizes.[146]

Event Three: The Presentation of a Garland Made of Myrtle

4§144. Another pre-eminent prize to be awarded at this festival was a garland made of myrtle (Uc). As we will see in this case as well, the ritual of awarding the garland took place as a culminating event of the festival, and the corresponding ritual that led up to this event was, in this case as well, the grand procession in honor of Hera. To repeat yet again, the word for this ritual lead-in is *pompē* 'procession' (Ud). Here too I add a related fact: a traditional term for referring to blossoms of myrtle was *kharites*, which is the plural form of *kharis* 'pleasurable beauty': in other words, the word *kharis* could refer metonymically to the festive use of myrtle blossoms in the making of garlands:

Extract 4-V

> Macedonians and Cypriotes use the word <u>*kharites*</u> [= plural of <u>*kharis*</u>] with reference to *myrtle blossoms* that are *compacted* and *curled* [around a garland]. We call them *garland-blossoms* [<u>*stephanitides*</u>].
>
> Scholia D (via Scholia A) for *Iliad* XVII 51[147]

4§145. We can actually see the same metonymic reference in Argive usage, as reflected in the diction of Pindar. In a song of his that celebrates the winner of a wrestling event at the festival of Hera in Argos, we find the plural of *kharis*, that is, *kharites*, personified as the 'Graces', and these divine attendants of Hera are invoked at the very beginning of the song (Pindar *Nemean* 10.1 Χάριτες).

4§146. There is a parallel metonymic reference reported by Pausanias (2.17.3–4): when this traveler enters the temple of Hera in Argos, he sees inside the *pronaos*, that is, when he gets inside the front third of the temple, he sees a set of archaic statues that are known to the Argives as the *Kharites*, which is also the word for the 'Graces', divine attendants of Hera who personify the pleasurable beauty of *kharis*; and, remarkably, Pausanias reports seeing next to the *Kharites* an archaic shield, presumably made of bronze, which once belonged to the hero Euphorbos.[148] In the Homeric *Iliad*, where the death of this hero is

[146] See also Hesychius s.v. *agōn khalkeios*.

[147] Μακεδόνες δὲ καὶ Κύπριοι <u>χάριτας</u> λέγουσι τὰς <u>συνεστραμμένας</u> καὶ <u>οὔλας</u> <u>μυρσίνας</u>, ἃς φαμὲν <u>στεφανίτιδας</u>. Commentary in *HPC* II§424 pp. 295–296.

[148] Commentary in *HPC* II§427 p. 296.

described, the flecks of blood that grace the hair of the dead Euphorbos are actually compared by way of simile to *kharites*, and the word seems to be referring in this context to red blossoms of myrtles:

Extract 4-W

> |$_{51}$ With blood bedewed were his locks of hair, looking like *kharites*, |$_{52}$ with the curls and all.
>
> *Iliad* XVII 51–52[149]

The Specific Argument Centering on the Shield of Achilles

4§147. So far, in terms of my general argument centering on the festival of Hera at Argos, we have seen that the ritual event of the *pompē* 'procession' held in honor of the goddess leads into three culminating ritual events: (1) the slaughter of one hundred cattle, (2) the awarding of bronze shields, and (3) the parallel awarding of myrtle garlands. But now I shift to my specific argument centering on the relevance of this same festival to the very idea of the Shield of Achilles. In making this shift, I will now highlight two further events taking place at the festival of the Heraia, which I will call Event Four and Event Five. As we will see, each one of these two events, just like the previous Events One, Two, and Three, is likewise a culmination that comes at the finishing-point of the *pompē* 'procession' honoring the goddess.

Event Four: The Choral Performance of Argive Girls

4§148. The procession in honor of Hera culminated in a choral performance of Argive girls who participated in that procession. This culminating ritual event can be reconstructed on the basis of what we read in the *Electra* of Euripides.

4§149. The role of the chorus that is singing-and-dancing in this drama is twofold: the performers in the chorus here represent not only the girls of Argos in the mythical past but also the girls of Argos who participated in the rituals of the seasonally recurring festival of Hera in the historical present of the drama. In the *Electra* of Euripides, the male Athenian chorus of his drama is representing a female Argive chorus participating in a contemporary version

[149] |$_{51}$ αἵματί οἱ δεύοντο κόμαι χαρίτεσσιν ὁμοῖαι |$_{52}$ πλοχμοί θ'. Commentary in *HPC* II§425 p. 296n80, where I analyze a modulation from red to white coloring in the complex simile of *Iliad* XVII 51–59. The simile extends from lines 51–52, focusing on the red color of myrtle blossoms, to lines 53–59, focusing on the white color of olive blossoms.

of Hera's festival, and this female Argive chorus is in turn representing their prototypical counterparts in the mythical past. Already back then, in that mythical past, a chorus of Argive girls is participating in the festival of the Heraia. In the *Electra* of Euripides, there are explicit references to the upcoming choral performance of these mythical girls at Hera's festival. And the festival itself, as we will now see, is explicitly called a *thusiā*, meaning literally 'sacrifice' (172). Here is the wording, as it is sung-and-danced by the chorus of Argive girls:

Extract 4-Xa

> $|_{167}$ O Electra, daughter of Agamemnon, I [= the chorus, speaking as a singular 'I'] have arrived $|_{168}$ at your rustic courtyard. $|_{169}$ He has come, a milk-drinking man, he has come, $|_{170}$ a Mycenaean, one whose steps lead over the mountains. $|_{171}$ He announces that, on the third day from now, $|_{172}$ a sacrifice [*thusiā*] is proclaimed $|_{173}$ by the Argives, and that all $|_{174}$ girls [*parthenikai*] to Hera must proceed [*steikhein*].
>
> Euripides *Electra* 167–174[150]

4§150. This word *thusiā* here (172) is referring to the ritual centerpiece of the festival, the *hecatomb*, which is a sacrifice of one hundred cattle. But the same word *thusiā* is also referring, by way of metonymy, to the entire festival. Each and every girl from each and every part of the Argive world must *steikhein* 'proceed' to Hera—that is, to the festival of Hera. Each girl personally must make the mental act of proceeding to the goddess. Each girl collectively must join in, that is, join the grand procession that will lead to the precinct of the goddess, where the hundred cattle will be slaughtered in ritual sacrifice. We see here the religious mentality that shapes the idea of the *pompē* 'procession' as mentioned in Extract 4-Ud. In that text we had already read about this procession of Argive girls that leads to the festival proclaimed by the people of Argos here at line 172 of the *Electra*. The key word in Extract 4-Ud, to repeat, was *pompē* for 'procession'. And now, at line 172 of the *Electra*, we see the other key word, *thusiā*, both in the specific sense of 'sacrifice' and in the metonymic sense of 'festival'. After the procession reaches the precinct of Argive Hera, what happens next is the sacrifice of one hundred cattle, followed by festive celebrations. *And these festivities will highlight the choral singing and dancing performed by the girls of Argos.* So, the *pompē* 'procession' extends into the choral performance, by way of the sacrifice that will take place after the entry of the procession into the precinct.

[150] $|_{167}$ Ἀγαμέμνονος ὦ κόρα, ἤλυθον, Ἠλέκτρα, $|_{168}$ ποτὶ σὰν ἀγρότειραν αὐλάν. $|_{169}$ ἔμολέ τις ἔμολεν γαλακτοπότας ἀνὴρ $|_{170}$ Μυκηναῖος οὐριβάτας· $|_{171}$ ἀγγέλλει δ' ὅτι νῦν τριταί$|_{172}$αν καρύσσουσιν θυσίαν $|_{173}$ Ἀργεῖοι, πᾶσαι δὲ παρ' Ἥ$|_{174}$ραν μέλλουσιν παρθενικαὶ στείχειν.

We see here a validation of the formula proposed by Anton Bierl concerning processions as represented in Greek theater: he argues that *any procession that leads into a choral performance will thereby become part of the choral performance.*[151] There is a metonymy at work here. Further, in the case of the drama composed by Euripides, Electra is potentially the *prima donna* who will lead the procession that will be transformed into the choral performance of the Argive girls when they reach the precinct of Hera. In fact, the word that Electra herself uses in referring to the upcoming performance of the girls at the precinct is *khoros* (χορούς 178). For the moment, though, Electra declines the "invitation to the dance" (178–180).

4§151. So, what is the subject of the choral song when the time comes for the Argive girls to sing-and-dance at the festival of Hera? In the *Electra* of Euripides, where the choral singing-and-dancing of these girls is dramatically anticipated, we find that this song is about the Shield of Achilles and, secondarily, about the rest of the hero's armor. Here are the choral words as sung-and-danced by the girls of Argos:

Extract 4-Xb

> $|_{432}$ I address you, O ships of glory [*kleos*], you that once with countless oars went to Troy, taking with you the songs-and-dances [*khoreumata*] of the Nereids, $|_{435}$ while the dolphin, loving the reed [that accompanies song-and-dance], was leaping as it circled around your blue prows, making a path for Achilles, the son of Thetis, whose dance-step is light as he leaps, $|_{440}$ along with Agamemnon, toward the banks of the Trojan river Simoeis. The Nereids, leaving the headlands of Euboea, brought from the anvil of Hephaistos the result of his labor over the shield [*aspis*], that choice part of the golden armament. They brought it up to Mount Pelion [...] where his father, the charioteer, was raising the son of Thetis as a beacon light for Hellas, $|_{450}$ sea-born, swift-footed for the sons of Atreus. I heard, from someone who had arrived from Ilion at the harbor of Nauplia, O son of Thetis, $|_{455}$ that on the circle [*kuklos*] of your shield [*aspis*] of glory [*kleos*] were made such signs [*sēmata*], a terror to the Phrygians: on the base enveloped by the shield's rim, there was Perseus the throat-cutter, traveling over the sea $|_{460}$ with winged sandals and holding forth the Gorgon's head, accompanied by Hermes, the messenger of Zeus and the rustic son of Maia. $|_{464}$ In the center of the shield [*sakos*] was shining the radiant $|_{465}$ circle [*kuklos*] of the sun, drawn by winged chariot-horses, and also the ethereal song-and-dance

[151] Bierl 2009:57n152, 107, 272–273, 284, 294–295, 318–319. See also Bierl 2011.

> ensembles [*khoroi*] of stars—Pleiades and Hyades—making the eyes of Hector turn away. $|_{470}$ And on top of his [= Achilles'] gold-forged helmet were sphinxes, bearing in their talons the prey that they had won by way of their singing. On his [= Achilles'] breast-plate a lioness, breathing flame, was bounding ahead, and the talons of her paws were showing, $|_{475}$ at the very moment when she caught sight of the colt [Pegasus] from Peirene. Pictured on the surface of his [= Achilles'] killer sword were horses prancing on all four hooves with black dust swirling behind them.
>
> Euripides *Electra* 432–477[152]

4§152. We see here that the myth of the bronze shield of Achilles is explicitly linked with the choral performance of Argive girls who sing-and-dance the myth on the occasion of Hera's festival.[153] And this shield is a synecdoche for the entire festival: as I have already noted, the word *Aspis*, meaning 'Shield', was actually the Argive name for this festival of Hera.

4§153. We can find further traces of this link between the myth of the original bronze Shield of Achilles and the ritual complex of the Heraia. I have in mind here two vase paintings that show Thetis, the divine mother of Achilles, in the act of presenting the bronze Shield—along with other pieces of armor—to the hero. In these paintings, the Shield is visually correlated with garlands, which I connect with the garlands of myrtle that we saw mentioned in Extract 4-Uc:[154]

152 $|_{432}$ κλειναὶ νᾶες, αἵ ποτ' ἔβατε Τροίαν τοῖς ἀμετρήτοις ἐρετμοῖς πέμπουσαι χορεύματα Νηρῄδων, |435 ἵν' ὁ φίλαυλος ἔπαλλε δελφὶς πρῴραις κυανεμβόλοισιν εἱλισσόμενος, πορεύων τὸν τᾶς Θέτιδος κοῦφον ἅλμα ποδῶν Ἀχιλῆ $|_{440}$ σὺν Ἀγαμέμνονι Τρωίας ἐπὶ Σιμουντίδας ἀκτάς. Νηρῇδες δ' Εὐβοΐδας ἄκρας λιποῦσαι μόχθους ἀσπιστὰς ἀκμόνων Ἡφαίστου χρυσέων ἔφερον τευχέων, $|_{445}$ ἀνά τε Πήλιον [...] ἔνθα πατὴρ ἱππότας τρέφεν Ἑλλάδι φῶς $|_{450}$ Θέτιδος εἰνάλιον γόνον ταχύπορον πόδ' Ἀτρείδαις. Ἰλιόθεν δ' ἔκλυόν τινος ἐν λιμέσιν Ναυπλίοις βεβῶτος τᾶς σᾶς, ὦ Θέτιδος παῖ, $|_{455}$ κλεινᾶς ἀσπίδος ἐν κύκλῳ τοιάδε σήματα δείματα Φρύγια τετύχθαι· περιδρόμῳ μὲν ἴτυος ἕδρᾳ Περσέα λαιμοτόμαν ὑπὲρ ἁλὸς $|_{460}$ ποτανοῖσι πεδίλοις κορυφὰν Γοργόνος ἴσχειν, Διὸς ἀγγέλῳ σὺν Ἑρμᾷ, τῷ Μαίας ἀγροτῆρι κούρῳ $|_{464}$ ἐν δὲ μέσῳ κατέλαμπε σάκει φαέθων $|_{465}$ κύκλος ἁλίοιο ἵπποις ἃμ πτεροέσσαις ἄστρων τ' αἰθέριοι χοροί, Πλειάδες Ὑάδες, Ἕκτορος ὄμμασι τροπαῖοι· $|_{470}$ ἐπὶ δὲ χρυσοτύπῳ κράνει Σφίγγες ὄνυξιν ἀοίδιμον ἄγραν φέρουσαι· περιπλεύρῳ δὲ κύτει πύρπνοος ἔσπευδε δρόμῳ λέαινα χαλαῖς $|_{475}$ Πειρηναῖον ὁρῶσα πῶλον. ἄορι δ' ἐν φονίῳ τετραβάμονες ἵπποι ἔπαλλον, κελαινὰ δ' ἀμφὶ νῶθ' ἵετο κόνις.

153 I recommend the relevant analysis of Zeitlin 1970.

154 *HPC* II§419 pp. 293–294.

Extract 4-Ya

Attic black-figure column krater: Thetis presenting shield and other pieces of armor to Achilles. Attributed to the Painter of London B76. Berlin, Staatliche Museen, Antikensammlungen, 3763. Line drawing by Valerie Woelfel.

Extract 4-Yb

Attic black-figure hydria: Thetis presenting shield and garland to Achilles. Attributed to the Tyrrhenian Group. Paris, Musée du Louvre, E869. Line drawing by Valerie Woelfel.

Event Five: The Presentation of the Robe of Hera

4§154. Here I return to my starting point. At the very beginning, when we first considered the festival of Hera, I had reconstructed a ritual event featuring the presentation of a robe that was pattern-woven for the goddess by the women of Argos; the word for this sacred robe, as we saw, was *patos* (Hesychius s.v.,

Callimachus F 66.3). This ritual event of presenting the robe, as I argued, was a culmination of the procession that led to the place where the festival was held, that is, to the sacred precinct of Hera. From the start, I viewed this presentation of a robe to the goddess Hera, which would have taken place at the finishing-point of the procession held in her honor, as a ritual event that matches the presentation of the Peplos to the goddess Athena, which took place at the finishing-point of the Panathenaic Procession.

4§155. Similarly, the presentation of the Shield to Achilles, as we see it represented in the paintings we have just viewed in Extracts 4-Ya and 4-Yb, is happening in the context of a procession. The mother of Achilles, together with her nymph sisters, the Nereids, are pictured at a moment that can best be described as the culmination of a procession of their own, marking the climactic moment when Achilles is presented with his Shield—just as the victors in the athletic events of the festival of Hera are presented with their own shields at the finishing-point of the procession held in honor of the goddess.

4§156. I see a most remarkable correlation here at the finishing point of the procession honoring Hera. One culminating ritual event is the presentation of the Shield, a masterpiece of metalwork, while another culminating ritual event—if my reconstruction holds—is the presentation of the robe of the goddess, which would be a masterpiece of pattern-weaving. Such a correlation of metalwork and pattern-weaving is strikingly similar to what we saw already at the very beginning of Part Four, in the very first line of Extract 4-A. In that line, *Iliad* XVIII 590, the performance of metalwork by the divine smith Hephaistos is expressed by way of a most powerful metaphor: the god's act of metalworking his narration into bronze is compared there to an act of pattern-weaving that same narration into fabric, as if the divine metalworker were pattern-weaving a *peplos*. And the word for *pattern-weaving* in that line, as we saw, is *poikillein*.

4§157. This metaphorical correlation between the metalworking that produces the Shield and the pattern-weaving that produces a *peplos* makes me think of the picture that must have been pattern-woven into the sacred web of Hera. This picture, I propose, was notionally the same picture that was metalworked into the Shield of Achilles. And such a picture, which could be represented in the paired visual arts of metalworking and pattern-weaving, could also be represented in the verbal art of singing-and-dancing the song that was sung-and-danced by the girls of Argos as they celebrated the festival of Hera. We have already read in Extract 4-Xb this song of these Argive girls, which is quoted, as it were, in the *Electra* of Euripides. In the drama, as I already noted, the singing-and-dancing is performed by a male Athenian chorus who are representing a contemporary Argive female chorus who are in turn representing the original Argive female chorus in the act of describing the bronze Shield of Achilles. As we read the words sung-and-danced by the Argive girls in Extract 4-Xb, we can visualize what was metalworked into the bronze of the Shield of Achilles—and also, if I am right, what was pattern-woven into the fabric of Hera's robe.

The Big Picture of the Two Shields of Achilles

4§158. By way of synecdoche, then, the Shield of Achilles as sung-and-danced by the girls of Argos is a verbalization of the big picture that comes together in the ritual complex we know as the festival of Hera. Clearly, this Argive Shield is not the same thing as the Homeric Shield of Achilles as verbalized in *Iliad* XVIII. Rather, what we see being verbalized in the singing-and-dancing of the chorus in the *Electra* of Euripides is a local Argive version of the Shield as visualized in the rituals and myths of the city of Argos. But this Argive Shield, as a synecdoche for the festival of Hera, is nevertheless comparable to the Homeric Shield, since it is pointing metonymically to an old world of ritual and myth that could be seen as a prototype—or, to say it more accurately, as one of many possible prototypes—for the brave new world that we see emerging in the big picture of the Homeric Shield.

4§159. The newness of the Homeric Shield of Achilles in *Iliad* XVIII is ostentatiously foregrounded by the epic narrative, since this centerpiece of the hero's armor is in fact new to the *Iliad*: after all, Hephaistos has to make a new Shield for Achilles after the original, as it were, had been captured by Hector when he killed Patroklos, the ritual substitute of Achilles who was wearing that hero's armor, including the old Shield. And the new narrative that is metaphorically pattern-woven into the bronze of the hero's new Shield recapitulates, in a stylized way, the festival of Hera, which had been the setting for the original shield. Just as the old shield, by way of synecdoche, stands for the entire festival of the Heraia, in that the very name of the festival is *Aspis*, meaning 'Shield', so also the new Shield in *Iliad* XVIII begins its own narrative by pattern-weaving a vision of a generic festival. At this festival as well, there is choral singing-and-dancing to be enjoyed by all, and that is why all the participants attending such a beautiful spectacle are *terpomenoi* 'feeling delight', as we saw at line 604 of *Iliad* XVIII, quoted already in Extract 4-A.

4§160. The festive merriment of the crowd attending the choral singing-and-dancing in *Iliad* XVIII is comparable to the happy mood of the chorus of Argive girls as represented in the *Electra* of Euripides:

> The sadness of Electra as an Argive Cinderella stands in sharp contrast with the happiness of young women celebrating the Feast of Hera and having the best time of their lives. As these Argive girls sing-and-dance

> the song of the bronze Shield of Achilles, we can just see them catching the attention of dashing young Argive warriors and perhaps even falling in love, fully sharing in the charisma of the pattern-woven fabric they offer to Hera. A metonymy for this charisma is the blossom of the myrtle, which as we saw is the flower of choice for making *stephanoi* 'garlands' to wear at the festival of the Heraia in Argos.[155]

4§161. In this formulation, I am drawing attention to what I had just said about young people falling in love on the occasion of such a festival. This is no speculation, as we will see when we read the Epilogue that follows Part Four, where I quote passages from an ancient erotic novel describing how a young girl and a young boy fall in love at a festival of the goddess Artemis. In this connection, I also draw attention to the word *charisma* that I had just used with reference to the garlands worn by the celebrants at the festival. I recall here the linguistic evidence we have already seen showing a metonymic link between the word *kharis* 'pleasurable beauty' and the plaiting of myrtle blossoms for the making of festive garlands. In the Epilogue, we will return to this image of a garland of blossoms gracing the hair of joyous celebrants at a festival.

Another Synecdoche for the Idea of a Festival

4§162. We have seen, then, that the word *Aspis*, meaning 'Shield', is a synecdoche that expresses the idea of the entire festival of Hera in Argos. Now I highlight another such example of synecdoche that we have seen. In the *Electra* of Euripides, at line 172 as quoted in Extract 4-Xa, the word *thusiā* likewise refers to the entire festival of Hera in Argos. But this word means literally 'sacrifice'. The noun *thusiā*, as I noted earlier, derives from the verb *thuein*, meaning 'sacrifice', which is actually used with reference to the ritual slaughter of one hundred cattle at the festival of Hera, as we had read in Extract 4-Ua. Earlier, I had also noted that this same noun *thusiā* is used in Plato's *Timaeus* (26e) with reference to the festival of the Panathenaia, and that this festival of Athena, like the festival of Hera, featured the culminating ritual event of slaughtering one hundred cattle. In that context, I referred to another example of such a spectacular ritual event: it was the Athenian *hekatombē* or 'hecatomb' that took place at the conclusion of the Panathenaic Procession, and I cited an attestation of this word *hekatombē* in an Athenian inscription concerning the quadrennial Panathenaia of 410/9 BCE (*IG* I^3 375 lines 5 ... 7: παναθεναια τα μεγαλα ... ες τεν εκατομβεν).

4§163. So, the use of this word *thusiā* in the general sense of 'festival' is another shining example of synecdoche. It is a metonymic visualization that

[155] *HPC* II§§423–454 p. 295.

extends from the slaughtering of the sacrificial animal to the cooking and distribution of the meat and to the consequent eating, drinking, and feasting in general. And here is where the parallelism of the word *thusiā* with the basic meaning of the Homeric word *dais* in the sense of a 'distribution' of sacrificial meat proves to be decisive.

4§164. I see the emergence of a remarkable parallelism here. Just as the *dais* 'feast' in *Odyssey* viii 429 is a stylized festival that becomes a prime venue for hearing the *humnos* or 'web' of song that is signaled in this Homeric line, so also the *thusiā* or 'festival' of the Panathenaia as mentioned in Plato's *Timaeus* (26e) becomes a prime venue for hearing what is called metaphorically a *humnos* or 'hymn' that is sung to honor the goddess Athena as the patroness of the Panathenaia. I will now describe here, within the shortest possible compass, the context of such a metaphorical *humnos*.

4§165. The dramatized occasion of Plato's *Timaeus* is the eve of the Panathenaia, and the wording refers to this grand festival as 'the *thusiā* of the goddess' (26e).[156] The story of Atlantis and Athens, about to be narrated by Critias, is described by him metaphorically as a *humnos* or 'hymn' to be sung as an encomium of the goddess Athena in celebration of her festival: to recall the story, Critias says, would be a fitting way both to please Socrates 'and at the same time to praise the goddess, on the occasion of her festival, in a righteous and truthful way, just as if we were making her the subject of a *humnos*' (21a2–3).[157]

4§166. The neo-Platonic philosopher Proclus, that passionate devotee of the goddess Athena, offers a most pertinent insight in his allegorizing commentary on the *Timaeus* of Plato.[158] Essentially, Proclus interprets the notional *humnos* of Plato's discourse, which is being dedicated to the goddess Athena, as a Peplos in its own right,[159] more real even than the cult object presented to the goddess every four years by the ancient Athenians.[160]

4§167. I find that this insight of Proclus meshes perfectly with the ancient ritual mentality of celebrating the festivals of goddesses like Athena and Hera. For example, in the *Iphigeneia in Tauris* of Euripides, the words of the chorus refer to choral singing-and-dancing at the festival of Hera in Argos (the choral medium is signaled by the word *melpein* 'sing-and-dance' at line 221)[161] as a ritual that is parallel to the ritual of pattern-weaving the Peplos of Athena at

[156] τῇ ... τῆς θεοῦ θυσίᾳ.

[157] καὶ τὴν θεὸν ἅμα ἐν τῇ πανηγύρει δικαίως τε καὶ ἀληθῶς οἷόνπερ ὑμνοῦντας ἐγκωμιάζειν. Commentary in *PR* 53.

[158] What follows is a recasting of what I argued in *PR* 97–98.

[159] Festugière 1966: vol. I, 122.

[160] Festugière 1966: vol. I, 182–183.

[161] τὰν Ἄργει μέλπουσ' Ἥραν 'singing-and-dancing [*melpein*] as the subject of my song the goddess Hera at Argos'.

the festival of the Panathenaia (the making of the Peplos is signaled by the word *poikillein* 'pattern-weave' at line 224).[162]

4§168. For Proclus, the ultimate Peplos is the web that is pattern-woven by that essence of intelligence, the luminous intellect of Athena.[163] Experts who study the *Timaeus* in our own time have suggested that Plato himself must have intended this masterpiece of his, this stylized *humnos*, as his very own Peplos for the goddess.[164] I suggest that the metaphor applies also to Homeric poetry, in that the ongoing *humnos* performed at the *dais* or 'feast' in *Odyssey* viii 429 can be viewed by Athenians as a Panathenaic *humnos* destined for eternal re-weaving in the eternally self-renewing context of Athena's festival.[165]

A Double Synecdoche for a Festival of Artemis

4§169. As I near the end of Part Four, I will conclude by studying a set of passages taken from one last text, which is an inscription concerning a festival of the goddess Artemis in the city of Eretria on the island of Euboea. The text of this inscription, dated to the year 341/340 BCE, is especially "good to think with" because it concerns what was going on not only at the main events at the festival but also in the procession that led up to these events. As we will see, the word *thusiā* is used in a double sense in this inscription. More generally, it refers to the entire festival, but, more specifically, it refers also to the animal sacrifice that takes place as a culminating ritual event at the festival. And, as we will also see, the use of the word *pompē* in this inscription is essential for understanding the very idea of what I have all along been calling a *culminating ritual event*. Here is what I mean. The *pompē* or 'procession' is a metonymic sequence that leads up to a *thusiā* or 'sacrifice', which would not and could not be a culminating ritual event if it were not for the fact that there exists a sequence of meanings that lead up, metonymically, to a culmination of meanings. In other words, there cannot really be a *thusiā* in the sense of a 'festival' if there is no *pompē* 'procession' that leads up to it. What I am arguing, then, is that the correlation of these two words, *pompē* in the sense of 'procession' and *thusiā* in the sense of 'sacrifice', is a double synecdoche that points metonymically to the entire experience of a festival.

[162] Here is the overall context, at lines 222–224: ἱστοῖς ἐν καλλιφθόγγοις | κερκίδι Παλλάδος Ἀτθίδος εἰκὼ | ⟨καὶ⟩ Τιτάνων ποικίλλουσ', which I translate as 'pattern-weaving, with my shuttle, on looms that have beautiful voices of their own, a picture of Athenian Pallas (Athena), and of the Titans'. In the stylized Panhellenic wording of Euripides, the 'Titans' are of course the 'Giants' of the Gigantomachy. See also Extract 2-V as quoted in 2§140. I translate *kerkis* here as 'shuttle', but a more accurate trasnlation would be 'pin-beater' (Edmunds 2012).

[163] Festugière 1966: vol. I, 183; cf. Hadot 1983:129.

[164] Hadot 1983:117.

[165] *PR* 98.

4§170. I start by quoting the first eight lines of the inscription:

Extract 4-Za

> $|_1$ Theoi [= an invocation addressed to the gods]. $|_2$ Exekestos son of Diodoros spoke: in order that the $|_3$ Artemisia [= Festival of Artemis] be conducted by us in the most beautiful way [*kallista*] possible and in order that people should make sacrifice [= *thuein*] $|_4$ —as many of them as possible, it was decided by the Council [Boule] and the People [Demos] $|_5$ that the city is to organize a competition [*agōn*] of *mousikē*, at the expense of 1000 $|_6$ drachmas, on the days Metaxu and Phulakē,[166] and that [the city] is to provide $|_7$ lambs [= *arnes*] on the day that is five days before the Artemisia, and, $|_8$ of these [lambs], two are to be *enkritoi* [specially selected (for sacrifice)].[167]
>
> *IG* XII ix 189.1–8[168]

4§171. In the wording here, we see references to not one but two culminating ritual events. Besides an animal sacrifice, as indicated by the verb *thuein* 'sacrifice' at line 3, there is also a competition in what is called *mousikē*. The word for 'competition' here at line 3 is *agōn*. As for the word *mousikē*, I am not yet ready to translate this word—beyond saying that it means literally the 'art' or *tekhnē* of the Muses.

4§172. I have already highlighted a comparable use of this word *mousikē* in the Aristotelian *Constitution of the Athenians* (60.1), with reference to the festival of the Panathenaia in Athens. That festival was the traditional venue for seasonally recurring performances of Homeric poetry in the context of competitions in *mousikē*, and the word for 'competition' in that context was likewise *agōn* (again, *Constitution* 60.1). Here in the inscription from Eretria, an analogous venue is being described by way of these same words, *mousikē* and *agōn*.

4§173. The inscription does not specify the content of the *mousikē* to be performed at this seasonally recurring festival of Artemis, but it is remarkably precise in its wording concerning the actual forms of *mousikē*. I quote here the relevant part of the text:

[166] My interpretation here is not certain.

[167] On the semantics of *en-krisis* in the sense of a "choice selection" in a competitive context, see LSJ pp. 473–474. In Herodotus 1.31.1–5, as I indicated earlier, we see a reference to the choice selection of two oxen in the sacrifice of one hundred oxen at the festival of Hera at Argos.

[168] $|_1$ [θ]εο[ί].$|_2$ Ἐξήκεστος Διοδώρου εἶπεν· ὅπωρ ἂν τὰ Ἀρ$|_3$τεμίρια ὡς κάλλιστα ἄγωμεν καὶ θύω[ριν ὡς π$|_4$λε]ῖστοι, ἔδοξεν τεῖ βουλεῖ καὶ τοῖ δήμοι$|_5$ ⟦.⟧ τιθεῖν τὴμ πόλιν ἀγῶνα μουσικῆς ἀπὸ χιλίων $|_6$ δραχμῶν τεῖ Μεταξὺ καὶ τεῖ Φυλακεῖ καὶ παρέχει$|_7$ν ἄρνας τεῖ πρὸ τῶν Ἀρτεμιρίων πέντε ἡμέρας, τ$|_8$ούτων δὲ δύο ἐγκρίτους εἶναι.

Extract 4-Zb

> |$_{10}$ ... and that [the city] is to organize the *mousikē* for rhapsodes [*rhapsōidoi*], |$_{11}$ aulodes [*aulōidoi* = *aulos*-singers], *kitharā*-players [*kitharistai*], citharodes [*kitharōidoi* = *kitharā*-singers], and parody-singers [*parōidoi*]; |$_{12}$ further, that those who compete [*agōnizesthai*] in the *mousikē* |$_{13}$ should all compete [*agōnizesthai*] in the *prosodion* [= processional song] for the sacrifice [*thusiā*] in the courtyard [*aulē*], |$_{14}$ having the same costume that they have in the competition [*agōn*] proper.
>
> *IG* XII ix 189.10–14[169]

4§174. I draw attention to the use of the word *thusiā* here at line 13. I interpret this word not only as 'festival' in general but also as 'sacrifice' in particular. The meaning of 'sacrifice' is most relevant to the wording that we read later on, where it is specified that all the *agōnistai* 'competitors' in the *mousikē* are required to join in the procession that leads up to the sacrifice:

Extract 4-Zc

> |$_{38}$ ... and may the competitors [*agōnistai*] who participate in the *mousikē* also join in the procession [*sun-pompeuein*], |$_{38}$ all of them.
>
> *IG* XII ix 189.38–40[170]

The verb used here for the idea of 'join in the procession' is *sun-pompeuein*, which is of course derived from the noun *pompē*, meaning 'procession'. Then, in the very next sentence, we see the explicit reason for this required participation in the procession:

Extract 4-Zd

> ... in order that the procession [*pompē*] and the sacrifice [*thusiā*] become the most beautiful [*kallistē*] possible
>
> *IG* XII ix 189.39[171]

4§175. Here, then, is what I have been calling the *double synecdoche*. The competitors in *mousikē* join in and become part of the entire religious program of this festival, which is a continuum extending from the beginning of the

[169] |$_{10}$ ... τὴν δὲ μουσικὴν τιθεῖν ῥαψωιδοῖς, |$_{11}$ αὐλωιδοῖς, κιθαρισταῖς, κιθαρωιδοῖς, παρωιδοῖς, |$_{12}$ τοὺς δὲ τὴν μουσικὴν ἀγωνιζομένους πάντα[ς] |$_{13}$ ἀγωνίζεσθαι προσόδιον τεῖ θυσίει ἐν τεῖ αὐλεῖ ἔ|$_{14}$[χο]ντας τὴν σκευὴν ἥμπερ ἐν τοῖ ἀγῶνι ἔχουρ[ι]

[170] |$_{38}$ ... συμπο|$_{39}$μπευόντων δὲ καὶ οἱ τῆς μουσικῆς ἀγωνισταὶ πάντ|$_{40}$ες...

[171] |$_{40}$ ...ὅπως ἂν ὡς καλλίσστη ἡ πομπὴ καὶ ἡ θυσίη γένηται.

procession all the way to the culminating event of the sacrifice. And a dominant feature of this continuum is the idea of absolute beauty as expressed by the word *kallistē* 'most beautiful', applied here to both the *pompē* 'procession' and the *thusiā* 'sacrifice'. This idea was already in effect at the beginning of the inscription, where we had read:

Extract 4-Ze (repeated from Extract 4-Za)

> ... in order that the $|_3$ Artemisia [= Festival of Artemis] be conducted by us in the most beautiful way [*kallista*] possible and in order that people should make sacrifice [= *thuein*] $|_4$ —as many of them as possible.
>
> *IG* XII ix 189.2–4[172]

This theme of absolute beauty is surely connected with the cult-epithet of Artemis, *kallistē* 'most beautiful' (as interpreted by Pausanias 1.29.2, 8.35.8 in other contexts involving the worship of the goddess).[173]

4§176. The homology of procession and sacrifice, as it plays out at the festival of Artemis in Eretria, reflects a religious mentality of metonymic sequencing, where the ritual event of the procession culminates in the ritual event of a sacrifice—and where every element connects in proper sequence with every other element. We see a comparable homology at work at the grand festival of Athena in Athens, the Panathenaia. On that seasonally-recurring occasion as well, though of course on a vastly larger scale, we see a procession that culminates in a sacrifice. The Panathenaic Procession, which is actually called a *pompē* in the Aristotelian *Constitution of Athens* (60.1), starts from the Kerameikos and passes through the Agora and ends up on the heights of the Acropolis, reaching its climax in a grand sacrifice of one hundred cattle within the sacred space of Athena on high.[174]

Homer's Music

4§177. Let us consider again the actual forms of *mousikē* as they are listed in the inscription from Eretria. As we see from the relevant wording that I quoted in Extract 4-Zb (lines 10–11), there are contests in *mousikē* for *rhapsōidoi* 'rhapsodes', for *aulōidoi* 'aulodes' or '*aulos*-singers', for *kitharistai* '*kitharā*-players', for *kitharōidoi* 'citharodes' or '*kitharā*-singers', and for *parōidoi* 'parody-singers'. So, these forms of *mousikē* include poetic recitation by competing rhapsodes as well as monodic song performed by competing singers and instrumentalists.

[172] $|_2$ ... ὅπωρ ἂν τὰ Ἀρ$|_3$τεμίρια ὡς κάλλιστα ἄγωμεν καὶ θύω[ριν ὡς π$|_4$λε]ῖστοι.
[173] *PR* 50.
[174] *PR* 50.

And, although the inscription does not indicate what poetry the rhapsodes performed at the festival in Eretria, we can in fact be sure that, in most such situations, the content of poetic recitation by rhapsodes was Homeric poetry. To put it another way, the *mousikē* of the rhapsodes was primarily the music of Homer. This formulation, as we will see, applies especially in the case of the premier festival of Athena in Athens, the Panathenaia.

4§178. At the festival of the Panathenaia, there were contests in *mousikē* for *rhapsōidoi* 'rhapsodes', for *kitharōidoi* 'citharodes' or '*kitharā*-singers', for *aulōidoi* 'aulodes' or '*aulos*-singers', for *kitharistai* '*kitharā*-players', and for *aulētai* '*aulos*-players'. A precious piece of evidence about these contests comes from an Athenian inscription dated at around 380 BCE, *IG* II^2 2311, which records the winners of Panathenaic prizes. In this fragmentary inscription, we find references to *kitharōidoi* (line 5), *aulōidoi* (line 12), *kitharistai* (line 15), and *aulētai* (line 20), but the expected reference to *rhapsōidoi* has broken off. Looking elsewhere, however, we find a most pertinent reference in Plato's *Ion*. This work is named after a rhapsode from Ephesus who comes to Athens in order to compete for first prize in rhapsodic performance at the festival of the Panathenaia (*Ion* 530b2), and Plato's wording makes it explicit that this festival featured a 'competition' among rhapsodes, an *agōn* (ἀγῶνα at *Ion* 530a5, picked up by ἠγωνίζου and ἠγωνίσω at a8). It is also made explicit that the agonistic art of the rhapsodes falls under the general category of *mousikē* (μουσικῆς at a7).

4§179. The reference in the wording I just cited from Plato (*Ion* 530a7) to an *agōn* 'competition' in *mousikē* supplements the reference in the Aristotelian *Constitution of the Athenians* (60.1) to an *agōn* 'competition' in *mousikē* (τὸν ἀγῶνα τῆς μουσικῆς) at the Panathenaia. In that elliptic reference, we do not get to see the correlation of rhapsodic contests with citharodic, aulodic, and other such contests, and this gap in information has led to some confusion about the so-called 'musical contests' of the Panathenaia. Needless to say, the conventional but anachronistic translation 'musical' confuses the matter even further, since the modern words 'music' and 'musical' suggest, misleadingly, an exclusion of rhapsodes and the inclusion only of citharodes, aulodes, and so on.[175] That is why I highlight what the passage I just cited from Plato (*Ion* 530a7) shows so clearly: that the art of *mousikē* includes the art of the rhapsode.[176]

4§180. That said, I return to my formulation: the *mousikē* of the rhapsode was the music of Homer. In the case of the *mousikē* performed by rhapsodes competing at the festival of the Panathenaia in the classical period of Athens, it appears from the wording of Plato's *Ion* that their repertoire was exclusively

[175] *PR* 41–42.

[176] Conversely, as I argue in *PR* 41–48, the art of *mousikē* does not technically include the overall art of the dramatist of tragedy or comedy.

Homeric poetry. The rhapsode Ion is portrayed as a virtuoso performer who is potentially a grand master in performing Hesiod and even Archilochus, not just Homer (531a), but he admits that he specializes in Homer only, and the rationale for this specialization is one simple but big idea, that Homer is the best poet (531a–532c). The wording here implies that Homer is the only poet worth performing for rhapsodes because it is his poetry and no one else's that gets to be performed by rhapsodes competing at the Panathenaia.[177] Another telling piece of evidence is a reference in the *Panegyricus* of Isocrates (159), who speaks of the 'contests [*athloi*] of *mousikē*' in Athens as the primary venue used by the State for showcasing the performance of Homeric poetry.[178]

4§181. In speaking here of Homer's music, I have in mind the title of my 2002 book *Plato's Rhapsody and Homer's Music*. This title represents the only place in all my publications where I have ever used—before now—the word 'music', without quotation marks, in referring to the art of the rhapsodes. By saying 'Homer's music' in the title of the book, I was making the same point I am making now, but I never said *music* explicitly in the actual argumentation I developed in that book. Now I am saying it here, at the end of the Martin Classical Lectures, and I do so because I find that the text of the inscription I am now studying, which is the last text here in Part Four, comes so close to the modern idea of *music*. I am thinking here of the way we use this word in contexts that idealize music as some kind of a universal force of nature. And I say it this way because the religious sentiment that drives the text of the inscription from Eretria is elevating the meaning of the Greek word *mousikē* to comparable levels of exaltation.

The Eternal Delight of Music Without End

4§182. The text of the Eretrian inscription comes to an end by reporting arrangements that had been made for the words of this text to be inscribed on a stele, which was to be placed inside the precinct of the goddess Artemis (40–41). And now, at the end of the text, the wording makes clear the express purpose of all these arrangements:

Extract 4-Zf

> $|_{42}$ ... so that, according to these arrangements, $|_{43}$ the sacrifice [*thusiā*] and the music [*mousikē*] for Artemis may last $|_{44}$ forever.

IG XII ix 189.42–44[179]

[177] See *HC* 3§48.

[178] ἐν ... τοῖς τῆς μουσικῆς ἄθλοις. See *PP* 111n24.

[179] $|_{42}$ ... ὅπως ἂν κατὰ τοῦτα γί $|_{43}$νηται ἡ θυσίη καὶ ἡ μουσικὴ τεῖ Ἀρτέμιδι εἰς τὸν ἀεὶ χ$|_{44}$[ρό]νον.

4§183. According to the solemn words that are spoken here, the music of this *mousikē* is eternal, since it will recur on each seasonally recurring occasion of a festive sacrifice at the festival of the goddess Artemis. So also, I say, the ongoing *humnos* performed at the *dais* or 'feast' in *Odyssey* viii 429 is eternal, since it will recur on each seasonally recurring occasion when Homer's music is heard once again at some festival in the future. The greatest of all these festivals, for the Athenians who heard Homer's music, was of course the Panathenaia, the Feast of the goddess Athena. But there were other festivals celebrated by others who heard this music. And, at all these festivals, the experience of hearing the music was utter delight.

Epilogue Without End

A Metonymic Reading of a Love Story

5§1. I bring this whole project to an end by experimenting with a text that has no real ending. The text is an erotic novel—or, to say it more generally, a love story—attributed to one Xenophon of Ephesus, who is conventionally dated to the second century CE.

5§2. In my experiment, I do two things. First, I produce a working translation of three passages that I have extracted from this novel and, second, I supplement this translation with an ongoing commentary—together with some special annotations that I have added at 5§6 and 5§9. Both the commentary and the annotations focus on my metonymic reading of the whole novel—and on the relevance of this reading to what I have said about metonymy in all four parts of my book.

5§3. The novel centers on a girl and a boy who fall in love with each other at a festival of the goddess Artemis in Ephesus and who are soon thereafter united in marriage—but who are then brutally separated from each other and experience many tribulations before they are finally reunited in their mutual love. I highlight, from the start, the fact that the young lovers in the story fall in love at one particular moment in the course of the festival of Artemis. That moment will come toward the end of the first passage that we are about to read, and it happens at the climax of a procession that is heading toward the sacred precinct of the goddess.

5§4. This procession and its climax, as we will see, reveals a fundamental truth about processions: *to process in a procession is to participate in the actual process of metonymy.*

5§5. As we are about to see in the first passage that I will be quoting, the girl and the boy who will soon fall in love cannot yet see each other while they are actually processing in the procession honoring the goddess Artemis, since all the girls and all the boys are processing separately. But then, when the procession finally reaches the sacred precinct, the separate groupings of girls and boys are finally merged, and the girl and the boy finally get a chance to take their first good look at each other. So, the climax of the procession coincides with the precise moment when the girl and the boy make eye contact.

5§5. That said, I am ready to start translating the first of the three passages that I will highlight. This passage will lead up slowly—ever so slowly—to the climactic moment of eye contact:

Extract 5-A

> 1.1.1 There was in Ephesus a man who was a member of the leadership of the city there, Lykomedes by name. To this man Lykomedes and his wife, Themisto, native [*epikhōrios*] of the city, was born a boy called *Habrokomēs* [= having a *komē* 'head of hair' that is *habrā* 'luxuriant'], who was a prodigy of beauty such as never happened before in all Ionia. 1.1.2 This Habrokomes was with every day becoming more and more beautiful, and there was a *synchronized blossoming* [= *sun*- plus verb of *anthos*] of the beauty of his body [*sōma*] with the nobility of his spirit [*psūkhē*]. He was well trained in all forms of upbringing [*paideiā*], and he practiced *the art of the Muses* [= *mousikē*] *in all its varieties* [adjective *poikilē*]. Hunting, horsemanship, and the skillful handling of weapons were customary gymnastic pursuits of his. 1.1.3 He was most highly regarded by all the people of Ephesus, along with all those who inhabited the rest of Asia [= Asia Minor], and they had great hopes for him that he would become an outstanding citizen. The way they *related* to the boy was as to a *god*. There were already those who *made proskynesis* to him *when they saw him* and prayed to him. 1.1.4 The boy thought very highly of himself and gloried in the successes of his spirit [*psūkhē*], but even more so in the beauty of his body [*sōma*]. And whatever beautiful things were said about all others, he would look down on them as inferior. For him there was nothing to be seen or heard that was worthy of Habrokomes. 1.1.5 And if he heard that a boy was beautiful or a girl had a good shape, he would laugh at those who said so, since they did not realize that he was the one beautiful person, all by himself. As for Eros, he [= Habrokomes] did not consider him to be a god. He cast him [= Eros] out of his mind altogether, thinking that he [= Eros] was nothing, and saying that no one would ever fall in love or be subjugated to the god if they did not want to. 1.1.6 And if he ever saw a sacred space or statue of Eros, he would mock it, declaring himself to be more beautiful than every Eros. And that is the way it really was. For wherever Habrokomes was seen, there was no beautiful statue in view, nor was there an image [*eikōn*] that could be praised. 1.2.1 In response to these things, Eros is now feeling anger [*mēnis*]. That god loves conflict, and he is inexorable toward the haughty. He was devising a *tekhnē* against the boy. For in

fact even to the god the boy appeared to be difficult to capture. So, arming himself with the full force of the charms of love, he [= Eros] started his war on Habrokomes. 1.2.2 A *native festival* [*epikhōrios heortē*] of Artemis was in progress, extending from the city all the way to the *sacred space* [*hieron*]. The distance is seven stadium-lengths. It was the regulation that there should be a *procession* [= verb of *pompē*] of all the native [*epikhōrioi*] girls, *who would be arranging* [*kosmeîn*] their looks in the most expensive ways [*polu-telōs*], and the same goes for all the ephebes [= boys in a fixed age-class] as well who were the same age as Habrokomes. He himself [= Habrokomes] was around the sixteen-year-old mark, and he joined up with the ephebes and won the first prize of first position in the *procession* [*pompē*]. 1.2.3 There was a huge crowd for the *viewing* [*theā*]. Many people were natives [*epikhōrioi*] of the city, while many others were from other cities. For in fact there was a custom, at that *festival* [*panēguris*], for bridegrooms to be found for the girls and for wives to be found for the ephebes. 1.2.4 The participants in the *procession* [*pompē*] went along in file formation. First in order were the sacred [*hiera*] objects and the torches and the baskets and the incense. After them came the horses and the hunting dogs and the hunting equipment—some of the equipment was connected with war but most of it was connected with peace. Each of the girls arranged [*kosmeîn*] her looks *in such a way as one does oneself up for one's lover.* 1.2.5 Leading the processional file of girls was *Anthiā* [derived from *anthos* 'blossom'], daughter of Megamedes and Euhippe, both *natives* [*enkhōrioi*] of the city. The beauty of Anthia was a thing to *marvel* at [= verb of *thauma*], and she far surpassed the other girls. She was fourteen years old. Her body was *blossoming* [= verb of *anthos*] *in response to* [= *epi*] her fine shape. And the manifold *self-arrangement* [*kosmos*] of her *pose* [*skhēma*] was put together in such a way as to achieve *perfect seasonality* [*hōrā*]. 1.2.6 Her *head of hair* [*komē*] was golden, and most of it was let down but some of it, just a little, was *plaited* [= verb *plekein*] and *set in motion to be picked up by the breezes.* Her eyes were fierce, bright like those of the divine Maiden [Kore], but forbidding, too, as of one who has good balance [*sōphrosunē*]. Her dress was a tunic [*khitōn*] treated with purple dye, and it was girded so as to show her knee, with loose sleeves that showed her arms. Draped over her dress was fawnskin. A quiver was slung over her shoulder. There were arrows and javelins in it. Hunting dogs attended her. 1.2.7 At that moment, as the people of Ephesus *saw* her reaching the *sacred space* [*temenos*], they started *making proskynesis* to her, over and over again, *as to Artemis.* At that moment, at the very *sight* of her, the crowd shouted out. *Varied* [poikilo-] were the voices coming from them as they were *viewing* [= verb of theā] her. Some, experiencing *astonishment* [ekplēxis], were saying that she is the goddess. Others were saying that she was some kind of surrogate for the goddess. But all prayed to her and *made proskynesis* to her and called her parents blessed. And all those who were *viewing* [= verb of theā] her shouted "Anthia the beautiful." 1.2.8 As the crowd of the other girls went by in the procession, no one said anything except "Anthia." And when Habrokomes, along with the other ephebes, appeared in the procession, from then on, although the *view* [theā] featuring the girls was so beautiful, everyone lost track of them when they saw Habrokomes, and they turned their *gaze* [opsis plural] at him and were shouting, experiencing astonishment [*ekplēxis*] at the *view* [theā] and saying "Habrokomes is beautiful" and "he is—like no one else—a *reenactment* [mīmēma] of the god." 1.2.9 Already there were those who added this to the formula: "what a wedding this would be, the wedding of Habrokomes and Anthia!" These things, then, were the initial practice runs [*meletēmata*] of the *tekhnē* of Eros. Rapidly did the news about the two of them reach each other. And Anthia conceived in her heart [*thūmos*] a desire to *see* Habrokomes, while Habrokomes, up to now free of eros, began wanting to *see* Anthia. 1.3.1 When the *procession* [pompē] finally reached its culmination [*telos*] and the whole crowd entered the sacred [*hieron*] space in order to *make sacrifice* [thuein] and when the *arrangement* [kosmos] of the *procession* [pompē] was finally dissolved and all the men and women entered the same space, as well as all the ephebes and girls, then it was that the two of them get to *see* one other, and Anthia is captured [= "captivated"] by Habrokomes, while Habrokomes is defeated by Eros. He was *looking* right *into* the maiden [*korē*], one moment right after another, and, though he wanted to break away from the view [*opsis*], he simply couldn't. He was held fast by the god, who was pressing on him. 1.3.2 Anthia too was feeling wickedly sick, *receiving with eyes wide open* the beauty of Habrokomes as it was *flowing into* her. She was already despising all those things that are proper things to do for girls. She was ready to chatter about anything, just so that Habrokomes would hear it, and she was ready to bare parts of her *body* [sōma] as far as she could, just so that Habrokomes could see it. And he gave himself up completely to the *view* [theā] and was captured as the god's prisoner of war. 1.3.3 Then, *having finished the sacrifice* [thuein], they departed from the [sacred] space in sadness and feeling resentful about the speed of the departure. Wanting to *look at* each other, they kept turning backwards and standing back, finding countless excuses for delay. $_{1.3.4}$ Each going in separate ways, they finally made their ways back to their homes, and only the moment they got back did each of the two realize just how far they had got themselves into trouble. The consciousness of the *sight* [*opsis*] of each other came over them, and eros was kindled in them. For the rest of the day, they were stoking the desire in their heart [*thūmos*], and, when they went into sleep, they made direct contact with the nasty thing, and the eros inside each of them was to be held back no more. $_{1.4.1}$ Then, reacting to all this, *Habrokomes grabbed his own head of hair* [*komē*] and *dismembered* [= made a *sparagmos* of] *the fabric* of his clothing, saying to himself: "oh, oh, am I in trouble!"

Xenophon of Ephesus 1.1.1–1.4.5[1]

1 $_{1.1.1}$ Ἦν ἐν Ἐφέσῳ ἀνὴρ τῶν τὰ πρῶτα ἐκεῖ δυναμένων, Λυκομήδης ὄνομα. Τούτῳ τῷ Λυκομήδει ἐκ γυναικὸς ἐπιχωρίας Θεμιστοῦς γίνεται παῖς Ἁβροκόμης, μέγα δή τι χρῆμα [ὡραιότητι σώματος ὑπερβαλλούσῃ] κάλλους οὔτε ἐν Ἰωνίᾳ οὔτε ἐν ἄλλῃ γῇ πρότερον γενομένου. $_{1.1.2}$ Οὗτος ὁ Ἁβροκόμης ἀεὶ μὲν καὶ καθ' ἡμέραν εἰς κάλλος ηὔξετο, συνήνθει δὲ αὐτῷ τοῖς τοῦ σώματος καλοῖς καὶ τὰ τῆς ψυχῆς ἀγαθά· παιδείαν τε γὰρ πᾶσαν ἐμελέτα καὶ μουσικὴν ποικίλην ἤσκει, θήρα δὲ αὐτῷ καὶ ἱππασία καὶ ὁπλομαχία συνήθη γυμνάσματα. $_{1.1.3}$ Ἦν δὲ περισπούδαστος ἅπασιν Ἐφεσίοις, ἅμα καὶ τοῖς τὴν ἄλλην Ἀσίαν οἰκοῦσι, καὶ μεγάλας εἶχον ἐν αὐτῷ τὰς ἐλπίδας ὅτι πολίτης ἔσοιτο διαφέρων. Προσεῖχον δὲ ὡς θεῷ τῷ μειρακίῳ· καί εἰσιν ἤδη τινὲς οἳ καὶ προσεκύνησαν ἰδόντες καὶ προσηύξαντο. $_{1.1.4}$ Ἐφρόνει δὲ τὸ μειράκιον ἐφ' ἑαυτῷ μεγάλα καὶ ἠγάλλετο μὲν καὶ τοῖς τῆς ψυχῆς κατορθώμασι, πολὺ δὲ μᾶλλον τῷ κάλλει τοῦ σώματος· πάντων δὲ τῶν ἄλλων, ὅσα δὴ ἐλέγετο καλά, ὡς ἐλαττόνων κατεφρόνει καὶ οὐδὲν αὐτῷ, οὐ θέαμα, οὐκ ἄκουσμα ἄξιον Ἁβροκόμου κατεφαίνετο· $_{1.1.5}$ καὶ εἴ τινα ἢ παῖδα καλὸν ἀκούσαι ἢ παρθένον εὔμορφον, κατεγέλα τῶν λεγόντων ὡς οὐκ εἰδότων ὅτι εἷς καλὸς αὐτός. Ἔρωτά γε μὴν οὐδὲ ἐνόμιζεν εἶναι θεόν, ἀλλὰ πάντη ἐξέβαλεν ὡς οὐδὲν ἡγούμενος, λέγων ὡς οὐκ ἄν ποτέ [οὔ] τις ἐρασθείη οὐδὲ ὑποταγείη τῷ θεῷ μὴ θέλων· $_{1.1.6}$ εἰ δέ που ἱερὸν ἢ ἄγαλμα Ἔρωτος εἶδε, κατεγέλα, ἀπέφαινέ τε ἑαυτὸν Ἔρωτος παντὸς καλλίονα [καὶ κάλλει σώματος καὶ δυνάμει]. Καὶ εἶχεν οὕτως· ὅπου γὰρ Ἁβροκόμης ὀφθείη, οὔτε ἄγαλμα καλὸν κατεφαίνετο οὔτε εἰκὼν ἐπῃνεῖτο. $_{1.2.1}$ Μηνιᾷ πρὸς ταῦτα ὁ Ἔρως· φιλόνεικος γὰρ ὁ θεὸς καὶ ὑπερηφάνοις ἀπαραίτητος· ἐζήτει δὲ τέχνην κατὰ τοῦ μειρακίου· καὶ γὰρ καὶ τῷ θεῷ δυσάλωτος ἐφαίνετο. Ἐξοπλίσας οὖν ἑαυτὸν καὶ πᾶσαν δύναμιν ἐρωτικῶν φαρμάκων περιβαλόμενος ἐστράτευεν ἐφ' Ἁβροκόμην. $_{1.2.2}$ Ἤγετο δὲ τῆς Ἀρτέμιδος ἐπιχώριος ἑορτὴ ἀπὸ τῆς πόλεως ἐπὶ τὸ ἱερόν· στάδιοι δέ εἰσιν ἑπτά· ἔδει δὲ πομπεύειν πάσας τὰς ἐπιχωρίους παρθένους κεκοσμημένας πολυτελῶς καὶ τοὺς ἐφήβους, ὅσοι τὴν αὐτὴν ἡλικίαν εἶχον τῷ Ἁβροκόμῃ. Ἦν δὲ αὐτὸς περὶ τὰ ἓξ καὶ δέκα ἔτη καὶ τῶν ἐφήβων προσήπτετο καὶ ἐν τῇ πομπῇ τὰ πρῶτα ἐφέρετο. $_{1.2.3}$ Πολὺ δὲ πλῆθος ἐπὶ τὴν θέαν, πολὺ μὲν ἐγχώριον, πολὺ δὲ ξενικόν· καὶ γὰρ ἔθος ἦν ἐκείνῃ τῇ πανηγύρει καὶ νυμφίους ταῖς παρθένοις εὑρίσκεσθαι καὶ γυναῖκας τοῖς ἐφήβοις. $_{1.2.4}$ Παρῄεσαν δὲ κατὰ στίχον οἱ πομπεύοντες· πρῶτα μὲν τὰ ἱερὰ καὶ δᾷδες καὶ κανᾶ καὶ θυμιάματα· ἐπὶ τούτοις ἵπποι καὶ κύνες καὶ σκεύη κυνηγετικὰ ὧν ⟨τὰ μὲν⟩ πολεμικά, τὰ δὲ πλεῖστα εἰρηνικά. Ἑκάστη δὲ αὐτῶν οὕτως ὡς πρὸς ἐραστὴν ἐκεκόσμητο. $_{1.2.5}$ Ἦρχε δὲ τῆς τῶν παρθένων τάξεως Ἀνθία, θυγάτηρ Μεγαμήδους καὶ Εὐίππης, ἐγχωρίων. Ἦν δὲ τὸ κάλλος τῆς Ἀνθίας οἷον θαυμάσαι καὶ πολὺ τὰς ἄλλας ὑπερεβάλλετο παρθένους. Ἔτη μὲν τεσσαρεσκαίδεκα ἐγεγόνει, ἤνθει δὲ αὐτῆς τὸ σῶμα ἐπ' εὐμορφίᾳ, καὶ ὁ τοῦ σχήματος κόσμος πολὺς εἰς ὥραν συνεβάλλετο· $_{1.2.6}$ κόμη ξανθή, ἡ πολλὴ καθειμένη, ὀλίγη πεπλεγμένη, πρὸς τὴν τῶν ἀνέμων φορὰν κινουμένη· ὀφθαλμοὶ γοργοί, φαιδροὶ μὲν ὡς κόρης, φοβεροὶ δὲ ὡς σώφρονος· ἐσθὴς χιτὼν ἁλουργής, ζωστὸς εἰς γόνυ, μέχρι βραχιόνων καθειμένος, νεβρὶς περικειμένη, γωρυτὸς ἀνημμένος, τόξα [ὅπλα], ἄκοντες φερόμενοι, κύνες ἑπόμενοι. $_{1.2.7}$ Πολλάκις αὐτὴν ἐπὶ τοῦ

5§6. Annotations:

1.1.1a ... **a boy called *Habrokomēs*.** This name *Habrokomēs* means 'having a *komē* [head of hair] that is *habrā* [luxuriant]'.

1.1.1b ... **in all Ionia.** Throughout the narrative, there is a sense of Ionian identity. More specifically, since the city of Ephesus is a pre-eminent city in the Ionian regions of Asia Minor and the outlying islands, there is also a sense of Ephesian identity, as expressed by the persistent use of the words *epikhōrios* and *enkhōrios*, both of which I translate as 'native'. Such references create the impression that the narration must be happening in Ionia in general and in Ephesus in particular.

1.1.3 ... **And there were already those who made proskynesis to him.** The noun *proskunēsis* and the corresponding verb *proskuneîn* both refer to a ritual act of 'worshipping a superhuman power'. We have already seen the verb *proskuneîn* in 1§131. The ritual act of *proskuneîn*, which I translate here simply as 'make proskynesis', is an indirect "kiss": the idea is to kiss whatever comes into contact with the one who is worshipped—as in the case of kissing the clothing, or the ground walked on, or the air between the worshipped and the worshipper, and so on.

τεμένους ἰδόντες Ἐφέσιοι προσεκύνησαν ὡς Ἄρτεμιν. Καὶ τότ' οὖν ὀφθείσης ἀνεβόησε τὸ πλῆθος, καὶ ἦσαν ποικίλαι παρὰ τῶν θεωμένων φωναί, τῶν μὲν ὑπ' ἐκπλήξεως τὴν θεὸν εἶναι λεγόντων, τῶν δὲ ἄλλην τινὰ ὑπὸ τῆς θεοῦ περιποιημένην· προσηύχοντο δὲ πάντες καὶ προσεκύνουν καὶ τοὺς γονεῖς αὐτῆς ἐμακάριζον· ἦν δὲ διαβόητος τοῖς θεωμένοις ἅπασιν Ἀνθία ἡ καλή. 1.2.8 Ὡς δὲ παρῆλθε τὸ τῶν παρθένων πλῆθος, οὐδεὶς ἄλλο τι ἢ Ἀνθίαν ἔλεγεν· ὡς δὲ Ἁβροκόμης μετὰ τῶν ἐφήβων ἐπέστη, τοὐνθένδε, καίτοι καλοῦ ὄντος τοῦ κατὰ τὰς παρθένους θεάματος, πάντες ἰδόντες Ἁβροκόμην ἐκείνων ἐπελάθοντο, ἔτρεψαν δὲ τὰς ὄψεις ἐπ' αὐτὸν βοῶντες ὑπὸ τῆς θέας ἐκπεπληγμένοι, "καλὸς Ἁβροκόμης" λέγοντες, "καὶ οἷος οὐδὲ εἷς καλοῦ μίμημα θεοῦ." 1.2.9 Ἤδη δέ τινες καὶ τοῦτο προσέθεσαν "οἷος ἂν γάμος γένοιτο Ἁβροκόμου καὶ Ἀνθίας." Καὶ ταῦτα ἦν πρῶτα τῆς Ἔρωτος τέχνης μελετήματα. Ταχὺ μὲν δὴ εἰς ἑκατέρους ἡ περὶ ἀλλήλων ἦλθε δόξα· καὶ ἥ τε Ἀνθία τὸν Ἁβροκόμην ἐπεθύμει ἰδεῖν, καὶ ὁ τέως ἀνέραστος Ἁβροκόμης ἤθελεν Ἀνθίαν ἰδεῖν. 1.3.1 Ὡς οὖν ἐτετέλεστο ἡ πομπή ἦλθον δὲ εἰς τὸ ἱερὸν θύσοντες ἅπαν τὸ πλῆθος καὶ ὁ τῆς πομπῆς κόσμος ἐλέλυτο ᾔεσαν δὲ ἐς ταὐτὸν ἄνδρες καὶ γυναῖκες, ἔφηβοι καὶ παρθένοι, ἐνταῦθα ὁρῶσιν ἀλλήλους, καὶ ἁλίσκεται Ἀνθία ὑπὸ τοῦ Ἁβροκόμου, ἡττᾶται δὲ ὑπὸ Ἔρωτος Ἁβροκόμης καὶ ἐνεώρα τε συνεχέστερον τῇ κόρῃ καὶ ἀπαλλαγῆναι τῆς ὄψεως ἐθέλων οὐκ ἐδύνατο· κατεῖχε δὲ αὐτὸν ἐγκείμενος ὁ θεός. 1.3.2 Διέκειτο δὲ καὶ Ἀνθία πονήρως, ὅλοις μὲν καὶ ἀναπεπταμένοις τοῖς ὀφθαλμοῖς τὸ Ἁβροκόμου κάλλος εἰσρέον δεχομένη, ἤδη δὲ καὶ τῶν παρθένοις πρεπόντων καταφρονοῦσα· καὶ γὰρ ἐλάλησεν ἄν τι, ἵνα Ἁβροκόμης ἀκούσῃ, καὶ μέρη τοῦ σώματος ἐγύμνωσεν ἂν τὰ δυνατά, ἵνα Ἁβροκόμης ἴδῃ· ὁ δὲ αὐτὸν ἐδεδώκει πρὸς τὴν θέαν καὶ ἦν αἰχμάλωτος τοῦ θεοῦ. 1.3.3 Καὶ τότε μὲν θύσαντες ἀπηλλάττοντο λυπούμενοι καὶ τῷ τάχει τῆς ἀπαλλαγῆς μεμφόμενοι· ⟨καὶ⟩ ἀλλήλους βλέπειν ἐθέλοντες ἐπιστρεφόμενοι καὶ ὑφιστάμενοι πολλὰς προφάσεις διατριβῆς ηὕρισκον. 1.3.4 Ὡς δὲ ἦλθον ἑκάτερος παρ' ἑαυτόν, ἔγνωσαν τότε οἷ κακῶν ἐγεγόνεισαν· καὶ ἔννοια ἐκείνους ὑπῄει τῆς ὄψεως θατέρου καὶ ὁ ἔρως ἐν αὐτοῖς ἀνεκαίετο καὶ τὸ περιττὸν τῆς ἡμέρας αὐξήσαντες τὴν ἐπιθυμίαν, ἐπειδὴ εἰς ὕπνον ᾔεσαν, ἐν ἀθρόῳ γίνονται τῷ δεινῷ, καὶ ὁ ἔρως ἐν ἑκατέροις ἦν ἀκατάσχετος. 1.4.1 Λαβὼν δὴ τὴν κόμην ὁ Ἁβροκόμης καὶ σπαράξας τὴν ἐσθῆτα "φεῦ μοι τῶν κακῶν" εἶπε, "τί πέπονθα δυστυχής;"

The ostentatious use of "already" here suggests that the episodic practice of making the gesture of proskynesis to Habrokomes in the past time of the narrative is a prototype for an ongoing ritual practice of worshipping Habrokomes in the present time of narrating the narrative in Ephesus.

1.1.6a ... **more beautiful than every Eros.** The rhetoric of mocking Eros here makes the god multiple.

1.1.6b ... **For wherever Habrokomes was seen, there was no beautiful statue in view, nor was there an image [*eikōn*] that could be praised.** By implication, the picturing of Eros is blocked by the view of Habrokomes in the past time of the narrative. That is, there are no statues or pictures of Eros to be seen in the past time of the narrative, as opposed to the present time of narrating the narrative. It is as if the narrative exists in a time frame in which there are no images of Eros. Habrokomes with his good looks has 'become' Eros. By contrast, in the present time when the story is being told in Ephesus, the antithesis of mutually exclusive viewing has given way to a synthesis of inclusive viewing. From the perspective of those who worship the god Eros, Habrokomes has exactly the same silhouette as Eros, while from the perspective of Eros as a god to be worshipped, the figure of Eros is projecting the figure Habrokomes—with the unfortunate result that no one can see Eros. So, those who are hearing the story are now in a world where they cannot see past Habrokomes. The blocking of the view of Eros by the view of Habrokomes is an eclipse, and only the penumbra of the light emanating from Eros can show through.[2]

1.2.1a ... **Eros is now feeling anger [*mēnis*].** The present tense suggests that this response of Eros is universal, not particular. That is, the response of Eros is not restricted to the past time of the narrative but extends to the present time of narrating the narrative.

1.2.1b ... **And he was devising a *tekhnē* against the boy.** The *tekhnē* is not only the 'art' of Eros in *capturing* Habrokomes: it is also the art of the narrative in *captivating* those who hear the narration.

1.2.2a ... **A native festival [*epikhōrios heortē*] of Artemis was in progress, extending from the city all the way to the sacred space [*hieron*]. The distance is seven stadium-lengths. It was the regulation that there should be a procession [= verb of *pompē*] of all the native [*epikhōrioi*]**

2 For the metaphor of the penumbra, I am grateful to David Kowarsky.

girls. Here we see a double synecdoche of *procession* and *festival*, parallel to what we saw most recently in 4§§169–176.

1.2.2b ... **who would be arranging [*kosmeîn*] their looks in the most expensive ways [*polu-telōs*].** The adverb *polu-telōs* 'in the most expensive ways' is derived from the adjective *polu-telēs*, meaning 'involving much expense'. But there is a deeper meaning underneath the surface, since the noun *telos* from which the adjective derives means not only 'expense' but also 'the perfecting of a ritual process'.[3] In the present context, the arrangement of each girl's outer appearance is a ritual necessity, and this necessity is conveyed by the verb *kosmeîn*, which refers to the ways in which someone 'arranges' her or his exterior appearance. This verb is derived from the noun *kosmos*, meaning 'order, arrangement, self-arrangement'. These same words *kosmos* and *kosmeîn* can refer not only to the microcosmic *self-arrangement* or *make-up* of a person whose outer appearance is beautifully put together for a public ritual event—hence the meaning of the modern word *cosmetic*—but also to the *macrocosmic putting together of the universe*, the *cosmos*. Later on, at 1.2.4 and at 1.2.5, we see another expression of this "cosmic" and "cosmetic" theme. Further, at 1.2.5, the *kosmos* or self-arrangement of Anthia is synchronized with *hōrā*, that is, with the seasonality of the entire universe.[4] Still further, at 1.3.1, we see that the very idea of a *procession* that leads into a *festival* is conceived as a *kosmos*—as a universal whole in the sense of the modern word *cosmos*. That is why, in the context of 1.3.1, the entire procession held in honor of Artemis is called a *kosmos*. In this same context, the self-arrangement of a participant in the ritual process of a procession is meant to be synchronized with the cosmos.

1.2.2c ... **all the ephebes ... who were the same age as Habrokomes.** The wording of the narrative implies that Habrokomes was a *model* of the age group, not simply a *member*, like the others. If the narrative, as myth, is an aetiology of the ritual of the *pompē* or 'procession', then Habrokomes becomes *ex post facto* a model for the ritual.

1.2.4a ... **First in order were the sacred [*hiera*] objects and the torches and the baskets and the incense.** I note the metonymy: those who process in the procession are indexed in terms of what they are carrying in the sequence of processing.

3 *H24H* 20§1.

4 On the further link between *hōrā* as seasonality and *telos* as perfection in ritual, see *H24H* 1§149, 13§15.

1.2.4b ... **After them came the horses and the hunting dogs and the hunting equipment—some of the equipment was connected with war but most of it was connected with peace.** We see here further metonymy by way of sequencing. The identities of the persons linked with these features of the procession are elided.

1.2.4c ... **Each of the girls arranged [*kosmeîn*] her looks in such a way as one does oneself up for one's lover.** Here, as I already noted, we see clearly the "cosmetic" aspect of *kosmos*. What is so deeply personalized, however, is also at the same time broadly universalized. I highlight the fact that the verb *kosmeîn*, referring to the self-arrangement of each girl, is used here in the pluperfect form. This pluperfect has a metonymic significance. As David A. Smith has shown, *when a verb in the pluperfect tense is inserted within a sequence of other verbs in the past tense, the pluperfect has the function of indicating a climactic moment in the narrative.*[5] In the context of describing the self-arrangement of each girl in the procession, the pluperfect here is highlighting, one at a time, a singular climactic moment in the personal experience of each girl participating in the procession.

1.2.5a ... **Leading the processional file of girls was Anthiā.** Here is the first mention of *Anthiā* in the narrative; the name derives from *anthos* 'blossom'. She is a perfect match for *Habrokomēs*, whose name as we have seen means 'having a *komē* [head of hair] that is *habrā* [luxuriant]'. The metonymy of the lovers' names, *Habrokomēs* and *Anthiā*, is symmetrical with the metonymy of a luxuriant head of hair and a beautiful garland of blossoms intertwined with the hair. Such a garland is to be worn at a festival. On the occasion of a festival, garlands and hair go together metonymically. I am reminded here of a modern aphorism: "Love and marriage go together like a horse and carriage."[6]

1.2.5b ... **And the manifold self-arrangement [*kosmos*] of her pose [*skhēma*] was put together in such a way as to achieve perfect seasonality [*hōrā*].** As I have already argued in an earlier annotation (at 1.2.2[b]), the *kosmos* or self-arrangement of Anthia—that is, the way in which she is put together—is synchronized with *hōrā*, that is, with the seasonality of the entire cosmos. Her self-arrangement is seen as the pose of a dancer. The ancient Greek term *skhēma* (which becomes the modern

5 Smith 1994.

6 Reardon 1982:24 cites this title of a song sung by Frank Sinatra (first recorded August 15, 1955).

word *scheme*) can refer to the "freeze-frame" or stop-motion pose of a dancer *or of a statue.*[7]

1.2.7a ... **There were arrows and javelins in it [= the quiver].** This detail is clarified by another detail mentioned earlier at 1.2.4, where it is said that the peacetime weapons of hunting outshine the wartime weapons.

1.2.7b ... **At that moment, at the very sight of her, the crowd shouted out. ... Some, experiencing astonishment [*ekplēxis*], were saying that she is the goddess.** This moment, which creates a personal as well as a communal experience of *ekplēxis* 'astonishment', marks a sight that can truly be described as an *epiphany*. I recall here my working definition of epiphany at 1§§128–129, elaborated at 2§§14–15.

1.2.7c ... **Others were saying that she was some kind of surrogate for the goddess.** The surrogacy is expressed by way of the verb *peripoieîsthai* in the sense of 'be encompassed': it is as if Anthia were 'encompassed' by the goddess. A distinction is being made here between the perception of a full-grade initiate, who recognizes the moment when a human becomes divine in the ritual climax of an epiphany, and the perception of a partial-grade initiate, whose powers of inductiveness have not yet reached the *telos* or 'ritual perfection' of full understanding.

1.2.8 ... **and they turned their gaze [*opsis* plural] at him and were shouting, experiencing astonishment [*ekplēxis*] at the view [*theā*].** Just as the viewers at 1.2.7 experience *ekplēxis* 'astonishment' in seeing Anthia as an epiphany of the goddess Artemis, so also now at 1.2.8 they experience *ekplēxis* 'astonishment' in seeing Habrokomes as an epiphany of the discreetly unnamed god Eros. The discretion is motivated by the overt virginity of the goddess Artemis. I must take this moment here to express my own personal sense of astonishment as I marvel at the ritual precision of the language that is used here in describing the double epiphany that is mediated by Anthia and Habrokomes.

1.3.1 ... **When the procession [*pompē*] finally reached its culmination [*telos*] and the whole crowd entered the sacred space in order to make sacrifice [*thuein*] and when the arrangement [*kosmos*] of the procession [*pompē*] was finally dissolved and all the men and women entered the same space, as well as all the ephebes and girls, then it was that the two of them get to see one other.** To show the symmetrical arrangement of the syntax here, I quote the original

7 *H24H* 13§14, following *HC* 1§47.

Greek, with special highlighting: Ὡς οὖν ἐτετέλεστο ἡ πομπή ἦλθον δὲ εἰς τὸ ἱερὸν θύσοντες ἅπαν τὸ πλῆθος καὶ ὁ τῆς πομπῆς κόσμος ἐλέλυτο ᾔεσαν δὲ ἐς ταὐτὸν ἄνδρες καὶ γυναῖκες, ἔφηβοι καὶ παρθένοι, ἐνταῦθα ὁρῶσιν ἀλλήλους. The highlighted form *e-te-teles-to*, which I translated as 'finally reached is culmination', is the pluperfect of the verb *teleîst-hai* meaning 'reach a *telos* or point of ritual completion'. This form is correlated, by way of the conjunction *kai* meaning 'and', with another highlighted form, *e-le-lu-to*, which I translated as 'was finally dissolved' and which is the pluperfect of the verb *luesthai* meaning 'be dissolved'. So, the when-clause here introduces two correlated pluperfect forms signaling a climax in the sequence of action, and both pluperfects mark the same climax, expressing it in two different ways. Further, these two pluperfects are each followed by consecutive clauses introduced by the conjunction *de* meaning 'and', where both clauses mean the same thing: (1) "and [*de*] the whole crowd entered the sacred space," which comes after "when the procession [*pompē*] finally reached its culmination [*telos*]," and (2) "and [*de*] all the men and women entered the same space, as well as all the ephebes and girls," which comes after "when the arrangement [*kosmos*] of the procession [*pompē*] was finally dissolved." In the logic of this sequence of events, the two pluperfects are expressing the same climactic ritual moment, which is when the *pompē* 'procession' reaches its culmination and can finally be dissolved, so that the participants may now finally enter the sacred space of Artemis, where they will now perform the sacrifice that is signaled by the verb *thuein* 'sacrifice'. This complex when-clause is then followed by the simplex main clause, where a verb in the present tense captures the moment when Anthia and Habrokomes finally get to see one another for the very first time. So, the trajectory of the *pompē* is not only the procession in and of itself but also the plot of the story, which climaxes in sacrifice, which in turn signals the moment when the two lovers finally get to see one another. I am ready to say, then, that *the plot of the story*, as a metonymic sequence, corresponds to *the order of the procession*, which is a parallel universe of metonymic sequencing. That said, I have come to the point that I anticipated in 5§4: *to process in a procession is to participate in the actual process of metonymy*. To put it another way, *a procession is a process of metonymy*.

1.3.2 ... **And he gave himself up completely to the view [*theā*] and was captured as the god's prisoner of war.** Again, a pluperfect here marks the climactic moment.

1.3.3 ... **Then, having finished the sacrifice [*thuein*], they departed from the [sacred] space in sadness and feeling resentful about the speed of the departure.** Clearly, the act of *thuein* 'sacrificing' here is not just the slaughtering and cooking and dividing and consuming of beef but rather, metonymically, it is also the whole festival and all the experiences that come with it. When the sacrifice is over, the party is over. So, the happy part of the story is finished for now. and the lingering aftereffect is a melancholic desire for a reprise of the story—for experiencing the story as a re-enactment of the whole myth-ritual complex that was the festival of Artemis in Ephesus.

1.3.4 ... **Only the moment they got back did each of the two realize just how far they had got themselves into trouble.** Again we see here a pluperfect of a climactic moment. In this case, the two characters are made to realize the climax of their own story.

5§7. Now I proceed, "fast-forward," to the second of the three passages I translate. I divide this passage, which is already nearing the end of the whole novel, into three subsets, which I label Ba, Bb, and Bc.

5§8. As we rejoin the action in subset Ba, we can see that the lovers Habrokomes and Anthia have already been separated from each other for a long time, and they have experienced many tribulations since their separation.[8] Here is the immediate context: at 5.11.1, a character named Hippothoös, who now owns Anthia as his slave, has decided to take her back with him from "Italia" to Ephesus. They have boarded a huge Ephesian ship and have set sail together, heading for Ephesus. As we reach 5.11.2, the ship has just now stopped over at the grand city harbor of the island of Rhodes. Hippothoös and Anthia stay overnight in a house where Anthia is chaperoned by an old woman named Althaia. On the next day, before Hippothoös and Anthia can set sail from Rhodes, something intervenes, as we see here in Subset Ba:

Extract 5-Ba

5.11.2 A major *festival* [<u>*heortē*</u>] was being celebrated at the public expense of the people of Rhodes in honor of the god Helios, and there was a *procession* [<u>*pompē*</u>] and a *sacrifice* [<u>*thusiā*</u>] and a huge crowd of citizens celebrating the *feast* [= verb of <u>*heortē*</u>]. 5.11.3 Present at this occasion were Leukon and Rhode [= faithful former retainers of Anthia], intending not

8 I recommend the study of Bierl 2014 for an analysis of the overall plot of this novel. On plot and metonymy in the ancient Greek novel, see Bierl 2007, especially pp. 255–258. For more on the novel of Xenophon of Ephesus: Bierl 2012.

so much to take part in the *festival* [heortē] as to go on a search in hopes of *finding out* something, anything, about Anthia. Right at that point Hippothoös arrived *in the sacred space* [hieron], bringing Anthia with him. And she, looking off at the displayed votive offerings and remembering things from the past, said: "I address you, O god Helios, you who look upon all things connected with all humans, you who have bypassed no one but me alone, unfortunate wretch that I am. The previous time I was in Rhodes, I was happy and with good fortune [*tukhē*] as *I gave* you *proskynesis* and *sacrificed* [thuein] *sacrifices* [thusiā plural] to you along with Habrokomes, and I was thought to be happy and well blessed by gods [*daimones*] back then. But now I am a slave instead of a free woman, and I am a prisoner of war, unfortunate wretch that I am, a woman no longer blessed by good fortune, and I am going to Ephesus all alone and I will be revealed to the members of my household as a woman who no longer has Habrokomes. 5.11.5 She said these things and *followed up* [= epi-] what she said with *many a tear* and asked Hippothoös to allow her to *part company* with some of *her own hair* [komē] and to offer it as a votive offering to the god Helios and to *utter some prayer* [eukhesthai] about Habrokomes. 5.11.6 Hippothoös complied. And she, *cutting off* from her *locks* [plokamoi] as much as she could and seizing an opportune moment when everyone else had departed [from the sacred space], she offered it up as an offering, *inscribing* [epigraphein] it: "On behalf of Habrokomes, husband. Anthia. Her *hair* [komē] she offered as an offering to the god." Having done these things and having *uttered a prayer* [eukhesthai] she was about to go away with Hippothoös. 5.12.1 But Leukon and Rhode, who had up to now been circulating around the *procession* [pompē], *now stop over at the sacred space* [hieron], and they *look at* [blepein] the offerings and recognize the names of their masters. The first thing they do is to *greet* the *hair* [komē] and *weep* over it many times over, *as if they were looking at [blepein] Anthia herself*, and then in the end [derivative of *telos*], when they were done, they started going around [the city] in hopes of being able to *find* that [*ekeinē*] woman herself.

Xenophon of Ephesus 5.11.2–5.12.1[9]

9 5.11.2 ἑορτὴ δέ τις ἤγετο μεγαλοπρεπὴς δημοσίᾳ τῶν Ῥοδίων ἀγόντων τῷ Ἡλίῳ, καὶ πομπή τε καὶ θυσία καὶ πολιτῶν ἑορταζόντων πλῆθος. 5.11.3 Ἐνταῦθα παρῆσαν ὁ Λεύκων καὶ ἡ Ῥόδη, οὐ τοσοῦτον τῆς ἑορτῆς μεθέξοντες, ὅσον ἀναζητήσοντες εἴ τι περὶ Ἀνθίας πύθοιντο. Καὶ δὴ ἧκεν ὁ Ἱππόθοος εἰς τὸ ἱερόν, ἄγων τὴν Ἀνθίαν· ἡ δὲ ἀπιδοῦσα εἰς τὰ ἀναθήματα καὶ ἐν ἀναμνήσει τῶν πρότερον γενομένη 5.11.4 "ὦ τὰ πάντων" ἔφησεν "ἀνθρώπων ἐφορῶν Ἥλιε, μόνην ἐμὲ τὴν δυστυχῆ παρελθών, πρότερον μὲν ἐν Ῥόδῳ γενομένη εὐτυχῶς τέ σε προσεκύνουν καὶ θυσίας ἔθυον μετὰ Ἁβροκόμου καὶ εὐδαίμων τότε ἐνομιζόμην· νυνὶ δὲ δούλη μὲν ἀντ' ἐλευθέρας,

5§9. Annotations:

$_{5.11.2}$ ... **A major festival [*heortē*] was being celebrated ..., and there was a procession [*pompē*] and a sacrifice [*thusiā*].** Here we see the double synecdoche of *pompē* 'procession' and *thusiā* 'sacrifice'.

$_{5.11.3}$ ... **to go on a search in hopes of finding out something, anything, about Anthia.** As of now, Anthia is a vision that has completely disappeared from the view of the searchers. But soon they will be contemplating the *komē* 'hair' as if they could see all of Anthia.

$_{5.12.1a}$ ... **They look at [*blepein*] the offerings and recognize the names of their masters.** The searchers, after having read the inscription that Anthia had left behind in the sacred place, can now recognize Anthia just by looking at [*blepein*] her offering of hair [*komē*].

$_{5.12.1b}$ ... **The first thing they do is to greet the hair [*komē*] and weep over it many times over, as if they were looking at [*blepein*] Anthia herself.** By way of metonymy, the big picture becomes visible merely by way of looking at [*blepein*] the hair of Anthia—as if they were looking at [*blepein*] Anthia herself. We have here a most striking example of ritualized synecdoche.

$_{5.12.1c}$ ... **in hopes of being able to find that [*ekeinē*] woman herself.** The pronoun *ekeinē*, referring to 'that' woman, visualizes the totality of Anthia in the discourse of the narrative. This pronoun *ekeinos*/*ekeinē* is conventionally used in contexts describing an epiphany.[10]

5§10. The story now continues to track what happens to Leukon and Rhode on that same day (5.12.2). The couple searches for Anthia but still cannot find her. Then they go back to the house where they are staying with Habrokomes, who is also on the island, unbeknownst to Anthia, and they tell him what they saw. He is filled with hopes of finding Anthia. Then, the story shifts to the next day (5.12.3). Anthia goes back to the sacred space with Hippothoös, since there

---

αἰχμάλωτος δὲ ἡ δυστυχὴς ἀντὶ τῆς μακαρίας, καὶ εἰς Ἔφεσον ἔρχομαι μόνη καὶ φανοῦμαι τοῖς οἰκείοις Ἁβροκόμην οὐκ ἔχουσα." $_{5.11.5}$ Ταῦτα ἔλεγε καὶ πολλὰ ἐπεδάκρυε καὶ δεῖται τοῦ Ἱπποθόου ἐπιτρέψαι αὐτῇ τῆς κόμης ἀφελεῖν τῆς αὐτῆς καὶ ἀναθεῖναι τῷ Ἡλίῳ καὶ εὔξασθαί τι περὶ Ἁβροκόμου. $_{5.11.6}$ Συγχωρεῖ ὁ Ἱππόθοος· καὶ ἀποτεμοῦσα τῶν πλοκάμων ὅσα ἐδύνατο καὶ ἐπιτηδείου καιροῦ λαβομένη, πάντων ἀπηλλαγμένων, ἀνατίθησιν ἐπιγράψασα ΥΠΕΡ. ΤΟΥ. ΑΝΔΡΟΣ. ΑΒΡΟΚΟΜΟΥ. ΑΝΘΙΑ. ΤΗΝ. ΚΟΜΗΝ. ΤΩΙ. ΘΕΩΙ. ΑΝΕΘΗΚΕ. Ταῦτα ποιήσασα καὶ εὐξαμένη ἀπῄει μετὰ τοῦ Ἱπποθόου. $_{5.12.1}$ Ὁ δὲ Λεύκων καὶ ἡ Ῥόδη τέως ὄντες περὶ τὴν πομπὴν ἐφίστανται τῷ ἱερῷ καὶ βλέπουσι τὰ ἀναθήματα καὶ γνωρίζουσι τῶν δεσποτῶν τὰ ὀνόματα καὶ πρῶτον ἀσπάζονται τὴν κόμην καὶ πολλὰ κατωδύροντο οὕτως ὡς Ἀνθίαν βλέποντες, τελευταῖον δὲ περιῄεσαν, εἴ που κἀκείνην εὑρεῖν δυνήσονται.

[10] *H24H* 5§39, 15§45.

is still no ship available for sailing on to Ephesus, and I quote here in Subset Bb the wording that captures what she does next:

Extract 5-Bb

> She [= Anthia] sits down ritually among the offerings, weeping and sighing.
>
> Xenophon of Ephesus 5.12.3[11]

5§11. It is as if Anthia herself, not only her lock of hair, became a votive offering in the sacred space of the temple. *She is becoming a ritual metonym.* Meanwhile, as we continue where we just left off (5.12.3), Leukon and Rhode enter the sacred space, having left Habrokomes behind in the house, since he is too disheartened to be searching for Anthia. I show here in Subset Bc what happens next:

Extract 5-Bc

> 5.12.3 Entering the space, they *see* Anthia and at first she was still *unrecognized* by them, *but then they put everything back together again*: the *eros*, the *tears*, the *votive offerings*, the *names*, the *form* [*eidos*]. 5.12.4 In this way, bit by bit, they begin to *recognize* her.
>
> Xenophon of Ephesus 5.12.3–5.12.4[12]

5§12. The disintegration of loss is followed up here by the reintegration of recovery, of finding the self again. And the key to this recovery is the metonymic sequencing of identifiable aspects of Anthia that have by now become all too familiar to anyone who has experienced her story: the *eros*, the *tears*, the *votive offerings*, the *names*, the *beautiful looks* [*eidos*].

5§13. Then, to continue (5.12.4), Leukon and Rhode identify themselves to Anthia and tell her that Habrokomes is safe and sound [= *sōizesthai*] (5.12.5). Hearing the news, Anthia experiences astonishment [*ekplēxis*] (5.12.6). Soon thereafter the two lovers are happily reunited in Rhodes, so that they may now sail to Ephesus together for *la grande finale* (5.13.1–5.15.1).

5§14. Now comes the third of the three passages that I am translating. This passage, which I label C, coincides with the ending of the novel—an ending that is really no ending at all:

11 προσκαθίσασα δὲ τοῖς ἀναθήμασιν ἐδάκρυέ τε καὶ ἀνέστενεν.

12 5.12.3 ἐλθόντες δὲ ὁρῶσι τὴν Ἀνθίαν καὶ ἦν μὲν ἔτι ἄγνωστος αὐτοῖς, συμβάλλουσι δὲ πάντα, ⟨τὸν⟩ ἔρωτα, ⟨τὰ⟩ δάκρυα, τὰ ἀναθήματα, τὰ ὀνόματα, τὸ εἶδος. 5.12.4 Οὕτως κατὰ βραχὺ ἐγνώριζον αὐτήν·

Extract 5-C

> $_{5.15.2}$ The whole city (of Ephesus) *had* already *found out in advance* about their [= the lovers'] *safe return* [sōtēriā]. As soon as they [= the lovers] emerged [from the ship that pulled into the city harbor], right then and there they went to the *sacred space* [hieron] of Artemis and *uttered* many *prayers* [eukhesthai] and, having *made sacrifice* [thuein], they offered many votive offerings to the goddess, especially *a piece of writing* [graphē] that narrated everything they experienced and did. $_{5.15.3}$ Having done this, they went up to the city and arranged for lavish funerals for their parents, who had in the meantime died of old age and heartbreak. And they [= the lovers] for the rest of time lived their lives celebrating the *festival* [heortē].
>
> Xenophon of Ephesus 5.15.2–5.15.3[13]

5§15. The *graphē* 'piece of writing' that the two lovers dedicate as a votive offering inside the temple of Artemis can be seen as the novel itself.[14] And the novel thus becomes a synecdoche for the overall sacrifice that is the festival. So, how does the novel end? Did the two lovers live happily ever after? No, better than that: for these two lovers *to live happily ever after is to celebrate a festival forever*. I repeat the actual wording that we have just read: *for the rest of time, they lived their lives celebrating the festival* [heortē]. So the party, as conveyed by the word *heortē* 'festival', will go on forever.

5§16. Already at an early stage of their story, back when the couple had made love for the very first time, it was said that they felt as if their whole life had now turned into one big party, and the word that was used there as well for the idea of a party was *heortē* 'festival' (1.10.2). Back then, of course, the story of all the tribulations that the couple would have to endure in the future had not yet even begun, and the fallacy of their feelings of permanent happiness was in fact duly noted by the story itself.[15] But now, as the story reaches its conclusion,

[13] $_{5.15.2}$ Προεπέπυστο δὲ τὴν σωτηρίαν αὐτῶν ἡ πόλις ἅπασα· ὡς δὲ ἐξέβησαν, εὐθὺς ὡς εἶχον ἐπὶ τὸ ἱερὸν τῆς Ἀρτέμιδος ᾔεσαν καὶ πολλὰ ηὔχοντο καὶ θύσαντες ἄλλα ⟨τε⟩ ἐνέθεσαν ἀναθήματα καὶ δὴ καὶ [τὴν] γραφὴν τῇ θεῷ ἀνέθεσαν πάντα ὅσα τε ἔπαθον καὶ ὅσα ἔδρασαν· $_{5.15.3}$ καὶ ταῦτα ποιήσαντες, ἀνελθόντες εἰς τὴν πόλιν τοῖς γονεῦσιν αὐτῶν τάφους κατεσκεύασαν μεγάλους (ἔτυχον γὰρ ὑπὸ γήρως καὶ ἀθυμίας προτεθνηκότες), καὶ αὐτοὶ τοῦ λοιποῦ διῆγον ἑορτὴν ἄγοντες τὸν μετ' ἀλλήλων βίον.

[14] There is an incisive commentary by Bierl 2014 3§4 on the idea that the book itself can be seen as a votive offering deposited inside a temple.

[15] The psychology of the couple's delusional optimism at this point in the narrative is analyzed by Bierl 2014 5§4.

it is said that the *heortē* 'festival' can truly recommence, so that the partying will now go on forever. So the conclusion of the story is not really a conclusion.[16]

5§17. And the synecdoche for this eternal celebration at a *heortē* 'festival' is the interweaving of a garland made of *anthē* 'blossoms', signaled by the name of *Anthiā*, with a *habrā* or 'luxuriant' *komē* or 'head of hair', signaled by the name of *Habrokomēs*. Once the luxuriant hair is reunited with the blossoms of the garland, the celebration can go on forever, and everyone who takes part will be sure to feel utter delight.

[16] On narrative strategies of bringing to a conclusion an open-ended story, as in this case, I cite the essay of Nimis 1999.

Bibliography

Bibliographical Abbreviations

ABV Beazley, J. 1956. *Attic Black-Figure Vase Painters*. Oxford.

BA Nagy, G. 1999. *The Best of the Achaeans: Concepts of the Hero in Archaic Greek Poetry*. Rev. ed. with new introduction. Baltimore (available online).

CPG Leutsch, E. L. von, and F. G. Schneidewin, eds. 1839–1851. *Corpus Paroemiographorum Graecorum*. Göttingen.

DELG Chantraine, P. 2009. *Dictionnaire étymologique de la langue grecque: Histoire des mots*. Edited by. J. Taillardat, O. Masson, and J.-L. Perpillou, with a supplement "Chroniques d'étymologie grecque," ed. A. Blanc, C. de Lamberterie, and Jean-Louis Perpillou, 1–10. Paris.

EH Nagy, G. 2006. "The Epic Hero." Expanded version of "The Epic Hero." In *A Companion to Ancient Epic*, ed. J. M. Foley, 71–89. Oxford, 2005 (available online).

FGH Jacoby, F. 1923–58. *Die Fragmente der griechischen Historiker*. 3 vols. Berlin.

GM Nagy, G. 1990b. *Greek Mythology and Poetics*. Ithaca, NY (available online).

H24H Nagy, G. 2013. *The Ancient Greek Hero in 24 Hours*. Cambridge, MA.

HC Nagy, G. 2009. *Homer the Classic*. Hellenic Studies 36. Washington, DC (available online).

HPC Nagy, G. 2010. *Homer the Preclassic*. Berkeley, CA (available online).

HQ Nagy, G. 1996b. *Homeric Questions*. Austin, TX (available online).

HR Nagy, G. 2003. *Homeric Responses*. Austin, TX.

HTL Nagy, G. 2004a. *Homer's Text and Language*. Urbana, IL.

IG Deutsche Akademie der Wissenschaften. 1873–. *Inscriptiones Graecae*. Berlin.

LSJ Liddell, H. G., R. Scott, and H. S. Jones. 1940. *A Greek-English Lexicon*. 9th ed. Oxford.

MW *Fragmenta Hesiodea*. Edited by R. Merkelbach and M. West. 1967. Oxford.

PH Nagy, G. 1990a. *Pindar's Homer: The Lyric Possession of an Epic Past*. Baltimore (available online).

PMG Page, D. L. 1962. *Poetae Melici Graeci*. Oxford.

PP Nagy, G. 1996a. *Poetry as Performance: Homer and Beyond*. Cambridge (available online).

PR Nagy, G. 2002a. *Plato's Rhapsody and Homer's Music: The Poetics of the Panathenaic Festival in Classical Athens*. Cambridge, MA, and Athens (available online).

SEG Gieben, J. C., et al. 1923–. *Supplementum Epigraphicum Graecum*. Amsterdam.

Bibliographical References

Albersmeier, S., ed. 2009. *Heroes: Mortals and Myths in Ancient Greece*. Baltimore.

Aleshire, S. B., and S. D. Lambert. 2003. "Making the Peplos for Athena: A New Edition of *IG* II² 1060 + *IG* II² 1036." *Zeitschrift für Papyrologie und Epigraphik* 142:65–86.

Alexiou, M. 1974. *The Ritual Lament in Greek Tradition*. Cambridge. 2nd ed. 2002, with new introduction by P. Roilos and D. Yatromanolakis. Lanham, MD.

Allen, T. W., ed. 1912. *Homeri Opera*. Vol. 5, *Hymns, Cycle, Fragments*. Oxford.

Aloni, A. 1989. *L'aedo e i tiranni: Ricerche sull'Inno omerico ad Apollo*. Rome.

Bakker, E. J. 1997. *Poetry in Speech: Orality and Homeric Discourse*. Ithaca, NY.

———. 2002. "The Making of History: Herodotus' *historiēs apodexis*." In *Brill's Companion to Herodotus*, ed. E. J. Bakker, I. J. F. De Jong, H. van Wees, 3–32. Leiden.

———. 2005. *Pointing at the Past: From Formula to Performance in Homeric Poetics*. Hellenic Studies 12. Washington, DC.

Barber, E. J. W. 1991. *Prehistoric Textiles: The Development of Cloth in the Neolithic and Bronze Ages, with Special Reference to the Aegean*. Princeton.

———. 1992. "The Peplos of Athena." In Neils 1992a, 103–117, with notes at 208–210.

Berczelly, L. 1992. "Pandora and Panathenaia: The Pandora Myth and the Sculptural Decoration of the Parthenon." *Acta ad archaeologiam et artium historiam pertinentia* 8:53–86.

Berenson Maclean, J. K., and E. B. Aitken, eds. 2001. *Flavius Philostratus. Heroikos*. Atlanta. The introduction, translation, and commentary are available at http://chs.harvard.edu/CHS/article/display/3565.

Bers, V., D. Elmer, D. Frame, and L. Muellner, eds. 2012. *Donum Natalicium Digitaliter Confectum Gregorio Nagy Septuagenario a Discipulis Collegis Familiaribus Oblatum: A Virtual Birthday Gift Presented to Gregory Nagy on Turning Seventy by his Students, Colleagues, and Friends*. http://chs.harvard.edu/CHS/article/display/4843.

Bershadsky, N. 2012. "A Picnic, a Tomb, and a Crow." *Harvard Studies in Classical Philology* 106:1–45.

Bierl, A. 2001. *Der Chor in der alten Komödie: Ritual und Performativität; Unter besonderer Berücksichtigung von Aristophanes' Thesmophoriazusen und der Phalloslieder fr. 851 PMG*. Munich.

———. 2006. "Räume im Anderen und der griechische Liebesroman des Xenophon von Ephesos: Träume?" In *Mensch und Raum von der Antike bis zur Gegenwart*, ed. A. Loprieno, 71–103. Colloquium Rauricum 9. Munich.

———. 2007. "Mysterien der Liebe und die Initiation Jugendlicher: Literatur und Religion im griechischen Roman." In *Literatur und Religion: Wege zu einer mythisch-rituellen Poetik bei den Griechen*, ed. A. Bierl, R. Lämmle, and K. Wesselmann, 2:239–334. MythosEikonPoiesis 1.2. Berlin.

———. 2009. *Ritual and Performativity. The Chorus in Old Comedy*. Translation by A. Hollman of Bierl 2001. Hellenic Studies 20. Washington, DC. http://chs.harvard.edu/CHS/article/display/4427.

———. 2011. "Prozessionen auf der griechischen Bühne: Performativität des einziehenden Chors als Manifestation des Dionysos in der Parodos der Euripideischen *Bakchen*." In *Medialität der Prozession: Performanz ritueller Bewegung in Texten und Bildern der Vormoderne (= Médialité de la procession: Performance du mouvement rituel en textes et en images à l'époque prémoderne)*, ed. K. Gvozdeva and H. R. Velten, 35–61. Heidelberg.

———. 2012. "Traumatic Dreams: Lacanian Love, Kubrick's *Eyes Wide Shut*, and the Ancient Greek Novel, or, Gliding in Phantasmagoric Chains of Metonymy." In Bers, Elmer, Frame, and Muellner 2012. http://chs.harvard.edu/CHS/article/display/4388.

———. 2013. "Maenadism as Self-Referential Chorality in Euripides' *Bacchae*." In *Choral Mediations in Greek Tragedy*, ed. R. Gagné and M. G. Hopman, 211–226. Cambridge. Abridged version of Bierl 2011.

———. 2014. "Space in Xenophon of Ephesus: Love, Dream, and Dissemination." Translation by M. Berrey of Bierl 2006. http://chs.harvard.edu/CHS/article/display/5637.

Blech, M. 1982. *Studien zum Kranz bei den Griechen*. Berlin.

Bravo, J. J. 2009. "Recovering the Past: The Origins of Greek Heroes and Hero Cults." In Albersmeier 2009, 10–29.

Brelich, A. 1958. *Gli eroi greci: Un problema storico-religioso*. Rome.

Bundy, E. L. 1972. "The 'Quarrel between Kallimachos and Apollonios' Part I: The Epilogue of Kallimachos's 'Hymn to Apollo.'" *California Studies in Classical Antiquity* 5:39–94.

———. 1986 [1962]. *Studia Pindarica*. Berkeley, CA.

Burkert, W. 1960. "Das Lied von Ares und Aphrodite: Zum Verhältnis von *Odyssee* und *Ilias*." *Rheinisches Museum fur Philologie* 103:130–144. Reprinted 2001 in *Kleine Schriften*, vol. 1: *Homerica*, ed. C. Riedweg and others, 105–116. Göttingen. Trans. by G. M. Wright and P. V. Jones in *Homer: German Scholarship in Translation*, 249–262 (Oxford 1997).

———. 1979. "Kynaithos, Polycrates, and the Homeric Hymn to Apollo." In *Arktouros: Hellenic Studies Presented to B. M. W. Knox*, ed. G. W. Bowersock, W. Burkert, and M. C. J. Putnam, 53–62. Berlin. Reprinted 2001 in *Kleine Schriften*, vol. 1: *Homerica*, ed. C. Riedweg et al., 189–197. Göttingen.

———. 1983. *Homo Necans: The Anthropology of Ancient Greek Sacrificial Ritual and Myth.* Trans. P. Bing. Berkeley, CA. Originally published 1972 as *Homo Necans*. Berlin.

———. 1985. *Greek Religion*. Trans. J. Raffan. Cambridge, MA. Originally published 1977 as *Griechische Religion der archaischen und klassischen Epoche*. Stuttgart.

———. 1992. *The Orientalizing Revolution: Near Eastern Influence on Greek Culture in the Early Archaic Age*. Translation of Burkert 1984 by M. Pinder and W. Burkert. Cambridge, MA.

Calame, C. 2001. *Choruses of Young Women in Ancient Greece: Their Morphology, Religious Role, and Social Function*. Trans. D. Collins and J. Orion. 2nd ed. Lanham, MD.

Chaniotis, A. 2009. "Dividing Art - Divided Art: Reflections on the Parthenon Sculpture." In *New Acropolis Museum*, ed. I. Mylonopoulos and A. Chaniotis, vol. 1:41–48. New York.

Chantraine, P. 2009. *Dictionnaire étymologique de la langue grecque: Histoire des mots*. Ed. J. Taillardat, O. Masson, and J.-L. Perpillou, with supplement "Chroniques d'étymologie grecque," ed. A. Blanc, C. de Lamberterie, and Jean-Louis Perpillou, 1–10. Paris.

Clader, L. L. 1976. *Helen: The Evolution From Divine to Heroic in Greek Epic Tradition*. Mnemosyne Supplement 42. Leiden.

Clay, D. 1983. "Individual and Community in the First Generation of the Epicurean School." *Syzetesis* (Naples) 1:255–79. Reprinted in Clay 1998:55–74.

———. 1986. "The Cults of Epicurus." *Cronache ercolanesi* 16:11–28. Reprinted in Clay 1998:75–102.

———. 1998. *Paradosis and Survival*. Ann Arbor, MI.

Collins, L. 1988. *Studies in Characterization in the Iliad.* Frankfurt.

Connelly, J. B. 1993. "The Parthenon Frieze and the Sacrifice of the Erechtheids: Reinterpreting the 'Peplos Scene.'" *American Journal of Archaeology* 97:309–310.

———. 1996. "Parthenon and *Parthenoi*: A Mythological Reinterpretation of the Parthenon Frieze." *American Journal of Archaeology* 100:53–80.

———. 2007. *Portrait of a Priestess: Women and Ritual in Ancient Greece*. Princeton.

———. 2014. *The Parthenon Enigma: A New Understanding of the West's Most Iconic Building and the People Who Made It*. New York.

De Martino, F. 1982. *Omero agonista in Delo*. Brescia.

Detienne, M. 1972. *Les jardins d'Adonis: La mythologie des aromates en Grèce*. Paris.

———. 1977. *The Gardens of Adonis*. Trans. by J. Lloyd of Detienne 1972. Sussex.

Deutsche akademie der Wissenschaften. 1873–. *Inscriptiones Graecae*. Berlin.

Dibbern, M. 2000. *The Tales of Hoffmann: A Performance Guide*. Vox Musicae: The Voice, Vocal Pedagogy, and Song No. 5. Hillsdale NY.

Ducrot, O., and T. Todorov. 1979. *Encyclopedic Dictionary of the Sciences of Language*. Trans. C. Porter. Baltimore.

Dué, C. 2002. *Homeric Variations on a Lament by Briseis*. Lanham, MD. http://chs.harvard.edu/CHS/article/display/4311.

———. 2006. *The Captive Woman's Lament in Greek Tragedy*. Austin, TX. http://chs.harvard.edu/CHS/article/display/5631.

Edmunds, S. T. 2012. "Picturing Homeric Weaving." In Bers, Elmer, Frame, and Muellner 2012. http://chs.harvard.edu/CHS/article/display/4353.

Ekroth, G. 2002. *The Sacrificial Rituals of Greek Hero-Cults in the Archaic to the Early Hellenistic Periods*. Liège.

———. 2009. "The Cult of Heroes." In Albersmeier 2009:121–143.

Elmer, D. F. 2010. "'It's Not Me, It's You, Socrates': The Problem of the Charismatic Teacher in Plato's *Symposium*." Martin Weiner Lecture, Brandeis University, November 10, 2010.

Exum, J. C. 1999. "How Does the Song of Songs Mean: On Reading the Poetry of Desire." *Svensk Exegetisk Årsbok* 64:47–63.

Ferrari, G. 1997. "Figures in the Text: Metaphors and Riddles in the *Agamemnon*." *Classical Philology* 92:1–45.

———. 2000. "The *Ilioupersis* in Athens." *Harvard Studies in Classical Philology* 100:119–150.

Festugière, A. J. 1966. *Proclus. Commentaire sur le Timée*. Vol. 1. Paris.

Frame, D. 1978. *The Myth of Return in Early Greek Epic*. New Haven. http://chs.harvard.edu/CHS/article/display/4317.

———. 2009. *Hippota Nestor*. Hellenic Studies 34. Washington, DC. http://chs.harvard.edu/CHS/article/display/4101.

Freedman, D. G. 1998. "Sokrates: The Athenian Oracle of Plato's Imagination." PhD dissertation, Harvard University.

Hadot, P. 1983. "Physique et poésie dans le *Timée* de Platon." *Revue de théologie et de philosophie* 115:113–133.

Heiden, B. 2007. "The Muses' Uncanny Lies: Hesiod, *Theogony* 27 and its Translators." *American Journal of Philology* 128:153–175.

Hollingdale, R. J., trans. 1982. *Friedrich Wilhelm Nietzsche. Daybreak: Thoughts on the Prejudices of Morality*. Cambridge.

Jacoby, F. 1923–1958. *Die Fragmente der griechishen Historiker*. Berlin.

Jakobson, R. 1931. "Über die phonologischen Sprachbünde." Reprinted in Jakobson 1971, 137–143.

———. 1949. "On the Theory of Phonological Affinities Between Languages." In Jakobson 1990, 202–213. For the date of the original article, see 1990:544 under RJ 1949b.

———. 1952. "Studies in Comparative Slavic Metrics." *Oxford Slavonic Papers* 3:21–66. Reprinted in Jakobson 1966, 414–463. The Hague.

———. 1956. "Two Aspects of Language and Two Types of Aphasic Disturbances." In Part II of *Fundamentals of Language*, by R. Jakobson and M. Halle. The Hague. Recast as Chapter 7 of Jakobson 1990.

———. 1957. *Shifters, Verbal Categories, and the Russian Verb*. Cambridge, MA. Reprinted in Jakobson 1971:130–147.

———. 1966. *Selected Writings*. Vol. 4. The Hague.

———. 1971. *Selected Writings*. Vol. 1. 2nd ed. Berlin.

———. 1990. *On Language*. Ed. by L. R. Waugh and M. Monville-Burston. Cambridge, MA.

Kaplan, J. 2000. *A Divine Love Song: The Emergence of the Theo-Erotic Interpretation of the Song of Songs in Ancient Judaism and Early Christianity*. PhD dissertation, Harvard University.

Kearns, E. 1989. *The Heroes of Attica*. London.

Kierkegaard, S. 1843 [1983]. *Fear and Trembling: Repetition.* Translated, with introduction and notes, by H. V. Hong and E. H. Hong. Princeton.

Kirk, G. S., ed. 1985. *The Iliad: A Commentary.* Vol. 1, *Books 1-4*. Cambridge.

———, ed. 1990. *The Iliad: A Commentary.* Vol. 2, *Books 5-8*. Cambridge.

Koller, H. 1956. "Das kitharodische Prooimion: Eine formgeschichtliche Untersuchung." *Philologus* 100: 159–206.

———. 1957. "Hypokrisis und Hypokrites." *Museum Helveticum* 14:100–107.

Kroll, W., ed. 1899/1901. *Procli Diadochi in Platonis rem publicam commentarii* I/II. Leipzig.

Lamberterie, C. de. 1997. "Milman Parry et Antoine Meillet." In Létoublon 1997, 9–22. Translated as "Milman Parry and Antoine Meillet" in Loraux, Nagy, and Slatkin 2001, 409–421.

Lamberton, R. 2012. *Proclus the Successor on Poetcs and the Homeric Poems. Translation, Notes, Introduction.* Society of Bibliocal Literature, Writings from the Greco-Roman World, Number 34). Atlanta.

Lang, C., ed. 1881. *Cornuti theologiae Graecae compendium*. Leipzig.

Lapatin, K. D. S. 2001. *Chryselephantine Statuary in the Ancient Mediterranean World.* Oxford.

Leach, E. R. 1982. Critical introduction to *Myth*, by M. I. Steblin-Kamenskij, 1–20. Trans. M. P. Coote. Ann Arbor.

Lee, M. M. 2004. "Evil Wealth of Raiment: Deadly πέπλοι in Greek Tragedy." *The Classical Journal* 99:253–279.

Leipen, N. 1971. *Athena Parthenos: A Reconstruction.* Toronto.

Lepschy, A. 1998. "Il colore della porpora." In *La porpora: Realtà e immaginario di un colore simbolico; atti del convegno di studio, Venezia, 24 e 25 ottobre 1996*, ed. O. Longo, 53–66. Venice.

Lessing, G. E. 1766. *Laokoon, oder Über die Grenzen der Mahlerey und Poesie.* Translated by E. A. McCormick as *Laocoön: An Essay on the Limits of Painting and Poetry* (Baltimore, 1962. Revised ed. 1984).

Leutsch, E. L. von, and F. G. Schneidewin, eds. 1839–1851. *Corpus Paroemiographorum Graecorum.* Göttingen.

Levaniouk, O. 2011. *Eve of the Festival: Making Myth in Odyssey 19.* Hellenic Studies 46. Washington, DC. http://chs.harvard.edu/CHS/article/display/4104.

———. 2012. "Sky-Blue Flower: Songs of the Bride in Modern Russia and Ancient Greece." In Bers, Elmer, Frame, and Muellner 2012. http://chs.harvard.edu/CHS/article/display/4647.

Liddell, H. G., R. Scott, and H. S. Jones. 1940. A Greek–English Lexicon. 9th ed. Oxford.

Loraux, N. 1982. "Donc Socrate est immortel." In *Le Temps de la Réflexion* 3:19–46. Recast as "Therefore Socrates is Immortal" in Loraux 1995, 145–167.

———. 1995. *The Experiences of Tiresias: The Feminine and the Greek Man.* Trans. P. Wissing. Princeton.

Loraux, N., G. Nagy, and L. Slatkin, eds. 2001. *Antiquities.* Postwar French Thought 3. New York.

Lord, A. B. 1960. *The Singer of Tales.* Harvard Studies in Comparative Literature 24. Cambridge, MA. See also Lord 2000.

———. 1991. *Epic Singers and Oral Tradition.* Ithaca, NY.

———. 1995. *The Singer Resumes the Tale.* Edited by M. L. Lord. Ithaca, NY.

———. 2000. 2nd ed. of Lord 1960. Edited, with new Introduction (vii–xxix) by S. Mitchell and G. Nagy. Cambridge, MA. http://chs.harvard.edu/CHS/article/display/5595.

Lyne, R. O. A. M., ed. 1978. *Ciris: A Poem Attributed to Vergil.* Cambridge.

Mango, C. 1963. "Antique Statuary and the Byzantine Beholder." *Dumbarton Oaks Papers* 17:53–57.

———. 1972. *The Art of the Byzantine Empire, 312–1453: Sources and Documents.* Toronto.

Mango, C., Vickers, M., and Francis, E. D. 1992. "The Palace of Lausus at Constantinople and Its Collection of Ancient Statues." *Journal of the History of Collections* 4:89–98.

Mansfield, J. M. 1985. "The Robe of Athena and the Panathenaic Peplos." PhD dissertation, University of California at Berkeley.

Martin, R. P. 1989. *The Language of Heroes: Speech and Performance in the Iliad*. Ithaca NY. http://chs.harvard.edu/CHS/article/display/4318.

———. 1993. "Telemachus and the Last Hero Song." *Colby Quarterly* 29:222–240.

———. 2000. "Synchronic Aspects of Homeric Performance: The Evidence of the *Hymn to Apollo*." *Una nueva visión de la cultura griega antigua hacia el fin del milenio* (ed. A. M. González de Tobia) 403–432. La Plata.

Meillet, A. 1921–1936. *Linguistique historique et linguistique générale*. 2 vols. Paris.

———. 1925. *La méthode comparative en linguistique historique*. Paris.

Merkelbach, R., and M. L. West, eds. 1967. *Fragmenta Hesiodea*. Oxford.

Mitchell, S., and G. Nagy, eds. 2000. Introduction. In Lord 2000, vii–xxix.

Muellner, L. 1996. *The Anger of Achilles: Mēnis in Greek Epic*. Ithaca, NY.

Mylonopoulos, I., and Chaniotis, A., eds. 2009. *The New Acropolis Museum*. Vol. 1. New York.

Nagy, B. 1972. "The Athenian Ergastinai and the Panathenaic Peplos." PhD dissertation, Harvard University.

———. 1978a. "The Ritual in Slab-V East of the Parthenon Frieze." *Classical Philology* 73:137–141.

———. 1978b. "The Athenian Athlothetai." *Greek, Roman and Byzantine Studies* 19:307–314.

———. 1980. "A Late Panathenaic Document." *Ancient World* 3:106–111.

———. 1983. "The Peplotheke." In *Studies Presented to Sterling Dow*, ed. K. Rigsby, 227–232. Greek, Roman, and Byzantine Monographs 10. Durham, NC.

———. 1991. "The Procession to Phaleron." *Historia* 40:288–306.

———. 1992. "Athenian Officials on the Parthenon Frieze." *American Journal of Archaeology* 96:55–69.

———. 1994. "Alcibiades' Second Profanation." *Historia* 43:275–285.

Nagy, G. 1972. Introduction, Parts I and II, and Conclusions. In *Greek: A Survey of Recent Work*, F. W. Householder and G. Nagy, 15–72. Janua Linguarum Series Practica 211. The Hague.

———. 1979. *The Best of the Achaeans: Concepts of the Hero in Archaic Greek Poetry*. Revised ed. with new introduction 1999. Baltimore. http://chs.harvard.edu/CHS/article/display/5576.

———. 1983. "*Sēma* and *Noēsis*: Some Illustrations." *Arethusa* 16:35–55. Recast as ch. 8 of *GM* = Nagy 1990b.

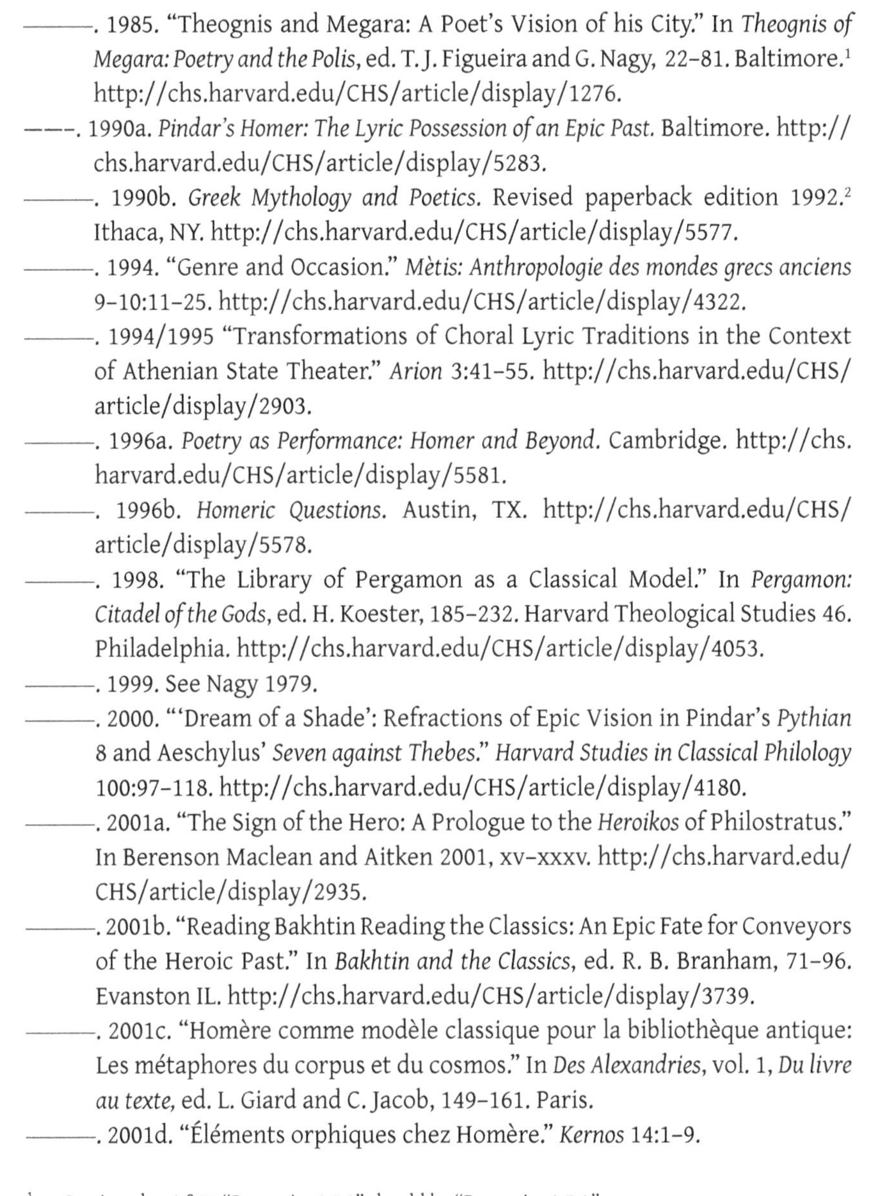

———. 1985. "Theognis and Megara: A Poet's Vision of his City." In *Theognis of Megara: Poetry and the Polis*, ed. T. J. Figueira and G. Nagy, 22–81. Baltimore.[1] http://chs.harvard.edu/CHS/article/display/1276.

———. 1990a. *Pindar's Homer: The Lyric Possession of an Epic Past.* Baltimore. http://chs.harvard.edu/CHS/article/display/5283.

———. 1990b. *Greek Mythology and Poetics.* Revised paperback edition 1992.[2] Ithaca, NY. http://chs.harvard.edu/CHS/article/display/5577.

———. 1994. "Genre and Occasion." *Mètis: Anthropologie des mondes grecs anciens* 9–10:11–25. http://chs.harvard.edu/CHS/article/display/4322.

———. 1994/1995 "Transformations of Choral Lyric Traditions in the Context of Athenian State Theater." *Arion* 3:41–55. http://chs.harvard.edu/CHS/article/display/2903.

———. 1996a. *Poetry as Performance: Homer and Beyond.* Cambridge. http://chs.harvard.edu/CHS/article/display/5581.

———. 1996b. *Homeric Questions.* Austin, TX. http://chs.harvard.edu/CHS/article/display/5578.

———. 1998. "The Library of Pergamon as a Classical Model." In *Pergamon: Citadel of the Gods*, ed. H. Koester, 185–232. Harvard Theological Studies 46. Philadelphia. http://chs.harvard.edu/CHS/article/display/4053.

———. 1999. See Nagy 1979.

———. 2000. "'Dream of a Shade': Refractions of Epic Vision in Pindar's *Pythian* 8 and Aeschylus' *Seven against Thebes.*" *Harvard Studies in Classical Philology* 100:97–118. http://chs.harvard.edu/CHS/article/display/4180.

———. 2001a. "The Sign of the Hero: A Prologue to the *Heroikos* of Philostratus." In Berenson Maclean and Aitken 2001, xv–xxxv. http://chs.harvard.edu/CHS/article/display/2935.

———. 2001b. "Reading Bakhtin Reading the Classics: An Epic Fate for Conveyors of the Heroic Past." In *Bakhtin and the Classics*, ed. R. B. Branham, 71–96. Evanston IL. http://chs.harvard.edu/CHS/article/display/3739.

———. 2001c. "Homère comme modèle classique pour la bibliothèque antique: Les métaphores du corpus et du cosmos." In *Des Alexandries*, vol. 1, *Du livre au texte*, ed. L. Giard and C. Jacob, 149–161. Paris.

———. 2001d. "Éléments orphiques chez Homère." *Kernos* 14:1–9.

[1] Corrigenda: at §77, "Pausanias 1.5.3" should be "Pausanias 1.5.4."

[2] Corrigenda. On p. 203 between "same line)" and "specified," insert "of the marital bed; similarly, she 'recognizes' (ἀναγνούσῃ xix 250) as *sēmata* (same line) the clothes ..." (in the present printed version, the reference to the marital bed as *sēmata* at *Odyssey* xxiii 206 is distorted by a mistaken omission of the wording that needs to be restored here: by haplography, the mention of the marital bed is omitted, and this omission distorts the point being made about the clothes and brooch of Odysseus as *sēmata* in their own right at xix 250). On p. 214n42, "Pausanias 9.44.44" should be "Pausanias 8.44.4."

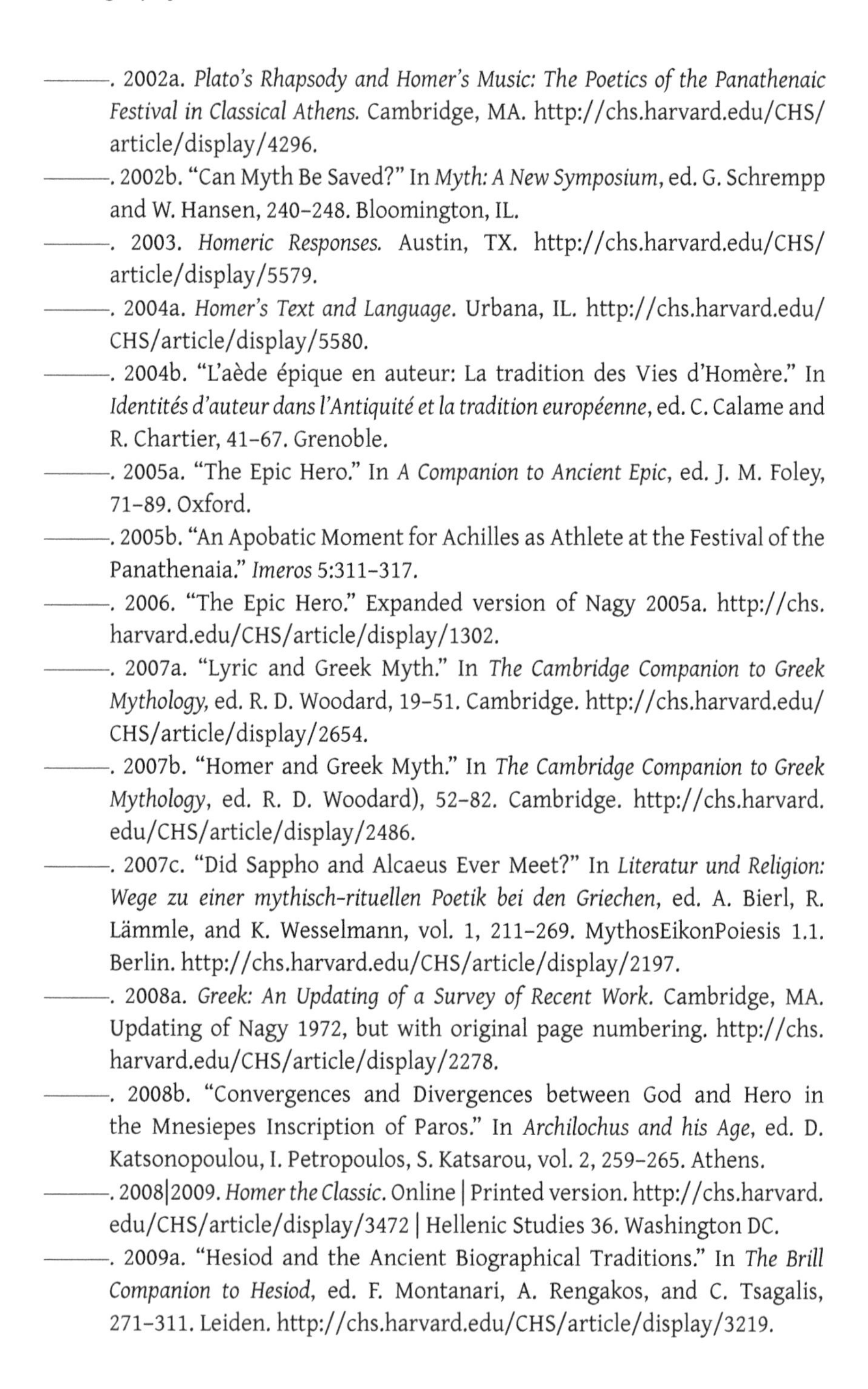

———. 2002a. *Plato's Rhapsody and Homer's Music: The Poetics of the Panathenaic Festival in Classical Athens.* Cambridge, MA. http://chs.harvard.edu/CHS/article/display/4296.

———. 2002b. "Can Myth Be Saved?" In *Myth: A New Symposium*, ed. G. Schrempp and W. Hansen, 240–248. Bloomington, IL.

———. 2003. *Homeric Responses.* Austin, TX. http://chs.harvard.edu/CHS/article/display/5579.

———. 2004a. *Homer's Text and Language*. Urbana, IL. http://chs.harvard.edu/CHS/article/display/5580.

———. 2004b. "L'aède épique en auteur: La tradition des Vies d'Homère." In *Identités d'auteur dans l'Antiquité et la tradition européenne*, ed. C. Calame and R. Chartier, 41–67. Grenoble.

———. 2005a. "The Epic Hero." In *A Companion to Ancient Epic*, ed. J. M. Foley, 71–89. Oxford.

———. 2005b. "An Apobatic Moment for Achilles as Athlete at the Festival of the Panathenaia." *Imeros* 5:311–317.

———. 2006. "The Epic Hero." Expanded version of Nagy 2005a. http://chs.harvard.edu/CHS/article/display/1302.

———. 2007a. "Lyric and Greek Myth." In *The Cambridge Companion to Greek Mythology*, ed. R. D. Woodard, 19–51. Cambridge. http://chs.harvard.edu/CHS/article/display/2654.

———. 2007b. "Homer and Greek Myth." In *The Cambridge Companion to Greek Mythology*, ed. R. D. Woodard), 52–82. Cambridge. http://chs.harvard.edu/CHS/article/display/2486.

———. 2007c. "Did Sappho and Alcaeus Ever Meet?" In *Literatur und Religion: Wege zu einer mythisch-rituellen Poetik bei den Griechen*, ed. A. Bierl, R. Lämmle, and K. Wesselmann, vol. 1, 211–269. MythosEikonPoiesis 1.1. Berlin. http://chs.harvard.edu/CHS/article/display/2197.

———. 2008a. *Greek: An Updating of a Survey of Recent Work.* Cambridge, MA. Updating of Nagy 1972, but with original page numbering. http://chs.harvard.edu/CHS/article/display/2278.

———. 2008b. "Convergences and Divergences between God and Hero in the Mnesiepes Inscription of Paros." In *Archilochus and his Age*, ed. D. Katsonopoulou, I. Petropoulos, S. Katsarou, vol. 2, 259–265. Athens.

———. 2008|2009. *Homer the Classic.* Online | Printed version. http://chs.harvard.edu/CHS/article/display/3472 | Hellenic Studies 36. Washington DC.

———. 2009a. "Hesiod and the Ancient Biographical Traditions." In *The Brill Companion to Hesiod*, ed. F. Montanari, A. Rengakos, and C. Tsagalis, 271–311. Leiden. http://chs.harvard.edu/CHS/article/display/3219.

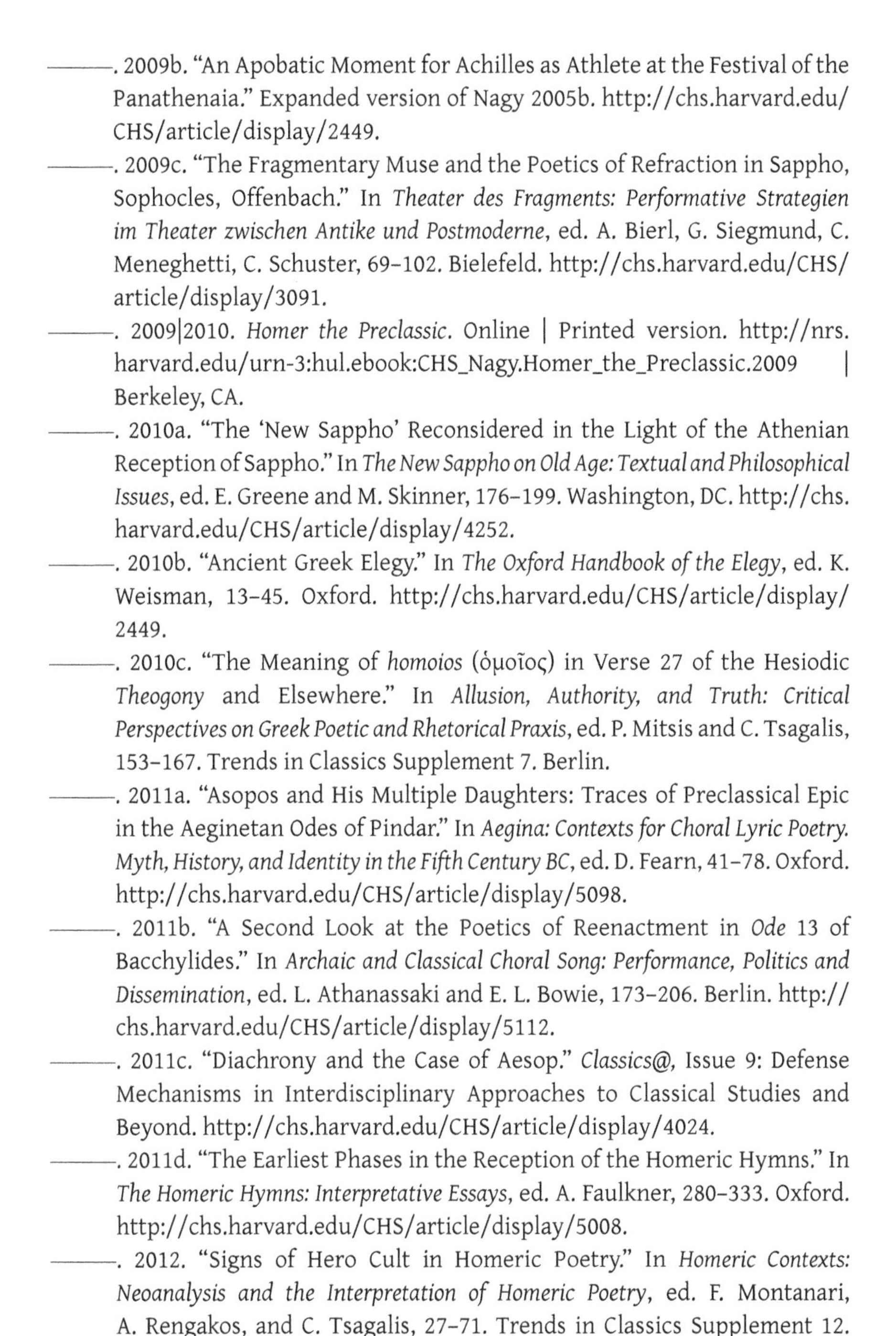

———. 2009b. “An Apobatic Moment for Achilles as Athlete at the Festival of the Panathenaia.” Expanded version of Nagy 2005b. http://chs.harvard.edu/CHS/article/display/2449.

———. 2009c. “The Fragmentary Muse and the Poetics of Refraction in Sappho, Sophocles, Offenbach.” In *Theater des Fragments: Performative Strategien im Theater zwischen Antike und Postmoderne*, ed. A. Bierl, G. Siegmund, C. Meneghetti, C. Schuster, 69–102. Bielefeld. http://chs.harvard.edu/CHS/article/display/3091.

———. 2009|2010. *Homer the Preclassic*. Online | Printed version. http://nrs.harvard.edu/urn-3:hul.ebook:CHS_Nagy.Homer_the_Preclassic.2009 | Berkeley, CA.

———. 2010a. “The ‘New Sappho’ Reconsidered in the Light of the Athenian Reception of Sappho.” In *The New Sappho on Old Age: Textual and Philosophical Issues*, ed. E. Greene and M. Skinner, 176–199. Washington, DC. http://chs.harvard.edu/CHS/article/display/4252.

———. 2010b. “Ancient Greek Elegy.” In *The Oxford Handbook of the Elegy*, ed. K. Weisman, 13–45. Oxford. http://chs.harvard.edu/CHS/article/display/2449.

———. 2010c. “The Meaning of *homoios* (ὁμοῖος) in Verse 27 of the Hesiodic *Theogony* and Elsewhere.” In *Allusion, Authority, and Truth: Critical Perspectives on Greek Poetic and Rhetorical Praxis*, ed. P. Mitsis and C. Tsagalis, 153–167. Trends in Classics Supplement 7. Berlin.

———. 2011a. “Asopos and His Multiple Daughters: Traces of Preclassical Epic in the Aeginetan Odes of Pindar.” In *Aegina: Contexts for Choral Lyric Poetry. Myth, History, and Identity in the Fifth Century BC*, ed. D. Fearn, 41–78. Oxford. http://chs.harvard.edu/CHS/article/display/5098.

———. 2011b. “A Second Look at the Poetics of Reenactment in *Ode* 13 of Bacchylides.” In *Archaic and Classical Choral Song: Performance, Politics and Dissemination*, ed. L. Athanassaki and E. L. Bowie, 173–206. Berlin. http://chs.harvard.edu/CHS/article/display/5112.

———. 2011c. “Diachrony and the Case of Aesop.” *Classics@*, Issue 9: Defense Mechanisms in Interdisciplinary Approaches to Classical Studies and Beyond. http://chs.harvard.edu/CHS/article/display/4024.

———. 2011d. “The Earliest Phases in the Reception of the Homeric Hymns.” In *The Homeric Hymns: Interpretative Essays*, ed. A. Faulkner, 280–333. Oxford. http://chs.harvard.edu/CHS/article/display/5008.

———. 2012. “Signs of Hero Cult in Homeric Poetry.” In *Homeric Contexts: Neoanalysis and the Interpretation of Homeric Poetry*, ed. F. Montanari, A. Rengakos, and C. Tsagalis, 27–71. Trends in Classics Supplement 12. Berlin. http://chs.harvard.edu/CHS/article/display/5500.

———. 2013a. *The Ancient Greek Hero in 24 Hours*. Cambridge, MA.

———. 2013b. "The Delian Maidens and their Relevance to Choral Mimesis in Classical Drama." In *Choral Mediations in Greek Tragedy*, ed. R. Gagné and M. G. Hopman, 227–256. Cambridge. http://chs.harvard.edu/CHS/article/display/5671.

———. 2013c. "Virgil's Verse *invitus, regina* ... and its Poetic Antecedents." In *More modoque: Die Wurzeln der europäischen Kultur und deren Rezeption im Orient und Okzident. Festschrift für Miklós Maróth zum siebzigsten Geburtstag*, ed. P. Fodor, G. Mayer, M. Monostori, K. Szovák, L. Takács, 155–165. Budapest. http://chs.harvard.edu/CHS/article/display/5167.

Nagy, J. F. 1986. "Orality in Medieval Irish Literature: An Overview." *Oral Tradition* 1:272–301.

Neils, J., ed. 1992a. *Goddess and Polis: The Panathenaic Festival in Ancient Athens*. Princeton.

Neils, J. 1992b. "The Panathenaia: An Introduction." In Neils 1992a, 13–27, with notes at 194–195.

———. 2001. *The Parthenon Frieze*. Cambridge.

Newton, R. M., trans. 2014. *Yiannis Ritsos. Epitaphios*. Middlesbrough.

Nick, G. 2002. *Die Athena Parthenos: Studien zum griechischen Kultbild und seiner Rezeption*. Mitteilungen des Deutschen Archäologischen Instituts. Athenische Abteilung. Beiheft 19. Mainz.

Nietzsche, F. 1885. "Morgenröthe." In *Sämtliche Werke, Kritische Gesamtausgabe*, ed. G. Colli and M. Montinari, vol. 3, *Morgenröte, Idyllen aus Messina, Die fröhliche Wissenschaft*. Munich 1980.

Nilsson, M. P. 1906. *Griechische Feste*. Leipzig.

Nimis, S. 1999. "The Sense of Open-Endedness in the Ancient Novel." *Arethusa* 32:215–238.

Nock, A. D. 1944. "The Cult of Heroes." *Harvard Theological Review* 37:141–174. Reprinted in Nock 1972.

———. 1972. *Essays on Religion in the Ancient World*. Edited by Z. Stewart. Cambridge MA.

Obbink, D., ed. 1996. *Philodemus. On Piety*. Part 1. Oxford.

Pache, C. O. 2004. *Baby and Child Heroes in Ancient Greece*. Urbana, IL.

———. 2009. "The Hero beyond Himself: Heroic Death in Ancient Greek Poetry and Art." In Albesmeier 2009, 88–107.

Page, D. L. 1962. *Poetae Melici Graeci*. Oxford.

Papadopoulou-Belmehdi, I. 1994. *Le chant de Pénélope: Poétique du tissage féminin dans l'Odyssée*. Paris.

Papadopoulou, I. 2004. "Poètes et (Philo)sophoi: Pour une archéologie de la mimesis." *Revue de philosophie ancienne* 24:3–16.

Parke, H. W. 1977. *Festivals of the Athenians*. Ithaca, NY.
Parry, A., ed. 1971. *The Making of Homeric Verse: The Collected Papers of Milman Parry*. Oxford.
Pasquali, G., ed. 1908. *Procli Diadochi in Platonis Cratylum commentaria*. Leipzig.
Patton, K. C. 2009. *Religion of the Gods: Ritual, Paradox, and Reflexivity*. Oxford.
Petropoulos, J. C. B. 1993. "Sappho the Sorceress: Another Look at fr. 1 (LP)." *Zeitschrift für Papyrologie und Epigraphik* 97:43–56.
Peponi, A. E. 2009. "*Choreia* and Aesthetics in the *Homeric Hymn to Apollo*: The Performance of the Delian Maidens (Lines 156–64)." *Classical Antiquity* 28:39–70.
Petrović, I. 2012. "Rhapsodic hymns and epyllia." In *Brill's Companion to Greek and Latin Epyllion and Its Reception*, ed. M. Baumbach and S. Bär, 149–176. Leiden.
———. 2013. "The Never-Ending Stories: A Perspective on Greek Hymns." In *The Door Ajar: False Closure in Greek and Roman Literature and Art*, ed. F. Grewing, B. Acosta-Hughes, and A. Kirichenko, 203–227 Heidelberg.
Pfeiffer, R. 1968. *History of Classical Scholarship: From the Beginnings to the End of the Hellenistic Age*. Oxford.
Pinney, G. F. 1988. "Pallas and Panathenaea." In *Proceedings of the Third Symposium on Ancient Greek and Related Pottery*, ed. J. Christiansen and T. Melander, 465–477. Copenhagen.
Power, T. 2010. *The Culture of Kitharōidia*. *Hellenic Studies* 15. Washington, DC. Available online at http://nrs.harvard.edu/urn-3:hul.ebook:CHS_Power.The_Culture_of_Kitharoidia.2010.
Prevelakis, P. 1983. *Ὁ ποιητὴς Γιάννης Ρίτσος. Συνολικὴ θεώρηση τοῦ ἔργου του*. Athens.
Pucci, P. 2007. ed. (with commentary). *Inno alle Muse (Esiodo, Teogonia, 1-115)*. Pisa.
Puhvel, J. 1988. "Hittite Athletics as Prefigurations of Ancient Greek Games." In *The Archaeology of the Olympics: The Olympics and Other Festivals in Antiquity*, ed. W. J. Raschke, 26–31. Madison, WI.
Reardon, B. P. 1982. "Theme, Structure and Narrative in Chariton." *Yale Classical Studies* 27:1–27.
Redfield, J. M. 2003. *The Locrian Maidens: Love and Death in Greek Italy*. Princeton.
Revermann, M. 1998. "The Text of *Iliad* 18.603–6 and the Presence of an ΑΟΙΔΟΣ on the Shield of Achilles." *Classical Quarterly* 48:29–38.
Rhodes, P. J. 1981. *A Commentary on the Aristotelian Athenaion Politeia*. Oxford.
Richardson, N., ed. 1993. *The Iliad: A Commentary* VI: *Books 21–24*. General editor G. S. Kirk. Cambridge.
Ridgway, B. S. 1992. "Images of Athena on the Acropolis." In Neils 1992a, 119–142.

Saffrey, H. D., Segonds, A.-P., eds. 2001. *Marinus: Proclus ou sur le bonheur*. With the collaboration of C. Luna. Paris.

Saussure, F. de. 1916. *Cours de linguistique générale*. Critical ed. 1972 by T. de Mauro. Paris.

———. 1966. *Course in General Linguistics*. Trans. W. Baskin. New York.

Scheid, J. and Svenbro, J. 1994. *Le Métier de Zeus: Mythe du tissage et du tissu dans le monde gréco-romain*. Paris.

Schmitt, R. 1967. *Dichtung und Dichtersprache in indogermanischer Zeit*. Wiesbaden.

Shear, J. L. 2001. "Polis and Panathenaia: The History and Development of Athena's Festival." PhD dissertation, University of Pennsylvania.

Simon, E. 1953. *Opfernde Götter*. Berlin.

Skjærvø, P. O. 2005. "Poetic and Cosmic Weaving in Ancient Iran: Reflections on Avestan *vahma* and Yasna 34.2." In *Haptačahaptāitiš: Festschrift for Fridrik Thordarson*, ed. D. Haug and E. Welo, 267–279. Oslo.

Slatkin, L. 1987. "Genre and Generation in the *Odyssey*." In *METIS: Revue d'anthropologie du monde grec ancien* vol. 2., 259–268.

———. 1991. *The Power of Thetis: Allusion and Interpretation in the Iliad*. Berkeley, CA.

———. 2011. *The Power of Thetis and Selected Essays*. Hellenic Studies 16. Washington, DC. Available online at http://nrs.harvard.edu/urn-3:hul.ebook:CHS_Slatkin.The_Power_of_Thetis_and_Selected_Essays.2011.

Smith, D. A. 1994. "Syntax and Narrative: The Historic Present in Herodotus." Harvard A. B. thesis.

Stern, D. 2008. "Ancient Jewish Interpretation of the Song of Songs in a Comparative Context." In *Jewish Biblical Interpretation and Cultural Exchange: Comparative Exegesis in Context*, ed. N. B. Dohrmann and D. Stern, 87–107. Philadelphia.

Stoneman, R. 1981. "Plowing a Garland: Metaphor and Metonymy in Pindar." *Maia* 33:125–138.

Tambiah, S. J. 1985. *Culture, Thought, and Social Action*. Cambridge, MA.

Theodoropoulou, M. 2012. "The Emotions Seek to be Expressed: Thoughts from a Linguist's point of view." In *Unveiling Emotions*, ed. A. Chaniotis, 433–468. Stuttgart.

Van Nortwick, T. 1992. *Somewhere I Have Never Traveled: The Second Self and the Hero's Journey in Ancient Epic*. New York.

Wace, A. 1948. "Weaving or Embroidery?" *American Journal of Archaeology* 52:51–55.

Walters, H. B. 1898. "On Some Black-Figured Vases Recently Acquired by the British Museum." *Journal of Hellenic Studies* 18: 281–301.

Waugh, L. R. 1982. "Marked and Unmarked: A Choice between Unequals in Semiotic Structure." *Semiotica* 38:299–318.

White, S. A. 2000. "Socrates at Colonus: A Hero for the Academy." In *Reason and Religion in Socratic Philosophy*, ed. N. D. Smith and P. Woodruff, 151–175. Oxford.

Wolf, F. A. 1795. *Prolegomena ad Homerum, sive de operum Homericorum prisca et genuina forma variisque mutationibus et probabili ratione emendandi.* Halle.

Wolf, F. A., ed. 1804, 1807. *Homerou epe: Homeri et Homeridarum opera et reliquiae.* 4 vols. Leipzig.

Zeitlin, F. I. 1970. "The Argive Festival of Hera and Euripides' *Electra*." *Transactions of the American Philological Association* 101:645–669.

Index

CPSIA information can be obtained
at www.ICGtesting.com
Printed in the USA
LVHW030720020223
738080LV00001B/3